A·N·N·U·A·L EDITIONS

Human Sexuality 02/03

Twenty-Seventh Edition

EDITOR

Susan J. Bunting

Lincoln College

Susan Bunting is a child, adolescent, and family counselor at Chestnut Health Systems, a consultant for Employment Development Associates, and an instructor in sociology and psychology at Lincoln College in Illinois. Dr. Bunting received her B.S. and M.S. in sociology and her Ed.D. in curriculum and instruction from Illinois State University. She has taught, counseled, trained, and developed curriculum in human sexuality, sexual abuse, substance abuse, domestic violence, self-esteem, child and human development, learning disabilities, behavior change, family, and intimate relationships. Dr. Bunting publishes pamphlets, instructional materials, articles, and books in these areas.

McGraw-Hill/Dushkin

530 Old Whitfield Street, Guilford, Connecticut 06437

Visit us on the Internet
http://www.dushkin.com

Credits

1. **Sexuality and Society**
   Unit photo—© 2002 by PhotoDisc, Inc.
2. **Sexual Biology, Behavior, and Orientation**
   Unit photo—© Sara Krulwich/New York Times Pictures.
3. **Interpersonal Relationships**
   Unit photo—© 2002 by Cleo Freelance Photography.
4. **Reproduction**
   Unit photo—© 2002 by Cleo Freelance Photography.
5. **Sexuality Through the Life Cycle**
   Unit photo—Courtesy of Louis P. Raucci.
6. **Old/New Sexual Concerns**
   Unit photo—Rick Brown/Picture Group.

Copyright

Cataloging in Publication Data
Main entry under title: Annual Editions: Human Sexuality 2002/2003.
1. Sexual behavior—Periodicals. 2. Sexual hygiene—Periodicals. 3. Sex education—Periodicals.
4. Human relations—Periodicals. I. Bunting, Susan J., *comp.* II. Title: Human sexuality.
ISBN 0–07–250690-3   658'.05   ISSN 1091–9961

Twenty-Seventh Edition

Cover image © 2002 by PhotoDisc, Inc.

Printed in the United States of America   1234567890BAHBAH5432   Printed on Recycled Paper

Editors/Advisory Board

Members of the Advisory Board are instrumental in the final selection of articles for each edition of ANNUAL EDITIONS. Their review of articles for content, level, currentness, and appropriateness provides critical direction to the editor and staff. We think that you will find their careful consideration well reflected in this volume.

EDITOR

Susan J. Bunting
Lincoln College

ADVISORY BOARD

John D. Baldwin
University of California, Santa Barbara

Janice I. Baldwin
University of California, Santa Barbara

Kelli McCormack Brown
University of South Florida

T. Jean Byrne
Kent State University

Jeffrey K. Clark
Ball State University

Maureen A. Clinton
Suffolk Community College

Linda J. Coleman
Salem State University

Donald R. Devers
Northern Virginia Community College

Harry F. Felton
Pennsylvania State University Worthington

Dan Goldman
Rancho Santiago College

Marylou Hacker
Modesto Junior College

Kathleen Kaiser
California State University, Chico

Gary F. Kelly
Clarkson University

John T. Lambert
Mohawk College Fennell

Bruce D. LeBlanc
Black Hawk College

Theodore J. Maroun
McGill University

Fred L. Peterson
University of Texas Austin

Dale Rajacich
University of Windsor

Mina Robbins
California State University, Sacramento

Martin S. Turnauer
Radford University

Deitra Wengert
Towson University

Staff

To the Reader

In publishing ANNUAL EDITIONS we recognize the enormous role played by the magazines, newspapers, and journals of the public press in providing current, first-rate educational information in a broad spectrum of interest areas. Many of these articles are appropriate for students, researchers, and professionals seeking accurate, current material to help bridge the gap between principles and theories and the real world. These articles, however, become more useful for study when those of lasting value are carefully collected, organized, indexed, and reproduced in a low-cost format, which provides easy and permanent access when the material is needed. That is the role played by ANNUAL EDITIONS.

*W*e all need to learn about sex. The healthy management of sex is essential to successful living and sex-happiness is a part of our total happiness.[1]

Sex lies at the root of life, and we can never learn to reverence life until we know how to understand sex.[2]

We must eradicate sexual illiteracy.[3]

All sane people ought to know about sex nature and sex functioning.[4]

We believe that sexual knowledge can lead to reasoned, responsible interpersonal sexual behavior and can help people make important personal decisions about sex. In short, learning about sexuality is an invaluable preparation for living.[5]

You have just read the words of several prominent sexologists. What they have to say quite forcefully and dramatically about the subject and study of sex seems pretty similar, doesn't it? Well, they were written in 1891, 1919, 1967, 1982, and 1995. Can you guess which is which?

As readers of the twenty-seventh edition of *Annual Editions: Human Sexuality*, it is important for you to get a broader perspective on the issues by trying a few more "guess the era" questions. This time, however, we'll make it a little easier. Which advice was given by a clergyperson in 1968 and which in 1998?

We need more sex, not less, but we need sex with soul.[6]

It's smart to know what you need to know (about sex).[7]

How about these three looks at "today's" challenge of society and sexuality—written in 1933, 1950, and 1969?

Today, the American people are trying to break out of this vicious circle of unhappy marriages, maladjusted children, desperate, bitter, frustrating lives; they are tired of evasions and ignorance. There is a strong desire to learn the truth about sex and its place in our lives.[8]

The atmosphere in which sex teaching takes place has gradually become more open, more accepting, less fearful and less likely to produce opposition.[9]

Sexual psychology, normal and abnormal, as well as sexual hygiene, nowadays attracts a general interest and attention heretofore undreamed of.[10]

And finally, a quote many of you can show your parents because it was written about them, not you:

In today's most technologically advanced societies, members of the younger generation are making it clear—
in dress and music, deeds and words—just how unequivocally they reject their elders' sexual world.[11]

So readers, as you begin your examination of human sexuality at the dawn of this new century, try to remember that some things have changed, some things will change, and many things are likely to stay much the same. Maybe that's why it's important to emphasize the human in human sexuality.

Annual Editions: Human Sexuality 02/03 is organized into six sections: *Sexuality and Society; Sexual Biology, Behavior, and Orientation; Interpersonal Relationships; Reproduction; Sexuality Through the Life Cycle;* and *Old/New Sexual Concerns*. This edition closes with a focus on a truly timeless topic: sexual morality and decision making.

The articles in this anthology have been carefully reviewed and selected for their quality, readability, currency, and interest. They present a variety of viewpoints. Some you will agree with, some you will not, but we hope you will learn from all of them.

Appreciation and thanks go to Loree Adams for her suggestions and expertise; to Michael Fatten, Joe Strano, Sue LeSeure, and Sarah Oberst for their willingness to act as two-way sounding boards; to Mary Roy for her organization and assistance, to Ollie Pocs for inspiration, and to those who have submitted articles and reviewed previous editions. We feel that *Annual Editions: Human Sexuality 02/03* is one of the most useful and up-to-date books available. Please return the postage-paid *article rating form* on the last page of this book with your suggestions and comments. Any book can be improved. This one will continue to be—annually.

[signature: Susan J. Bunting]

Susan J. Bunting
Editor

1. F. Caprio, 1967 2. H. Ellis, 1891 3. R. Westheimer, 1995 4. H. Long, 1919 5. Masters, Johnson & Kolodny, 1982 6. T. Moore, 1998 7. C. Shedd, 1968 8. Lewin & Gilmore, 1950 9. Broderick & Bernard, 1969 10. H. Ellis, 1933 11. McLuhan & Leonard, 1967.

Contents

UNIT 1
Sexuality and Society

Eight selections consider sexuality from historical and cross-cultural perspectives and examine today's changing attitudes toward human sexual interaction.

Part A.   Historical and Cross-Cultural Perspectives

Part B.   Changing Society/Changing Sexuality

The concepts in bold italics are developed in the article. For further expansion, please refer to the Topic Guide and the Index.

UNIT 2
Sexual Biology, Behavior, and Orientation

Eight selections examine the biological aspects of human sexuality, sexual attitudes, hygiene and sexual health care, and sexual orientation.

The concepts in bold italics are developed in the article. For further expansion, please refer to the Topic Guide and the Index.

UNIT 3
Interpersonal Relationships

Six selections examine the dynamics of establishing sexual relationships and the need to make these relationships responsible and effective.

Unit Overview   84

The concepts in bold italics are developed in the article. For further expansion, please refer to the Topic Guide and the Index.

UNIT 4
Reproduction

Seven articles discuss the roles of both males and females in pregnancy and childbirth and consider the influences of the latest birth control methods and practices on individuals and society as a whole.

The concepts in bold italics are developed in the article. For further expansion, please refer to the Topic Guide and the Index.

UNIT 5
Sexuality Through the Life Cycle

Five articles consider human sexuality as an important element throughout the life cycle. Topics include responsible adolescent sexuality, sex in and out of marriage, and sex in old age.

Unit Overview   **146**

The concepts in bold italics are developed in the article. For further expansion, please refer to the Topic Guide and the Index.

UNIT 6
Old/New Sexual Concerns

Nine selections discuss ongoing concerns of sexual abuse, violence, and harassment, gender roles and issues, and sex in the media.

The concepts in bold italics are developed in the article. For further expansion, please refer to the Topic Guide and the Index.

The concepts in bold italics are developed in the article. For further expansion, please refer to the Topic Guide and the Index.

Topic Guide

This topic guide suggests how the selections in this book relate to the subjects covered in your course. You may want to use the topics listed on these pages to search the Web more easily.

On the following pages a number of Web sites have been gathered specifically for this book. They are arranged to reflect the units of this *Annual Edition*. You can link to these sites by going to the DUSHKIN ONLINE support site at *http://www.dushkin.com/online/*.

ALL THE ARTICLES THAT RELATE TO EACH TOPIC ARE LISTED BELOW THE BOLD-FACED TERM.

World Wide Web Sites

The following World Wide Web sites have been carefully researched and selected to support the articles found in this reader. The easiest way to access these selected sites is to go to our DUSHKIN ONLINE support site at *http://www.dushkin.com/online/*.

AE: Human Sexuality 02/03

The following sites were available at the time of publication. Visit our Web site—we update DUSHKIN ONLINE regularly to reflect any changes.

General Sources

National Institutes of Health (NIH)
http://www.nih.gov

Consult this site for links to extensive health information and scientific resources. The NIH is one of eight health agencies of the Public Health Service, which, in turn, is part of the U.S. Department of Health and Human Services.

SIECUS
http://www.siecus.org

Visit the Sexuality Information and Education Council of the United States (SIECUS) home page to learn about the organization, to find news of its educational programs and activities, and to access links to resources in sexuality education.

UNIT 1: Sexuality and Society

Human Rights Practices for 1998 Report: India
http://www.usis.usemb.se/human/human1998/india.html

Read this U.S. Department of State USIS (U.S. Information Service) report on India's human rights practices for an understanding of the issues that affect women's mental and physical health and well-being in different parts of the world.

Q Web Sweden: A Women's Empowerment Base
http://www.qweb.kvinnoforum.se/index.htm

This site will lead you to a number of pages addressing women's health issues and discussing societal issues related to sex. It provides interesting cross-cultural perspectives.

SocioSite: Feminism and Women's Issues
http://www.pscw.uva.nl/sociosite/TOPICS/Women.html

Open this University of Amsterdam Sociology Department's site to gain insights into a number of issues that affect both men and women. It provides biographies of women in history, an international network for women in the workplace, and links to family and children's issues, and more.

Women's Human Rights Resources
http://www.law-lib.utoronto.ca/Diana/

This list of international women's human rights Web sites provides interesting resources on marriage and the family; rights of girls; sexual orientation; slavery, trafficking, and prostitution; and violence against women.

UNIT 2: Sexual Biology, Behavior, and Orientation

Bibliography: HIV/AIDS and College Students
http://www.sph.emory.edu/bshe/AIDS/college.html

This Emory University site contains an in-print bibliography of articles dealing with HIV/AIDS and college students. Some 75 articles addressing sexual behaviors and behaviors related to HIV/ AIDS, primarily from academic and professional journals, are listed.

The Body: A Multimedia AIDS and HIV Information Resource
http://www.thebody.com/cgi-bin/body.cgi

On this site you can find the basics about AIDS/HIV, learn about treatments, exchange information in forums, and gain insight from experts.

Healthy Way
http://www.ab.sympatico.ca/Contents/health/

This Canadian site, which is directed toward consumers, will lead you to many links related to sexual orientation. It also addresses aspects of human sexuality over the life span, general health, and reproductive health.

Hispanic Sexual Behavior and Gender Roles
http://www.caps.ucsf.edu/hispnews.html

This research report from the University of California at San Francisco Center for AIDS Prevention Studies describes and analyzes Hispanic sexual behavior and gender roles, particularly as regards prevention of STDs and HIV/AIDS. It discusses gender and cultural differences in sexual behavior and expectations and other topics of interest.

James Kohl
http://www.pheromones.com

Keeping in mind that this is a commercial site with the goal of selling a book, look here to find topics of interest to nonscientists about pheromones. Links to related material of a more academic nature are included. Check out the diagram of "Mammalian Olfactory-Genetic-Neuronal-Hormonal-Behavioral Reciprocity and Human Sexuality" for a sense of the myriad biological influences that play a part in sexual behavior.

Johan's Guide to Aphrodisiacs
http://www.santesson.com/aphrodis/aphrhome.htm

"The Aphrodisiac Home Page" provides links to information about a multitude of substances that some believe arouse or increase sexual response or cause or increase sexual desire. Skepticism about aphrodisiacs is also discussed.

UNIT 3: Interpersonal Relationships

American Psychological Association
http://www.apa.org/psychnet/

By exploring the APA's "PsychNET," you will be able to find links to an abundance of articles and other resources related to interpersonal relationships throughout the life span.

Bonobos Sex and Society
http://songweaver.com/info/bonobos.html

This site, accessed through Carnegie Mellon University, includes an article explaining how a primate's behavior challenges traditional assumptions about male supremacy in human evolution.

The Celibate FAQ
http://mail.bris.ac.uk/~plmlp/celibate.html

Martin Poulter's definitions, thoughts, and suggested resources on celibacy, created, he says, "in response to the lack of celibate stuff (outside of religious contexts) on the Internet," and his perception of the Net's bias against celibacy can be found on this site.

Go Ask Alice

http://www.goaskalice.columbia.edu

This interactive site provided by Healthwise, a division of Columbia University Health Services, includes discussion and insight into a number of personal issues of interest to college-age people—and those younger and older. Many questions about physical and emotional health and well-being in the modern world are answered.

Sex and Gender

http://www.bioanth.cam.ac.uk/pip4amod3.html

Use the syllabus, lecture titles, and readings noted in this site to explore sexual differentiation in human cultures, the genetics of sexual differentiation, and the biology of sex roles in nonhumans.

UNIT 4: Reproduction

Ask NOAH About Pregnancy: Fertility & Infertility

http://www.noah-health.org/english/pregnancy/fertility.html

New York Online Access to Health (NOAH) seeks to provide relevant, timely, and unbiased health information for consumers. At this site, the organization presents extensive links to a variety of resources about infertility treatments and issues.

Childbirth.Org

http://www.childbirth.org

This interactive site about childbirth options is from an organization that aims to educate consumers to know their options and provide themselves with the best possible care to ensure healthy pregnancies and deliveries. The site and its links address a myriad of topics, from episiotomy to water birth.

Medically Induced Abortion

http://content.nejm.org/cgi/content/short/333/9/537

Read physician Richard Hausknecht's *New England Journal of Medicine* article about medical abortion using methotrexate and misoprostol.

Planned Parenthood

http://www.plannedparenthood.org

Visit this well-known organization's home page for links to information on the various kinds of contraceptives (including outercourse and abstinence) and to discussions of other topics related to sexual and reproductive health.

UNIT 5: Sexuality Through the Life Cycle

American Association of Retired Persons (AARP)

http://www.aarp.org

The AARP, a major advocacy group for older people, includes among its many resources suggested readings and Internet links to organizations that deal with the health and social issues that may affect one's sexuality as one ages.

National Institute on Aging (NIA)

http://www.nih.gov/nia/

The NIA, one of the institutes of the National Institutes of Health, presents this home page to lead you to a variety of resources on health and lifestyle issues that are of interest to people as they grow older.

Teacher Talk

http://education.indiana.edu/cas/tt/tthmpg.html

This home page of the publication *Teacher Talk* from the Indiana University School of Education Center for Adolescent Studies will lead you to many interesting teacher comments, suggestions, and

ideas regarding sexuality education and how to deal with sex issues in the classroom.

World Association for Sexology

http://www.tc.umn.edu/nlhome/m201/colem001/was/wasindex.htm

The World Association for Sexology works to further the understanding and development of sexology throughout the world. Access this site to explore a number of issues and links related to sexuality throughout life.

UNIT 6: Old/New Sexual Concerns

Abortion Law Homepage

http://members.aol.com/_ht_a/abtrbng/index.htm

This page explains the background and state of abortion law in the United States. *Roe v. Wade, Planned Parenthood v. Casey,* feticide cases, and statutes are among the important subects discussed.

Infertility Resources

http://www.ihr.com/infertility/index.html

This site includes links to the Oregon Health Sciences University Fertility Program and the Center for Reproductive Growth in Nashville, Tennessee. Ethical, legal, financial, psychological, and social issues are discussed.

Men's Health Resource Guide

http://www.menshealth.com/new/guide/index.html

This resource guide from *Men's Health* presents many links to topics in men's health, from AIDS/STDs, to back pain, to impotence and infertility, to vasectomy. It also includes discussions of relationship and family issues.

Other Sexual Violence Resources on the Web

http://www.witserv.com/org/ocrcc/resource/resource.htm

Open this useful site for Links to Other Sexual Violence Pages. For example, it has a link to "Men Against Rape," a site maintained by the D.C. Men Against Rape organization, providing men's perspectives on sexual violence.

Sexual Assault Information Page

http://www.cs.utk.edu/~bartley/saInfoPage.html

This invaluable site provides dozens of links to information and resources on a variety of sexual assault–related topics: child sexual abuse, date rape, incest, secondary victims, and offenders.

Third Age: Love and Sex

http://www.thirdage.com/romance/

This interactive site explores a current topic: relationships forged on the Internet. Browse here to hear various viewpoints on the issue. Advice columnists and psychologists add their perspectives.

Women's Studies Resources

http://www.inform.umd.edu/EdRes/Topic/WomensStudies/

This site from the University of Maryland provides a wealth of resources related to women's studies. You can find links to such topics as body image, comfort (or discomfort) with sexuality, personal relationships, pornography, and more.

We highly recommend that you review our Web site for expanded information and our other product lines. We are continually updating and adding links to our Web site in order to offer you the most usable and useful information that will support and expand the value of your Annual Editions. You can reach us at: *http://www.dushkin.com/annualeditions/.*

UNIT 1
Sexuality and Society

Unit Selections

1. **Child Sex Trade Rises in Central America**, Serge F. Kovaleski
2. **AIDS Has Arrived in India and China**, Ann Hwang
3. **AIDS: 20 Years of Terror**, Bernard Otabil
4. **The New Gender Wars**, Sarah Blustain
5. **Parasites in Prêt-à-Porter**, Peggy Orenstein
6. **Never Too Buff**, John Cloud
7. **"The Uniform for Today Is Belly Buttons"**, Gigi Guerra
8. **The Second Sexual Revolution**, Jack Hitt

Key Points to Consider

- Have you ever spoken to a young person from another culture/country about sexuality-related ideas, norms, education, or behavior? If so, what surprised you? What did you think about their perspective or ways?

- Do you feel that the American culture is too permissive or too rigid with respect to sexual norms, expectations, and laws? Why? What changes would you recommend?

- What do you think can and should be done about HIV/AIDS in developing countries?

- In what ways does it matter whether the source of gender differences is biological or cultural? What is your prediction about the likelihood that these differences will diminish?

- Would you ever consider visiting a nude recreation resort or beach? Why or why not? Do you think your answer would be different if you were in your 30s? 40s? 50s? Why?

 **Links: www.dushkin.com/online/**
These sites are annotated in the World Wide Web pages.

Human Rights Practices for 1998 Report: India
http://www.usis.usemb.se/human/human1998/india.html

Q Web Sweden: A Women's Empowerment Base
http://www.qweb.kvinnoforum.se/index.htm

SocioSite: Feminism and Women's Issues
http://www.pscw.uva.nl/sociosite/TOPICS/Women.html

Women's Human Rights Resources
http://www.law-lib.utoronto.ca/Diana/

People of different civilizations in different historical periods have engaged in a variety of modes of sexual expression and behavior. Despite this cultural and historical diversity, it is clear that human sexuality is a dynamic and complex force that involves psychological and sociocultural as well as physiological facets. Our sexuality includes our whole body and personality while we learn what it means to be sexual and to behave sexually within the structure and parameters of our era through our family, social group, and society. By studying varying cultures and eras we see more clearly the interplay between the biological, psychological, and sociocultural, as well as between the person, generation, and society.

For several centuries, Western civilization, especially Western European and, in turn, American cultures, have been characterized by an "antisex ethic." This belief system includes a variety of negative views and norms about sex and sexuality, including denial, fear, restriction, and the detachment of sexual feelings and behavior from the wholeness of personhood or humanity. Indeed, it has only been in the last 50 years that the antisex proscriptions against knowing or learning about sex have lost their stranglehold so that people can find accurate information about their sexual health, sexual functioning, and birth control without fear of stigma or even incarceration.

One generalization on which sociologists and others who study human behavior anywhere in the world can agree is that social change in beliefs, norms, or behavior—sexual or otherwise—is not easily accomplished. When it does occur, it is linked to significant changes in the social environment and usually happens as a result of interest groups that move society to confront and question existing beliefs, norms, and behavior. Changes in the social environment that have been most often linked to changes in sexuality and its expression include the invention of the car, the liberation of women from the kitchen, changes in the legality and availability of birth control, the reconsideration of democratic values of individual freedom and the pursuit of happiness, the growth of mass media, and the coming of the computer age. The social groups that have been involved in the process of this sexual/social change have also been far-reaching. In the United States they include the earliest feminists, the suffragettes; Margaret Sanger, the mother of the birth control movement; mainstream religious groups that insist that "sexuality is a good gift from God"; publishers of sex education curricula for youth; pioneering researchers like Alfred Kinsey, Havelock Ellis, William Masters, Virginia Johnson, and others; and a panorama of interest groups who have advocated changes, demanded rights, or both. Many events, people, and perspectives have played a role in sexuality beliefs and behaviors today.

Still it is clear that many things have changed with respect to sexuality and society. One of the most dramatic is from the "don't-talk-about-it" to an "everyone's-talking-about-it" communication norm. Current examples range from baby-boomer women and menopause, to prominent politicians or athletes and oral sex, adultery, prostate cancer, or impotency. However, it is also clear that some things have not changed as much as we might expect, given the increased talk, information, and availability of birth control and other sexual health products and services. It is not characteristic for the majority of people of any age to feel comfortable with and communicate about sexual feelings, fears, needs, and desires. Negotiating, even understanding, consent and responsibility seems even harder today than when we were not talking. The incidence of unplanned, unwed, and teenage pregnancies, sexually transmitted diseases (some life-threatening), molestation, incest, rape, and sexual harassment continue to be troubling. At the same time, despite more knowledge than ever before and the efforts of many in the educational, medical, and political spheres, the dream of healthy, positive, and fulfilling sexuality still eludes individuals and society as a whole.

This unit overviews historical, cross-cultural, and current issues and trends in order to illustrate the connectedness of our values, practices, and experiences of sexuality. In so doing it is meant to challenge readers to adopt a very broad perspective through which their examination of today's sexuality, and their experience of it, can be more meaningful. Only in so doing can we hope to avoid a fear-based return to the "antisex ethic" of the past while striving to evaluate the impact and value of the social changes that have so profoundly affected sexuality at the dawn of the twenty-first century.

The articles in the first subsection, *Historical and Cross-Cultural Perspectives*, address a wide range of sexual issues, including several stark and tragic realities of sexuality in less developed and prosperous countries. The opening article examines the sociocultural reasons for a geographical shift in child sexual abuse from southeastern Asia to Central America. The last two articles focus on the AIDS epidemic in three regions—India, China, and Africa—where rates and fatalities are highest and resources and hope are lowest.

The five articles that make up the second subsection, *Changing Society/Changing Sexuality*, address pivotal issues of sexuality today. Each attempts to place these changes within a historic perspective while discussing the conflicting assessments and uncertain future of these changes. The opening article, "The New Gender Wars" revisits the age-old nature versus nurture question with a few new twists for the new millennium. The next article gives us an intriguing look at a society-jarring trend in present-day Japan: over half of its women at age 30 remain single, and many still in their parents' homes. The next two articles with attention-grabbing titles, "Never Too Buff" and "'The Uniform for Today Is Belly Buttons'" explore two apparent trends in the U.S.: increased body focus for males and an increase in visits to nudist resorts among young adults. The closing article addresses a "revolutionary" topic, the increased medicalization of sexual function and dysfunction that exploded nationally and internationally just before the turn of the twenty-first century. According to many, this societal and cultural change fits the definition of "The Second Sexual Revolution."

Child Sex Trade Rises in Central America

By Serge F. Kovaleski
The Washington Post, January 2, 2000

SAN JOSE, Costa Rica—The sexual exploitation of girls and boys, largely by American men, has reached alarming proportions in Central America, according to children's rights advocates who say the region is now a priority in their struggle against child prostitution and pornography.

A major reason for growth in the Central American child sex business, child rights advocates say, is that traditional destinations such as Thailand and the Philippines have cut into the sex tourism trade over the last two years by enacting public awareness campaigns, stricter laws and enforcement measures.

Prostitution among the children who live and work on the streets of Latin America, whose number as been estimated as high as 40 million, has long been a consequence of the region's poverty. But as countries such as Guatemala, El Salvador, Costa Rica and Nicaragua increase promotion of their beaches, volcanoes and natural beauty as tourist destinations, they are attracting greater numbers of men from North America, Europe and other Latin American countries who are interested in buying sex from children.

"What we are seeing is the dark side of tourism," said Heimo Laakkonen, the head of UNICEF in Costa Rica. Laakkonen said that while sexual exploitation of minors is not a new problem in

the region, "with the increase in tourism, the problem has gotten worse."

Sitting at the bar in the dingy Del Ray Hotel here one recent evening, a 33-year-old Californian named David said he was on his second trip to Costa Rica in as many years. He spoke brazenly about how he had scanned several Web pages advertising youthful-looking female prostitutes in Costa Rica in his efforts to purchase sex with a girl who had no previous sexual experience.

David, who insisted only his first named be used, boasted of how he had arranged for one of the many taxi drivers connected with the sex trade to bring a 13-year-old girl from her parents' home in a poor San Jose neighborhood to his hotel. The girl's mother and father asked for $400, which David said he eagerly paid.

Costa Rican law only allows women 18 and older to work as prostitutes. Stiffer penalties enacted recently threaten prison terms of up to 10 years for anyone convicted of buying sex from a minor. The prospect did not seem to alarm David.

"I am living out a fantasy.... And nobody looks like they have a real problem with it," he said. As the stocky, unkempt bartender spoke, adult prostitutes mingled with foreigners in the hotel lobby as younger sex workers strolled the streets outside.

Costa Rica, the region's leader in tourism and the country in Central America where child prostitution is believed to be most pronounced, has drawn more than 1 million foreign visitors this year for the first time.

Children's rights activists have accused governments in Central America, where about 54 percent of the population is below the age of 18, of being slow to confront the region's burgeoning child prostitution and pornography industry.

"It involves a certain level of political maturity on the part of governments to acknowledge the severity of the problem, as opposed to the ostrich syndrome of keeping your head stuck in the sand," said Bruce Harris, regional director of Covenant House (Casa Alianza) Latin America, an organization that helps street children.

Although there are no statistics to quantify the sexual exploitation of children in Central America, anecdotal evidence, surveys and a string of recent arrests of Americans, as well as other foreigners and locals, support the contention that the problem is growing.

The increased demand for child prostitutes in this region and others stems partly from fears of contracting AIDS from older prostitutes and the mistaken impression that young people are less likely to be infected, experts say.

Carlos Roverssi, the former executive president of Costa Rica's National Child Trust, the government's child welfare agency, acknowledged last year there had been "an accelerated increase in child prostitution" in the country that he blamed largely on the unofficial promotion of sex tourism in Costa Rica over the Internet.

In Nicaragua, a recent UNICEF report said, there has been significant growth in the prostitution of children between the ages of 12 and 16 in towns where taxi drivers were reported to serve as middlemen.

Several months ago, agents of the international police organization Interpol operating out of El Salvador discovered a prostitution network that was trafficking young girls from several countries in Central America to work in bars along the border of El Salvador and Guatemala. Interpol also said that it had rescued about 20 Salvadoran girls from such prostitution rings during the past three years.

While some minors are pushed into prostitution by families that are unable to support themselves, most underage sex workers in Central America are street children, many of whom, studies show, had fleed sexual abuse at home. In Honduras, the number of homeless minors has grown sharply in the aftermath of Hurricane Mitch last year.

Drug abuse has become a prevalent factor as well. In a recent study of 300 street children in Nicaragua by the government's Family Ministry , more than 80 percent said they had started to work as prostitutes over the last year, with most saying they did so to buy drugs. About a third said they needed the money to buy crack.

Standing on a corner near the Del Rey Hotel in San Jose, Juana Rojas, 14, who said she became a sex worker about nine months ago, was offering to have sex for $15. "A few tricks and I can buy some [crack] rocks up the street," she said.

She added, "I started going with men when I got hooked on crack a while ago, and since then I must have been with more than a hundred" foreigners.

Some child prostitutes offered other explanations. "I can live well, buy nice clothes and go out dancing on the nights I do not work," said Maria, 15, who shares a house here with a 14-year-old prostitute and works for a woman who sends them clients. They are paid between $50 and $200 a night.

Maria said she became a sex worker two years ago after her father committed suicide and her relationship with her mother unraveled. "Much of the time I am sad," she said. "It is hard on my self-esteem when you hear people refer to prostitutes as filthy little whores."

AIDS Has Arrived in India and China

How will the world's two most populous countries cope with the pandemic?

by Ann Hwang

In 1348, the Black Death arrived in Europe from its probable home in Central Asia, and over the next couple of years it is believed to have killed 25 million people. Sometime soon, mortality from AIDS will exceed the death toll of that worst outbreak of bubonic plague. Since the start of the AIDS pandemic roughly 20 years ago, 20 million people have died and over 50 million have been infected. Every 11 seconds, someone dies from AIDS. According to statistics compiled by the World Health Organization, AIDS is now killing more people each year than any other infectious disease. AIDS has become one of the greatest epidemics in the history of our species.

The AIDS epidemic took much longer to build momentum than did the Black Death, but AIDS has far more staying power. For all their intensity, the bubonic plague epidemics were relatively short: *Yersinia pestis*, the plague bacterium, tends to burn itself out quickly. And in any case, *Y. pestis* and *Homo sapiens* are no longer caught up in an intense epidemic cycle. Plague still kills people in various parts of the world, but it does not spark epidemics on a continental scale. Even if it did, antibiotics have made it far less deadly than it was 650 years ago. But HIV, the virus that causes AIDS, shows no sign of releasing us from its grip. Indeed, it has evolved into several new forms, even as it continues to burn through humanity. And although there are now drugs that can prolong the lives of its victims—or at least, those who can afford treatment—there is no cure for the disease and no vaccine for it. (See box, "An AIDS Vaccine?")

Within the AIDS pandemic, sub-Saharan Africa has become the equivalent of mid-14th century Europe. Ignorance of the disease, poverty, war, and frequently, a rather relaxed attitude toward sexual activity (especially when it comes to men)—such factors have allowed HIV to explode through some African societies. In 1996, the Joint United Nations Programme on HIV/AIDS (UNAIDS) predicted that by 2000, over 9 million Afri-

cans would be infected with HIV. The actual number turned out to be 25 million. Though Africa is home to less than 9 percent of the world's adults, it has more than two-thirds of adult HIV infections. In Botswana, the county with the world's highest infection rate, one in three adults is now infected. And as the infected continue to die, places like Botswana may become increasingly unstable for lack of farmers, teachers, community leaders, even parents.

But in large measure, the course of the pandemic will depend on what happens not in Africa but in Asia, the continent that is home to nearly 60 percent of the world's people. AIDS is already well established in Asia, although no one knows precisely when or where it first arrived. By the mid-1980s, however, infections were beginning to appear in several Asian counties, including Thailand and India. A few years later, it was obvious that HIV infection was increasing dramatically among two of the best known "high risk populations"—prostitutes and users of injection drugs. As its incidence increased, the disease began to travel the highways of Asia's drug trade, radiating outward from the opium-producing "Golden Triangle," where Myanmar (Burma), Laos, and Thailand converge. The infecting of the world's most populous continent had begun.

That process may now be reaching a kind of critical mass. AIDS has arrived in the two most heavily populated countries in the world: India and China. With populations of 1 billion and 1.3 billion respectively, these countries are home to over a third of the world's population and nearly 70 percent of Asians people. Thus far, neither has suffered the kind of explosive epidemic that has ravaged sub-Saharan Africa. Each still has important opportunities to stem the epidemic. What will the giant societies of Asia make of those opportunities? This is one of the greatest social and ethical issues of our era.

Mapping the Epidemic

Reported Risk of HIV infection in India and China, 1999

Caveat lector: the data in this map, which derive from official country sources, do not give a complete picture of the epidemic. In particular, information on high risk groups is incomplete. The high risk data do not include homosexuals in either India or China, or blood sellers in China. Because the latter group is omitted, the map does not accurately portray the epidemic in central China.

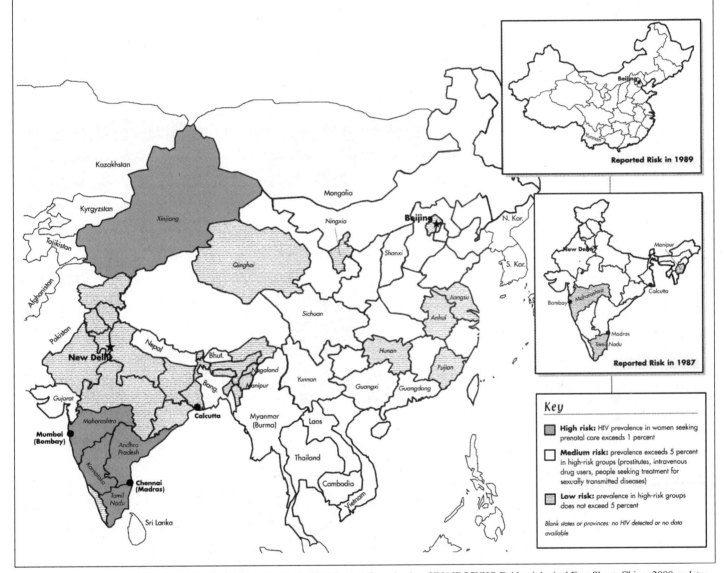

Key

High risk: HIV prevalence in women seeking prenatal care exceeds 1 percent

Medium risk: prevalence exceeds 5 percent in high-risk groups (prostitutes, intravenous drug users, people seeking treatment for sexually transmitted diseases)

Low risk: prevalence in high-risk groups does not exceed 5 percent

Blank states or provinces: no HIV detected or no data available

Sources: Indian Ministry of Health and Family Welfare, National AIDS Control Organization; UNAIDS/WHO Epidemiological Fact Sheet: China, 2000 update; UNAIDS Country Profile: China

Four Million Infected in India

India is home to an estimated 4 million people with HIV—more than any other country in the world. Because of India's huge population, the level of infection as a national average is very low—just 0.4 percent, close to the U.S. national level of 0.3 percent. But this apparently comfortable average masks huge regional disparities: in some of India's states, particularly in the extreme northeast, near the Myanmar border, and in much of the south, the rate of infection among adults has reached 2 percent or more—five times the national rate and more than enough to kindle a widespread epidemic.

Among these more heavily infected regions, there is another kind of disparity as well, in the way the virus is spreading. In southern India, AIDS fits the standard profile of a sexually transmitted disease (STD), with particularly high infection rates among prostitutes. Sex is big business in India, generating revenues of $8.7 billion each year, according to the Centre of Concern for Child Labour, a Delhi-based non-profit. Mumbai (Bombay), the country's largest west coast city, has twice the population of New York yet almost 20 times the number of prostitutes. By 1997, over 70 percent of those prostitutes were HIV positive. The prostitutes' clients, in addition to risking infection themselves, put their wives or other sex partners in jeopardy, thereby creating a bridge that allows the virus to spread from a high-risk enclave to the general population.

In some segments of Indian society, that bridge is now very broad. Long-distance truck drivers, for example, are usually away from home for long periods and many visit prostitutes en route. For one study, published in the *British Medical Journal* in 1999, nearly 6,000 long-distance truckers were interviewed and nine out of ten married drivers described themselves as "sexually promiscuous," defined as having frequent and indiscriminate change of sexual partners. Not surprisingly, HIV incidence is now rising among married Indian women. A study from 1993 to 1996 found that over 10 percent of female patients at STD clinics in Pune, near Mumbai, were HIV positive; over 90 percent of these women were married and had had sexual contact only with their husbands. (See box, "Increasingly, A Women's Disease.")

In India's northeast, the epidemic has a very different character. This region has an extensive drug culture—which is hardly surprising, given its proximity to the Golden Triangle. Here, the epidemic has been driven by intravenous drug use, particularly among young unemployed men and students. By sharing contaminated needles, addicts are injecting the virus into their bloodstreams. Data are scarce, but according to government estimates, there are 1 million heroin users in India, and roughly 100,000 of them reside in the comparatively small states that make up the northeast.

In the northeastern state of Manipur, on the Myanmar border, HIV among intravenous drug users and their sexual partners increased from virtually nothing in 1988 to over 70 percent four years later. By 1999, 2.2 percent of pregnant women attending prenatal care clinics in Manipur tested positive for HIV. Because the infection risk in women seeking prenatal care should be roughly representative of the general population, epidemiologists often use this group to estimate trends in the general population. In the northeast, as in the south, HIV is apparently moving into mainstream society.

Perhaps One Million Infected in China

In China, the shadow of AIDS is at present just barely discernable. Current estimates put the number of HIV infections at 500,000 to 1 million. In a country of 1.3 billion, that works out to an infinitesimal national level of infection: eight one-hundredths of a percent at most. But even though the virus is very thinly spread, it seems to be present nearly everywhere: all of the country's 31 provinces have reported AIDS cases.

As with India, the character of this incipient epidemic differs greatly from one region to the next. China's original HIV hotspot is in the south: Yunnan province, which borders Laos and Myanmar, had almost 90 percent of the country's HIV cases in 1990. Yunnan lies on the periphery of the Golden Triangle and is home to a large (but not readily definable) proportion of China's intravenous drug users. Today, however, the virus has moved well beyond Yunnan, in part because of a surge in the popularity of injection drugs. By the middle of the 1990s, half of new infections in intravenous drug users were occurring outside Yunnan, mostly in other southern provinces. Guangxi province, which borders Yunnan to the east, saw infection levels in surveyed drug users climb from zero in 1993 to 40 percent by 1997.

An AIDS Vaccine? No Magic Bullet

"People expect a magic bullet," says Chris Collins, president of the board of the AIDS Vaccine Advocacy Coalition, a network of U.S. activists that seeks to increase funding for HIV vaccine research. But he cautions, "the AIDS vaccine probably isn't going to be that."

It is true that vaccine researchers have made substantial progress over the past few years. A California-based company known as VaxGen is now conducting the first ever large-scale tests in humans of a possible vaccine. An interim analysis of the tests, which involve 8,000 volunteers on three continents, is scheduled for November 2001. Many experts believe that such efforts will eventually pay off, but the results are not likely to compare with the smallpox vaccine, which eventually eliminated that earlier global pandemic.

One big obstacle is the virus's mutation rate. Mutations appear to occur in at least one of the virus's genes each time it replicates, once every 8 hours. In HIV, as in any other organism, most mutations prove to be evolutionary dead ends. But not all of them: the virus has already spawned more than a dozen different subtypes around the globe, and it is unclear whether a single vaccine would be effective against every subtype. China in particular has a very heterogeneous epidemic, with nearly all known subtypes represented. This global mosaic of subtypes may exacerbate the medical North-South divide. How much industrialized-country R&D will be invested in developing vaccines for strains that predominate in developing countries?

Even when a viable vaccine is discovered, researchers are likely to face formidable challenges in determining its use. Suppose, for example, that a vaccine is only 50 percent effective: should it be licensed, given the possibility that people receiving it may be less inclined to have safe sex or use clean needles? Assuming that a strong general case could be made for the use of such a vaccine, who is going to pay for the inoculation of the developing world's high-risk populations? Vaccine researchers may find the sociology of the epidemic as difficult to deal with as the biology of the virus itself. No doubt, an effective vaccine will be a valuable tool against the pandemic, but it is not likely to replace any of the other tools already in use.

Last year, China's official count of registered intravenous drug users reached 600,000—more than double the number in 1992. And as the number of users has grown, so has the custom

Increasingly, A Women's Disease

In the developing world, women now account for more than half of HIV infections, and there is growing evidence that the position of women in developing societies will be a critical factor in shaping the course of the AIDS pandemic. In general, greater gender inequality tends to correlate with higher levels of HIV infection, according to the World Bank researchers who track literacy rates and other general indicators of social well-being.

As in the AIDS-ravaged countries of sub-Saharan Africa, India and China offer women far fewer social opportunities than men. Both countries score in the lower half of the "Gender-Related Development Index," a measure of gender equity developed by the United Nations Development Programme.

Double sexual standards that demand female virginity while condoning male promiscuity put many women at risk. Studies in India and Thailand, by the Washington D.C.-based International Center for Research on Women (ICRW), have found that young, single women are expected not only to be virgins but also to be ignorant of sexual matters. As a result, young women lack basic knowledge about their bodies and are poorly prepared to insist on the use of condoms to protect themselves from HIV or other sexually transmitted diseases (STDs).

Even within marriage, women may have little influence over sex. "A woman does not have much say in the house," said one Indian woman participating in an ICRW focus group. "He is the husband. How long can we go against his wish?" Without adequate legal protection or opportunities for economic independence, such women may have little choice but to remain in abusive marriages and follow their husbands' dictates, Of 600 women living in a slum in Chennai (Madras), a major city on India's east coast, 90 percent said they had no bargaining power with their spouses about sex and couldn't convince them to use condoms. And 95 percent of these women were financially dependent on their husbands.

Women's risk is compounded by biological factors. During vaginal intercourse without a condom, transmission of HIV from an infected man to a woman is two to four times more likely than transmission in the opposite direction. The two key factors appear to be the surface area of exposed tissue and the viral load. Women lose on both counts: the virus concentrates in semen, and the surface area of the vagina is relatively large and subject to injury during sex. Tears in the lining of the vagina or cervix may admit the virus more readily. Women suffer another biological disadvantage as well. In general, STDs are harder to detect in women because the symptoms are more likely to be internal. Lesions from unrecognized STDs can increase a woman's susceptibility to HIV.

Once infected, women are less likely to be treated. In couples where both partners are infected with HIV but where treatment can be afforded only for one, it is the husband who almost invariably gets the drugs. Subhash Hira, director of Bombay's AIDS Research and Control Center, explained it this way to an AP reporter: "It is the woman who is stepping back. She thinks of herself as expendable." A 1991–93 study in Kagera, Tanzania found that in AIDS-afflicted households, more than twice as much, on average, was spent caring for the male victims than for the female victims: $80 versus only $38.

The stigma of infection also seems to fall more heavily upon women. Unease over female sexuality appears to translate readily into a tendency to see infection in women as punishment for sexual promiscuity. Women are sometimes even blamed for being the source of the disease. Suneeta Krishnan, an expert on AIDS in southern India, notes that the local languages contain few words for STDs, but the most commonly used formula is "diseases that come from women." One man explained the term to her: "The man may be the transmitter of the disease, but the source is the woman. She is the one who is blamed. For example, if a well is poisoned, and a man drinks from it and falls ill, people do not blame him. They blame the well. In the same way, people blame women for sexually transmitted diseases."

—*Ann Hwang*

of sharing needles. Information on this habit is hard to come by, but based on the most recent data the government has provided, UNAIDS estimated that 60 percent of users shared needles in 1998, up from 25 percent the year before.

In many parts of China, and particularly in the countryside of the central provinces, the virus is spreading through a very different form of injection. Selling one's own blood is a common way for poor people to make a little extra money, but it puts them at high risk for HIV infection. The government banned blood sales in 1998 (the blood supply in China is supposed to come from voluntary donations). But growing demand for blood virtually ensures the continuation of the practice. In some illegal collection centers, blood of the same blood type may be pooled, the plasma extracted to make valuable clotting and immune factors, and the remaining cells re-injected into the sellers. (Re-injection shortens the recovery period, allowing people to sell their blood more frequently.) The needles and other collection equipment are often reused as well. A January 2000 raid on one such center in Shanxi province, southwest of Beijing, turned up 64 bags of plasma, all of which tested positive for HIV and hepatitis B.

The extent of the black market in blood is unknown. China's news media are banned from reporting on the topic, outside researchers have been prevented from studying it, and government officials won't discuss it. But it's a good bet that the system is not about to be weaned off black market blood anytime soon; official donations are apparently inadequate even though their "voluntary" character is already badly strained. Inland from Hong Kong, for instance, in the city of Guangzhou, work groups are fined if they do not meet their blood donation quotas. Workers sometimes avoid the fines without donating by hiring "professional donors" to take their place. One could argue that such quotas still work, albeit in a somewhat indirect and callous way. But the system is riddled with flaws. The general cultural reluctance to give blood in China has been exacerbated by a widespread perception that donation is dangerous. And unfortunately, that perception is probably justified, since even official blood collection centers may reuse needles and tubing. (Such reuse is not necessarily intentional; sometimes unscrupulous dealers collect used equipment, repackage it, and sell it as new.) Another unfortunate consequence follows when the blood is actually used: apart from the larger urban hospitals, the Chinese blood supply is probably not adequately screened for HIV or other diseases, and "professional donors" have much higher levels of infection than the general public.

In the major cities and especially along China's highly developed southeastern coast, AIDS is primarily an STD. At least in the cities, sexual mores appear to have loosened considerably over the past couple of decades. Not surprisingly, prostitution is becoming more common. For the country as a whole, prostitution arrests now number about 500,000 annually; China's Public Security Department estimates the number of prostitutes to be between 3 and 4 million, a figure that has been increasing since the 1980s. STDs, such as syphilis and gonorrhea, were virtually eradicated in the 1960s under an aggressive public health campaign, but have returned with a vengeance. Infection rates are increasing by 30 to 40 percent each year, according to the Ministry of Health. That portends an increase in AIDS, not only because of what it suggests about the growing sexual permissiveness, but also because the genital sores caused by other STDs make people more vulnerable to HIV.

Sexual contact, intravenous drug use, blood selling—in many parts of the country, these and perhaps other modes of transmission are increasingly likely to "overlap" as the virus spreads. The results may be difficult to anticipate, or to counter. For example, in 1998, the most recent year for which statistics were available, the province reporting the largest number of new HIV infections was not Yunnan or Guangxi, but the remote Xinjiang, in China's arid and lightly populated northwest. Why? In part, the answer appears to be drugs. Despite its apparent isolation, Xinjiang is enmeshed in the opium trade. Some studies have found infection levels of about 80 percent among the province's intravenous drug users. Local prostitutes seem to be heavily infected as well. And HIV has begun to appear in women coming to clinics for prenatal care—a strong indication that the virus is starting to leak into the province's general population. But despite the fact that it has become an HIV hotspot, Xinjiang has attracted little official attention, and that suggests another reason for the province's plight. Most of Xinjiang's inhabitants are Uigur, a people of Turkish descent. (The area is sometimes called "Chinese Turkestan.") Like some of China's

other ethnic minorities, the Uigur suffer disproportionately from HIV. The country's AIDS prevention and education programs, very small to begin with, may be even less effective among ethnic minorities. Lack of official interest in minorities may be a factor Xinjiang's epidemic; perhaps also there is some sort of cultural "communications gap."

In early 2000, a group of concerned Chinese scientists—including some members of the Chinese Academy of Sciences—submitted a report to the government that warned, "The spread of AIDS is accelerating rapidly and we face the prospect of remaining inert against the threat." Without decisive action, according to China's National Center for AIDS Prevention and Control (NCAIDS), 10 million people in China could be infected with HIV by 2010.

Death on the Margins

In China and most of India, AIDS is still concentrated among socially marginal high-risk groups—groups engaged in activities that attract mainstream disapproval and that are often illegal. One of the most obscure of these groups is male homosexuals. Despite the prominence of homosexuality in the AIDS controversies of the industrialized countries, very little is known about gay life in China or India. But studies in Chennai (Madras), the largest city on the southeast coast, reveal one ominous characteristic of the Indian homosexual underground: most participants do not appear to be exclusively homosexual. Most are married.

Gay men who are married, heterosexual men who patronize prostitutes, intravenous drug users and their sexual partners: AIDS may still be a disease of the social margins, but in both India and China there are several major bridges between the margins and mainstream society. It's possible that the virus will tend to cross those bridges relatively slowly. If it remains largely in the fringe populations, it should be easier to control. But even this scenario entails serious risk, since it could encourage callousness towards the victims and complacency towards the disease.

Take the complacency potential first: if AIDS is portrayed as a disease of marginalized groups, people who are not in those groups may be reluctant to acknowledge their own vulnerability. Suneeta Krishnan, a researcher at the University of California at Berkeley, has studied HIV for the past three years in southern India and seen this reluctance first hand. "The perception is that AIDS is only a problem of female commercial prostitutes sitting in Bombay," she said. "It's only a problem for us if we have sex with them." Such attitudes could easily heighten the risk of contagion.

The "us-them" mentality can also greatly increase the suffering of those who are already infected. One effect of stigmatizing AIDS-prone minorities is that *all* AIDS sufferers tend to end up stigmatized. Rajesh Vedanthan, one of the founders of Swasthya, a nonprofit that provides HIV counseling to women in the southern Indian state of Karnataka, recalls the story of a pregnant woman who sought care at a hospital for profuse vaginal bleeding. Without her consent or knowledge, she was tested for HIV and found to be infected. The hospital doctor—without informing her of her HIV status—placed gauze to soak up the blood, discharged her from the hospital without treatment, and told her never to return. By the time she came to Swasthya, she had a raging infection. Such inhumanity can greatly compound the contagion of the disease itself.

"Avoiding Unnecessary Agony"

In Beijing, the streets are swept clean by women wielding brooms made from twigs. Licensed taxis queue at the airport waiting for uniformed guards to assign them passengers. But you needn't go far from China's capital before all the taxis have inexplicably broken meters, and beggars crowd the trash-covered streets. A similar duality is apparent in the country's efforts to deal with AIDS. As a totalitarian state with a strong tradition of public health and social services, China would appear to be in good shape to control the AIDS epidemic. But China spends only about seven tenths of 1 percent of its GDP on health care. (The United States is at the other end of the spectrum, with public health care expenditures amounting to 6 percent of its GDP.) China's anti-AIDS efforts thus far have amounted to little more than crackdowns on prostitution, drug use, and blood sales—strong-arm tactics that have had negligible effect.

Public education about the epidemic has been stalled by censorship. The language of official AIDS announcements reflects a deep awkwardness in discussing sexual issues. "The government calls to the attention of its citizens whether their words and deeds conform to the standards of the Chinese nation," explained one official declaration dating from the beginning of the epidemic. The announcement added, with muffled urgency, that citizens should "know what to do and what not to do when making sexual decisions and avoiding unnecessary agony." Though times are changing, China's first nationally televised advertisement promoting condom use to prevent AIDS was taken off the air in December 1999, after just two days of broadcast, because it violated a ban on ads for sex products.

Technical infrastructure for treating and tracking the epidemic is also in short supply. In its most recent report, released in 1997, NCAIDS noted that China had only 400 labs capable of testing for HIV, or roughly one for every 3 million people. There is also a shortage of medical personnel trained to treat people infected with HIV or other STDs. When workers at STD clinics in the southern city of Shenzen were tested on their medical knowledge, only 23 percent passed, according to Xinhua, the official Chinese news agency. According to Zeng Yi, an AIDS researcher and member of the Chinese Academy of Sciences, local officials in various parts of the country are reluctant to collect data on HIV, for fear that their province will be blackballed as a highly infected area. Even more alarming is the apparent drop in resources committed to fighting the epidemic. Following budget cuts of 40 percent, the number of HIV screening tests in disease surveillance programs fell from 3.4 million in 1997 to 1.3 million in 1998.

India, the world's largest democracy, has little reason for complacency either. Early in the epidemic, some Indian politicians were calling for banning sex with foreigners, isolating HIV-positive people, and urging a return to traditional values—cries that were being heard in other countries as well. The proposal to ban sex with foreigners was put forth in 1988 by A.S. Paintal, the government's chief medical researcher, but was scuttled immediately under a barrage of domestic and international criticism. In Goa state, on India's west coast, a law permitting the resting and isolation of anyone suspected of being HIV-positive was overturned only after repeated protests. On the federal level, an unsuccessful 1989 "AIDS Prevention Bill" called for the forcible testing and detention of any HIV-positive person or anyone suspected of being HIV-positive.

In 1992, India's Ministry of Health and Family Welfare established the National AIDS Control Organisation (NACO) to carry out AIDS prevention and education. NACO has put into place a surveillance system to monitor disease trends, but limited resources have hampered prevention and made treatment impossible. Anti-retroviral therapy, the "drug cocktail" that can slow the progression of AIDS, costs $270 to $450 per month. The country's average per capita income is only $444 per year. Even among India's rapidly expanding middle class, the average per capita income is only about $4,800 per year—roughly the same as a year's worth of the cocktail. Nor is there preventive care for the many opportunistic infections that ultimately kill people whose immune systems are ravaged by AIDS, even though in industrialized countries, these infections can usually be held at bay for years with relatively inexpensive medications. Like China, India spends only about 1 percent of its GDP on health care—a number that Jeffrey Sachs, a professor of international trade at Harvard University, calls "shockingly low."

The Sonagachi Prostitutes and the Future of AIDS

In 1989, when surveys of Thai brothels turned up rising levels of HIV infection among prostitutes, the Thai government collaborated with several non-governmental organizations to launch a massive public information campaign urging condom use. The "100% Condom Program" distributed condoms to brothels and massage parlors, and enforced use by tracking the contacts of men who sought care for STDs. Over the course of the next three years, condom use in brothels increased from 14 to 90 percent. By 1995, the number of men treated at government clinics for new sexually transmitted infections had dropped tenfold. A year later, HIV prevalence among conscripts to the army had dropped below 2 percent—less than half of what it had been in mid-1993.

The lesson from the early stages of the epidemic in Thailand is clear: it's worth dispensing with moral scruples to give people a clear sense of the medical issues. Public education works, at least when it's backed by some degree of enforcement. There's no reason to think this approach would be any less effective in China or India. Consider the prostitutes of Calcutta's Sonagachi district. Against considerable odds, these women have managed, not just to inform themselves about AIDS, but to organize themselves. The over 30,000 dues-paying members in their informal union have improved working conditions, educated other prostitutes about AIDS, started reading classes, and reduced the number of child prostitutes. They understand the need for condoms and have even threatened collective action against brothel owners reluctant to require condom use. As a result, their HIV infection levels remain at 5 percent—very low compared to the 60 or 70 percent levels typical of prostitutes in other Indian cities.

Frank talk about condoms and safe sex is of course just a start. An effective AIDS program must also have a reliable, confidential, and voluntary HIV testing program. It must protect the rights of infected people and secure treatment for them. But perhaps the greatest challenge of all is the need to build some form of long-term support for those marginalized, high-risk groups—support that invites the kind of initiative shown by the Sonagachi prostitutes. As Suneeta Krishnan puts it, "HIV is intimately linked to social and economic inequality and deprivations. As long as these problems persist, HIV is going to persist."

That is perhaps one of the lessons from the latter stages of the Thai epidemic. The Asian financial crisis dried up funding for Thailand's AIDS programs. Spending fell from $90 million in 1997 to $30 million in 1998 before rebounding somewhat, to $40 million in 1999 and 2000. The drop in funds has made the weak points in the Thai approach more apparent. Among populations other than brothel workers and their clients, the epidemic has proceeded largely unchecked. Male homosexuals have not generally been included in the program. Neither have intravenous drug users—a group whose infection level has passed 40 percent. And the worst news of all is that the infection level among women receiving prenatal care is now climbing.

In India and China as in many other places, prostitutes, homosexuals, and drug addicts are frequently the objects of contempt and legal sanction. But these are the people who should be top priorities for any serious AIDS program, for both practical and humanitarian reasons. How much of an investment are we really willing to make in the egalitarian principles upon which every public health program is built? AIDS is an acid test of our humanity. Over and over again, the virus teaches its terrifying lesson. There is no such thing as an expendable person.

Ann Hwang is a medical student at the University of California, San Francisco and a former intern at the Worldwatch Institute.

AIDS: 20 years of terror

AIDS—Africa's looming disaster

Bernard Otabil

Another brave HIV/AIDS campaigner has finally succumbed to the disease. Nkosi Johnson, the brave 12-year-old South African died on June 1. Certainly, he is not the only person who died as a victim to the deadly disease on that day. What makes Nkosi Johnson's death so unique is his fight and bravery—that despite the despair and a shattered world that accompanies AIDS, he found the strength that made him one of the best campaigners on this deadly disease. Nkosi symbolised hope. Hope that the disease will certainly be overcome. He strove hard for the removal of stigma and discrimination that so many people suffer as a result of this disease. And at the 13th International AIDS Conference in Durban in July 2000, he called for HIV-positive people to be treated as equals. This, according to many commentators, was the turning point in the fight against AIDS on the continent.

The world has lost a true champion, a hero in the fight against AIDS. This is the human reality of the disease in the African continent. There are many like the late Nkosi who are willing to champion the cause of the fight against the deadly disease in the African continent. But who will listen to them? Gradually, deliberation on the epidemic has occupied the priority sessions at most international meetings of the powerful institutions of the world. Money—the lack of it and its mobilisation—has become the most actively discussed topic. According to some experts, international institutions and creditor organisations should tie debt relief and aid to some developing countries to an AIDS epidemic reduction strategy as in the case of the numerous poverty reduction and strat-

egy papers. But is this the real solution? Certainly, it could help. But those actually suffering from the disease know that it is not only the lack of funds which is the problem, but also the need to have a properly integrated community that treats HIV/AIDS patients as no different in society. Many are really suffering from emotional abuse. And African leaders have a great deal of work to do in addressing this issue.

In the campaign to win the masses at elections, many politicians go to great length to reach remote parts of their countries' extremely difficult to reach areas. But such political will is often absent in the fight against the spread of HIV/AIDS. The taxpayer's money should be used to cater for their own needs. The state of the health sector in most African countries is not supportive of programmes aimed at fighting the spread of the disease. In Ghana for instance, expectant mothers in the main maternity ward of the country's leading hospital, Korle Bu Teaching Hospital, sleep on the floor. So how will HIV/AIDS sufferers be treated? In some parts of Africa, the isolation of AIDS patients has led to early deaths of sufferers. Most patients have lost the will to fight on, preferring to die rather than go through the humiliation of being a sufferer. The consequence is now there for everybody to see. The disease is now alarming. Many sufferers prefer to keep the knowledge to themselves, infecting others instead.

As the impact of HIV/AIDS has placed increased strain on health institutions, HIV care will increasingly fall onto the homes as primary care givers, and onto the communities as support services. This is where the role of African governments is much more crucial. The important role of gov-

ernment in providing basic health care and support to people living with HIV/AIDS or to those affected by other disease could prove vital as an effective strategy for home care or community-based response. The talking must now be left with the bureaucrats and the academicians, now is the time to act.

President Obasanjo of Nigeria, as part of his numerous overtures, organized a seminar on the subject in Abuja in April this year. The attendance was good and the conference was termed a success. But will it help the sufferers—most of whom live in shantytowns and villages with very poor hygienic conditions? The very surroundings of most sufferers even increase the death rate. The sad reality is that the continent of Africa is on the way to extinction, if this issue is not properly addressed. Africans have a fighting instinct, and indeed, this is the only way that the continent can be protected.

President Festus Mogae of Botswana has sounded a battle cry. "We really are in a national crisis. We are threatened with extinction," he said. He is completely alarmed by the rate of infection in his country. Experts say about 36 per cent of the population is HIV-positive. And this figure is bound to double within the next 20 years if the spread is not checked. Botswana is not a poor country. The country has foreign reserves of over $6 billion and in the past 20 years, it is the only country that has been able to graduate from least-developed status. The diamonds industry is growing and Botswana's capital market is now one of the most cherished by foreign portfolio managers. So why is it that the scourge is eroding all the gains that it has made over the past years? Money certainly is not an issue. The disease, from the current trend in the African continent, could still be controlled by basic grassroot level initiatives. Volunteers could play a vital role in this regard and African governments should take the leading role. It is all too easy to blame cash-strapped economics in Africa as the driving force behind the spread. But the failure of most African governments to properly address the issue is as responsible a factor as the big pharmaceutical companies willing to put profits before human lives. The subject

in some parts of Africa is treated more like malaria. But AIDS is more deadly, crucial to the continent's growth and survival.

Sadly, even some scientists and respected learned people in the continent have gone to great length to prove that Africa's AIDS pandemic is not as it is told. Many of these so-called experts attribute the continent's death rate problems to tuberculosis but not HIV/AIDS. Sad indeed. The bare facts are that in many developing countries, people are suffering from the double burden of poverty combined with the explosion of communicable diseases,

which are responsible for around 60 per cent of all illnesses.

AIDS is now the number one killer—and that is official! The pandemic is now reducing life expectancy in some countries. Last year alone, it is estimated that HIV/AIDS was responsible for two million deaths in Africa, while more than one million lives were lost through malaria and tuberculosis. A country like Zambia is one that is at the brink of total disaster. The issue is now at such a critical stage that Africans are the best people to put an end to the pandemic.

AIDS: not all about money

*Brigitte Syamalevwe has lived with HIV/AIDS for the past 10 years.
Here, she explains how Africans can help fight the disease without necessarily waiting
for more money, in this interview with Bernard Otabil*

When the epidemic assumed such an alarming proportion on the African continent, the issue of money took centre stage. Yes, Africans are poor. So raising well over $5,000 a year for the cocktail of drugs needed to fight against the bout of infection that accompanies a suppressed immune system would surely be a problem for many Africans. But according to Brigitte Syamalevwe, it is not all about money.

Brigitte, an educationist and mother of 11 children, was diagnosed as being HIV-positive 10 years ago. She certainly knows what she is talking about. As a United Nations Volunteer, she is an international consultant and speaker on HIV/AIDS issues, particularly in her native country of Zambia. And though she struggles at times to complete her speech at conferences, she is never short of making her mark.

At a press conference in Brussels during the Third United Nations Conference on Least Developed Countries, the reality of the disease dawned on many. "My speech is not going to be one of the most fantastic ones that you have become used to all day," she said. "But rather, one that appeals to your conscience, and the fact that it takes you and me to properly address this issue of AIDS on the African continent," she continued. And she did indeed appeal to the conscience of the many gathered in the room.

As one of the privileged few to spend some time with her after her presentation, it was really a relaxing moment. Was she

really ill? Certainly, you couldn't tell without asking. She really looked younger than her age, bright and very apt. Her thoughts were very focused and very sharp. Brigitte emphasised repeatedly the fact that living with AIDS is not all about money, but rather the very little help that one can get in terms of education as to how one can take preventive measures. "The lack of HIV/AIDS education is rather going to kill and destroy Africans. At present, there is no cure for the disease and the infection rate is increasing by the day. Our behavior [with respect] to the disease is still very negative," she explained.

The illiteracy rate and the growing poverty problems on the continent are certainly aggravating the issue of AIDS in Africa. The issue is now multidimensional. It is now a development issue. When the South African President, Thabo Mbeki stressed the fact that HIV does not cause AIDS, his message was misinterpreted or rather he missed the point slightly. Perhaps, as he is not suffering from the disease, many did not see the logic in what he was trying to portray. Mbeki's stand, I suppose, was the belief that the continent of Africa has several depressing factors, all playing different parts in the spread of the disease. The ultimate immune deficiency syndrome and the resulting problems are only a manifestation of the many problems of malnutrition, hunger, starvation and the numerous diseases on the African continent.

Brigitte sees along the same lines. Africans, she says, do not treat the epidemic with the kind of attention needed to properly control the disease.

"In many parts of Africa, the political will that is needed to support the structures… and to ensure that it is directed to the communities where HIV/AIDS is much more rampant is not there," she stressed. She believes that most of the time, African governments and indeed some in the Western world have spent time on the bench, writing and campaigning, "but the sad reality is that the house is burning". African governments, she says, have spent most of the time talking about the disease without taking that needed decisive action that would ensure that people are properly made aware of the dangers of the epidemic. And although the Executive Director of UNAIDS, Peter Piot, may agree otherwise when he said at Abuja: "The political momentum is there, let nobody question the strong commitment of Africa's leadership to fight AIDS", he also stressed the need for commitment to be expanded at all levels in society, and turned into action and budgets.

In fact, up until as recently as the Abuja meeting in April, African governments had not made that much noise about the disease. Most of the campaign has been done by some nongovernmental and voluntary organisations. And Brigitte believes that the lack of involvement of African governments has only helped spread the disease.

Discrimination and the stigma associated with a declaration that one is infected with HIV/AIDS ensured that people stayed put and infected other people—causing the pandemic on the African scene. "The stigma associated with AIDS is the biggest worry… the government's support is very much needed," she said. Married to a pastor and health worker, Brigitte voluntarily decided to go for the AIDS test. Her reason? As a secondary school teacher of French, she was greatly alarmed by the rate at which some of her students were losing their parents and loved ones. It was therefore necessary, according to her, to take the test to ensure that she would not leave her children in sorrow one day. But though the results did not go the way she wanted, she never lost hope.

"We all have two instincts—an instinct to fight back and an instinct to flee," she said. And certainly, she had the courage to fight back and help others in her community. However, it wasn't all that rosy in the beginning. "The initial stages were tough. I did not have all the support I needed. Again, it is not all about money. The only support I had was sympathy. You know sympathy will only kill you. Sympathy… makes you addicted to only the good things that you would supposedly be missing," she said. "I had to be angry. An anger that stirred up my spirit in order to fight on all the way. That is why I have now channelled all my energies towards the creation of the necessary awareness that would help the future generation."

The AIDS epidemic rate of spread on the African continent is attracting more lip service than actual help from the international community. Quite often, the international agencies like the IMF have called for the reduction of the price of drugs, thereby making it affordable for the ordinary African. But the issue is far more than that. If the IMF and its sister organisation, the World Bank are so committed to the plight of Africans, then why can't they step in? This is not necessarily infringing on the rights of the pharmaceutical companies but rather buying the drugs at a specially agreed price and selling them cheaply to most African countries. Such a strategy does not sound as cosy as HIPC (the Heavily Indebted Poor Countries Initiative), so one does not expect much attention from the international institutions. And the way some Western pharmaceutical companies attempted a lawsuit to prevent the use of cheaper drugs in South Africa leaves much to be desired.

According to Brigitte, the international community is still largely unaware of the extent of the problem. "HIV/AIDS has diminished the gains that we (Zambia) managed in the late sixties and early seventies. To date, we are losing about three teachers a day in Zambia. And if you look at the fact that it takes 25 years to train and equip a teacher in Zambia, then we are effectively losing 75 years of trained skilled manpower," she stressed. It is really going to take much of a struggle to reverse this trend in Zambia. There is a crisis. The very fabric of society is now destroyed. The education system in most African countries is now getting worse and worse, with most social amenities like healthcare fully stretched. Some key sectors of some countries will collapse if these issues are not properly addressed. With a breakdown in the educational system, it is more likely that the rate of infection of children will increase.

The denial of the reality in most parts of Africa, according to Brigitte is a big threat to the control of the disease on the continent. "It saddens me that there is a total denial of the reality in most African countries. As a result, in most of these countries, people are not empowered enough to plan strategies and devise policies aimed at combating the issue," she stressed. "We declared last year the need for all African countries to declare HIV/AIDS as an emergency or a crisis situation that needed prompt action. But government commitment is not as it would have been thought. There is commitment at the community level as people living with AIDS and have seen the death of loved ones have tried to help each other. But the resources, mobilisation mechanisms, that would have ensured more volunteers and care workers needed to run these communities are not there," she explained.

The African culture, perhaps, needs some serious attention if the issue of AIDS is to be addressed in the manner befitting for all. In Zambia, the Copperbelt region is one of the areas with the highest infection. According to some commentators, the earthy behaviour of the mineworkers is what is driving the infection rate up. And according to Brigitte, it is all to do with poverty and education. Brigitte also believes that the length of denial in the country and the lack of political will of past presidents have all aggravated the problem. "The country has a history of inconsistency in its political life. Governments have not shown that boldness enough, and until the son of our president Kenneth

Kaunda died of AIDS, not many people really had the knowledge about the disease," she stressed.

But that is not all. The very nature of the social organisation in most African countries, and for that matter the man-woman relationship, all have a negative impact on the disease. "In most African countries, women, for example, are not part of the decision making process at home. The men always dominate. And this in a way has transcended across all aspects of society so much so that even in the bedroom, the woman is even powerless to ask a man to put on a condom even to protect both parties," she said.

This cultural issue needs to be addressed if the AIDS pandemic is to be controlled. No matter the amount of money that is raised through funds and donations from the international community, the conduct of people in the continent in terms of sexual relationship can only cause the infection rate to increase. The new generation holds the key to addressing some of these cultural issues. The abject poverty on the continent is pushing more people onto the street, causing most of them to be vulnerable to the disease. The definition of masculinity in most African countries has much to be blamed for the spread of HIV/AIDS on the continent. The male African may sometimes use his position in such a way that puts all his family members at risk of infection.

It is all down to the policy makers. And Brigitte believes that if people with responsibilities in society tackle these issues critically, then we will have a different set of behaviour in the future. "The cultural issues are a problem. As a mother and an African, I see this as a severe pain on both our present society and the future children. We need a different approach and attitude towards this particular wrath. It is all about building the right relationships, attitudes and approach."

So wearing the hat of a United Nations Volunteer, Brigitte has been able to affect the community in which she lives. She runs an orphanage and has played leading roles in ensuring that people with HIV/AIDS play an active part in the community. Brigitte believes in the work of volunteers, believing that money is necessary, but not the only factor that can help address the issue on the African continent. The future, according to Brigitte is very bleak, unless African governments and indeed individuals put their act together to properly address this issue.

Africans are fighting back

Interview by B. A. Otabil with Sharon Capeling-Alakija, Executive Co-ordinator, United Nations Volunteers

WA: Looking at the emotional appeal made by most of the speakers at this session [of the Third United Nations Conference on LDCs], how certain are you that the international community will give the needed funds to fight the global AIDS epidemic?

SC-A: I truly wish I knew or had the answer to that. The answer I have to give you, truly, is that I'm not sure. Certainly, I feel that the knowledge of the cost of this pandemic on Africa is well understood. We cannot hide behind any ignorance any longer because I think that the problem has been articulated in eloquent and passionate terms. Certainly, here... the information is available. But whether or not this time, we are really going to be able to create the momentum that is necessary and sustain it, for me is still a question. I am cautiously optimistic, very cautious because, as the representative from the WHO said,... for this new funding to be positive and meaningful, more is needed. There are some criteria here. There is the need for this new money (funding) and it needs to be sustained over a long period of time. So that once we do build up the momentum of getting people aware and willing to come forward, the funds must be there to support the programmes. This is because part of it will be given to African people themselves. When the resources are not available for testing, for giving care, for education that is going to be necessary for the use of condoms; if the resources are not there once you build the momentum, you are really going to disappoint. So, it is a big question as to whether or not the donors are going to come forward. I certainly think that there are no excuses any longer.

WA: Looking at the rate of spread of AIDS and its impact on Africa, one can see that it needs more of a grass root approach. What is your organisation doing with regard to getting African governments to support your initiatives at this level?

SC-A: You know, you are absolutely right. These problems will be solved within countries themselves by mobilising the population to address the issue. However, as a part of international solidarity, we are all on one planet, there are responsibilities for the global community to support the efforts of countries in Africa and also to help countries in Africa build the capacity so that they can address the question themselves. As the UNV, we have a very excellent mechanism called national volunteers. We are mobilising people within countries in West Africa, sometimes to go to the countries on the continent and sometimes to stay and work in their own countries as national United Nations volunteers. Particularly people who are already HIV-positive and this set of people are part of our whole campaign of volunteers in Africa. This is to encourage people who are HIV-positive to speak out. What can be more compelling with respect to prevention is to listen to the words of someone who is HIV-positive, who may not see his or her own children grow. Those kind of issues are really compelling and these people who are not United Nations volunteers [are] doing this advocacy work or also engaged in counselling people and helping people who are HIV-positive to form community associations for the care of each other, also dealing with the whole phenomenon we now see in Africa. So I think that our UNV are able to support the mobilisation of people within countries themselves. The volunteers are often able to give some form of protection. As you know, people are often very afraid of people with AIDS. They tend to stigmatise, so any UNV helps people come out from this stigma to help fight against this pandemic. It also helps to give them some self-esteem because you often see them marginalised in the community in which they live. We are really helping Nigerians, Ghanaians, Sierra Leoneans and Malians to help themselves. You know, we all need solidarity, we all need friendship.

WA: Do you think African governments have been forthright in their fight against AIDS?

SC-A: I think what we have seen, for example in Abuja... where we had a summit of African leaders is that this issue was very much on the agenda. I think we have had a breakthrough now. I remember the tragedy when one of the first African leaders to come forward and really speak out on this was Kenneth Kaunda of Zambia. And of course what provoked it was actually the death of his own son. He began to realise that his countrymen and women were dying and it was his responsibility as the president to come out, but it takes tremendous amount of courage because it is the most intimate of subjects. The disease is transmitted through intimate sexual relations which people are not comfortable to talk publicly about and... people are afraid. There are all sorts of taboos and myths associated with the disease, how it is contracted and the contagious nature of it. It, therefore, takes tremendous amount of courage for people to come out and talk. I think we have seen African leaders beginning to give each other a little bit of courage to speak about the disease. Now, they are helping to mobilise the others. You need both a two-way means of communication from the top down and from the bottom up. You need people to be mobilised in the struggle, which will need the leadership that is creative enough to speak out candidly about the disease because it is still very sensitive.

WA: How would you say your partnership with UNCTAD and UNAIDS is helping to fight the disease globally?

SC-A: We have a very close working relationship with UNAIDS. In fact, they have been a major source of funding for us through this programme of getting greater involvement of people with AIDS. And in fact, with the current role of Ex-President Rawlings of Ghana, they have been very active in helping him with preparing briefings and preparing him for this new endeavor. We are working very close with them. I think the very major contribution of UNAIDS has been an advocacy and getting the issue on the agenda of governments and decision makers around the world. I think they have really done that. UNCTAD's contribution as the main secretariat running the LDCs, has been in term of development. This conference, for example, has not been only about trade issues, but rather... a conference about the whole myriad of changes that need to happen in order for the LDCs to enjoy the benefit that the rest of the world is beginning to experience from economic growth and globalisation.

WA: What do you think the future holds for the African continent?

SC-A: I have lived in Africa for 10 years myself, eight years in West Africa.

Besides, ... I am married to a Nigerian and I have strong ties to West Africa to this day. One of the lasting things that I have seen all of these years since I left West Africa is the resilience of the people. No matter what besets West Africa, somehow, people will fight back and I believe Africans will fight and find solutions. I am not so optimistic about the world community, I am more optimistic about the resilience of African people. They deserve better.

---

20 years of HIV/AIDS

In June 1981, scientists in the United States reported the first clinical evidence of a disease that would become known as Acquired Immunodeficiency Syndrome or AIDS. Twenty years later, the AIDS epidemic has spread to every corner of the world. Almost 22 million people have lost their lives to the disease and over 36 million people are today living with HIV, the virus that causes AIDS. But two decades of struggle to control the epidemic have also yielded a growing arsenal of breakthroughs.

1981

The first cases of unusual immune system failures are identified among gay men in the USA.

1982

Acquired Immunodeficiency Syndrome (AIDS) is defined for the first time. In the course of the year, the three modes of transmission are identified; blood transfusion, mother-to-child, and sexual intercourse.

1983

The Human Immunodeficiency Virus (HIV) is identified as the cause of AIDS. In Africa, a heterosexual epidemic is revealed.

1985

The scope of the growing epidemic becomes manifest. By 1985, at least one case of HIV/AIDS has been reported in each region of the world. Film star Rock Hudson becomes the first international icon to disclose he has AIDS. In the USA, the Food and Drug Administration (FDA) approves the first HIV antibody test. HIV screening of blood donations begins in the USA.

1987

Africa's first community-based response to AIDS (The AIDS Support Organisation or TASCO) is formed in Uganda. It becomes a role model for similar activities around the world. The International Council of AIDS Service Organisations (ICASO) and the Global Network of people living with HIV/AIDS are founded. In February, the World Health Organisation (WHO) establishes the Special Programme on AIDS, later to become the Global Progamme on AIDS. The first therapy for AIDS—azidothymidine (AZT)—is approved for use in the USA.

1988

In London, health ministers from around the world meet to discuss the HIV/AIDS epidemic for the first time.

1991–1993

In 1991–1993, HIV prevalence in young pregnant women in Uganda begins to decrease—the first significant downturn in a developing country. The success is attributed to countrywide mobilisation against the epidemic.

1994

Scientists develop the first treatment regimen to reduce mother-to-child transmission.

1995

An outbreak in Eastern Europe is detected among injecting drug users.

1996

The joint United Nations Programme on HIV/AIDS (UNAIDS) is created. Evidence of the efficacy of Highly Active Antiretroviral Therapy (HAART) is presented for the first time.

1998

Brazil becomes the first developing country to provide antiretroviral therapy through its public health systems. The first short-course regimen to prevent mother-to-child transmission is announced.

1999

The first efficacy trial of a potential HIV vaccine in a developing country starts in Thailand.

2000

The UN Security Council discusses HIV/AIDS for the first time.

2001

UN Secretary-General Kofi Annan launches his call to action, including the creation of a global fund on AIDS and health.

From *West Africa* (London), June 11-17, 2001, pp. 10-16. © 2001 by West Africa (London). Reprinted by permission.

THE NEW GENDER
WARS

EXPERTS AGREE THAT MEN AND WOMEN HAVE MORE THAN JUST BIOLOGICAL DIFFERENCES. BUT WHAT DOES THAT MEAN FOR SOCIETY? CULTURE? FAMILY? WORK? WITH PRIMARILY WOMEN RESEARCHERS ON ONE SIDE AND MEN ON THE OTHER, THE BATTLE OF THE SEXES RAGES ON.

BY SARAH BLUSTAIN

It's boys against girls yet again. Schoolyard taunting, but the stakes are higher. In place of spitballs, though, this time they're hurling serious research at one another.

The latest skirmish in the war between the sexes has flared up between psychologists studying the origins of gender differences. Research has shown that despite feminist advancements, gender differences persist. The question no longer is whether there are differences between the sexes but what to make of them.

This gender split raises important questions about the current research. Each of these social scientists has looked at hundreds of studies to support his or her claims.

On one side are those who claim that it is evolution and biology that make us significantly different, and that no amount of feminist agitation will change that. Men will continue to be philandering, non-nurturing and sex-focused, and women will continue to be mothering keepers-of-the-hearth. On the other side are those who claim there's a lot more variation to our gender roles. Society, they say, and not our genes, determines how we react to our biological course. Change, this latter group says, is possible and evident.

So to what extent *does* biology, despite feminist objections, mean destiny? How willingly does our biology respond to our environment? And even if biology plays a role, how much of the male/female split is nonetheless reinforced by the culture we live in? During this era of great change in women's and men's roles—as we work out collectively who we will be in the coming generations—we need to know: Where do these differences come from and where might they go?

No little amount of rancor has been stirred up in the attempt to answer these questions, in no small measure because the psychologists themselves who are studying the origins of gender differences seem divided along gender lines. In undertones, some researchers suggest that all the evolutionary psychologists (EPs) are men, and those with theories about more varied etiology are women. Some accuse male EPs of seeing feminists as "the enemy," while others accuse female researchers of dismissing evolutionary theories which seem to reinforce male dominance out of hand. Each side tries to take the scientific high ground, pointing to the gender split with a cough or a sly look. They mean that, perhaps, these details are no accident: Maybe men, who still hold positions of relatively high status in American society, are promoting theories that maintain the patriarchal status quo; women, some of them self-described feminists, see a science that allows for more change.

This gender split raises important questions about the current research. Each of these social scientists has looked at hundreds of studies to support his or her claims.

There's relevant data from cultures on every continent, from cultures in every era dating back hundreds of thousands of years, and from every species from chimps to phalaropes (a small shorebird) to mice. Faced with thousands of studies, each theorist must look selectively at the data. And if theory drives research, we need to ask how much of the narratives of human development we read come from the way the personal narratives of the individual researchers color their world view.

The latest round of hostilities in this gendered war started in the mid-1990s, when a group of evolutionary psychologists began publishing research that looked at the origins of gender differences through Darwin's eyes. These EPs claimed (and continue to claim) that differences between the sexes do exist and that, try as we might, we can't change them. (That's the spark in the political tinder-box.) Whether in pre-modern Africa or current-day America, they say, gender-specific skills come from distinct psychological mechanisms that can be traced back directly and very nearly wholly to the Darwinian principle of sexual selection. In other words, it's in our genes.

The narrative of sexual selection goes something like this: In the mating and survival game, we all have a choice. One option, as David Geary, Ph.D., of the University of Missouri-Columbia puts it, "is to take all your energy and focus it on competing to get as many mates as you can. The other option is to have few mates and invest your reproductive energies on raising [offspring]." Men—who for biological reasons can have as many children as women they impregnate—follow the former path. Women, bound to their offspring by pregnancy and nursing, follow the latter.

True in many species, this drama is complicated among humans because many men parent their children, albeit not as much as women. Women, for their part, will compete for those men who invest in their children, thus raising their value. While the impact of these elements varies from one culture to the next, the pattern remains: Women invest in children more than men, and men, all other things being equal, prefer more sexual partners than do women.

Given these facts, the EPs suggest, men will naturally be inclined to pursue multiple partners. Their efforts, from an evolutionary point of view, will be put into finding a beautiful woman (genetically more appealing), finding as many partners as possible, and honing their physical skills in order to battle with other men for desirable women. Emotional skills that might lead to long-term relationships, in this view, have little role. Women, on the other hand, will pursue men who are more likely to stick around the morning after and help provide the food and protection mother and child will need to survive.

Sounds a lot like gender stereotypes today: a species of aggressive philandering men and nurturing, monogamous women. (Much cited research to bolster this view by David Buss, Ph.D., a leader in this field at the University of Michigan, found that male college students who were offered the chance to sleep with a beautiful stranger that night, were more likely than their female counterparts to say yes.)

The situation may vary among cultures but, says Geary, culture will never change the fact that men can potentially reproduce more frequently than women. "It will always lead to some level of conflict of interest between men and women. Women want men to invest in their kids and them, and by doing so, men lose the opportunity to have multiple mates." And, he adds, there is no culture in which there is equality between men and women in childcare. "Women," he adds, "hate to hear that."

He's right. Women do hate to hear that. Not only women of the general public, but women researchers as well. Riled psychologists, many of them women, sat up in alarm when the evolutionary psychology theories started snowballing in academic journals and in the popular press as well. Articles appeared, television shows hosted EP spokespersons. Social conservatives started using the "biological" evidence of gender differences to claim validity for the women-as-natural-homemaker model of society.

Upsetting to critics of EP theories is the suggestion, popularized in the press, that what is biological is unchangeable. "One of my objections to evolutionary psychology," explains Mary Gergen, Ph.D., professor of psychology and women's studies at Pennsylvania State University-Delaware County and a hard-core believer that gender is primarily a social construct, "is that it tends to stabilize and justify existing patterns of social relationships. They say they are presenting 'just the facts ma'am,' but it justifies the status quo"

Certainly, the idea put forth by evolutionary psychologists about the origins of gender differences is a conservative take on the matter. Conservative in the old sense of the word: inclined to preserve existing conditions and to resist change. Conservative, too, in the political sense of the word, as these debates quickly descend from the ivory tower and onto the ground, where policy is determined and intimate relationships are worked out. It's a position that offers an in-your-face challenge to feminists and other women activists who have tried to move American society in the direction of the egalitarian ideal, bolstered by the philosophical perspective that human psychology is eminently mutable.

Women harassing their men [over childcare] will lead to more investment in their children.

Researchers, a good number of them self identified feminists, who had been happily testing sex differences, suddenly felt called to action not only to "put out fires," as one said, but to come up with alternative solutions to the question of origins.

"I started to address [the origins question] because it was being addressed very directly by evolutionary psychologists," explains Alice Eagly, Ph.D., a professor of psychology at Northwestern University who had been working on questions of sex differences for 20 years. To her, their explorations of evolution were becoming "imperial," suggesting that all sex differences had biological basis.

All of these researchers agree on some theoretical basics: the nature-versus-nurture debate is moot; the differences between men and women are the result of humanity moving through the environment. Even EPs, though they believe change is slow, agree that "evolution," as Geary explains, "does not lead to a fixed point. Women harassing their men [over childcare] will lead to more investment in their children. There's some kind of wiggle-room."

"This is more than wiggle room," Eagly insists, and it's there that the battles begin. "Yes, there is a lot of sexual selection for the biological side of things," agrees Janice Juraskca, Ph.D., professor of psychology at the University of Illinois, "but one of the things that got selected that these guys [EPs] often forget is a flexible human brain." It's the flexibility question that's key, and it's on that question—a question that has major political and personal implications—that all battle-lines between the girls and the guys are drawn.

Eagly and a former student, Wendy Wood, Ph.D., now a professor at the Texas A&M University, have been working together to offer an alternative, what they call their "bio-social" model. Their work spans the fields of psychology, investigating hormones, cultural bias and other cross-cultural and cross-species evidence to determine what they consider a more complex understanding of gender differences.

Like the EPs, Eagly and Wood reject social constructionist notions that all gender differences are created by culture. But to the question of where they come from, they answer differently: not our genes but our roles in society. This narrative focuses on how societies respond to the basic biological differences—men's strength and women's reproductive capabilities—and how they encourage men and women to follow certain patterns. If you're spending a lot of time nursing your kid, explains Wood, "then you don't have the opportunity to devote large amounts of time to developing specialized skills and engaging tasks outside of the home." And, adds Eagly, "if women are charged with caring for infants, what happens is that women are more nurturing. Societies have to make the adult system work [so] socialization of girls is arranged to give them experience in nurturing."

According to this interpretation, as the environment changes, so will the range and texture of gender differences. At a time in Western countries when female reproduction is extremely low, nursing is totally optional, childcare alternatives are many, and mechanization lessens the importance of male size and strength, women are no longer restricted as much by their smaller size and by child-bearing. That means, argue Eagly and Wood, that role structures for men and women will change and, not surprisingly, the way we socialize people in these new roles will change too. (Indeed, says Wood, "sex differences seem to be reduced in societies where men and women have similar status," she says. If you're looking to live in more gender-neutral environment, try Scandinavia.)

Certainly these are more optimistic theories for women who have themselves moved into the "male" world of work outside the home. "I think," continues Eagly, that "we would expect the shift only toward women taking on masculine qualities, because that's where the social change has been in terms of roles," she explains. "Women have moved into a lot of male-dominated [areas]. You don't see the reciprocal shifts psychologically—men becoming kinder and more nurturing," she says, because the social changes haven't produced more contact between men and babies. What's critical for more equality, she says—equality being one of her goals—is a "less sharp division of labor."

In a footnote in his book *Civilization and Its Discontents*, Sigmund Freud offers a bizarre account of the origin of differences between the sexes. When left alone with a campfire, he explains, primitive man could not help but urinate on it. It was in his nature, a working out of his homosexual struggle with a competitive penis-symbol, the flame. It was part of being anatomically able and competitively-prone. See a fire, piss it out. That's how women—clearly less able in this sport—become the tenders of the hearth.

Certainly no one would debate that—were we able to put Freud on his own couch—this theory would tell us more about its author than about the origins of gender differences. We might interpret the theories of some liberal psychologists in a similar vein. In the heady revolutionary 1960s and '70s, they believed you could banish gender differences with a little re-education. "We thought," explains Diane Halpern, Ph.D., a professor of psychology at California State-San Bernadino, who began her research in the late 1970s, "that there weren't going to be many [differences], that they weren't going to be significant, and those that there were could be attributed to bias." (She has since revised her thinking.)

In the development of current theories, there's a lot more research going on. Eagly and Wood are working on a series of papers to prove their "social roles" theory. In his recent book, *Male, Female* (APA, 1998), Geary used some 1,200 references. "I had to do overkill in order to prove the point," he reflects, "because there's so much resistance to the idea that there are real biological differences."

But even with all this research, dramatic differences in interpretation come into a relief, along with a clear gender divide over the question of whether men and women must—biologically—adhere to certain behaviors. That story of philandering fathers developed by the EPs, for instance, could be just a story.

Indeed, says Lynn Miller, Ph.D., professor of communication and psychology at the University of Southern California, it's possible to tell an entirely different evolutionary tale. Forget the abandoning fathers. To her, "we were adapted for the important role of fathers as well as mothers." Miller argues that because human birthing is so difficult—the newborn's head is larger than the birth canal—and because human infants are so fragile, humans depend on fathers' active involvement. "We probably are the descendants of men who gave that additional care," she says. And, she adds, "When you look across cultures, where fathers are more heavily involved with offspring, their children are more likely to delay sexual activity, less likely to be violent, and more likely to be in a monogamous and more enduring relationship."

Raises eyebrows, doesn't it? The guys are telling us that men will naturally wander, and the gals, whether they follow evolutionary, social-role or social-constructionist theory, are telling us that's not so. They've all got something to back up their narrative, but there's one thing to remember: Each of these narratives was born creatively, at least in part, from the head of the researcher who promotes it. So before we are drawn into their battle of the sexes, perhaps we should be putting today's gender explorers on the couch as well.

READ MORE ABOUT IT

Gender Differences At Work, C. Williams, Neil Smelser (Univ. California Press, 1991)

Sarah Blustain is associate editor of Lilith Magazine *and a freelance writer living in New York.*

Parasites in Prêt-à-Porter

By Peggy Orenstein

Japan's young women are shunning marriage, spending big and still living with their parents. Are these 'Parasite Singles' the harbingers of a feminist revolution, or have they just gone *wagamama*?

On a Sunday afternoon, the Omotesando neighborhood in Tokyo swarms with women in their 20's and 30's. They spill out of stores with bags marked Gucci, Jil Sander, Issey Miyake, Comme des Garçons. They crowd cafes and snack on coffee and cake specials. They finger sleek tchotchkes on the shelves of home design stores, occasionally shouting, "*Kawaaaaaiiiii!*" the compliment supreme, which means, essentially, "cuuuuuuute!" As I cross the main thoroughfare, three women in their late 20's pass by, arms linked. They are actually singing "Girls Just Want to Have Fun."

Sumiko Arai waits for me at the Anniversaire cafe. Her hair is lightened to an of-the-moment reddish brown, cut in a layered bob. She carries a trendy canvas purse with sequined straps and is shod in high-heeled, animal- print mules with cripplingly pointed toes. Fish-net stockings? Of course. She even has the makeup right: neutral, with clear lip gloss and a bit of shimmer across the eyes. She waves when she spots me, a cell phone in her manicured hand, her right cheek dimpling in a grin.

Anniversaire, arguably Omotesando's most popular cafe, is attached to a department store specializing in weddings. Brides can shop for trousseau jewelry on the first floor, register for gifts on the second and third and buy frothy, Western-style dresses on the appointment-only upper levels. There is even a quaint wooden chapel where ceremonies are performed. Yet when a pair of cake-perfect newlyweds glide past the cafe, store clerks ringing hand bells behind them, the fashionable young women sipping cappuccino take little notice. Few of them are married or want to be any time soon. "If I were married," Arai says, "I'd have to worry about what my husband thinks, about cooking for him, cleaning. And if I had kids. . . . " She shrugs. "Child-rearing takes up so much time." Arai's cell phone chimes, a bell she always heeds. "Right now," she adds before answering it, "I don't have to worry about anything."

MORE THAN HALF OF JAPANESE WOMEN are still single by 30—compared with about 37 percent of American women— and nearly all of them live at home with Mom and Dad. Labeled "Parasite Singles" (after "Parasite Eve," a Japanese horror flick in which extraterrestrial hatchlings feed off unsuspecting human hosts before bursting, "Alien"-style, through their bellies), they pay no rent, do no housework and come and go freely. Although they earn, on average, just $27,000 a year, they are Japan's leading consumers, since their entire income is disposable. Despite Japan's continuing recession, they have created a boom in haute couture accessories by Louis Vuitton, Bulgari, Fendi and Prada, as well as in cell phones, minicars and other luxury goods. They travel more widely than their higher-earning male peers, dress more fashionably and are more sophisticated about food and culture.

While their spending sprees keep the Japanese economy afloat, their skittishness about traditional roles may soon threaten to capsize it. Japan's population is aging more rapidly than any on the planet—by 2015 one in four Japanese will be elderly. The birthrate has sunk to 1.34 per woman, well below replacement levels. (The birthrate in the United States, by contrast, is 2.08.) Last year, Japan dropped from the eighth-largest nation in the world to the ninth. The smallest class in recorded history just entered elementary school. Demographers predict that within two decades the shrinking labor force will make pension taxes and health care costs untenable, not to mention that there will not be enough workers to provide basic services for the elderly. There are whispers that to avoid ruin, Japan may have to do the unthinkable: encourage mass immigration, changing the very notion of what it means to be Japanese.

Politicians, economists and the media blame parasite women for the predicament. (Unmarried men can also be parasitic, but they have received far less scrutiny.) "They are like the ancient aristocrats of feudal times, but their parents play the role of servants," says Masahiro Yamada, a sociologist who coined the derogatory but instantly popular term "Parasite Single." (The clock on his 15 minutes of fame has been ticking ever since.) "Their lives are spoiled. The only thing that's important to them is seeking pleasure."

He may be right: parasite women may indeed be a sign of decadence, a hangover from the intoxicating materialism of the Bubble years of the 80's. But that conclusion, the most common one in the Japanese press, misses something more substantive: an unconscious protest against the rigidity of both traditional family roles and Japan's punishing professional system.

"Maybe they appear to be spoiled," says Yoko Kunihiro, a sociologist who studies dissatisfaction among women in their 30's, "but you could also perceive Parasite Singles as the embodiment of a criticism against society. Seen from the perspective of conventional values, even feminist values, they seem like a very negative force, but I see something positive in them."

THERE WAS A TIME WHEN A WOMAN SUMIKO Arai's age would have been dismissed as "Christmas cake": like a holiday pastry, her shelf life would have expired at 25. But sell-by dates have changed in Japan, along with male predilections: high-profile sports heroes like the Seattle Mariner Ichiro Suzuki and the sumo grand champion Takanohana are married to women several years their senior. Instead of calling her a stale sweet, Arai's parents, with more affection than disapproval, call her *para-chan* ("little parasite": "chan" is the diminutive in Japanese). "They tell me to get married and leave the house," she says. "But if they really thought that, they'd try to set me up on *omiai*"—matchmaking meetings. "My mom has said to me, 'Make sure you find the right guy.' I think she's speaking from personal experience. Maybe she feels she did find the right guy. But I think sometimes she's telling me because she wishes she'd chosen better herself."

Arai is in her late 20's, the younger of two children—her older brother is married but childless. Her mother is a housewife, her father a salaryman whom she speaks of fondly. That is somewhat unusual; most of the women I met felt little connection to their dads, whose careers took precedence over family life. "We don't have an emotional bond," one woman explained. "I try to be nice to him now that he's retired, but I hardly saw him growing up."

Arai is the publicist for Girlsgate.com, one of several Web sites for women that have sprung up over the last year in Japan. Girlsgate hopes to lure the discerning parasite with articles on the history of

Hermès fashions and tips on customizing designer shoes. The editor in chief, Yoshiko Izumi, 31, is a former Miss Fairlady, the generic term for a woman who stands smilingly next to new-model vehicles at car shows. Although not a parasite herself—Izumi has been married to her business partner for seven years—she says she understands the parasite psychology. "They're not dependent on men financially," she explains as we huddle around an i-Mac at Girlsgate headquarters, touring the site. "They're enjoying their lives. They don't want to give up that pleasure for marriage." She turns to Arai. "Isn't that right?"

> 'Maybe I am *wagamama*. I don't know. I do want to get married eventually, but I have to find the right guy. **Meanwhile, I want to look cool.**'

Like employees of dot-com start-ups anywhere, Arai frequently clocks 12-hour days, sometimes more, which separates her from the parasite pack. "I didn't expect that when I took the job," she confides later. Although she finds the work satisfying and is carefully politic in her enthusiasm for the company, the long hours are, quite simply, tedious. She never set out to be the woman in the gray flannel kimono. "You have to put in a ridiculous amount of time to succeed in Japanese society," she says. "But if you have a typical office lady job, you work regular hours. After work you can take lessons, spend time with friends, have dinner. That's why women in Japan have much better lives than men."

Girlsgate was launched last year on March 3, which in Japan is Girls' Day: families with daughters display dolls representing the ancient royal court, eat foods symbolizing purity and pray for their girls' happiness. Legend has it that if mothers don't pack the dolls away promptly after the holiday, their daughters will be slow to find a husband. Apparently, in Sumiko Arai's generation, there were a lot of lazy moms. "No one is actually rejecting marriage," Izumi says quickly. "Not even Sumiko. They all think they'll probably get married some day. It's just..." She breaks off and laughs. "Women today are *wagamama*."

Her word choice is significant. *Wagamama* means selfish, willful; in a culture where personal sacrifice is the highest virtue, the connotation is far harsher, especially for women. Yet, as the parasite trend has emerged, women like Arai have taken on the word *wagamama*, albeit slightly tongue in cheek, as a term of defiance—somewhat like the way American women use "girl" or African-Americans say "nigga"—transforming its meaning in the process to something closer to "choosy" or even "self-determining." Makiko Tanaka, Japan's first female foreign minister, who has been flayed in the press as "rude" and "incompetent," is *wagamama*. Princess Masako, whose sole purpose is to produce an heir to the throne, is not. Women's magazines have caught the trend, featuring headlines like "Restaurants for the Wagamama You." One afternoon, I even walked by an office building on which WAGAMAMA was painted in English letters 10 stories high. Although women would initially startle when I asked if they were wagamama, they would, with some self-mockery, accept the label: it had clearly become a kind of resistance against expectations.

"Maybe I am *wagamama*," Arai says. "I don't know. I do want to get married eventually, but I have to find the right guy." She grins mischievously. "Meanwhile, I want to look cool."

If you were a 30-ish parasite in the spring of 2001, you would mix your Uniqlo T-shirts (Uniqlo being the Japanese version of the Gap) with high-end designer accessories. You would be considering the purchase of a wide belt. You would take lessons in English or French. You would frequent galleries. You would be planning a vacation to Vietnam. You would be tiring of Italian restaurants and returning to Japanese, served in a Western setting. In a nation where the G.D.P. is driven by consumer spending, you would be part of an economic powerhouse. The entertainment, travel and fashion industries would cater to your slightest whim. Consider: Since the current recession began in 1994, the G.D.P. has dropped nearly 20 percent. Japanese sales of Louis Vuitton products, meanwhile, have soared from $36 million to $863 million annually, accounting for a full third of the company's worldwide sales.

"We're heading into a market in which mothers in their 50's and daughters in their 20's and 30's are the main consumers," explains Jun Aburatani, founder of the Tokyo marketing firm Gauss. He calls it the New 50 Pattern Society. "The mothers are beginning to live their lives after long years spent child-rearing. The daughters are liberated from social pressure to get married, so they, too, are beginning to live their lives. You can see it already: even during the recession we're in now, entertainment, designer products and healthy products are strong sellers: red wine, olive oil, vitamins, travel, performing arts, diet products. Young women are very positive about enjoying their lives. They go to hot-springs resorts. They buy clothes, shoes, purses, cosmetics. Men don't. And that reflects a difference in attitude between fathers and mothers. The women are much more vivacious." According to Gauss, men over 50 want to die before their wives—and their wives want them to as well. Widowhood, the women say, is the best time of their lives.

Switch on Japanese TV, and you'll see this new trend mirrored in advertising. In America, where there has been a second baby boom, children symbolize satisfaction and fulfillment. Soft-focus images of infants or families are used to hawk cars, insurance, coffee, prescription drugs. Japanese ads are comparatively baby-free. "We're becoming a society that excludes children," Aburatani says. "Whether you think it's good or bad, that's the way it is. Many women over 50 found marriage to be a disappointment and motherhood to be a burden. They tell that to their adult daughters, and that makes their daughters want to stay single. They doubt whether husbands and children are worth it."

As I leave Gauss, the woman who served the obligatory tea during my meeting with Aburatani stops me. "Would you like to ask me some questions?" she says. "I fit into your demographic—I'm 26 years old with no plans to marry." I agree, and we head downstairs to a Subway sandwich shop. Because she has her own apartment, Chiho Kashiwagi is not strictly speaking a Parasite Single, although she would be if her parents didn't live so far from Tokyo. She points out that those who condemn parasites tend to overlook the fact that women in Japan, as in most countries, earn less than men

and that Tokyo rents are prohibitively expensive. Not to mention that until 1986, many employers required single women to live with their parents, and some continue to look askance at those who don't.

Kashiwagi can't imagine modeling her life on her mother's, who is a housewife. "I see her dissatisfaction," she says. But would she like to live like her father? Kashiwagi laughs and tucks her hair behind her ears. "How can I answer that?" she says. "I'd like to be like him in the sense that he's independent, but if you mean working like a traditional Japanese man, no. He worked very long hours and devoted his life almost exclusively to his work. He has no hobbies, no outside interests. That conflicts with other things I want to do."

Kashiwagi admires Makiko Tanaka's political career, especially the very qualities that have drawn fire from the press: her outspokenness and common touch. Kashiwagi confides that her secret ambition is to pursue a career in politics, but since she'd also like to be a mother, she's not sure it's a realistic dream. Women like Tanaka—a prominent public figure who identifies herself as a "housewife"—are still the exception. For most women, it's still nearly impossible to have both a family and a career. "There's a term in Japan called the *ie*," Kashiwagi says. "It's like the household, but it means more than that." The word feels weighty, implying the family as institution. "Even now, Japanese marriage isn't between two individuals, but two ies. And that's the reason I'm single now. If I were married, I'd be influenced by the idea of the ie, by the expectations I'd feel."

> In Japan, where women for centuries were raised to be 'good wives and wise mothers,' Kashiwagi's simple assertion—
> ## 'I want to enjoy my life'
> —is itself a radical act.

Kashiwagi wants to put off taking her place in the *ie* for as long as possible—perhaps until her mid-30's. Why would she be more willing to relinquish her professional goals then? "Well, I won't have much time left to have children, and I don't want to be a single mother," she says. We sit in silence a moment, then

she perks up. "For now, though, I want to live for myself and enjoy my life."

"Live for myself and enjoy my life." I heard that phrase, articulated precisely that way, from every single woman I interviewed. It was as if they had all read it in the same magazine (which is, in fact, possible). They said it with such finality, as if it explained something. When pressed, they would cite the freedom to go to nice restaurants, hang out with friends, buy clothes on a whim, do what they want. But listening to Kashiwagi, it dawns on me: for American women, self-determination may be the bedrock on which we build our dreams, but in Japan, where women for centuries were raised to be "good wives and wise mothers," simply asserting "I want to live for myself" or "I want to enjoy my life" is itself a radical act—even if it's unclear where it may lead.

I ask Kashiwagi, If I come back to visit her in 10 years, where will she be? "I wonder," she muses. "I suppose I could be a politician. But maybe I'll just be an ordinary housewife."

LONG BEFORE MAKIKO TANAKA THERE WAS Mariko Bando, one of Japan's best-known female politicians; she is currently director general of the Gender Equality Bureau Cabinet Office and a regular on the pundit circuit. Her bureau is charged with the amorphous task of "encouraging other ministries to look at gender issues" as well as strategizing on how to better support mothers in the workplace. So far, she has generated lots of paper with few results, which has been frustrating.

Rather than dismissing the parasites as merely spoiled children, overindulged by their parents, Bando says she believes there is also an economic explanation for the phenomenon. "We understand why Japanese women don't want to have children," she says. "Once they're married, they have to do all the housework. Japanese husbands may help some, but they won't share the burden. Also, if women work as hard as men they can be promoted—not always, but it's possible—but if they have children and stop working, it's virtually impossible to re-enter the work force. Many well-educated women quit and become housewives whether they want to or not. So instead, women are postponing marriage and/or childbirth."

The typical employment pattern for women in Japan is age-related, following an M curve: it peaks by 24, drops sharply, then spikes again in the early 50's (when former housewives take low-level part-time jobs) before falling off for good at 55. By comparison, American women's employment stays steady from their 20's until around 60. Some Japanese economists believe that boosting women's labor-force participation rate to U.S. levels during their 30's, 40's and 50's would lower inflation and raise the G.D.P. It would offset the labor shortage caused by the declining birthrate and revitalize Japan's economy. But that doesn't appear to be an argument either government or business is heeding; according to the Economic Planning Agency, working conditions for women have actually worsened in Japan since the 1980's. "They agree in principle," Bando says, "but a lot of men in the government are themselves uncomfortable with working mothers as colleagues."

Meanwhile, the psychological impact of the M curve, which Kashiwagi and Arai are preparing for, goes a long way toward explaining the parasite phenomenon. If, because of social pressures and discrimination—not to mention long, inflexible working hours, grueling commutes, lack of support from her husband and limited child care—a woman has to quit her job after having children, and never return, what is the motivation for someone who wants kids to push herself professionally? What is the motivation for an ambitious woman to contemplate motherhood? I recalled something that Yumi Matsushita, a 33-year-old interpreter, said to me: "You commute long hours in unfashionable trains and eat bad canteen food and for what? Do these men have good lives? And even if you get promoted, you have more drinking to do, more time at the office, more time away from family. And if you have a child, it will become even more difficult. So you have to wonder, what's the point in pushing harder?

"At the same time, once you become a mother, you're a mother. That's it. You're not a woman anymore. You can't work anymore. And the father's not involved. It's very confining. It limits your activities, your financial freedom. It's really not attractive."

So far, the government's main response to the baby bust has been to hike child allowances to about $2,400 a year per child for six years. Some conservative politicians would like to go further, increasing them tenfold. The idea is to offer an incentive for women to stay home,

making larger reforms unnecessary. Bando scoffs at that. "Women don't need a child allowance, they need services," she says, especially more day-care centers open longer hours. (Japanese nannies are virtually nonexistent, and hiring foreigners is illegal.) But creating more places to park the kids would not challenge the system a whole lot more than child subsidies do. Business meetings would still start at 8 p.m. Leaving work to tend to a sick child would still be considered a sign of disloyalty. "It's a workaholic culture," Bando agrees. "We have to change the structure of Japanese companies." And how will that be done? "This is the most difficult challenge," she says, shaking her head.

Bando is herself the mother of a 28-year-old Parasite Single who works in a pharmaceutical laboratory. Her dreams for her daughter often seem muddled. "Like many mothers, we think of our daughters as another version of ourselves," she says. "Most of my college friends quit their jobs to become housewives. They encouraged their daughters to have careers, and some do. My friend's daughter is a rising star in her profession, but she's single. And my friend says: 'I pity her. She can't marry and have children.' Even though this career is what my friend wanted for her. Maybe we can change it. I'm hoping it will change. But I'm not seeing it. Not yet."

If you watch TV, it seems like American women feel a lot of pressure to marry or to be in couples," says Shuko Sadamoto, a single 34-year-old economist. "Do you think they just marry because it's *time*?"

Mihoka Iida, a 34-year-old magazine editor who lives with her parents, adds: "That obsession with having a boyfriend. . . . We just don't feel that paranoia. I mean, I enjoy 'Ally McBeal'"—which recently came to Japan as "Ally My Love"—but she seems so extreme. That dancing baby?" She rolls her eyes. "I think I'm doing Japan a favor by not having children. There are too many people in this country anyway." They both laugh.

Sadamoto and Iida have each traveled widely in Asia, Europe and North America. Sadamoto, who is shy and a little tomboyish, attended graduate school at Columbia University. Iida, tall and elegant in Comme des Garçons, spent her high-school years in Vancouver. They

say it's easier to be single in Japan, removed from America's pervasive "couples culture." "In the U.S. you're supposed to be together with your boyfriend or husband all the time," says Iida. "In Japan, women have their ways of having fun and men have their ways. You're not expected to bring a date everywhere, and you don't feel excluded if you're not involved with someone."

We are having drinks after work at Shunju, a restaurant at the top of a new skyscraper with a panoramic view of the city. Pinpoints of light beam down on our plates from artfully placed halogens, refracting onto our faces with a flattering glow. We are drinking wine and joking, but then Iida suddenly turns serious. "In a way, the men have to pay for what they've created in Japan," she says. "They hire all these educated, intelligent, even bilingual women in their companies, but then they don't utilize them the way they could. So that means the men have to work 24 hours a day, but the women don't. I suppose if this were America, women in that position would feel discriminated against, and they'd try to do something about it. We just react by going out and having fun, by not being part of it."

Of course women would like to have broader professional opportunities, they say, but not under the current conditions. "I don't know how men do it," Iida says. "When I first started working, I looked at the guys above me—and they were all guys—and I thought, I don't aspire to that. Living and working like men in Japan is not something to dream of. But then, I think that's related to the difficulty of having dreams in general."

Ever since the Bubble economy burst, Iida says, young people in Japan—both women and men—have lost hope. The Parasite Single phenomenon is merely a symptom of their pessimism. Women do tend to defer marriage and children during economic downturns: America's birthrate reached a historic low during the Great Depression. Perhaps in Japan it just looks different, with women deflecting despair by pursuing the perfect pair of shoes. "It's easy to blame women for the declining birthrate," Iida says. "To blame so-called Parasite Singles. But this isn't our making. We didn't create all these problems with the economy that have brought us to where we are now, where women have no hope for the future."

Sadamoto admits that she's not optimistic about the future. "Maybe if I were,

I'd have children," she says. "It's difficult to have dreams when the economy is so bad."

Iida says: "I don't really understand how Americans can be optimistic about marriage and children. It's possible, even probable, that it won't work out, but you do it anyway. I don't get it. We don't idealize family life. We never had a Japanese version of 'The Brady Bunch.'"

Sadamoto adds: "That's why being single doesn't feel like a sacrifice. It's the other way around—you have your own time and your own income. You weren't forced to get married to someone you didn't really like just because you were supposed to. That seems like a good thing."

THOSE WHO HAVE TRIED TO MAKE PARASITE singles the whipping girls for Japan's declining birthrate tend to believe that the solution is a return to the traditional family, in which men work and women stay home. In fact, the two factors that are keeping birthrates up in the United States are both distinctly nontraditional. One is single motherhood, which in America accounts for one-third of births. The second, according to World Bank data, is female employment. Women's earning power appears to raise confidence in the future: it gives young couples hope. Economic conditions in the West helped push women into the workplace; perhaps the situation in Japan will need to become significantly more dire before that solution is seriously considered. "In the United States and other countries, the economy went through gut-wrenching pain and got to a point where you couldn't afford one income to support a family," said Kathy Matsui, an analyst for Goldman Sachs in Tokyo. "That forced change."

Japan is nothing if not adaptable. It is a country with near-archaeological layers of tradition that can, nonetheless, change as quickly as Tokyo fashions. Consider: One day Japan operated on the feudal system. The next day it did not. One day the emperor was a god. The next day he was not. One day it was unthinkable for a woman to hold a cabinet post. Today Makiko Tanaka is the country's most popular politician. If such vast, deep transformation can happen so rapidly, there may yet be hope for breaking the deadlock between Parasite Singles and a government that needs more bodies.

One spring afternoon, I visited Mitsuko Shimomura, a pioneering female journalist who, in her 60's, has taken over for her 90-year-old mother as administrator of her family's health clinic in Tokyo. She is also director of the Gender Equity Center in Fukushima prefecture, about an hour and a half outside Tokyo. "I don't regret the decline in the birthrate," Shimomura told me. "I think it's a good thing. The Parasites have unintentionally created an interesting movement. Politicians now have to beg women to have babies. Unless they create a society where women feel comfortable having children and working, Japan will be destroyed in a matter of 50 or 100 years. And child subsidies aren't going to do it. Only equality is."

Peggy Orenstein is a contributing writer for the [*New York Times* Magazine] and author of "Flux: Women on Sex, Work, Love, Kids and Life in a Half-Changed World."

NEVER TOO BUFF

A new book reveals a troubling obsession:
How male self-worth is increasingly tied to body image

By JOHN CLOUD Boston

POP QUIZ. WHO ARE MORE LIKELY TO BE dissatisfied with the appearance of their chests, men or women? Who is more likely to be concerned about acne, your teenage son or his sister? And who is more likely to binge eat, your nephew or your niece?

If you chose the women and girls in your life, you are right only for the last question—and even then, not by the margin you might expect. About 40% of Americans who go on compulsive-eating sprees are men. Thirty-eight percent of men want bigger pecs, while only 34% of women want bigger breasts. And more boys have fretted about zits than girls, going all the way back to a 1972 study.

A groundbreaking new book declares that these numbers, along with hundreds of other statistics and interviews the authors have compiled, mean something awful has happened to American men over the past few decades. They have become obsessed with their bodies. Authors Harrison Pope and Katharine Phillips, professors of psychiatry at Harvard and Brown, respectively, and Roberto Olivardia, a clinical

psychologist at McLean Hospital in Belmont, Mass., have a catchy name to describe this obsession—a term that will soon be doing many reps on chat shows: the Adonis Complex.

The name, which refers to the gorgeous half man, half god of mythology, may be a little too ready for *Oprah*, but the theory behind it will start a wonderful debate. Based on original research involving more than 1,000 men over the past 15 years, the book argues that many men desperately want to look like Adonis because they constantly see the "ideal," steroid-boosted bodies of actors and models and because their muscles are all they have over women today. In an age when women fly combat missions, the authors ask, "What can a modern boy or man do to distinguish himself as being 'masculine'?"

For years, of course, some men—ice skaters, body builders, George Hamilton—have fretted over aspects of their appearance. But the numbers suggest that body-image concerns have gone mainstream: nearly half of men don't like their overall appearance, in

contrast to just 1 in 6 in 1972. True, men typically are fatter now, but another study found that 46% of men of normal weight think about their appearance "all the time" or "frequently." And some men—probably hundreds of thousands, if you extrapolate from small surveys—say they have passed up job and even romantic opportunities because they refuse to disrupt workouts or dine on restaurant food. In other words, an increasing number of men would rather look brawny for their girlfriends than have sex with them.

Consider what they're spending. Last year American men forked over $2 billion for gym memberships—and another $2 billion for home exercise equipment. *Men's Health* ("Rock-hard abs in six weeks!" it screams every other issue) had 250,000 subscribers in 1990; now it has 1.6 million. In 1996 alone, men underwent some 700,000 cosmetic procedures.

At least those profits are legal. Anabolic steroids—the common name for synthetic testosterone—have led to the most dramatic changes in the male form in modern history, and more and more average

BODY BOOSTERS Here are some of the substances some men use to bulk up:

PROTEINS

Protein is the building block of muscle growth. It repairs muscle tissue broken down while training. It's sold in powders and bars under names like MET-Rx and Myoplex. These are acceptable sources of protein, but there is little evidence that they are superior to ordinary foods like skim milk or lean meat. Long-term use of very high doses of protein may cause kidney and liver damage.

FAT BURNERS

Include the drug ephedrine, which comes from the plant Ephedra. Ephedrine is a powerful stimulant used in diet pills, herbal ecstasy and energy-booster products. It promotes fat loss, but weight is quickly retained when use stops. It has caused seizures and strokes, especially among those with high blood pressure and diabetes. The FDA says it has been associated with at least 58 deaths since 1994.

CREATINE

A nutrient found in red meat, it produces energy and helps restore muscle tissue after strenuous exercise. Several studies show it increases lean body mass, though some of this gain is probably water. Long-term use of high doses of creatine hasn't been studied, though there are no known short-term dangers. It comes in many forms: powder, liquid, gum.

ADRENAL HORMONES

Naturally produced in humans and animals, these hormones are partly metabolized into testosterone in the body, and thus are claimed to promote muscle growth. Mark McGwire said he had used them to get a more efficient workout and a faster recovery from weight lifting. (He says he no longer uses them.) It may increase levels of cholesterol and help develop female breast tissue. Long-term dangers are unknown.

DUBIOUS DRUGS

Anabolic steroids classified as controlled substances are synthetic testosterone that is injected into muscle tissue or taken orally to promote muscle growth and enhance athletic performance. Serious side effects include liver damage, cancer and heart disease. Other prescription products are growth hormones like GHB, which is thought to stimulate natural hormone secretion but is also used as an alternative to ecstasy.

    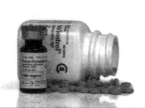

men want those changes for themselves. Since steroids became widely available on the black market in the 1960s, perhaps 3 million American men have swallowed or injected them—mostly in the past 15 years. A 1993 survey found that 1 Georgia high school boy in every 15 admitted having used steroids without a prescription. And the Drug Enforcement Administration reports that the percentage of all high school students who have used steroids has increased 50% in the past four years, from 1.8% to 2.8%. The abuse of steroids has so alarmed the National Institute on Drug Abuse that on Friday it launched a campaign in gyms, malls, bookstores, clubs and on the Internet to warn teenagers about the dangers. Meanwhile, teenagers in even larger numbers are buying legal but lightly regulated food supplements, some with dangerous side effects, that purport to make you bigger or leaner or stronger.

As they infiltrated the body-building world in the '70s and Hollywood a decade later, steroids created bodies for mass consumption that the world had literally never seen before. Pope likes to chart the changes by looking at Mr. America winners, which he called up on the Internet in his office last week. "Look at this guy," Pope exclaims when he clicks on the 1943 winner, Jules Bacon. "He couldn't even win a county body-building contest today." Indeed, there are 16-year-olds working out at your gym who are as big as Bacon. Does that necessarily mean that today's body builders—including those 16-year-olds—are 'roided? Pope is careful. "The possibility exists that rare or exceptional people, those with an unusual genetic makeup or a hormonal imbalance," could achieve the muscularity and leanness of today's big body builders, he says.

But it's not likely. And Pope isn't lobbing dumbbells from an ivory tower: the professor lifts weights six days a week, from 11 a.m. to 1 p.m. (He can even mark historical occasions by his workouts: "I re-member when the *Challenger* went down; I was doing a set of squats.") "We are being assaulted by images virtually impossible to attain without the use of drugs," says Pope. "So what happens when you change a million-year-old equilibrium of nature?"

A historical loop forms: steroids beget pro wrestlers—Hulk Hogan, for one, has admitted taking steroids—who inspire boys to be just like them. Steroids have changed even boys' toys. Feminists have long derided Barbie for her tiny waist and big bosom. The authors of *The Adonis Complex* see a similar problem for boys in the growth of G.I. Joe. The grunt of 1982 looks scrawny compared with G.I. Joe Extreme, introduced in the mid-'90s. The latter would have a 55-in. chest and 22-in. biceps if he were real, which simply can't be replicated in nature. Pope also points out a stunning little feature of the three-year-old video game Duke Nukem: Total Meltdown, developed by GT Interactive Software. When Duke gets tired, he can

VIEWPOINT • Joel Stein

I BLED FOR THIS COLUMN

ICANNOT WAIT TO LATHER UP MY NAKED, HAIRY BODY IN AN IN-flatable pool full of testosterone gel. I have felt testosterone deficient since I was five, when, surrounded by female friends, I spent my days compiling my sticker collection, listening to the *Annie* sound track, baking in my Easy-Bake Oven and arranging my glass-animal collection. Peggy Fleming had a more masculine childhood than I did.

But I needed to know precisely how unmanly I am, so I went to my doctor to get my T count checked. Unfortunately, my doctor could not administer the test via saliva; he would need a blood sample. That made me consider canceling my appointment, which in and of itself delivered the result I needed. But I made the appointment anyway. In 48 hours I would know how much man was in me.

For a long time, I've overcompensated for my lack of manliness through sportswriting, porn watching and stock buying, but deep down I know I'm a little shy on T. I cannot yell at other drivers, raise my voice, pick up women in a bar or grow a full beard. All whiskey, no matter how expensive, just tastes like burning. Yet deep inside I long to sleep around, to kick some ass, to release my first rap album. As I saw it, I had little choice but to score some of that testosterone gel when it comes out this summer. I could keep it in my jacket pocket for emergency situations, next to my lip balm and antibacterial hand gel. I'm thinking about marketing this as a first-aid kit for wusses.

Waiting for my results, feeling especially insecure, I called my masculinity mentor, Adam Carolla, the host of Comedy Central's *The Man Show*. "I'm guessing you're a little light," Carolla said. He suggested that I sign up for the AndroGel now. "A little extra aggres-sion, a couple of extra inches on the biceps, a little body hair could help you," he said. When I mentioned my concern about taking un-prescribed medication, Carolla suggested that I just eat a lot of beef jerky. "I believe there is a lot of testosterone in jerky. That would be the most logical food to put it in, anyway," I suggested I might enjoy it more as a pasta with a light tomato-basil sauce, which I could mar-ket as "testosteroni." Carolla said he had to go.

Still anxious about my results, I called a former girlfriend, figur-ing she'd make me feel better. "I bet it's freakishly low," she said. "You're afraid of dogs; you once owned an Easy-Bake Oven; and you've never been much for fighting." Now I remembered there were good reasons our relationship didn't work out (one of them be-ing that I told her about the Easy-Bake Oven).

After two neurosis-filled days, my doctor called and told me my testosterone level was totally normal. When I pressed him for a num-ber, he said it was within the normal range of 260 to 1,000. When I really pressed him for a number, he told me it was 302. When I start-ed to freak out about being in the bottom 10%, he again reassured me that it was completely normal. Yeah, normal in that I don't have breasts.

One of my female friends tried to comfort me, saying that women may have hot, wild flings with high-testosterone men, but they settle down with hormonally balanced guys. This did not make me feel better. You'd have to have a T count of 20 for this to make you feel any better. All I could think about was that now I have one less ex-cuse for having an affair. Unless, of course, I'm all hopped up on man gel.

---

find a bottle of steroids to get him going. "Steroids give Duke a super adrenaline rush," the game manual notes.

To bolster their argument, the *Adonis* authors developed a computerized test that allows subjects to "add" muscle to a typical male body. They estimate their own size and then pick the size they would like to be and the size they think women want. Pope and his colleagues gave the test to college students and found that on average, the men wanted 28 lbs. more muscle—and thought women wanted them to have 30 lbs. more. In fact, the women who took the test picked an ideal man only slightly more muscular than average. Which goes a long way to-ward explaining why Leonardo DiCaprio can be a megastar in a nation that also ide-alizes "Stone Cold" Steve Austin.

But when younger boys took Pope's test, they revealed an even deeper sense of inadequacy about their bodies. More than half of boys ages 11 to 17 chose as their physical ideal an image possible to attain only by using steroids. So they do. Boys

are a big part of the clientele at Muscle Ma-nia (not its real name), a weight-lifting store that TIME visited last week at a strip mall in a Boston suburb. A couple of teen-agers came in to ask about tribulus, one of the many over-the-counter drugs and body-building supplements the store sells, all legally.

A FRIEND OF MINE," ONE BOY BEGINS, fooling no one, "just came off a cycle of juice, and he heard that tribulus can help you produce testosterone naturally." Patrick, 28, who runs the store and who stopped using steroids four years ago because of chest pain, tells the kid, "The s___ shuts off your nuts," meaning steroids can reduce sperm produc-tion, shrink the testicles and cause impo-tence. Tribulus, Patrick says, can help restart natural testosterone production. The teen hands over $12 for 100 Tribulus Fuel pills. (Every day, Muscle Mania does $4,000 in sales of such products, with protein supple-ments and so-called fat burners leading the pack.)

Patrick says many of his teen customers, because they're short on cash, won't pay for a gym membership "until they've saved up for a cycle [of steroids]. They don't see the point without them." The saddest customers, he says, are the little boys, 12 and 13, brought in by young fathers. "The dad will say, 'How do we put some weight on this kid?' with the boy just staring at the floor. Dad is going to turn him into Hulk Hogan, even if it's against his will."

What would motivate someone to take steroids? Pope, Phillips and Olivardia say the Adonis Complex works in different ways for different men. "Michael," 32, one of their research subjects, told TIME he had always been a short kid who got picked on. He started working out at about 14, and he bought muscle maga-zines for advice. The pictures taunted him: he sweated, but he wasn't getting as big as the men in the pictures. Other men in his gym also made him feel bad. When he found out they were on steroids, he did two cycles himself, even though he knew they could be dangerous.

But not all men with body-image problems take steroids. Jim Davis, 29, a human-services manager, told TIME he never took them, even when training for body-building competitions. But Davis says he developed a form of obsessive-compulsive disorder around his workouts. He lifted weights six days a week for at least six years. He worked out even when injured. He adhered to a rigid regimen for every session, and if he changed it, he felt anxious all day. He began to be worried about clothes, and eventually could wear only three shirts, ones that made him look big. He still felt small. "I would sit in class at college with a coat on," he says. You may have heard this condition called bigorexia—thinking your muscles are puny when they aren't. Pope and his colleagues call it muscle dysmorphia and estimate that hundreds of thousands of men suffer from it.

Even though most boys and men never approach the compulsion of Davis or Michael (both eventually conquered it), they undoubtedly face more pressure now than in the past to conform to an impossible ideal. Ripped male bodies are used today to advertise everything that shapely female bodies advertise: not just fitness products but also dessert liqueurs, microwave ovens and luxury hotels. The authors of *The Adonis Complex* want guys to rebel against those images, or at least see them for what they are: a goal unattainable without drug use.

Feminists raised these issues for women years ago, and more recent books such as *The Beauty Myth* were part of a backlash against the hourglass ideal. Now, says Phillips, "I actually think it may be harder for men than women to talk about these problems because it's not considered masculine to worry about such things." But maybe there is a masculine alternative: Next time WWF comes on, guys, throw the TV out the window. And order a large pizza.

From *Time*, April 24, 2000, pp. 64–68. © 2000 by Time Inc. Magazine Company. Reprinted by permission.

"THE UNIFORM FOR TODAY IS BELLY BUTTONS"

The number of nudist women our age has doubled over the past six years. Gigi Guerra strips down to uncover the scoop.

I don't get excited about being naked in group situations. Sure, I've skinny-dipped, played strip poker, streaked, and gone on my fair share of gyno visits—but it's not as if these things helped define who I am as a person. I did what I had to do and then put my pants back on. Simply put, I love wearing clothes. I love buying clothes even more. Strip me of the joy of shopping and you've removed half the woman.

So now I hear that nudism is trendy. Not for old hippies, but for people our age. The American Association of Nude Recreation says the number of their 18- to 34-year-old members has increased by 50 percent since 1994. According to Nicky Hoffman, the administrative director of the Naturist Society (another organization for nudists), almost a third of their members are in their 20s and 30s. And though there are still more guys than girls, Nicky says she wouldn't be surprised if women soon start to outnumber men. To see what the big deal is, I flew to suburban Sacramento, Calif., site of Laguna del Sol, one of the biggest nudist resorts in the country. Needless to say, packing was a breeze.

"I never want to buy a swimsuit again."

"Most people come here for the first time out of curiosity," explains 36-year-old Patty Sailors, a perky, intelligent brunette who, along with her husband, manages Laguna. "The relaxing atmosphere keeps them here." I'm standing with her in the carpeted main office. We're both clothed, defying the hand-painted sign on the wall announcing: THE UNIFORM FOR TODAY IS BELLY BUTTONS. People around us are forking over four bucks a night for campsites, $12 for RV hookups and 90 bills for modern, air-conditioned rooms. Patty says she expects a crowd of at least 500 this weekend.

Tie-dye T-shirts hang on a rack in the back of the room. They're promoting Nudestock, a yearly Laguna blowout that brings hot dogs, a cover band, and vast expanses of uncovered genitals together under the sun. Nudists seem to like theme events. There's even a Truman Capote-esque Black-and-White Ball in April. I ask Patty how a nudist can properly "dress" for such an event. "Oh, people use lots of body paint," she laughs. "Some guys even draw their tuxes on." Is that with or without the cummerbund?

Patty gives me a tour of the grounds in a silver golf cart that looks like a mini Rolls-Royce. As we putt along, she explains that all guests are taken on tours like this—not just as a courtesy, but also to weed out freaks. "We make sure this is not a sexual environment," says Patty. Laguna bills itself as a family resort, and everything here whiffs of kids, couples and young singles keeping their hands to themselves. But about one in 70 people is turned away because they're married and try to come without their spouse. Occasionally, Patty says, others are denied entry because they gawk too much, make crude jokes, or give off weird vibes.

"Most have their first taste of nudism by getting N.I.F.C.," says Patty, as we cruise by a row of mobile homes. I see my first naked person and giggle to myself. "That means Nude In Front of the Computer," she continues, reining in my amusement. "Or, they'll walk around the house nude." We pass a volleyball game. One guy—clad only in a cropped T-shirt—jumps up to spike the ball. His penis follows. I'm simultaneously mesmerized and horrified. Does it hurt?

Patty's first taste of nudism came when she stopped wearing pj's in high school. "Then I started skinny-dipping," she explains. "The main reason I became a nudist is because I don't ever want to have to buy a swimsuit again." She's serious: Bathing attire is one of the

29

biggest taboos in the world of nudism. Resort-wear designers, take note.

"Clothing hides who you are."

I stay in one of the motel-like rooms. It's spacious and clean, with a huge bed, generic art and a switch-on fireplace. There's even an indoor pool down the hall. It feels like I'm at the Marriott—except for the naked people who keep walking by my door. A water volleyball game is in full swing. (No, not that kind of swing. Get your mind out of the gutter.) I realize that this is the perfect time to get naked—I can run and hide in the pool; everyone will be too busy to notice.

I'm buck-naked in a room full of imperfection, and strangely, it feels comforting.

I strip, grab my towel and leave the room. Within seconds, I have a panic attack. I've never had issues with my body, but now I start to obsess: My butt feels too bony, and suddenly a Brazilian bikini wax doesn't seem like such a bad idea. I pray nobody looks at me.

But as soon as I enter the pool area, I'm relieved. Two women on lounge chairs have 10 times the pubic hair I do. A college-aged girl sitting by the hot tub has cellulite. Droopy breasts abound. The variety of penis sizes and shapes is astounding. I'm buck-naked in a room full of imperfections, and strangely, it feels sort of comforting.

Late Friday evening, a DJ kicks off a dance in the clubhouse. I'm perched by the bar, clad only in a gauzy cotton top (it's a little chilly). Though it's strange to socialize with my pubes showing, it's also refreshing to be around broads who aren't constantly in the rest room inspecting their asses in the mirror. Emily, a curly-haired accountant in her early 30s, couldn't care less about pathetic preening. She's been dancing all night with only a sky-blue butterfly clip in her hair, a big diamond ring on her finger and the determination to have a good time. She's here with her daughters, her brother and her fiancé, whom she met through a dating game on the radio. Emily tells me that one of her girls, who has a surgery scar on her chest, likes coming to Laguna because nobody is freaked out by her body. "I don't think [women] should be ashamed to be naked," she shouts over the pounding beat. "Here, it doesn't matter what your body looks like. Clothing is a way for people to hide who they really are."

Back in my room, I stare at my pajamas. I put them on and feel like I'm committing some kind of terrible crime.

"We're naked, not nuts."

It's Saturday. The temperature is supposed to top 100 degrees. Outside there's a sea of flesh that's 50 times more tan than mine. Thank God for SPF 45—I slather it on every square inch of my pasty white body. *Every* square inch.

On my way to Laguna's restaurant for breakfast, I feel beyond exposed. This is my first time fully naked in the light of day. Strangers wave and say hi, but nobody stares. By the time I arrive, I'm feeling unusually relaxed. I spread a towel down on a vinyl booth (nudist etiquette) and eat my melon, cottage cheese and muffin platter.

Post-dining, I walk to the main lawn. There's a volleyball match going on. The organizers are Neil, a tall, tanned engineer, and his 34-year-old wife, Gigi (hey, nice name!), a shy costume designer with long blond hair. Between games, Gigi tells me that nudism helped her become comfortable with her body. Back when she was 20, she and some friends came across a nude beach. Her friends joined in but Gigi thought she was "too fat" to participate. So she sat on a towel all day, sulking. "By the afternoon, I gave in and took all my clothes off," she explains.

Today, she and Neil participate in some form of nude recreation every summer weekend. Gigi has, at last count, windsurfed, square-danced, hiked, biked, and Jet Skied in the buff. Oh, and played volleyball. The couple has a Web site, *www.nakedvolleyball.com*, dedicated to the sport. "People e-mail us and say we need more pornography on the site," Gigi says, rolling her eyes. "They don't understand that nudism is not a sexual thing. We're naked, but not nuts."

Even though I suck at volleyball, I decide to give it a try. Gigi has inspired me. I forget that I'm naked as I jump around, run and punch. It's actually kind of liberating to feel the wind whistle through new places. Then I dive to catch a low ball. I end up sliding across the grass on my butt. A spiky burr wedges itself into one cheek. No more volleyball.

I head off court and run into Lisa. She's 23 years old and about to graduate from college with a degree in business management. She's stunning—sort of a Natalie Wood/Katie Holmes hybrid. But surprisingly, she hasn't been getting unwanted attention from any of the guys. Lisa says her real problem is dealing with the judgments of clothed people. For example, her roommate: "She saw my ass [one day]," says Lisa, "and asked me why I don't have any tan lines." Lisa doesn't think she'll tell her she's a nudist. "People can be really immature about it when they find out," she sighs.

Nudist myths: Guys walk around with erections. I did not see a single one. *All nudists like volleyball.* A survey of nudists found that they most favor swimming, walking and hiking. *Nudists are white trash.* Almost a quarter have a masters or Ph.D. and nearly half make upwards of $50K a year.

"This whole place is a dressing room!"

Late in the afternoon, I stop by the boutique, which is run by Lois, a spirited redhead. As I sift through racks of chiffon floral wraps and try on a Nipple Necklace—a tiny spray of colorful beads that dangles from your dockyard rivets—Lois makes small talk. "Some women ask where the dressing room is," she says, taking a sip of her Koozie-housed Diet Coke. "I tell them that this whole place is a dressing room!"

Next, I head to the river. The trail is gorgeous—fields of tall grass spread in one direction, willow trees dot the landscape in the other. In the distance I see a sign tacked to a fence. It's a warning: YOU ARE LEAVING LAGUNA DEL SOL. CLOTHING REQUIRED BEYOND THIS POINT. I later hear that farm workers on the other side of the fence snoop on the nudie people.

I jump into the cool water of the river. It feels great to swim naked. I climb up on some rocks, and think about how I'm actually starting to enjoy being nude. It now feels liberating. But then yelling interrupts my meditative moment. It's the photographer. I can't hear her over the rushing water. She points at my leg in desperation. I see a big bug crawling up my inner thigh, inches from my genitals. The insects here seem more sexed than the people do.

"I had a nude bridal shower."

"The good thing about being nude," says India, a bubbly 24-year-old with chunky highlighted hair, "is that when [my baby] spits up on me, I just hop in the shower." We're sitting outside the mobile home that she lives in year-round with her 30-year-old husband, Bobby, and their cute son. It's the end of the day and everything is moving slowly. Cows loll about in a nearby field. A big American flag flaps lazily from a pole in their immaculately groomed yard.

Bobby is Laguna's groundskeeper, and India works in town as a hairdresser. They met a few years ago when she gave him a cut. He soon brought her to Laguna for a weekend with his parents. "I grew up strictly religious," she says. "I wouldn't even wear a spaghetti-strap tank top in public." But she appreciated the nudists' nonjudgmental attitude. By Sunday, India was naked. "At first it was weird being naked around my boyfriend's parents, though," she notes.

Bobby proposed to India, nude, at Laguna. "I even had a nude bridal shower," she adds, smiling. India wants to stay here for a long time. She likes the "gated community" feel. "And each weekend, we meet a new young couple," she says excitedly. "I see more people our age here. It doesn't matter who you are or what you do."

Nudist truths: Tampons are acceptable attire. "But we advise women to tuck the cord," explains Patty. *Nudists are clean.* One woman told me that she showers up to five times a day. *Nudity is more accepted in Europe.* In France, there's a summer community of 40,000. Everything is done in the buff, from banking to grocery shopping.

"Attitudes are changing."

I think about what India says. I haven't heard one person start a conversation with: "Where do you work?" Instead, people chat about simple things like, "How are you today?" or "What SPF you got on?" It's nice to be at a place where your career (or lack thereof) doesn't dictate who you are—housewives and CEOs are on equal footing here. But perhaps the main reason why we women are drawn to nudism is because it makes us feel good about our bodies. Emily, Gigi, Lisa and India all told me as much. And pop culture might actually be helping the call.

"Attitudes are changing," says Nicky. "Larger-sized models and actresses are out there. Nudist organizations are popping up on campuses. At U Penn, there's a Naturalist Student Association. Wesleyan University has a clothing-optional dorm. I even saw an ad for salad dressing that showed a young naked couple on the beach. What does nudity have to do with salad dressing? I have no idea, but it sends a message that naked bodies are okay."

By late Sunday, I've forgotten that I'm naked. At first, I thought nudism was freaky. Now I realize that it's just a way for people to get comfy with themselves. And if you ask me, that's a way better way to go about it than dieting or getting plastic surgery.

Nudists also seem to have found a safe way to escape the pressures of daily life. For me, that's an appealing concept. I'm simultaneously trying to make it on my own, establish my career, pay off debt, and figure out what the hell it is I'm headed for—just like anyone my age. It's weird, but when you take away your clothes, it's like you take a vacation from a lot of your worries. Too bad I'm still addicted to shopping.

From *Jane*, August 2000, pp. 144–147. © 2000 by Fairchild Publications. Reprinted by permission.

The Second Sexual Revolution

Viagra was just the beginning. Soon we will all be medicated and wired for high-performance romance.

By Jack Hitt

It was only two years ago that Bob Dole went on "The Larry King Show" to discuss his prostate-cancer operation. During a commercial break, so the story goes, King leaned over to ask his old friend, confidentially, how he was dealing with the operation's grimmest side effect, impotence. Dole cheerfully informed the talk-show host that there was a new drug, Viagra, and miraculously, it had cured the problem. King asked Dole if he would discuss it on the air, and Dole said sure, why not?

The world was about to become a very different place. Viagra would cycle through the expected paces of pop-culture acceptance with stunning speed. Leno and Letterman got an entire summer's worth of monologues off the subject. For a while the papers regularly pumped out clowning (and possibly true) stories about the drug—there was Frank Bernardo, 70, who left his wife, declaring, "It's time for me to be a stud again"; there was also Gen. Sani Abacha of Nigeria, who died in the midst of a Viagra-fueled encounter with two women in his magisterial bed.

But the jokes are over. Viagra's sales topped $1 billion in the first year, and Pfizer is now the second-largest drug company in the world. The drug's use has leveled off, but consider the level: nearly 200,000 prescriptions are filled each week, and 17 million Americans have used the drug. Viagra has been embraced by the well off (4 percent of the total population of Palm Beach County has a prescription), but not only by the well off. Not long ago, Wal-Mart and Kmart had a Viagra war that drove the per-pill price down from $10 to $7.80.

And so, no one talks about it anymore.

Welcome to the lull. It's as if a freak 20-foot swell crashed on the beach, leaving a few new gullies. It's over. Go back inside. Everything is back to normal. Everything except that tsunami on the horizon.

Though most of us are taught to believe that the totality of sex is unknowable, the mechanics of it aren't lofty. Compared to a kidney, our genital rig is the corporeal equivalent of a 1968 VW Beetle engine.

At this moment, there are at least a dozen new Viagra-like medicines and devices currently in clinical trials. Many of these drugs are for men, but this time around, there are just as many for women—specifically, for a new phylum of illness, female sexual dysfunction, which will soon cycle through the same paces as "erectile dysfunction," setting the word "frigidity" alongside impotence in our dictionary of merry old archaisms. "Our knowledge of sexual health is in revolutionary mode," says Dr. Irwin Goldstein, a Boston University urologist and pioneer in the field.

Sexual Healing

Soon, a variety of remedies for sexual dysfunction—and ways to enhance sexual performance—will become available to men and women.

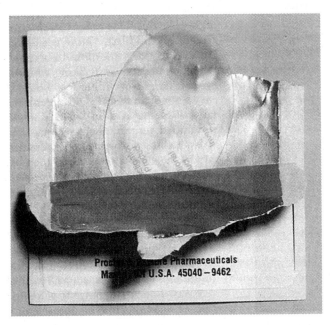

Testosterone patch This device, made by Proctor & Gamble, delivers testosterone to the pelvic region. But it's not for men only. Several companies are working on a version for women whose testosterone production and sex drive have decreased after hysterectomies or other sex-organ surgery.

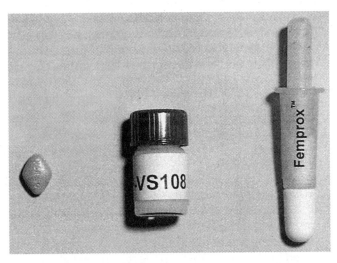

Viagra The granddaddy of pharmaceutical sex medicine, the little blue pill was introduced to the market in 1998. Its popularity has helped to make its producer, Pfizer, the second-largest drug company in the world.

Prostaglandin E-1 cream To stimulate blood flow to the genital area, Vivus is developing a topical cream for women that contains this ingredient. It is intended to alleviate arousal and orgasm dysfunction and enhance vaginal lubrication.

Alprostadil cream NexMed is working on its own topical cream for women, similar to prostaglandin E-1. It is also developing a topical therapy for male impotence.

Clitoral device Beyond pills or hormonal creams, one company is taking a nonpharmacological approach to treating women with sexual dysfunction. UroMetrics is developing the Eros Clitoral Therapy Device, a small pump with a cup, about the size of a thimble, that fits over the clitoris. It is designed to stimulate blood flow to the organ, thereby enhancing sensation and lubrication and enabling its user to achieve orgasm more easily.

With $1 billion in sales for Viagra, the research pressure is intense, yielding paper titles like "The Ejaculatory Behavior in Sexually Sluggish Male Rats...." Scientists, doctors and pharmaceutical companies are racing to discover newer and better drugs. Who doubts they will improve the lives of those who suffer from the newly discovered sexual disorders now showing up in the medical journals? But these drugs will also have, some say, an "enhancing" effect on normally functioning people. More important, the temptation for anyone to obtain these drugs will be more easily satisfied than ever before, since the family of pharmaceuticals inspired by Viagra is entering the market at a time when medicine is decentralizing, slipping the reins long held by doctors. There is already telling evidence that these new sex drugs may well do for medicine what porn did for the Internet—constitute the killer ap that reshapes the industry in an age of patient choice and turboconsumerism.

THOUGH MOST OF US ARE INCULCATED WITH THE belief that the totality of sex is unknowable, maybe even divine, once you've spent some time with the new sex researchers, you learn that the actual mechanics of it all aren't that lofty. Compared to a kidney or a lung, our genital rig is basic stuff, the corporeal equivalent of a 1968 VW Beetle engine. Ensure that the "hormonal milieu" is properly gauged and that there is enough blood flow, and the engineering work is pretty much done—for men and women alike. (Then there needs to be passion, romance and love perhaps, but urologists continue to leave these areas of research to poets and musicians. So far.)

"Not to discount psychological aspects," said Goldstein, who was a member of the team that treated Bob Dole, "but at a certain point all sex is mechanical. The man needs a sufficient axial rigidity so his penis can penetrate through labia, and he has to sustain that in order to have sex. This is a mechanical structure, and mechanical structures follow scientific principles." Goldstein, seated in his office at Boston University Hospital's Sexual Health Clinic, poked his forefinger into the palm of his hand and explained that the "typical resistance" posed by the average vagina is a measurable two pounds. The key is to create an erection that doesn't "deform" or collapse when engaging that resistance.

"I am an engineer," noted Goldstein, who in fact collaborated with Boston University's department of aerospace engineering in formulating his theories. "And I can apply the principles of hydraulics to these problems. I can utilize medical strategies to assess, diagnose and manipulate things that are not so straightforward in psychiatry."

That's something new. For most of the 20th century, any sexual complaint was treated on the couch, not in the lab. Only comparatively recently has impotence been understood to be an organic disease—potentially identifiable and treatable with medicine.

The change is part of a cultural shift that dates back to the birth control pill, when mostly young people were liberated to experiment with sex fearlessly outside of marriage. Many moral conservatives continue to condemn the era for unleashing the Pandoran epidemics of teenage pregnancy, sexually transmitted disease and moral decline. But this telling of the story ignores a more subtle and significant shift. Average folks—young and old, liberal and conservative—began to accept that sex was not a biblical imperative whose sole aim is procreation, but a lively part of good health—something to be enjoyed, like great food and laughter, well into old age. This is the revolution that Bob Dole has joined at the barricades.

The distinction is not just medical; it's metaphysical. Psychological problems carry with them the full freight of personal responsibility. But a physical problem seems more like a cosmic error, something unrelated to a person's actions. It's no flaw in your manhood or womanhood if your sexual organs don't work. It's a "disorder"—and by being labeled as one, it becomes something detached from your own true self and easier for a patient to emotionally confront and for a doctor to treat.

Breaking through the wall of the patient's superego, though, was only half the challenge for researchers like Goldstein. Medical approaches to sexual problems have been thwarted by another obstacle: there wasn't anything medicine could do about them. "Unless you have a treatment, you don't have a condition," Goldstein said. "If there is nothing for me to say except, 'See a psychiatrist,' then what is the rush to accurately describe and research your condition?"

For the longest time the only treatments were for men, and they were practically medieval. Outside the opaque world of aphrodisiacs, medicine had come up with only one solution for male impotence: the penile implant, a surgical procedure developed by urologists in 1973.

"I can remember," Goldstein said of the slow progress. "It was 1983, when a doctor named Giles Brindley came up with the first drug-induced erection. At a urology meeting, he was wearing sweat pants. He excused himself for a minute and went to the men's room and injected himself. When he came back, he lowered his pants to show us a stunning and natural erection. He walked down the aisle and let us touch it. People couldn't believe it wasn't an implant."

Goldstein noticed a look of considerable distress on my face, and added something that he thought might comfort me: "It was a bunch of urologists."

Not long after Dr. Brindley's performance, a company based in California, Vivus, perfected an erectile suppository called MUSE (medicated urethral system for erection). Although it is effective, it requires that the suppository be inserted in the tip of the penis. Pfizer's truly great breakthrough with Viagra was inventing an erectile treatment that didn't make the average person double over in horror.

As the cures have become more user-friendly, the discourse among the general population has become more comfortable, too. The morning I was meeting with Goldstein, a patient showed up and allowed me to join his consultation on the condition that I would not publish his name.

The patient, a Dominican-born social worker in his 30's, was accidentally kicked in the groin years ago. The damage was severe. A beefy, rounded man, he sits on the examination table sidesaddle, his ankles crossed coyly. Both he and his Rubenesque wife curl their shoulders inward and keep their heads bowed, as if in shame. It's clear that the ripple effect of this simple injury has affected every part of their lives and marriage.

When Goldstein asks the patient what happens when he makes love to his wife, he says, "I don't know." He looks at me with the same tepid smile and pinched eyes that Bob Dole has in that magazine ad. "I don't know," he repeats. It's fascinating to watch Goldstein work this tiny room, this miniature stage, trying to determine just what mix of clinical authority and just-us-guys informality will make this doctor-patient interview work. He has the uncanny ability to radiate locker-room crassness and professional etiquette almost in the same sentence. He's dressed in a crisp gray pinstriped suit, but he possesses a soft casual voice that lopes amiably around his words, like Donald Sutherland's. One wall of his office is covered with half a dozen sheepskins, proving his professional bona fides to anyone who needs that. Over his door is a walrus penis bone, two feet long—a conversation starter for a certain kind of person. The wall plate of his light switch is a cartoon of a doctor and the switch itself doubles as the doctor's… well, funny stuff for an altogether different kind of person.

The formal "make love" query isn't working, so Goldstein tries again: "When you lie down naked to fool around with your wife, describe what happens." The social worker's eyes pinch harder. I involuntarily curl my shoulders—as if to acknowledge our common genomic humanity. (I feel certain my face resembles, at this time, the Greek mask of tragedy.)

"It takes a long time, a long time to get ready, you know," he says quickly, as if he fears Goldstein might become even more "street" in his queries. Again, he looks at me. "A long time, you know." I nod furiously and make a noise similar to a kitten coming upon a saucer of milk.

Goldstein says: "Here's what's happening. Normally when you get an erection, the blood flows like this." He walks to a sink and turns the spigot on full blast. "Now what's happening is this." He slows the flow to a trickle. "Everything works. It's just taking too long. One of your arteries to your penis is blocked. The good news is we can fix that with a penis bypass operation." He punches in a video showing a highly magnified surgery, the screen all liquidy pinks. We watch as doctors take a redundant piece of artery from the stomach and then use it to bypass the damaged artery in the penis. "I've done 600 of these operations. You have a highly significant chance for a full recovery."

The patient laughs involuntarily—the kind of irrepressibly giddy laughter that accompanies extremely good fortune on par with winning $100 million or being selected by NASA to fly to the moon. The wife laughs. It's absolutely infectious. I start laughing. It is a small celebration of unadulterated laughter. This news puts everyone in the peppiest mood. We all shake hands, awkward but well meaning, like passing the peace in church.

"I am going to prescribe Viagra for him," Goldstein told me back in his office. "Not for sex. But as a sleeping pill." Goldstein explained that the average male gets five erections per night in his sleep. "Our belief is that the night erection is the battery recharging time. Your penis is guaranteed to have one and a half to three hours of erection time every night. You know how doctors now recommend taking a single aspirin a day to prevent heart attack? I predict one day there will be evidence to support a medication—something like Viagra—that enhances erections. Call it erectogenic."

HYPOTHESES AND FRESH IDEAS SEEM COMMONPLACE in this new field now that Bob Dole has made the world safe for sexual-health research. Some of them are simple. For instance, Goldstein has made it a minicrusade to banish the standard bicycle seat, which crushes the main nerve cluster leading to the genitalia and, Goldstein believes, accounts for the relatively high incidence of sexual dysfunction among bikers. But a great deal of the cutting-edge discoveries are occurring for women. Last year, the Journal of the American Medical Association published a study reporting that 43 percent of women experience some kind of sexual dysfunction. Just a few weeks ago, the Network for Excellence in Women's Sexual Health was organized to help doctors and health care professionals who want to enter this emerging field.

A lot of the revelations about women stem directly from studies on men. Women also have four or five nightly clitoral "erections," Goldstein said, which are crucial for the maintenance of their sexual health. Yet even among these researchers, the presumption still persists that men's sexuality is mere hydraulics and that women's sexuality is more complex. "We're being forced to realize that men aren't so simple either," Goldstein said, "because of what we've learned about women."

Take, for example, the case of a Boston professor who participated last year in a clinical trial to measure Viagra's efficacy on women and spoke to me only on the condition of anonymity.

"Female sexual dysfunction is a very real problem for some people," the 55-year-old told me, recalling the day in 1994 when she learned she had breast cancer. She endured a lumpectomy, an oophorectomy (removal of ovaries) and finally a hysterectomy. When it was over, she said, "it was as though my mind was capable of being sexual but it was disconnected from my body. There was no there there. I felt like I had been neutered."

Admitting to a "a strong libido," she went to her doctor to find out what she could do. He told her "more or less, women at your age don't care about sex anymore." So she read up, asked around and soon heard about the Boston University clinic run by Goldstein and his two partners, Jennifer Berman, a urologist; and her sister Laura Berman, a sex therapist.

The doctors selected the professor for the early trials, in part because her problem is complex. Viagra achieves its effect by increasing blood flow to the genitals, but that would not be enough. According to the Bermans, the pathways connecting the professor's desire (she felt it cerebrally) with her physical arousal (she felt nothing genitally) had been interrupted. Such communications are facilitated by hormones, specifically the right levels of estrogen and testosterone. She began testosterone cream applications accompanied by an estrogen ring inserted in the vagina like a diaphragm for slow release of the hormone. While this adjustment helped reconnect the brain with the genitals, there still wasn't enough blood flow during stimulation to regularly effect an orgasm. So Viagra, too, was tested.

"The combination was so successful," she said. "With Viagra I have orgasms, much more intense orgasms."

This case reveals just how detailed sexual disorder studies have become in a fairly short time. In fact, in the October 1999 issue of the journal Urology, the three partners at the Boston clinic broke down the four basic kinds of female sexual dysfunction that either are or will soon be treatable. The professor's basic condition is known as Sexual Arousal Disorder. (It even has an Oprah-ready acronym.) Sexual thoughts occur, but they aren't communicated to the genitals.

The other ailments are Orgasmic Disorder which includes inorgasmia (inability to have orgasm) and the unnamed condition of "muffled" orgasms. The third new subdisease is Sexual Pain Disorder, which includes vaginismus (involuntary muscle spasms) and dyspareunia (general genital pain). The final one is Hypoactive Sexual Desire Disorder, more or less the opposite of the professor's condition, in which the genitals may or may not work but it hardly matters because the patient lacks libido and the usual sexual thoughts or fantasies that precede a sexual encounter.

Many of these conditions overlap and are often accompanied (or caused) by emotional problems like depression. "It's more of an algorithm," Berman said. But in the overwhelming majority of her patients' cases, she added—and there's a furious debate embedded in the rest of this sentence—the organic disorder precedes the emotional ones.

This is not to say psychological sex problems don't exist. "There is no drug," Laura Berman said, "that will restore a satisfactory sex life to a woman who hates her husband." But she estimated that only about 20 percent of her patients have purely psychogenic problems; for the other patients, there is a raft of new procedures to measure their sexual health.

In many clinics, a typical female patient would first submit to a photoplethysmography. According to James Yeager, chief research scientist with the drug company NexMed, the device is a "black box with wires coming out of it with a kind of penlight that is inserted in the vagina."

The woman then stimulates herself while a photo cell in the penlight measures the change in redness of the vaginal tissue and then calibrates blood flow. There are drawbacks to this procedure, which are obvious, and if they're not, send me a postcard and I'll drop you a line. I'm moving on.

At the Boston University Hospital clinic, genital blood flow is measured with a "high-frequency laser duplex Doppler," Laura Berman said, "which is like a sonogram." Then the clinicians also measure vaginal pH (using a digital pH probe), the structural architecture of the organ or "vaginal compliance" (using a Schuster balloon) and finally, clitoral and labial vibratory threshold (using a biothesiometer). "We record these measurements at baseline and after sexual stimulation with a standardized 15-minute erotic video and vibrator," the authors write in their Urology article.

When we operated on the female pelvis,' says one doctor, 'we just cut everything out. And I would ask, Where are the nerves? And you know what? No one even knew.'

With men, the entire process is quite similar. In the old days, men were outfitted with a "penis cuff"—a wraparound device like a petite blood-pressure gauge. Today, a sonogram is more accurate and yields a photograph mapping out the geographies of blood flow. Once the doctors examine the differentials in these measurements, a diagnosis follows and, when appropriate, medical treatment.

DISCOVERING THOSE TREATMENTS IS THE PROVINCE of researchers, and one of the most pre-eminent of them is Goldstein's colleague and Laura Berman's sister, Dr. Jennifer Berman, one of the nation's few female urologists. Berman agreed to see me under extraordinary circumstances. Only three days before, she had given birth to her son, and the birth was difficult. Still, amazingly trim in her slacks and sailor's peacoat, Dr. Berman said she was happy to come to her office since she also wanted to check on the status of a new grant application for a major research program, which she was eager to explain.

"When I was trained in urology," she said, walking briskly down the street to her lab, "I was struck at the lengths surgeons went to, when operating on men, to preserve the nerves and blood vessels that are connected to the penis. But when we operated on the female pelvis, we just cut everything out. And I would ask, 'Where are the nerves?' And you know what? No one even knew." She said this, strangely, not with anger but with an explorer's excitement. "So we need fresh cadavers. They're about $3,000 each. You know, if you look in any anatomical text, there are 20 pages on male sexual anatomy and 2 pages on the female. And there are conflicting reports as to how one should describe the female anatomy. We know there is a major plexus of nerves along the cervix but how they connect to the clitoris and vagina is not understood at all. In men, we know that there is a cluster of nerves along the lateral side of the prostate. That's why there's a special operation."

I didn't say anything for a while. It wasn't the usual male-feminist discomfort, although it's never easy being the sole representative of the sex when one of those grotesque inequities pops into view. No, rather, it was an acknowledgment of the air of frontier desperation that characterizes so much of this research: so many obvious things to do, so many cultural obstacles. I imagine there was a similar feeling surrounding anatomy in Dickensian England, when early surgeons robbed graves to find corpses to practice on. Or in the early days of organ transplantation (in the 60's), when doctors would occasionally get caught slipping really nice kidneys from the nearly dead. These dissonances occur in medicine when doctors have sneaked ahead of the culture in redefining something holy—the sanctity of the dead, respect for the living and now: the mystery of sex.

Berman led me into a modern brick building, where we passed through a number of security checks. We stepped into a recovery room, where two surgeons were working on one of Dr. Berman's projects. Five white New Zealand rabbits had just undergone oophorectomies to surgically induce menopause. A sixth was feeling the anesthesia take effect. Her head was flopped forward, now too heavy to lift. Her eyes had gone slack.

Afterward, Berman will test a new treatment. A lot of Sexual Pain Disorder is caused by "inadequate secretion in the vaginal canal," Berman said. So she will administer an agent that will naturally switch on the body's mucosal membranes to start producing lubrication.

In another wing of the lab, she opened a refrigerator and pulled out a tray holding a few dozen capped test tubes.

"These are rabbit cervixes that were removed after the drug test," she said. "They'll be tested to see if there's been an increase in mucosal activity."

She then showed me an "organ chamber." In outsize tubes are clips that hold stretched segments of the smooth muscle from the clitorises, vaginas and penises removed from animal specimens or discarded human tissue after surgery.

"I can do any kind of smooth muscle test," Berman said. "The tissues are placed in these chambers and you look at how they respond to drugs. I can show you how tissue contracts or relaxes. I can stimulate it electronically and look at the reactions in the presence or absence of different drugs. And it's all recorded here." She pointed to a needle scratching across an unscrolling cylinder of paper, like a seismograph.

These tests represent the experiments now being conducted in university labs and corporate R-and-D facilities all over the country. The cumulative lesson of much of this research is leading to two categories of treatments—hormone therapy, which restores desire, and various drugs, which amplify the sensation of arousal. Many companies are researching hormone medicines. Solvay already mar-

kets one called Estratest. Organon is in trials with a treatment called tibolone, which is believed to increase desire. Dr. Glenn Braunstein, an endocrinologist at Cedars-Sinai Medical Center in Los Angeles, is working on a "testosterone patch" under grants from the marketing giant Procter & Gamble.

But the real gold rush is occurring in the other field of research—creating a drug to increase blood flow to the genitals. And just as Viagra as a pill was a kind of psychological breakthrough, the researchers looking for other blood-flow solutions want something simple—a tablet or perhaps even better, a quick-acting cream that is stabilized at room temperature so that women can carry it in a purse like lipstick or men can just toss it into a shaving kit. The competition is furious among small firms, each with a blood-flow drug—some for men, some for women—that are anywhere from one to five years from getting to market. Herewith a sampling, complete with active ingredients:

- Vivus: prostaglandin E-1 cream.
- MacroChem: a gel, using a version of prostaglandin E-1 called Topiglan.
- NexMed: alprostadil, a variant of prostaglandin cream.
- Tap Pharmaceuticals: an apomorphine treatment formulated into a small tablet placed under the tongue.
- Pentech Pharmaceutical: ditto.
- Zonagen: phentolamine, in tablets and suppositories.
- Pfizer: Viagra for women (sildenafil).
- Palatin Technologies: a peptide molecule derivative called PT-14; in the earliest test stages.
- ICOS Corporation: a tablet code-named IC351. (That's all they would reveal.) Bill Gates, who may be telling us something, owns almost 13 percent of the company.

I WANTED TO COMPILE A COMPLETE LIST OF EACH and every sex drug currently in trials. But it became an endless pursuit, the research being so frenetic, and the line between legitimate and illegitimate being so confusing. Obviously, once hard science ratified the actual existence of a drug like Viagra, the very reality of it was a wake-up call to America's snake-oil salesmen.

Infomercials have shifted from vegetable slicers and wrinkle tonics to "natural" aphrodisiacs. There is scarcely a tree left standing in the rain forest whose bark hasn't been stripped and tested for the alternative-health industry. The Internet is teeming with unsolicited ads for products with vaguely homonymic names, though none of them come close to Pfizer's allegedly unintended melding of "vital" and "Niagara" to generate the best product name since Coke. Some long-touted aphrodisiacs are now being tested, too. A derivative of chili peppers is in legitimate trials. Does this count as a drug?

NitroMed, a company based in Massachusetts, is working on a mixture of an old passion powder called yohimbe (stripped from the inner bark of the Corynanthe yohimbe tree in tropical West Africa) combined with an amino acid called L-Arginine to see if the two can work effectively as a vasodilator—that is, a chemical that increases blood flow. Then there are the nondrug inventions. A company called UroMetrics is working on a vacuum device, fitted with a small cup the size of a thimble, and intended to draw blood directly to the clitoris. It might be easy to dismiss this as a sex toy, except that it's also in trials for Food and Drug Administration approval, and UroMetrics intends to distribute it only as a medical device via prescription.

While cruising the Patent Office's Web site (www. uspto.gov), I discovered that Vivus's claim to prostaglandin E-1 cream has been challenged by a Tennessee doctor named Michael Wysor. According to his patent attorney, Michael Ebert in New York, Wysor may have filed his invention after the original patent was granted to Vivus, but he believes there are technical challenges that support his claim.

Wysor, who ran two sexual-health clinics, in Knoxville and Johnson City, that have since gone bankrupt, has just finished a book proposal on erectile dysfunction. He has tried his cream on women informally, but refused to elaborate on his methods. That's just how crowded the field has become. Garage inventors are in on it.

With the enraged pace of daily life, who doubts that a drug-enhanced four-minute sexual encounter among harried day traders could become the norm?

The pace of change inside this small research world also means that almost no one is stopping to reflect on the implications of the drugs that are marching—and there really is no stopping them now—toward the marketplace. When I spoke to Leland Wilson, the C.E.O. of Vivus, about his company's new prostaglandin cream, he happily suggested that most women would be able to experience orgasm after just a few minutes of vaginal intercourse. Such a development seemed fraught with truly significant implications—both good and bad—but obviously fraught. When I pressed him to imagine some of the implications, he sputtered through several change-of-subject tactics.

"That is beyond the realm of medicine," he said. There was a quality to the conversation reminiscent of Werner von Braun, who supposedly once said, "I send the rockets up; where they come down is not my business."

IT WOULD BE NICE IF ALL MEDICAL BREAKTHROUGHS were just for the medical complaints outlined by the doctors. But that's not how the world works. With couples holding down two jobs and the enraged pace of modern life, who doubts that a drug-enhanced four-minute sexual

encounter among harried day traders could become the norm? The very idea of a long slow evening probably won't completely disappear. It'll just go the way of sitting on the porch, the 3 o'clock dinner and the literary novel—something experienced over the holidays or on vacation.

"I find it simply incredible this whole thing is happening," said Leonore Tiefer, a psychologist at the New York University School of Medicine and pretty much the only critic of all this research I could find.

"There is no such thing as 'female sexual dysfunction,'" she added. "It's a social construction invented to benefit the drug companies." Tiefer believes that a kind of "magical thinking" infects the way most of us imagine our sexuality. That it can always be better, and that we resist the natural changes that define the arc of a well-lived life: "That's where this disorder comes in and says, 'If there is a change'—and invariably there is a change in life—'then change is bad.' Ah, a problem! So we invent a universal model, a normative view of sex. If you don't get wet for X period of seconds from Y pressure of stimulation, then you have a problem."

Tiefer was evasive when I asked her about the existence of real medical conditions being cured by these new drugs. "What about the placebo effect?" she asked, when I offered up the Boston professor's case as an example. Tiefer believes the medicalization of sex gives people an out—a way to avoid the root cause of their sexual problems. "I don't see many women depressed about the blood flow to the genitalia. They are depressed about many other things about sex, but not that. This research should be done, of course, but with a few dollars, by a few people, in a few places. But it should not be this Boeing of sex research."

Not surprisingly, many researchers dismiss Tiefer's ideas as rear-guard propaganda to protect the sex concession that therapists have held for so long. Fears that the medical establishment will big-foot the psychologists' business is not an imaginary concern these days. The central theme of Peter Kramer's "Listening to Prozac" is the observation that, in the treatment of depression, drug therapy has driven talk therapy right out of business.

"Every disease pharmacology has attacked in the last 50 years," Vivus's Wilson said bluntly, "has at some point been treated by psychologists, and as soon as pharmacology discovers the real organic reason for the disease and a method for treating it, then psychologists moved on to treat something else. That's exactly what's happening here." Precisely because "psychologists have never successfully treated sexual dysfunction in anybody," Wilson said, "business" was the real source of much of the current professional "squabbling." But not all of Tiefer's critics dismiss her apprehensions.

"There is a fear that Viagra might be used like Prozac," Laura Berman said, "as a sort of Band-Aid approach to therapy. And it's a risk, especially in men, that you might be treating the symptoms, not the problem."

But Tiefer also believes that the medical model of research is just too reductive: "They don't look at sex in a robust way. It's the narrowest possible view: does it twitch once or twice? O.K., then, twice is statistically more significant than once. Good girl."

"Viagra does make sex into a very goal-oriented act," Berman conceded. "The question is, What is sex in general? Is the goal to have an orgasm? Or is it to make yourself vulnerable to someone, communicate with them, share yourself with someone? Sex is often the mirror of the larger relationship. So now we have the possibility of the four-minute encounter. What does that do to intimacy?" She paused for a moment, and it was possible to see her concern metamorphose into a new argument: "Maybe a couple would be better off if they combined four-minute sex with a two-hour conversation over wine." This research, she concluded, suddenly finding her voice, will ultimately allow for different choices. "You will also be able to have hours of sex with multiple orgasms," she added, offering up a future of "quickies and slowies, and a whole range of options."

CHOICE. YOU WONDER, WHAT TOOK SO LONG? THE language of the marketplace that has conquered every other domain in contemporary life has at last found a vehicle to enter the bedroom. "This work," Berman said, "is putting something mysterious and uncontrollable under our control. It can be a liberating and exciting shift, or a confining one, depending."

And that's where Viagra and its progeny are truly revolutionary. They enable us to control our own sexual health, pushing the idea of sexuality far beyond the lab or the couch. The Tiefer debate presumes that these medical inventions will stay under the strict control of doctors, that the old rules of the medical-industrial complex still apply.

But the Golden Age of the A.M.A. is over. The appearance of Viagra has taken place at a time when medicine itself is in the process of decentralizing and allowing market forces to guide many decisions. Increasingly, patients are told to take charge of their own health care; politicians debate a "patient's bill of rights." H.M.O.'s themselves are built on the idea that individuals will decide the general direction of their care. Doctors are increasingly called health care "providers" as drugs are now marketed directly to patients. Viagra was one of the first new drugs introduced to the world alongside the slogan: "Ask your doctor about...."

In this loosey-goosey environment, Viagra has already slipped into the recreational underground—far beyond the reach of both psychologists and doctors. Club kids in the big cities use it as a party drug. The practice of poly-pharmacy, taking a couple of different rave drugs, say, Ecstasy or Special K, kills the sex drive. For heavy partiers, Viagra solves the problem; it allows a night of Dionysian dancing to end the way it used to.

Viagra has also found its way into gay subculture. "You have to realize that a lot of men come out of the closet when they are 30 or even 40, and then go nuts," said Eston Dunn, the health education coordinator for the Gay and Lesbian Community Center in Fort Lauderdale, Fla. "If you're heterosexual, you discover your sexuality at 15, and then you go nuts. That's why a lot of older gay men behave like 15-year-olds. In many ways, they really are 15, and a lot of them turn to Viagra to keep up with their own new-found enthusiasm." In the gay party scene, Dunn said, "you used to hear that cocaine lines were put out with straws. Now it's Viagra, like jelly beans in little candy dishes."

The third group using Viagra on the sly is nonimpotent heterosexuals. I found out about this niche accidentally one night at my own dinner table. An old acquaintance stopped over for the night. He's an ambitious man, in his late 30's, the chairman of a well-regarded department of a prestigious university. On about our third glass of wine, he leaned over and asked, "So have you tried Viagra?"

I bolted back. "No, no," he said. "I mean for fun." But I was confused. Pfizer's official pronouncements state clearly that Viagra doesn't really "work" on potent men. My friend, who would not allow his name to be used, said he wasn't talking about the stated effect of Viagra. Although he did in fact get what he thought were unflagging erections, there is another side effect of Viagra. Beside maximizing blood flow, for the three to five hours that the drug is in the body, it also blocks the enzyme that stymies erections just after orgasm.

"My girlfriend always knows when I use it," explained my friend, who has tried the drug roughly 15 times in the last year. "Instead of this carefully choreographed single episode, suddenly I'm a nuclear reactor of love. Definitely. Multiple orgasms in one night." (So female drugs eliminate foreplay, shortening sex, and male drugs lengthen intercourse, extending sex. Once again, men and women pass like ships in the night.)

Pfizer makes it plain that the company does not agree with this kind of cavalier use of Viagra. But Pfizer is being somewhat disingenuous. Just look at the ads for Viagra. The originals in 1998 and 1999 featured what were clearly old men. One image was a barrel-chested fellow with whitening hair wearing a big winter sweater stretched across the healthy bulk of a well-lived life. He is standing in a meadow, hugging his wife, a women in her 60's looking quite good in a pair of jeans. The slogan reads, "Let the Dance Begin."

The new ad, which I clipped in January from a national magazine, has a trim fellow who could be a character on "Friends." He has a mop of brown hair above a smooth forehead. He's embracing a young woman in a white blouse, tossing her mane of pretty red hair. He might be 35, maybe. The slogan reads, "Take the First Step." More elaborate versions speak of a new disease: "If you're not satisfied with your sex life due to poor erections during recent months, talk to your doctor. You may be suffering from mild E.D.—and Viagra can help."

"Not satisfied with your sex life"—now there's a market segment. And what is "mild" E.D.? It's not really defined and could encompass just about any complaint imaginable. Perhaps it's what my friend was describing. He wanted his "maximum" erections to last for as long as he wanted to spend in bed with his lover. Viagra, he said, "lets me do this for hours without ever having to even think about it." And how did he get his prescription? He told his doctor that since he practices safe sex, he'd have less "trouble keeping a condom on" if his penis maintained a maximum blood-flow erection. His "provider" wrote the prescription.

The appeal Viagra has for some of these subgroups has meant that the blue pill is showing up in the underground drug economy. There have been numerous drug busts reported in which Viagra was found individually packaged among cocaine, Ecstasy and pot—ready for dealers to market. In England, according to several published reports, the drug goes by the street name "poke."

I'm skeptical of the "poke" lingo, in part because the street is probably the most inaccessible place to get Viagra. Why go to some dingy corner in a bad part of town when the Internet is filled with sites that sell it easily and cheaply. Of course, the authorities have tried to crack down on the practice of selling pharmaceuticals online. A family-practice doctor in Ohio named Daniel L. Thompson was charged in July with 64 felonies, including 17 counts of drug trafficking for providing Viagra and other prescriptions over the Internet. And in December, President Clinton called on the F.D.A. to take measures to stop the practice. But controlling the Web is futile, as I discovered one day last winter when I typed "Viagra and aphrodisiac" into a search engine and was offered hundreds of choices. The Web sites sound like jokes: drugman.com and my-webdr.com and viagraguys.com. I opted to get my fix from a Web site called kwikmed.com.

After I signed on—I waited while this message scrolled by: "Brought to you by Tide Detergent"—I was instructed to fill out an online medical interview. I was asked obvious questions, like "Are you taking any heart medication?" I told the truth and said no. I was asked only a couple of private questions, but I admitted to no dysfunction whatsoever. Only one question was devoted to ascertaining my "problem." So I wrote: "Life is not as good as it should be"—a philosophical statement I have pretty much always lived by. When I clicked the box marked Send, I instantaneously received a message back saying my doctor had "approved me for Viagra," unless of course my credit card didn't clear. The next morning, at the crack of the workday, barely 12 hours after I had clicked the send button, the FedEx guy appeared with an envelope that rattled when he handed it to me. In a brown bottle were 10 of the famous blue diamond-shaped pills. The crooked label looked as if it had been produced on an Officemax printer. My doctor was someone named "A. Guzman."

As we permit more and more market forces to take command of the health care industry, it shouldn't surprise anyone that the new drug dealer will not be found in the shadows, offering sinsemilla under his breath. He's already sitting right on our desks, his cursor winking at us. As I started to cruise the Internet looking for this underground world, it quickly became clear that, like the culture at large, Viagra had almost instantaneously colonized this frontier, too. One or two hyperlinks from Viagra, and I came upon a book called "Better Sex Through Chemistry."

"The idea of exotic herbal aphrodisiacs has been around forever," said the book's co-author, John Morgenthaler, when I reached him on the telephone. "But people thought they were akin to eating raw oysters. A neat idea, but really just the placebo effect." Viagra, in his mind, changed all that. Morgenthaler's book, and a 1999 sequel, "The Smart Guide to Better Sex From Andro to Zinc," chronicles the new levels of proof that hard science is bringing to the reputations of some of the old folklore remedies. This is evidence-based medicine at its simplest, separating the wheat from the chaff with double-blind placebo-controlled tests. Many of the old remedies hold no interest to researchers—like camel hump fat or jackal bile or dong chong xia cao, a Chinese fungus that grows on dormant worms. (One day, naturalists may credit Viagra for saving the rhinoceros, now on the cusp of extinction due to the popularity of its supposedly aphrodisiacal horn.)

Other traditional remedies, like yohimbe, are being seriously considered. But the rethinking of sex caused by Viagra, according to Morgenthaler, merely signals a much bigger change that the drug is effecting.

"Viagra has opened the subject and legitimized the idea of enhancement drugs," Morgenthaler said. "This is the way it works with Western medicine: first there is this idea that if you have a 'disease' then you need a medicine to treat it. Then some forward-thinking doctor says, 'Why wait for the disease to start?' So we get to talking about 'prevention.' The third step is, 'Why be disease-oriented at all?' Let's just enhance ourselves beyond normal and average." This new era will be brought about by the consumerization of medicine, Morgenthaler noted. By allowing patients to have more of a say in what "medicine" means, we are redefining its purposes.

"What is cosmetic surgery?" Morgenthaler asked. "Isn't it just medicine bent entirely toward enhancement? The other breakthrough area is sports medicine. It's almost entirely about enhancement." Two years ago, Mark McGwire of the St. Louis Cardinals revealed that he was a regular user of an enhancing drug called androstenedione. Many critics weighed in to denounce the corrosive effect of a role model proclaiming the virtues of a drug. Morgenthaler, however, sees McGwire as a brave pioneer, like Dole—someone who has come out of the closet to speak honestly about the brave new worlds these medicines hail.

"There really is an obvious parallel here," said Rachel Maines, author of the highly regarded book "The Technology of Orgasm." Her sober account of the industrial history of the electric vibrator shows how it was invented by a doctor, Joseph Mortimer Granville, in the 1880's and was used exclusively by doctors as a sexual-medical device to better cure hysteria in women by effecting a "hysterical paroxysm." The machine had the added benefit of moving patients more quickly through the office by shortening the old manual method of inducing a paroxysm to an industrial-age 10 minutes. The earliest vibrators easily stayed within the bounds of medicine since "they were steam-powered and you had to keep shoveling coal into the engine," Maines said. But eventual refinements in the machinery meant the vibrator "was democratized—it started with doctors and then slowly became available to everyone."

When I raised with Goldstein the possibility of these new drugs spilling over into the general population, he was outraged. He hardly believed me when I told him I had Viagra in my hands less than a day after going online to find it. When I insisted that it was that easy to obtain, he simply asserted that the government should do something about it. When I told him that I had talked to people who were enjoying Viagra recreationally and that the drug had another life below the surface of medicine's officialdom, he shrugged and said, "It's not right."

Instead he gave me a lecture, outlining the future as he saw it: "When you go to medical school, you can go into ob/gyn, urology, general surgery, endocrinology, cardiology, gastroenterology—but can you find a department of sexual medicine? No. But sexual medicine will find its place in medical schools. There will be a sexual medical specialty with multidisciplinary inputs from many fields. Why? Because all human beings have only several things in common. When they get thirsty, they drink. When they get hungry, they eat." He paused for a minute. "And all are very interested sexual beings. This is the principle upon which I am dedicating my academic career."

No doubt sexual medicine will one day be taught at medical schools. But in permitting that to happen we have defined a certain kind of pleasure as a branch of health (although perhaps not as radically as, say, the Netherlands, where government-financed prostitutes are made available to people with disabilities). Still, the pressure is on to improve something that was once understood to be a lucky side effect to procreation.

The generation that will first sample all these drugs and creams and pills as they come off the R.-and-D. conveyor belts in the next few years is the same one that, in the pop history of America, broke ground by smoking pot in the 1960's and 70's for enlightenment and set off the sexual revolution. It is the same generation whose interest in long-term health gave us jogging and workout spas; the same generation that is perpetually accused of being permanent adolescents; the same generation that has accelerated this economy into overdrive. Does anyone believe that regulation will prevent this same generation from employing drugs, in the words of Leonore Tiefer, "to maintain a 20-year-old vagina to go with their husband's 20-year-old penis"? The underground markets of John Morgenthaler and the Main Street clinics of Irwin Goldstein are not two choices. They are flip sides of the same coin—an inevitable result of the impulse to bring the wonderful world of chemistry into the bedroom.

My bottle of Viagra sits on the second shelf of my medicine cabinet, unopened—a totem of the future. But what's in it? Medicine? Preventive therapy? Enhancement pills? Recreational drugs? The marketplace will let us know soon enough. I look at the little brown bottle every morning and see the name of my new provider, A. Guzman—a genie of turboconsumerism heralding the conquest of choice over the last redoubt of privacy.

Jack Hitt is a contributing writer for the magazine.

UNIT 2

Sexual Biology, Behavior, and Orientation

Unit Selections

Key Points to Consider

• How do you rate yourself with respect to knowing how your body works sexually on a scale from one (very uninformed, not even sure of correct names for parts and processes) to six (well-informed and can troubleshoot sexual health conditions and figure out how to improve sexual response)? What has held your score down or increased it?

• How have (or would) you react if a friend confided in you that he or she was having sexual functioning problems, for example, erections or painful intercourse problems? What if the person confiding in you was a coworker? A stranger? Your mother or your grandfather? Who would you talk to if it were you with the problem, and what response would you want from the other person?

• Let's assume you were shown research that predicted that behaviors you currently engage in could cause you to have serious health problems in the future. What likelihood of future problems and what nature of problems would make you change the behaviors in question?

• What is your opinion about the following statement: "There is no such thing as sexual addiction. Those people are just making excuses for being irresponsible"?

• It is rare for people to wonder why someone is heterosexual in the same ways as we wonder why someone is homosexual or bisexual. What do you think contributes to a person's sexual orientation? Do you think it is possible for people not to feel threatened by sexual orientations different from their own? Why or why not?

 **Links: www.dushkin.com/online/**
These sites are annotated in the World Wide Web pages.

Bibliography: HIV/AIDS and College Students
  http://www.sph.emory.edu/bshe/AIDS/college.html

The Body: A Multimedia AIDS and HIV Information Resource
  http://www.thebody.com/cgi-bin/body.cgi

Healthy Way
  http://www.ab.sympatico.ca/Contents/health/

Hispanic Sexual Behavior and Gender Roles
  http://www.caps.ucsf.edu/hispnews.html

James Kohl
  http://www.pheromones.com

Johan's Guide to Aphrodisiacs
  http://www.santesson.com/aphrodis/aphrhome.htm

Human bodies are miraculous things. Most of us, however, have less than a complete understanding of how they work. This is especially true of our bodily responses and functioning during sexual activity. Efforts to develop a healthy sexual awareness are severely hindered by misconceptions and lack of quality information about physiology. The first portion of this unit directs attention to the development of a clearer understanding and appreciation of the workings of the human body.

Over the past decade and a half, the general public's awareness of, and interest and involvement in, their own health care has dramatically increased. We want to stay healthy and live longer, and we know that to do so, we must know more about our bodies, including how to prevent problems, recognize danger signs, and find the most effective treatments. By the same token, if we want to stay sexually fit—from robust youth through a healthy, happy, sexy old age—we must be knowledgeable about sexual health care.

As you read through the articles in this section, you will be able to see more clearly that matters of sexual biology and behavior are not merely physiological in origin. The articles included clearly demonstrate the psychological, social, and cultural origins of sexual behavior as well.

Why we humans feel, react, respond, and behave sexually can be quite complex. This is especially true regarding the issue of sexual orientation. Perhaps no other area of sexual behavior is as misunderstood as this one. Although experts do not agree about what causes our sexual orientation—homosexual, heterosexual, or bisexual—growing evidence suggests a complex interaction of biological or genetic determination, environmental or sociocultural influence, and free choice. In the early 1900s sexologist Alfred Kinsey introduced his seven-point continuum of sexual orientation. It placed exclusive heterosexual orientation at one end, exclusive homosexual orientation at the other, and identified the middle range as where most people would fall if society and culture were unprejudiced. Since Kinsey, many others have added their research findings and theories to what is known about sexual orientation. John Money, a Johns Hopkins University researcher, who for the last 30 years has done research and writing on what he calls the sexology of erotic orientation, and Anne Fausto-Sterling, a professor of biology and women's studies at Brown University, who for the last 10 years has been an advocate for intersexuals (people not clearly male or female by anatomy or behavior), recommend that we consider sexuality and sexual orientation as even more multidimensional than Kinsey's continuum. They stand with others who suggest that we pluralize our terms in this area: human sexualities and orientations.

That the previous paragraph may have been upsetting, even distasteful, to some readers emphasizes the connectedness of psychological, social, and cultural issues with those of sexuality. Human sexuality is biology, behavior, and much, much more. Our sexual beliefs, behaviors, choices, even feelings and comfort levels, are profoundly affected by what our culture prescribes and proscribes, which has been transmitted to us by the full range of social institutions and processes. This section begins our attempt to address these interrelationships and their impact on human sexuality.

The subsection *The Body and Its Responses* contains three informative and thought-provoking articles that illuminate the interplay of biological, psychological, cultural, and interpersonal factors that affect sexual functioning. The first two articles, "Man Power" and "Male Sexual Circuitry" focus on male bodies and functioning. The third, "The Science of Women & Sex" focuses on female bodies and functioning. All can be viewed as owner's manuals for each sex. However, we believe all readers should read all three to learn a great deal of interesting and practical information about sexual health and functioning.

The subsection *Hygiene and Sexual Health Care* opens with an interesting article "Sex, Drugs and Rock and Roll" that gives today's college-aged readers an opportunity to learn from the mistakes (or experiences) of their cohorts of the 1970s. Next, "Improved AIDS Treatments Bring Life and Hope—at a Cost" summarizes the current state of HIV/AIDS treatment, addressing advances, problems, and hopes for the future. Finally, the subsection concludes with a tour of The Meadows, a treatment center for sexual addicts, and the stories of people for whom sexual desire and behavior have led to dire consequences.

The *Human Sexualities and Orientation* subsection contains two articles that dramatically demonstrate the changes that have occurred during the last decade with respect to sexual orientation. In the past few years, growing numbers of scientific findings have identified biological, genetic, and hormonal differences between heterosexual and homosexual people. However, these findings have not significantly weakened an American culture often called fundamentally homophobic (or homosexual-fearing). At the same time, more gay, lesbian, bisexual, and transgendered people have publicly acknowledged their orientation, and have become more visible in the public eye via popular magazine stories, television, and movies. They are asserting their desires to be understood and accepted. In this subsection readers will meet some of these people, as well as some of their families, supporters, and critics. At the end, readers can make their own predictions about whether the first decade of the new century will bring a greater understanding and acceptance of the wide range of human sexualities, further entrenchment of homophobia, or an increased polarization of both.

MAN POWER

ONE GUTSY GUY CHECKS OUT THE NEW **TESTOSTERONE GEL** AND FINDS THAT MASCULINITY IS FAR MORE THAN SKIN DEEP

BY JIM THORTON

THE PHARMACIST HANDS ME A SMALL BOX CONTAINING 30 foil pouches that resemble those miniature ketchup packets at a fast-food joint. In exchange for this one-month supply of AndroGel, the new easy-to-use testosterone supplement, I fork over $170—an expense I'm positive my insurance company won't cover.

The pharmacist tells me to rub the goo on my shoulder every day, preferably in the morning. "Don't accidentally get any on your wife," he adds, explaining this could "virilize" her—give her facial hair, deepening voice, and whatnot. "Make sure to wash your hands after applying it. And it's probably a good idea to wear a T-shirt during sex."

I tell him my first stop won't be the bedroom but the golf course, where I've challenged my prescribing urologist and former college buddy, Jay Hollander, to a round of match play at a club near his home in Detroit. The pharmacist chortles and says, "In that case, put some on right away and get your Big Bertha out!" I know he's joking, but part of me hopes there's a kernel of truth here. Since AndroGel hit the market last June, the media has been awash in hoopla about this latest magical elixir and its alleged fountain-of-youth effects on everything from sex drive to muscle mass.

Testosterone replacement isn't new, but earlier delivery systems had major drawbacks. Pills, for example, were linked to liver toxicity and are no longer recommended for use in men. Intramuscular injections require large needles and can be quite painful. Testosterone patches cause skin irritation in many men, and because they're so large—about a four-inch-by-four-inch square—it's hard to keep it private at the gym.

AndroGel is invisible and as easy to apply as lotion. Its main drawback is cost—as much as $180 per month versus $9 to $20 for injections. It's intended for men whose bodies fail to make enough natural testosterone, but we heard similar blather about Viagra, and now there's a whole subculture of nonimpotent users, from swingers to escorts, who reportedly pop the pills like sexual vitamins.

Might not AndroGel turn a hormone-normal guy into a turbocharged super male?

The experts say no. I say, let me find out for myself.

A half-hour after leaving the pharmacy, Jay and I stand on the first tee, surveying the fairway. Jay plays golf every other day; I play every other year. Still, I have a confidence bordering on cockiness that I'll win. My shoulder, after all, is well-anointed with man juice, which even now is leaching from my skin into my bloodstream, where it will join forces with the no-doubt whopping quantities my testicles—the body's testosterone factory—are already making.

'Will the gel turn me into a turbocharged super male?'

I almost feel sorry for Jay, who has only his pathetic endogenous testosterone to aid him in our match. Two hours earlier, he ran me through a battery of tests (see "Before You Go for the Goo…") to make sure there were no reasons, other than general foolhardiness, for me not to attempt this trial. My blood samples have been sent to the lab and will take a week or so to analyze. Still, both of us are confident this will be a formality. I'm in good shape. I've been swimming competitively since high school. In one month, I'll be competing in the U.S. Masters Swimming national championships in Baltimore. My physical exam and medical history both look fine. As the good doctor dictated into his recorder, "James Thornton is in excellent health, and his review of systems is entirely unremarkable."

As a lifelong hypochondriac, I'm thrilled by the word "unremarkable." And over the next few hours, I proceed to win the golf match by a comfortable four holes. In the rush of triumph, the high of victory, I can almost feel the testosterone surging through me.

Testosterone. Say it slowly and the syllables emanate sexual muscularity like a fine-tuned Italian race car.

BEFORE YOU GO FOR THE GOO...

Think you're a candidate for hormone replacement? Symptoms of low testosterone include erectile difficulty, reduced libido, fatigue, osteoporosis, breast enlargement, small testicles, infertility, reduced musculature, the loss of facial or body hair, and a lowered sense of well-being. According to Alvin Matsumoto, M.D., a professor of medicine at the University of Washington School of Medicine, you may need to undergo the following tests before taking testosterone supplements:

BLOOD TEST If your symptoms suggest low testosterone levels, most physicians will follow with a relatively inexpensive "total testosterone" test. If this comes back low or borderline, you may be asked to undergo more sophisticated tests for the "free" form of testosterone. Ideally, all such testing should be done in the morning when testosterone levels are highest. If the results point to hypogonadism, your doctor may want to repeat the tests. Testosterone levels often fluctuate, and changes can be triggered by everything from diet to stress. One low score doesn't mean you have a problem. (Men concerned with infertility may want to undergo a sperm count.)

ANALYSIS OF OTHER HORMONE LEVELS Your doctor may attempt to determine if your low testosterone problem is primary (the testicles aren't functioning normally) or secondary (the testicles aren't getting the right signals). Depending on what's happening, it may be possible to correct the problem without supplements.

PROSTATE EXAM Testosterone's chemical descendant, called DHT, fuels the growth of both healthy and cancerous prostate tissue. Because of this, men with known or suspected prostate cancer should probably not receive supplements. Ditto for men suffering from breast cancer. Even if you're cancer-free, you should have your PSA levels monitored if you use a supplement, since older men commonly have BPH (benign prostatic hyperplasia).

BLOOD COUNT AND LIPID PROFILE The phrase "red-blooded male" has a basis in fact. Testosterone, it turns out, increases the percentage of red blood cells in a man's bloodstream. If your hematocrit is high, supplemental testosterone can overly "thicken" your blood. There's also a slight chance that it can lower your "good" HDL cholesterol levels. Men with heart, kidney, or liver disease should be closely monitored if they receive testosterone. —J.T.

When sufficient quantities circulate in the blood of men, it turbocharges libido, sprouts beards, beefs up muscles, hardens bones, and inclines our minds toward the kind of rambunctious competitiveness that is both the signature blessing and occasional curse of masculinity.

Men start producing testosterone when we're still in the womb—as early as the twelfth week of pregnancy. But the real tsunami comes in adolescence. Testosterone circulates from the testicles to the blood, turning on the genes that make us men. By the time we turn 30, testosterone levels begin to decline at the rate of about 1 percent a year, though most men still produce enough for a healthy libido and healthy erections (that said, it's definitely more a hormone of desire than performance). The "normal" range for testosterone is quite broad—somewhere between 240 to 1,000 nanograms of the stuff per deciliter of blood. Trying to boost your level within the normal range can backfire.

"The key point to realize is that the human body balances," says Harvard researcher Richard Spark, M.D., author of *Sexual Health for Men* (Perseus, 2000). "When you give a normal man testosterone supplements, it just causes him to shut down his own internal production. Over time, his testicles will start to shrink."

Fortunately, this shrinkage is reversible once you stop taking supplements. There are other risks—from prostate problems to breast development to overly thickened blood—that make testosterone supplements ill-advised for men with normal levels, though the risk-to-benefit calculus shifts dramatically when your testosterone levels dip below normal. And by age 70, an estimated 10–25 percent of men have testosterone levels low enough to affect their sex drive and other aspects of mood and body physiology.

"When people hear 'low testosterone' they usually think about impaired sex drive, but that's really just the tip of the iceberg," says Ronald Swerdloff, M.D., chief of the division of endocrinology at Harbor-UCLA Medical Center. "Hypogonadism [low testosterone] can cause osteoporosis and decreased muscle strength in men, leaving them susceptible to falls and fractures. It can lead to abdominal obesity, low energy, and depressed mood and possibly even affect their thinking ability. With replacement therapy, these men often can enjoy a truly improved quality of life."

Multicenter studies presented by Swerdloff and his colleague, Christina Wang, M.D., at the Endocrine Society's annual meeting last June found that testosterone, whether administered by a patch or gel, did indeed improve sexual function, mood, muscle strength and mass, and body fat in hypogonadal men. Yet, according to the society, less than 200,000 of the four to five million American men who suffer hypogonadism are currently being treated for it. AndroGel may change that. Men may soon be slapping on testosterone like after-shave lotion. And based on the information I received from my urologist, I'm horrified to say this might include men like me.

It's a week later, and I'm staring in disbelief at my test results, which Jay's secretary has just faxed to my home in Pittsburgh. I skip over the few items that are normal and zero in on the many that aren't. Bottom line: My red blood cells, hemoglobin, and hematocrit (a measure of your blood's oxygen-carrying capacity) are all low—the telltale signature of anemia. Even worse, my pretreatment "free" testosterone (a form that isn't bound to other molecules and is readily available for use) is frighteningly close to the absolute bottom of the normal range.

"If it falls any farther," I tell my wife, Debbie, "you'd better start thinking about changing your sexual orientation."

Even to me, this forced levity rings with false bravado. I read on: lousy total cholesterol, sky-high "bad" LDL cholesterol, elevated chloride and BUN levels (whatever these might be). With intimations of mortality rattling my brain, I do what no hypochondriac should ever do: go on the Internet to learn about my conditions. I'll fast-forward through the details and simply say that of the dozens of explanations for my infirmities, the only ones that offer me any hope for survival are aspirin and alcohol abuse.

For much of my adult life, I've capped off each day with three or four beers, followed by a chaser of three or four aspirins. Doctors have long understood that hardcore alcoholic men frequently see their testosterone levels sink as a result of wretched nutrition and hormonal changes. But even worse for my system (though not necessarily my testosterone levels) is the aspirin. On one obscure Web site, I find the following: "In men and postmenopausal women, anemia is usually due to gastrointestinal blood loss associated with ulcers or the use of aspirin or [other] nonsteroidal anti-inflammatory medications [like ibuprofen]."

I decide on the spot to stop drinking and throw away my jumbo bottles of generic aspirin and ibuprofen. I also resolve to keep anointing myself with testosterone. I begin, as well, to fill out the paperwork to get reimbursed by my insurance company for the AndroGel. Disheartening as it is to admit, it looks like I have a legitimate need for it. I also try to console myself. Some experts say that diminishing testosterone may not be such a bad thing.

"I think you can make the case that some young men have too much testosterone and only when they get a little older do they become reasonable," says Stanley Korenman, M.D., a reproductive endocrinologist at UCLA School of Medicine. "Throughout history, the world has been run by older men. Young men make better soldiers because they're stronger, more aggressive, and more impulsive. Older men are wiser, they make more sense, and they are the ones who go into positions of leadership."

Georgia State psychology professor James Dabbs, Ph.D., says his research supports the idea that high testosterone hurts occupational achievement. Unemployed men, he found, have higher average testosterone levels than blue-collar workers, who in turn have higher average levels than white-collar workers. Waning testosterone may also make men better husbands and fathers. "It's very clear in birds," says Dabbs, "that the testosterone levels of the males drop dramatically once they start nesting." A study presented at the Endocrine Society's meeting last summer showed a similar drop in men following the birth of a child. Lowering testosterone with age, Dabbs speculates, may help predispose men to the gentler activities of parenthood. Bottom line: Men may need high testosterone to get a mate—and lower testosterone to keep her.

As much as I love my wife, I still want high testosterone levels. The supplements clearly work in hypogonadal men. But what about borderline cases like me? Will we enjoy at least a subtle variation of these benefits? It's this hope for rejuvenation that keeps me slathering on the AndroGel every morning for the next three weeks.

It's Sunday, August 20, the final day of the four-day U.S. Masters Swimming national championships. My legs and deltoids screaming with lactic acid, I surge forward the final dozen agonizing strokes to the wall and hit the automatic timing pad hard. The scoreboard flashes the finishing times for all eight swimmers in this one-of-many heats of the men's 100-meter freestyle. I'm too tired to look up to see how poorly I've swum this race, which, in my mind, is swimming's marquee event. Some 1,380 swimmers have traveled to Baltimore to test themselves against the nation's best age-group swimmers. Participants range in age from 19 to 91 and include at least nine former Olympians. The competition is brutal. Seventy-seven new national records and 51 new world age-group marks have been set over the first three days.

Medals are awarded to the top ten competitors in each event in each age group. Riddled as I am with iron-poor blood and pathetic natural testosterone production, I have no delusions of grandeur. If I finish in the top 15 of men 45—49, it will be a miracle of the Lazarus variety. Earlier I asked officials to add a third gender category to the competition: pink-blooded guys like me who, in the spirit of fairness, really should be swimming against the more muscular women. The officials declined my request.

When the starter's horn signaled the start of my heat, I leapt off the blocks, already exhausted. For several hours before the race, a photographer shot endless pictures of me flexing my eel-like muscles, pictures meant to illustrate the considerable power conferred upon me by AndroGel.

Truth be known, after four weeks of religious self-anointment, I'd noticed no changes whatsoever, be they physical, emotional, sexual, or cognitive. The fact that the photographer could make me appear even a tad muscular is testimony less to the AndroGel than to his genius. Unfortunately, all that flexing also left my muscles tight and fatigued, precisely the opposite state I had hoped for.

An hour after the race is over, the final results are posted. It's like the *Twilight Zone*—by some mad fluke,

I've finished seventh in my age group! What's more, my time is only a second or so off my best college performance 30 years ago.

When I pick up my medal, I keep all thoughts of AndroGel to myself. The last thing I want now is to attract the attention of urine-testers.

A couple of days after my return home, I smear my shoulder with the final dose of AndroGel and head to a local lab for retesting. My beer-and-aspirin sobriety has now stretched out for three weeks, and I'm anxious to learn if my body's begun slouching its way back toward good health. The nurse siphons off four tubes of my blood. Perhaps I'm deluding myself, but it looks a wee bit darker than last time.

A week later when the fax comes in, I'm guardedly overjoyed: The hemoglobin has clawed its way into the thick of the normal range, and red blood cells and hematocrit appear to be following fast. My testosterone has also climbed, though the change is modest. Before, I stood on the precipice of abnormality; with a little help from AndroGel, I've taken one baby step closer to the middle of the "low normal" quadrant.

When I reinterview the experts about why the AndroGel had little effect on me, they echo their earlier sentiments: Low-normal is still normal. Momentarily, I toy with asking my doctor to renew the prescription at a higher dose. But just as quickly, I dismiss this notion. I have never felt any symptoms associated with low testosterone, so I'm not sure what I'm hoping to improve. Of course, if I lose my next golf match, I just may call my pharmacist.

Jim Thornton won a National Magazine Award for health writing in 1998.

Male Sexual Circuitry

by Irwin Goldstein
and the Working Group for the Study of Central Mechanisms in Erectile Dysfunction

Five hundred years ago Leonardo da Vinci made an observation about the penis that rings true even today for many men and their partners. The Renaissance scientist, inventor and artist—one in a long line of investigators who have attempted to solve the riddle of penile rigidity—observed that this seemingly wayward organ has a will of its own. "The penis does not obey the order of its master, who tries to erect or shrink it at will, whereas instead the penis erects freely while its master is asleep. The penis must be said to have its own mind, by any stretch of the imagination," he wrote.

Da Vinci, who dissected cadaverous penises from men who had been executed by hanging, was the first scientist to recognize that during an erection, the penis fills with blood. In his perception that the penis acts of its own free will, however, this multitalented scholar was wrong.

Far from having a mind of its own, the penis is now known to be under the complete control of the central nervous system—the brain and spinal cord. As William D. Steers, chair of the department of urology at the University of Virginia, has noted, any disturbance in the network of nerve pathways that connects the penis and the central nervous system can lead to erection problems.

In the past few decades the study of erections has been redefined. Thanks to advances in molecular biology, we now have a better understanding of the processes within the penis that lead to erection and detumescence, the return of the penis to a flaccid state. Armed with this knowledge, we have begun to explore how the brain and spinal cord control erections and other sexual functions. The field is still young, but we are optimistic that these efforts will lead to new therapies for the millions of men who suffer from sexual dysfunction—and we expect that some of these findings will also inform treatments for women. Although research on women has lagged far behind that on men, we are beginning to elucidate the striking similarities—as well as differences—between the sexes in regard to sexual function.

An erection is a carefully orchestrated series of events, with the central nervous system in the role of conductor. Even when the penis is at rest, the nervous system is at work. When a man is not sexually aroused, parts of the sympathetic nervous system actively limit blood flow to the penis, keeping it limp. The sympathetic nervous system is one of two branches of the autonomic nervous system—the part of the central nervous system that controls largely "automatic" internal responses, such as blood pressure and heart rate.

Dynamic Balance

Within the penis, and throughout the nervous system, a man's sexual response reflects a dynamic balance between excitatory and inhibitory forces. Whereas the sympathetic nervous system tends to inhibit erections, the parasympathetic system—the other branch of the autonomic nervous system—is one of several important excitatory pathways. During arousal, excitatory signals can originate in the brain, triggered perhaps by a smell or by the sight or thought of an alluring partner, or by physical stimulation of the genitals.

Regardless of where the signals come from, the excitatory nerves in the penis respond by releasing so-called proerectile neurotransmitters, including nitric oxide and acetylcholine. These chemical messengers signal the muscles of the penile arteries to relax, causing more blood to flow into the organ. Spongy chambers inside the penis fill up with blood. As these expand, they compress the veins that normally drain blood from the penis. This pressure squeezes the veins until they are nearly closed, trapping blood within the chambers and producing an erection. (Viagra—also known as sildenafil—works by slowing the breakdown of one of the chemicals that keeps the muscles relaxed, thereby holding blood in the penis.)

During an erection, the penis not only receives nerve signals but also sends them to the spinal cord and brain. The penis has an unusually high density of specialized tactile

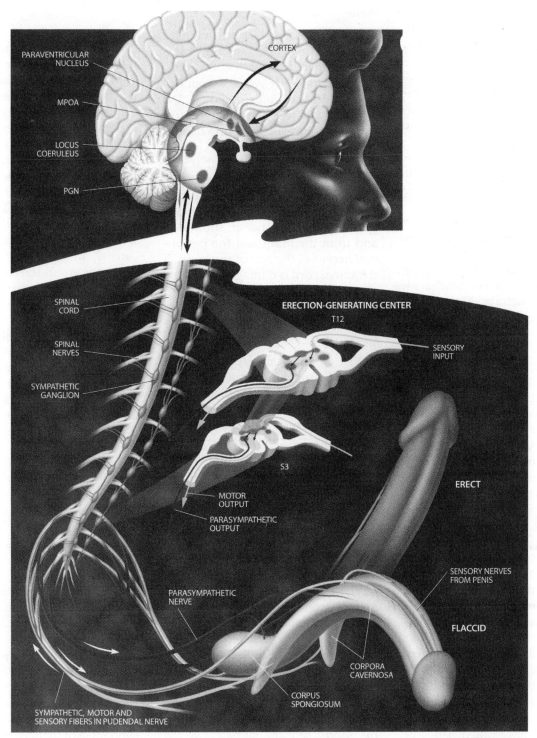

Labels within the illustration:

PARAVENTRICULAR NUCLEUS

CORTEX

MPOA

LOCUS COERULEUS

PGN

SPINAL CORD

SPINAL NERVES

SYMPATHETIC GANGLION

ERECTION-GENERATING CENTER
T12

SENSORY INPUT

S3

MOTOR OUTPUT

PARASYMPATHETIC OUTPUT

ERECT

SENSORY NERVES FROM PENIS

FLACCID

PARASYMPATHETIC NERVE

CORPORA CAVERNOSA

CORPUS SPONGIOSUM

SYMPATHETIC, MOTOR AND SENSORY FIBERS IN PUDENDAL NERVE

JOHN W. KARAPELOU

ERECTION is orchestrated by the central nervous system. Erections are continuously inhibited by the sympathetic nervous system During REM sleep, however, when the sympathetic neurons in the locus coeruleus are turned off, erections occur spontaneously. The other brain structure that inhibits erections is the paragigantocellular nucleus (PGN). Conversely, the parasympathetic nervous system is excitatory. Tactile stimuli or stimuli processed in the cortex may be integrated in the paraventricular nucleus and the medial preoptic area (MPOA), triggering an erection. Some erections (called reflexive) occur entirely in the erection-generating center of the spinal cord, which runs from vertebra S3 to vertebra T12.

receptors; when these receptors are stimulated, their signals course to the spinal cord and brain, where they influence nerve pathways from these higher centers. So although the penis does not "think" for itself, it keeps the brain and spinal cord well apprised of its feelings. After a man climaxes or the arousal has diminished, the erection quickly subsides. The sympathetic nervous system again limits blood flow into the penis, which returns to its soft state.

Circumstances that increase the activity of the sympathetic nervous system—such as stress or exposure to cold—can temporarily shrink the penis by making it more flaccid. Conversely, switching off the activity of the sympathetic nervous system enhances erections. Nocturnal erections are a good example of this phenomenon. These occur primarily during rapid eye movement (REM) sleep, the stage in which dreaming occurs. During REM sleep, sympathetic neurons are turned off in the locus coeruleus, a specific area of the brain stem, the part of the brain that connects to the spinal cord. According to one theory, when this sympathetic brain center is quiet, proerectile pathways predominate, allowing nocturnal erections to occur. We often refer to such erections as "battery-recharging mechanisms" for the penis, because they increase blood flow, bringing in fresh oxygen to reenergize the organ. (Episodes of nocturnal arousal also occur in women. Four or five times a night—that is, during each episode of REM— women experience labial, vaginal and clitoral engorgement.)

Some erections, called reflexive erections, are generated entirely in the spinal cord. Much like touching a finger to a hot burner triggers a rapid withdrawal of the hand, physical stimulation of the penis can set off a spinal erection reflex in some situations. So crucial is reproduction to our perpetuation as a species that it appears that the capacity to create an erection has been wired into nerve circuits near the base of a man's spine.

In humans, most of the evidence for this finding has come from observations of soldiers with spinal cord injuries, particularly veterans wounded in World War II. Before then, the general belief was that men with spinal cord injuries were permanently and completely impotent and sterile. Although we now know that this view is mistaken, it is understandable. The spinal cord is the information superhighway for the nervous system, shuttling nerve stimuli to and from the brain and the peripheral nerves of the rest of the body. If the spinal cord is damaged, this flow of nerve impulses can be interrupted in myriad ways, depending on where the injury occurs and how extensive it is.

Yet, as physician Herbert Talbot reported in a classic study in 1949, men with severe or complete spinal cord injuries often continue to have erections. In his examination of 200 men with paraplegia, two thirds were able to achieve erections, and some were able to engage in vaginal intercourse and have an orgasm. Even though devastating war injuries left these men paralyzed and unable to control many basic bodily functions, the ability to have erections was often preserved.

These observations—and information from studies in laboratory animals as far back as the 1890s—led to the discovery that an "erection-generating center" is located in the sacral segments of the spinal cord (that is, just above the tail end of the spine, between the S3 and T12 vertebrae). Physical stimulation of the penis sends sensory signals via the pudendal nerve to this erection center. The incoming signals activate connector nerve cells called interneurons, which then stimulate nearby parasympathetic neurons. These neurons send erection-inducing signals from the sacral spine to the penile blood vessels. As long as this reflex arc remains intact, an erection is possible.

The Brain's Brakes

Observations of men and laboratory animals with spinal cord damage have led to another intriguing finding: when the brain is disconnected from the erection-generating center in the spinal cord, erections typically occur more frequently and with less tactile stimulation than they did before the injury. For instance, Benjamin D. Sachs, an experimental psychologist at the University of Connecticut, found in 1979 that spinal transaction in rats caused an increase of more than 1,000 percent in the number of erections and a 94 percent reduction in the time it took for the animals to become erect.

It seemed as if, in the disconnection of the brain from the body, some inhibitory control over erections was removed. This proved to be the case. In 1990 physiologists Kevin E. McKenna and Lesley Marson, then at Northwestern University, identified the brain center that keeps the brakes on spinal-mediated erections. They found that a specific cluster of neurons in the hindbrain (an evolutionarily ancient part of the brain that controls such basic functions as blood pressure and heart rate) is in charge of this central inhibition. When McKenna and Marson destroyed this group of neurons— called the paragigantocellular nucleus, or PGN—in a male rat's brain, the inhibition disappeared, causing more frequent and intense erections.

These researchers then made another significant discovery about the brain's role in suppressing erections. They found that the PGN neurons send most of their axons down to the erection-generating neurons in the lower spinal cord. There the PGN nerve endings release the neurotransmitter serotonin—a chemical messenger that inhibits erections by opposing the effects of proerectile neurotransmitters.

This discovery may have important implications for the millions of men and women who take serotonin-enhancing drugs to treat depression and other mental health problems. Drugs such as Prozac and Paxil, which belong to the widely used class of drugs called selective serotonin reuptake inhibitors (SSRIs), work in part by increasing brain levels of serotonin. These drugs often cause sexual dysfunction as an unwanted side effect, most commonly delayed or blocked ejaculation in men and, in women, reduced sexual desire and difficulty reaching orgasm.

The work of McKenna and his colleagues provides an explanation for how this side effect may occur. By increasing serotonin in the central nervous system, SSRIs may tighten the brain's built-in brakes on erection, ejaculation and other sexual functions in some people.

As often happens in medicine, however, one person's side effect can be another's therapy. The inhibitory properties of SSRIs have been shown to be helpful for men with premature ejaculation, a condition in which a man climaxes too quickly, typically before vaginal penetration or a few seconds thereafter. SSRIs are effective in delaying orgasm in these men, most likely because they increase central inhibition. Although more research is needed, SSRIs may also hold promise in treating sexual disorders that are associated with excessive or inappropriate sexual urges, such as paraphilias—for example, pedophilia, a sexual interest in children.

Considering that sex makes the world go 'round, or at least keeps us on the planet, it is not clear why these elaborate inhibitory controls have evolved. Although no one knows for sure, some intriguing theories have been advanced. John Bancroft of Indiana University believes that for most men this central inhibition is adaptive, keeping them out of trouble that might arise from excessive or risky pursuit of sexual enjoyment. These internal brakes also may help prevent a man from having repeated ejaculations during sexual encounters, which could lower his sperm store and reduce fertility.

Also, as with many pleasures in life, an erection can become too much of a good thing if it lasts too long. An erection that persists longer than four hours—a phenomenon that may occur in men with sickle cell anemia and in those who use certain drugs—is considered a medical emergency. Called priapism, this condition traps blood within the erect penis, leading to permanent damage if not treated promptly: if freshly oxygenated blood is not brought in, tissue starvation can occur.

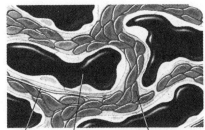

NERVE   SINUSOID   SMOOTH MUSCLE CELL CONTRACTED

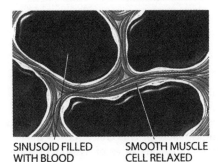

SINUSOID FILLED WITH BLOOD   SMOOTH MUSCLE CELL RELAXED

JOHN W. KARAPELOU

ENGORGEMENT begins when nerves release transmitters that diffuse into the smooth muscle cells around the arteries in the penis, causing the normally contracted cells to relax and blood to flow in (top). As they relax, the muscles elongate, pushing against the veins that drain blood from the penis. The blood becomes trapped in sinusoids--the chambers between muscle cells--and the penis becomes erect (bottom).

Despite the benefits of central inhibition for most men, Bancroft believes it can cause problems for others if it is too strong or too weak. If a man has too much central inhibitory control—if, say, his brain serotonin levels are too high—he may develop sexual dysfunction. Conversely, if his central inhibition is too low, he may be more inclined to engage in high-risk sexual behaviors, such as recklessly ignoring the threat of sexually transmitted diseases in the pursuit of sexual gratification.

Inside the Brain

Many regions throughout the brain contribute to the male sexual response, ranging from centers in the hindbrain, which regulates basic body functions, to areas of the cerebral cortex, the organ of higher thought and intellect. The brain sites we have identified so far appear to be extensively interconnected. We now think the brain's control of sexual function works as a unified network, rather than as a chain of relay sites. In other words, the control of erection does not appear to be organized in a tightly linked chain of command centers but rather is distributed throughout multiple areas in the brain and spinal cord. Therefore, should injury or disease destroy one or more of these regions, the capacity for erections often remains intact.

One of the important brain regions regulating sexual behavior is the hypothalamus. This small area plays a vital role in linking the nervous and endocrine, or hormonal, systems and is involved in the control of certain basic behaviors, such as eating and aggression. A cluster of neurons in the hypothalamus, called the medial preoptic area, or MPOA, seems to have a crucial role in sexual function and, accordingly, is being intensively studied at the moment.

Researcher François Giuliano of the Faculté de Médecine of the Université Paris-Sud and his colleagues have recently shown that electrical or chemical stimulation of the MPOA causes erections in rats. The MPOA appears to integrate stimuli from many areas of the brain, helping to organize and direct the complex patterns of sexual behavior.

Some scientists speculate that the MPOA may also be involved in the recognition of a sexual partner.

The hypothalamus also contains the paraventricular nucleus, another group of neurons with an important role in male sexual function. Like the MPOA, this nucleus is a processing center that sends and receives messages from different parts of the brain and spinal cord. During sexual arousal, the paraventricular nucleus releases oxytocin. This hormone has long been known to stimulate the release of milk in breast-feeding women and uterine contractions during delivery of a baby; in many species, oxytocin is a chemical "love" messenger that promotes bonding and social attachments. But it also proves to be a brain neurotransmitter that has a powerful proerectile effect in men. Like other neurotransmitters, oxytocin binds to target neurons and regulates the conduction of nerve impulses. In this case, oxytocin activates excitatory nerve pathways running from the spinal erection-generating center to the penis.

Higher brain centers are involved in male sexual response as well, but we know much less about them. Nevertheless, the few studies to date have provided some intriguing results. Researcher Serge Stoleru of Inserm in Paris recently used positron emission tomography (PET) to reveal which parts of the cerebral cortex are activated when men are sexually aroused. He compared PET scans in a group of men who were presented with three kinds of films: sexually explicit, humorous and emotionally neutral (such as a documentary on the Amazon). Stoleru found that when men were sexually aroused, specific parts of the cerebral cortex were activated, including regions associated with emotional experiences and control of the autonomic nervous system.

In addition, scientists are exploring how higher brain functions, such as memory and learning, help to control erections. Psychologist Raymond Rosen of Robert Wood Johnson Medical School in New Brunswick, N.J.,

showed that healthy men can be taught to have erections on demand, in response to mental imagery or nonsexual cues. In one study, men were instructed to use their minds to arouse themselves in exchange for a financial reward. When they were given feedback on their performance via a light display, they rapidly learned to increase their erections—in the absence of direct physical stimulation—through the use of imagery and fantasy techniques. To keep their motivation high, the men earned financial bonuses that depended on the number and degree of erections they achieved.

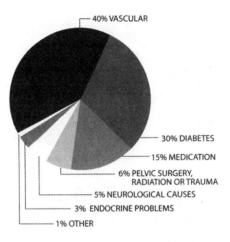

LAURIE GRACE

ERECTILE DYSFUNCTION has many causes, ranging from stress and other psychological concerns to purely physiological factors. This chart depicts the main physical causes of dysfunction and reveals that vascular problems underlie a vast number of cases.

This experiment was one of many that have shown that learning and memory strongly influence erections. Indeed, the ability of the brain to associate sexual arousal and orgasm with cues helps to explain why an astounding number of fetish objects—such as high-heeled shoes, leather whips and lingerie—can often enhance sexual arousal.

When Things Go Wrong

By understanding the role of the central nervous system in control-

ling erection and other sexual functions, we hope to set the stage for new therapies. Erectile dysfunction, which is defined as a consistent inability to get or keep an erection that is satisfactory for sexual performance, is an increasingly common health problem. A study we conducted a few years ago in the Boston area estimated that some degree of erectile dysfunction affects about 40 percent of men over age 40 and up to 70 percent of men 70 years old. As baby boomers grow old and the global population ages, we estimate that the number of men who have this condition will more than double in the next 25 years—ultimately affecting more than 330 million men worldwide.

If nerve stimuli cannot reach the penis for any reason, an erection problem is inevitable. Such dysfunction can also be an unfortunate complication of surgery to remove the prostate gland to treat prostate cancer, because this procedure can damage penile nerves. Diabetes can lead to nerve and blood vessel damage in the penis as well. Many neurological conditions—including spinal cord injury, Parkinson's disease, multiple sclerosis and stroke—can cause problems. And because a man's moods and mental well-being affect the flow of nerve messages to the penis, it is not surprising that stress, depression, anxiety or anger often underlies erection difficulties.

Using their growing knowledge of central nervous system control, researchers have begun to develop medications that target the central nervous system. A drug called apomorphine will most likely be the first in a new generation of therapies that acts directly on the brain as opposed to the penis, as Viagra does. Apomorphine—brand name Uprima—mimics the neurotransmitter dopamine, enhancing erections by binding to specific receptors on nerve cells in the paraventricular nucleus and the MPOA, thereby turning on proerectile pathways.

Apomorphine is under review by the U.S. Food and Drug Administra-

SIDE VIEW	FRONT VIEW	TOP VIEW
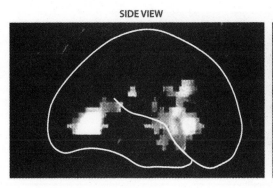	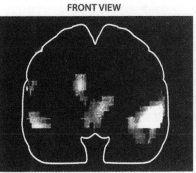	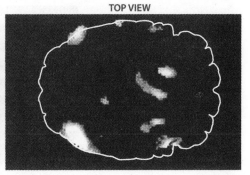

COURTESY OF SERGE STOLERU *INSERM*

AROUSAL has been mapped in these PET scans of men watching sexually explicit films. Although research on the sexual organization of the higher brain is just beginning, these scans show that several areas of the cerebral cortex are clearly involved.

tion for approval, and a final decision is expected soon. Although the compound has been used in medicine for more than a century—for the treatment of Parkinson's disease, among other disorders—it was not until the mid-1980s that investigators, including R. Taylor Segraves, a psychiatrist at Case Western Reserve University, and Jeremy P. W. Heaton, a urologist at Queen's University in Ontario, began investigating it for the treatment of erectile dysfunction. Since then, clinical studies have evaluated apomorphine in more than 3,000 men and found that it can successfully treat those with many different types of erectile dysfunction.

Like all drugs, apomorphine can cause unwanted side effects. Whereas Viagra, the most widely prescribed drug for erectile dysfunction, can give rise to headaches, nasal stuffiness and facial flushing, apomorphine can induce nausea during its initial use. In the future, we may be able to treat some men more effectively by combining apomorphine with therapies that act directly on the penis.

Sex and the Sexes

Until recently, most research on sexual function focused in large part on men and the control of penile erection. Fortunately, this is chang-ing, as we increasingly recognize that sexual dysfunction is extremely common—and treatable—in both sexes. In fact, a recent survey of more than 3,000 Americans reported that the number of women with sexual complaints was greater than the number of men: 43 percent as opposed to 31 percent.

Many researchers are studying the mechanisms that control sexual function in women and are testing therapies to treat female sexual disorders. Our laboratory is conducting a clinical trial to determine whether apomorphine can enhance sexual arousal in women with such problems. We also are testing a new FDA-approved device called the EROS-Clitoral Therapy Device, which is used to provide gentle suction to the clitoris, causing engorgement. In women with sexual dysfunction, it has been shown to safely improve sexual sensation, lubrication, orgasm and sexual satisfaction.

This research has made us aware of some similarities between the sexes in the central nervous system's control of arousal, orgasm and various sexual functions. Preliminary evidence suggests that the central control of sexual function in men and women is remarkably similar. For instance, as noted earlier, both sexes experience nocturnal arousal responses, and both are vulnerable to SSRI-induced sexual dysfunction.

Of course, there are also dramatic differences—as in the postorgasmic refractory period, the normal delay after an orgasm before arousal can occur again. Women can have multiple orgasms and therefore have virtually no refractory period, but most men have a refractory period that lasts from several minutes to many hours.

We have come a long way since da Vinci's discovery that the penis fills with blood—not air or spiritual essences—during an erection. The past decade has revolutionized not only the field of erection research but also our societal attitudes about sexual health. Only a few years ago erectile dysfunction went generally untreated.

Today this condition and other sexual problems are more openly recognized and discussed. Millions of men are receiving care for erection troubles, thanks to a burgeoning appreciation of the importance of sexual health and the availability of more effective and convenient treatments. In the near future we anticipate that there will be an even wide array of therapies for men and women. With our increasing insight into the brain's role in controlling our sexuality, we are also moving toward a more holistic view of sexual well-being—one that integrates mind and body and responds to the unique needs of both sexes.

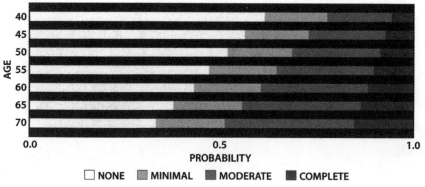

LAURIE GRACE

IMPOTENCE increases with age, according to several surveys. In 25 years, given the aging of the world's population, it is estimated that the condition may affect more than 330 million men.

Further Information

IMPOTENCE AND ITS MEDICAL AND PSYCHOLOGICAL CORRELATES: RESULTS OF THE MASSACHUSETTS MALE AGING STUDY. H. A. Feldman et al. in *Journal of Urology*, Vol. 151, No. 1, pages 54–61; January 1994.

NEURAL CONTROL OF PENILE ERECTION. F. Giuliano, O. Rampin, G. Benoit and A. Jardin in *Urology Clinics of North America*, Vol. 22, No. 4, pages 747–766; November 1995.

THE BRAIN IS THE MASTER ORGAN IN SEXUAL FUNCTION: CENTRAL NERVOUS SYSTEM CONTROL OF MALE AND FEMALE SEXUAL FUNCTION. K. McKenna in *International Journal of Impotence Research*, Vol. 11, Supplement 1, pages 548–555; 1999.

SEXUAL DYSFUNCTION IN THE UNITED STATES: PREVALENCE AND PREDICTORS. E. O. Laumann, A. Paik and R. C. Rosen in *Journal of the American Medical Association*, Vol. 281, No. 6, pages 537–544; February 10, 1999.

The Authors

IRWIN GOLDSTEIN is a urologist at Boston University. He is a member of the Working Group for the Study of Central Mechanisms in Erectile Dysfunction, which was formed in 1998. The other members are John Bancroft of Indiana University; François Giuliano of the Faculté de Médecine, Université Paris-Sud; Jeremy P. W. Heaton of Queen's University, Ontario; Ronald W. Lewis of the Medical College of Georgia; Tom F. Lue of the University of California, San Francisco; Kevin E. McKenna of Northwestern University; Harin Padma-Nathan of the University of Southern California; Raymond Rosen of the Robert Wood Johnson Medical School; Benjamin D. Sachs of the University of Connecticut; R. Taylor Segraves of Case Western Reserve University; and William D. Steers of the University of Virginia. All the authors consult or investigate (or have done so in the past) for one or more pharmaceutical companies—among them Abbott, Eli Lilly, Merck, Pfizer and TAP; Sachs owns stock in Abbott; Heaton shares several patents on apomorphine.

The Science of **Women & Sex**

INSPIRED BY VIAGRA, researchers are rushing to unlock the mysteries of female desire. The answers are turning out to be much more complex than anyone expected.

BY JOHN LELAND

For Ellen, a 45-year-old college professor in rural Maryland, the music of the bedroom has never been as harmonious as it is in magazines. She cannot reach orgasm with her husband, and has only tepid interest in sex. "Frankly, it's the one fly in the ointment of our marriage, she says. Sexual couples counseling didn't help; her gynecologist, "immanently unhelpful," told her nothing could be done. Then she heard about a Baltimore urologist named Toby Chai who was conducting a small trial of Viagra among women with sexual complaints. She'd read of the miraculous results in men and thought this might finally dispel the "iceberg" intruding on her marital life. "It's not something we talk about every day, but it's always there." Returning home with six pills—three placebo, three Viagra—Ellen became a pilgrim in the increasingly frenzied search to unlock the mysteries of female desire.

How do we define sexual dysfunction in women?

It's both a mind and body thing, and many women have a problem at some point in their lives. Doctors say sexual woes rise to the level of dysfunction only when they are persistent and—most important— cause personal distress.

Women's sexuality, Sigmund Freud opined, is the "dark continent" of the soul: an uncharted netherworld receding behind folds of flesh and muscle. Among the Big Ideas of the last century, few were as asinine as Freud's on sex and women, most notably his theory of penis envy. Yet in the decades that followed, science has continued to put forward as much ignorance as bliss. Until the late '20s, doctors manually stimulated women as a treatment for "pelvic disorder;" the vibrator, originally coal-fired, caught on as a way to shorten office visits.

In the 1950s and '60s, Alfred Kinsey and the team of Masters and Johnson began exploring female sexuality through the prism of its male counterpart. "We are still in a culture which has defined sexuality, sexual pleasure and [sexual goals] in male terms," says Dr. John Bancroft, current head of the Kinsey Institute. "Then we apply the same paradigm to women. That is a mistake." The male paradigm is simple: erection and release. Women's satisfactions and drives are more complex, organized as much around the health of the relationship as the majesty that is orgasm.

Add science to this simple insight and it becomes a program for revolution. Sparked by the stunning success of Viagra, and the prospect that it might be duplicated with women, a new era of sexual experimentation is now taking shape— this time not in the bedroom, but in the laboratory. "It's such a Wild West frontier of new discovery," says Dr. Irwin Goldstein, the media-friendly Boston urologist and pioneer in research on men and women. (Like many doctors interviewed for this article, Goldstein is a paid consultant and gets research money from one or more of the drug companies, but does not own stock in any.)

How does loss of testosterone affect women?

Women produce testosterone in their adrenal glands and ovaries. Around the time of menopause, the amount produced declines, which may lead to a loss of desire, as well as fatigue and thinning hair.

As many as four in 10 American women experience some form of sexual dissatisfaction, a figure likely to grow as the 41 million women of the baby boom, for whom unencumbered sex seemed a birthright, make the passage through menopause. The shadow cast by dysfunction can spread far beyond the bedroom, darkening a woman's entire sense of well-being. "It was probably in some ways more devastating than breast cancer," says a 55-year-old college professor who lost her ability to become aroused after hysterectomy. "This huge piece of who I am had just gone." Drug companies, research clinicians and traditional therapists are all leaping into the fray. Their work, still in its embryonic stages, is already starting to yield a radical new understanding of anatomy, dysfunction—and even the evolutionary meaning of orgasm.

The Risks of **Estrogen**

AFTER MENOPAUSE, changes in women's bodies can make sex painful. But new studies raise doubts about hormone therapy. BY SHARON BEGLEY

How much risk will a woman accept in return for good sex[&stop]? Many women approaching or past menopause view estrogen-replacement therapy (ERT) as a foundation of youth in a pill. By pumping up blood concentrations of estrogen to near-youthful levels, ERT vanquishes the hot flashes and night sweats responsible for libido-killing insomnia and irritability. It also prevents the thinning and drying out of vaginal tissue that comes with plummeting estrogen levels, notes Dr. Margery Gass, an Ob-Gyn at the University of Cincinnati College of Medicine. After menopause, thinner, less flexible vaginal tissue can make sex so painful that the body recoils even when the heart is willing. Virtually any form of estrogen—the pill Premarin, a patch, vaginal creams or vaginal rings kept in place for three months—"improves vaginal tissues, says Gass.

Why do we know so little about sex and older women?

In the past, women (and men) simply accepted dysfunction as a natural part of aging. After the spectacular success of Viagra, researchers began focusing on ways to help women remain sexually active.

Because estrogen alone stimulates the uterine lining and increases the risk of endometrial cancer, women with an intact uterus are advised to pair estrogen with progestin—which blocks this effect—in a regimen called hormone-replacement therapy (HRT). Estrogen alone has long had a dark side: it is associated with an increased risk of breast cancer. Now, in one of those you-can't-win cases, it appears that progestin may increase the risk of breast cancer even more than estrogen alone, says Dr. Ronald Ross of the University of Southern California. Scientists now think that estrogen-progestin increases the risk of breast cancer 53 percent compared with not taking hormones; estrogen by itself raises the risk 34 percent. The longer a woman takes HRT, the greater her risk.

The standard retort to concerns about breast cancer has been, "Sure, but estrogen reduces the risk of osteoporosis. That remains pretty much unquestioned: estrogen decreases the amount of bone that is resorbed in the constant process of skeletal building and demolishing. But estrogen's killer app is supposed to be preventing heart disease. It lowers bad LDL cholesterol and raises good HDL. (Creams and rings are not effective because their estrogen is absorbed directly by the bloodstream, bypassing the liver, where cholesterol levels are adjusted.) That heart benefit was supposed to swamp the risk of breast cancer, especially since heart disease kills nine times as many American women every year as does breast cancer. But results of the newest, best-designed studies are dismaying. They find that HRT provides no heart benefits to women with existing cardiovascular disease; it may actually increase their risk of heart attacks. And it may not protect healthy women from developing heart disease: in April, researchers at the Women's Health Initiative, run by the National Institutes of Health, warned that HRT seems to raise the risk of heart attacks and stroke in healthy women, at least initially. "Women with heart disease should not take estrogen with the expectation that it will help their heart, says Dr. David Herrington of Wake Forest University. Not even great sex can fix a broken Heart.

A dozen drug manufacturers, including Pfizer, the maker of Viagra, are rushing headlong into research and development, mostly on drugs originally intended to treat impotence in men. Both male and female genitals have smooth muscle tissue that engorges with blood during arousal. Researchers hope Viagra will relax this tissue in the clitoris, as it does in the penis, allowing the vessels in the organ to swell with blood. The early prognosis, though, is less than thrilling. In the most comprehensive female trial of Viagra to date, released this week, the drug proved no more effective than a placebo. Nonetheless, Cheryl Bourque, an analyst at Decision Resources, projects that by 2008, the market for treatments for women, including testosterone and estrogen (sidebar), could hit $1.7 billion. Drugs conceived specifically for women, still perhaps decades away, could make this figure seem minuscule.

Jennifer Berman is one of the few female urologists working on the cutting edge of this research. At the Women's Sexual Health Clinic in Boston not long ago, Berman received a 54-year-old woman who, since menopause and a mastectomy, suffered vaginal dryness and pain during intercourse, and lost all interest in sex. "I feel like I'm less than a woman," the woman says. Berman wanted to test the flow of blood to the woman's genitals. Supplied with a pair of 3-D glasses and a vibrator, the woman watched an erotic videotape while an ultrasound probe resembling an electronic tampon monitored her blood flow—an attempt to tease out the physical component of dysfunction. Berman and her sister, Laura, a sex therapist, have become the telegenic faces of female sexual dysfunction, a two-headed Oprah for the erotically aggrieved. Together they tag-team the mind and body, a synergy many doctors believe will provide the best relief for female sexual dysfunction. For women, more so than for men, simply "medicalizing" the problem is too reductive. While many Viagra-enhanced men are happy just to get erections, fixing women's blood flow will cure little if libido-killing stresses still assail the relationship, the home life and the woman's self-esteem. Women presenting identical complaints might require a drug, a weekend retreat or a sex toy, or some combination of the three.

Even so, medical advances promise important keys. Anatomists are finding that we haven't even mapped the basic body parts. In a conference room at Boston University, Trudy Van Houten stops an unsuspecting medical student. *The clitoris*, she challenges the young woman, a fourth-year med student: *how big is it?* The woman looks momentarily stunned. *Would you say it's one centimeter or 10?* By the fourth year of medical school, students should know the gross details of the body, but this seemingly simple question has the woman in a pickle. "It can't be as big as 10, she tries. Oh, but it is, it is. "It's here, it's here, it's here, it's here, says Van Houten, tracing a finger across an anatomical drawing. "Wow," says the student. "Thank you."

The new research borders on the macabre: Goldstein talks of "harvesting" clitorises, labia and vaginas from cadavers, surgery patients or animals to study the microprocesses of sexual response; Cindy Meston, a psychologist at the University of Texas at Austin, has reported that stimulating the same branch of the nervous system that shuts down sexual arousal in men seems to facilitate it in women. Researchers like Van Houten are only now starting to map the myriad nerves that spider through the pelvic region, hoping ultimately to spare hysterectomy patients from nerve damage, as surgeons do when they remove men's prostate glands.

As they learn about the body, scientists are also rethinking the types and roots of dysfunction. They have identified four sexual woes: a low sex drive or aversion to sex, difficulty becoming aroused, inability to reach orgasm and pain during sex. Healthy women might experience any of these on occasion. They rise to the level of dysfunction only

when they are persistent or recurring, and—most important—when they cause personal distress. Root causes can be physical (diabetes, obesity or other strain on the circulatory system), emotional (stress, fatigue or depression) or an interplay between the two. A cruel irony is that many drugs used to fight depression also dampen libido. For women now in middle age, the biggest threat to their sexual satisfaction may be social: after the age of 60 half of all women are without a partner.

> For women, the relationship and the context of sexuality can be even more critical to satisfaction than the majesty that is orgasm.

Real help for many women is still far off. In his frenzied office at the New York Center for Human Sexuality, Dr. Ridwan Shabsigh proudly shows off a color photograph of dense, tangled tubes. His lab team, he explains, injected a hardening resin into the bloodstream of a live rat, then dissolved the rodent in acid, leaving only the solidified resin where the blood vessels used to be. The image, created with an electron microscope, describes the vascular system of a rat vagina. "This is big," he said—one giant leap for science, one bad date for Queen Rat.

Shabsigh's team of head and body doctors uses an updated theoretical framework for female sexual response. In the 1970s, the influential psychiatrist Helen Singer Kaplan sorted women's responses into three successive phases—desire to arousal to orgasm—a one-way arrow pointing straight to nirvana. The arrow model, says Shabsigh, ignores the more reciprocal play between the various states of pleasure. "We think of female sexual function not as a line but as a circle" joining the four points of desire, arousal, orgasm and satisfaction. Turbulence or interruption at any point affects the weather at all the others. In other words, today's frustration about orgasm dampens next week's libido.

Though libido is the most common complaint, most of the drugs currently being tested target arousal. Many doctors think this will limit the pills' future impact. But for women like Ellen, the Maryland professor, this is splitting sexual hairs. The quiet disconnect of her marital bed, she says, caused emotional stress for both her and her husband. She was hoping Viagra would jump-start her libido, but she wanted an orgasm, as well. "It'd be nice to have your cake and eat it, too," she says. Unfortunately, the pills did not work for her. "I haven't given up," she says.

Many of the drugs in development—VasoFem, Alista, FemProx—act a lot like Viagra, and this week's discouraging trial results are a potential wet blanket for the industry. "We're definitely continuing our research," says Heather Van Ness, a Pfizer rep. "We feel this [area] is significantly more complicated than erectile dysfunction." One researcher in the Viagra trials, Dr. Rosemary Basson, says the study may have incorporated too broad a range of ages and complaints to be definitive. Viagra may work for some conditions but not others. A more targeted study, limited to post-menopausal women, is now gearing up in the United States. Also being tested is a "dopamine agonist" called apomorphine, recently recommended for approval for use in men, which sends electrical impulses from the hypothalamus to the genitals to trigger increased blood flow.

Do female orgasms serve any biological function?

Evolutionary biologists haven't yet figured that one out, and it's a controversial subject. One possible theory: orgasms in women have no function and are just a development vestige, like male nipples.

Drugs, however, aren't the only potential stairway to heaven. Earlier this month the FDA approved an apparatus called EROS-CTD, a clitoral suction de-

It's Really Not Just a Headache, Honey

As researchers learn more about the causes and types of female sexual dysfunction, they're uncovering new ways to help. There's no female equivalent to Viagra yet, but women have new reason to hope.

DYSFUNCTION TYPES

• **Desire:** A lack of libido can have both physical and psychological roots. Stress and depression (as well as some medications) are major causes.

• **Arousal:** Critical to sexual response, it may be expressed as a lack of subjective excitement or genital lubrication

• **Lack of orgasm:** It's a more common problem than previously believed: a substantial number of women have never experienced the sensation

• **Pain:** This condition can occur at any age, but it is especially troublesome after menopause, when natural lubricants dry up

DYSFUNCTION CAUSES

• **Psychological:** These range from depression and past sexual abuse to unsatisfactory relationships and a bad body image

• **Physical:** Factors include vaginal atrophy at menopause, nerve damage, diabetes, heart disease, smoking and obesity

TREATMENT OPTIONS

Researchers are looking at a wide range of medications and devices, most still in the experimental stage. For many women, the most effective treatment may combine drugs, hormones and counseling.

Viagra: The pill was no better than a placebo in women with a wide range of symptoms. New trials will target post-menopausal women.

Prostaglandin E-1 cream: Still in early clinical trials, this 'vasodilator' dilates arteries, increasing blood flow to genital tissues.

Alprostadil cream: Another version of prostaglandin E-1 and still under study, this compound is being tested for improved arousal and lubrication

Dr. K's Dream Cream: Sold 'off label' by Dr. Jed Kaminetsky, this combination of vasodilators may increase genital engorgement and arousal

Clitoral device: Approved earlier this month by the FDA, this prescription device creates a 'genital suction' over the clitoris in order to increase blood flow and sensation

Testosterone patch: Women whose hormone levels have declined apply the patch (still in clinical trials) to their abdomen to increase libido

Natural aids are popular, but not subject to FDA oversight

For arousal

L-arginine	an amino acid
Yohimbe	made from the bark of a tree

For libido

DHEA	helps fuel testosterone production

SOURCES: THE JOURNAL OF THE AMERICAN MEDICAL ASSOCIATION, NEWSWEEK REPORTING.

WHO SUFFERS

Problems* with physical intimacy affect more women than men and vary by age, education, race and marital status. The reasons are still unclear.

Sexual dysfunction

Women	Low sexual desire	22%
	Arousal problems	14
	Pain during intercourse	7
Men	Premature ejaculation	21%
	Erectile dysfunction	5
	Low sexual desire	5

*PROBLEMS THAT HAVE OCCURRED OVER THE LAST 12 MONTHS.

Health factors
These may contribute to sexual dysfunction

- Poor health
- Emotional problems or stress
- Urinary-tract symptoms
- A history of STDs

Low interest in sex

By age	Women	Men
18–29	32%	14%
30–39	32	13
40–49	30	15
50–59	27	17

Painful intercourse

By age	Women
18–29	21%
30–39	15
40–49	13
50–59	8

Absence of orgasm

By age	Women	Men
18–29	26%	7%
30–39	28	7
40–49	22	9
50–59	23	9

By race

	Women
White	29%
Black	44
Hispanic	30
Other	42

By marital status

Married	14%
Never married	17
Divorced, widowed, separated	16

High–school education

Less than	34%
Graduate	29

College

Some	24
Graduate	18

vice the size of a computer mouse that draws blood to the organ. The device is available by prescription only and costs about $360. The best part of participating in the EROS trials, says a 35-year-old at-home mother in St. Paul, Minn., "is that we get one for free.

Hormone therapy is also promising, but can be a wild ride. Testosterone, for reasons no one quite understands, is involved in the sex drive of both men and women. In their 30s and 40s, most women experience a 15 percent drop in testosterone levels. Removal of the ovaries, often a part of hysterectomy, reduces production to near zero. At the University of California, San Francisco, Dr. Louann Brizendine has been experimenting with testosterone replacement therapy, in both oral form and patches. This is the tricky end of the erotic medicine cabinet: side effects include increased risk of heart disease and liver damage, and long-term consequences are unknown. Also, the surges of biochemical desire can leave patients reeling. One woman unwittingly doubled her dosage and had to excuse herself every few hours just to seek relief.

As biologists expand their grasp of amatory nitty and gritty, the thorniest riddle may be more global: why, from an evolutionary point of view, do women have orgasms? Unlike the male O, women's climax does not appear to be necessary for reproduction. The traditional answer, phrased by anthropologist Don Symons in 1979, is that female orgasm is a relic of Darwinian sloppiness, like male nipples: evolution had no good motive specifically to cut one gender out of the fun. If you think this argument has passed unchallenged, you haven't breathed the air on campus lately. Proclaiming orgasmic empowerment, anthropologists speculated that the sweet paroxysm kept women supine after sex, facilitating insemination—a dubious argument, since nature did not design most women to climax reliably through intercourse, especially in the missionary position. The evolutionary biologist Sarah Blaffer Hrdy proposed that this skittishness was itself an evolutionary adaptation: our unsatisfied ancestresses would seek remedy from multiple partners—in turn tapping each for protection and resources, and counting on confusion about paternity to multiply the generosity. Or maybe orgasm allows women to influence which mate will father their children. British biologists Robin Baker and Mark Bellis, who went so far as to attach micro video cameras to the ends of men's penises, found that women retained more of their partners' ejaculate if they reached orgasm as well. In an only-in-America study at the University of New Mexico, researchers Randy Thornhill and Steven Gangestad found that, other things being equal, women were more likely to climax when their partners' bodies were symmetrical, a marker of desirable genes. "It's all consistent with female choice, says Thornhill. Since competing explanations arise, you are free to accept this as gospel or just another reminder that the mysteries of sex won't be solved overnight.

The new science of sex, though, is not wholly academic. Revolutions in the lab will likely rearrange the bedroom, perhaps even the surrounding communities, in ways unforeseeable. As Jared Diamond describes in his book "Guns, Germs and Steel," new technologies often create societies' needs for them, rather than the other way around. Invention, in other words, can be the mother of necessity. Right now we are just approaching the cusp of that maternity. The dark continent is growing brighter and more electric with each turn of the circle.

With Claudia Kalb *and* Nadine Joseph

Sex, Drugs & Rock'n'Roll

The Damage Done: A HEALTH REPORT

By Sue Woodman

DO YOU EVER WONDER IF YOUR DAILY HUNT for your glasses has anything to do with those magic mushrooms you took in 1971? Or whether the painful years of infertility you endured could be linked to the stranger you went home with after a party one night when you were 22?

For most of us, the days of multiple sex partners, fistfuls of drugs and cranking Led Zeppelin up to maximum decibels are long gone. Today, we try to at least exercise and take vitamins and, most of the time, feel we're holding our own against mortality.

So what became of the dire predictions that drugs would demolish our brain cells, that changing sexual partners would harm us and that rock music would blow out our eardrums?

We're not the only ones wondering. Across the country—in universities and hospitals, in cancer labs and neurobiology centers—medical and social scientists are examining the alleged fallout of sex, drugs and rock 'n' roll on our brains, organs and well-being.

The results are complex, sometimes influenced as much by politics as by science. The short answer: If you did it then but don't do it now, you're probably fine. "The human body is amazing in its ability to heal over time," says Richard Seymour, managing editor of the *Journal of Psychoactive Drugs*. The longer answer, though, is often not as optimistic. Below is the latest information on the potential lingering effects of your crazy, hazy youth.

sex: The sexual revolution brought some important gains, notably the birth of the women's health movement, with its emphasis on sexual, as well as reproductive, well-being. But that freedom came at

a price. Baby boomers have lived through numerous medical disasters as a result of their sexual habits—including injuries and pelvic inflammation from contraceptives such as the Dalkon Shield IUD and from epidemics of sexually transmitted diseases (STDs). Many of these STDs have contributed to serious illnesses that are surfacing only now.

For example, women who contracted the human papillomavirus (HPV) are at higher risk for developing cervical cancer, which strikes some 12,800 women a year. This disease often develops when women are between the ages of 40 and 60, and HPV is now recognized as its leading cause, says Dr. Richard Rothenberg, a physician at Emory University School of Medicine in Atlanta. Fortunately, an annual Pap smear can detect abnormal cervical cells before they become malignant.

It's been a long, strange trip... What have we done to our bodies?

Experts strongly suspect that the rise in chlamydia, a common bacterial STD, may have contributed to the increase in couples who suffered fertility problems in the 1980s.

"Women were also postponing having children at that time [and fertility declines with age], so there were other causes," says Dr. Ward Cates, president of Family Health International, a nonprofit health research and information organization in North Carolina. "But we know that there was suddenly a time in the mid-eighties when visits to infertility specialists went

up. A lot of women in their thirties were trying to get pregnant and couldn't."

Far worse, many physicians believe that the powerful infertility drugs women took may have increased their risk of ovarian cancer. Fertility drugs cause ovulation, and the more a woman ovulates, the greater her risk of developing cancerous cellular changes in her reproductive organs, according to the National Cancer Institute. The drugs also raise certain hormone levels that may heighten the cancer risk. The data are still inconclusive, but there is evidence that women who used fertility drugs but didn't conceive have an increased chance of ovarian cancer. (Women who became pregnant show no higher incidence of the disease.)

"I have come to believe there's a link (between fertility drugs and ovarian cancer), though in my circles, it's not politically correct to say so," concludes Dr. Mitchell Essig, a New York City gynecologist and infertility specialist. If you underwent infertility treatment, inform your doctor and be vigilant about having regular, thorough gynecological examinations.

drugs: Marijuana, LSD, speed, cocaine, mescaline, mushrooms, Quaaludes... they made us high, they changed our perception, they blew our minds. But did they do lasting harm?

It's difficult to say, because all drug studies are to some degree political. Many are funded by parties with their own axes to grind, such as pharmaceutical companies or the National Institute on Drug Abuse. Other studies were conducted on animals or very small groups, which makes them unreliable. But certain conclusions have emerged.

HEROIN: If you experimented with heroin in your youth, get a blood test to make sure you're not carrying a potentially deadly souvenir: hepatitis C.

About four million Americans—many of them over 45—are estimated to be harboring this sometimes-fatal virus. The symptoms, which include lethargy, jaundice and abdominal pain, may take up to three decades to appear. As many as 70 percent of cases result in chronic liver disease, and nearly one in four of those patients will develop cirrhosis.

Hepatitis C can be spread through sex, but its main transmission routes are syringes shared during IV-drug use. Blood transfusions were also a culprit until a new screening test finally flagged tainted blood in 1992. A staggering 90 percent of IV-drug users may have contracted hepatitis C—even if they shot heroin infrequently. "Most don't know they have it," says Seymour. "I fear that within the next decade, this disease will outstrip AIDS as a public health crisis."

LSD: In the four decades since LSD appeared on the street, between 1 and 1.5 million "teens, Deadheads and hippies" have tried it, estimates Seymour. While some people saw God on acid, others glimpsed madness.

There's disagreement about how long the effects of LSD may linger. A 1993 study, published in the journal *Addiction*, reported that hallucinogen persisting perceptual disorder (HPPD) could occur for as long as five years after using the drugs. But Seymour claims that he's seen almost no lasting problems from psychedelic-drug use as the first generation to try them reaches 60 and beyond. "Most middle-aged people seem to have left the experience behind long ago," he says. Of course, see your doctor if you have any symptoms oddly akin to those vibrantly colored journeys of yesteryear.

COCAINE: For a few reckless years starting in the late 1970s, cocaine became the drug of choice: chic, sharp and addictive. Today, our generation seems to be over that love affair. According to the 1998 National Household Survey on Drug Abuse, cocaine use has dropped by 90 percent since its peak in 1985.

The immediate risks of snorting coke, such as a stroke or heart attack, are well-known. But new studies suggest that some of cocaine's effects on the brain may be irreversible and lead to chronic problems later on.

For many, speed was the first drug—and probably the most dangerous.

"Cocaine causes long-term, possibly irreversible, alterations in brain blood flow," says Dr. Jonathan Levin, an assistant professor at Harvard Medical School, who has been studying cocaine's effect on blood flow and brain function for almost a decade. Brain scans of cocaine users show distinct areas where blood flow is diminished, and this may be related to the problems associated with long-term cocaine use: memory loss, shortened attention span, sleep disorders and depression, among others.

Does this brain damage repair itself in the years after you stop sniffing cocaine? "Abstinence does repair some of the abnormalities, but it's not clear to what extent," says Levin. Luckily, researchers haven't found any concrete proof that casual cocaine users who did a few lines at parties 20 years ago caused lasting harm to their brains.

SPEED: For many, speed was the first drug—the one they started taking as students simply to pull a few all-nighters—and new findings show it was likely the most dangerous. Methamphetamine, or speed, has become fashionable again among young drug takers, so there's been a glut of new research on the substance. Frighteningly, it shows that speed might be more destructive to the brain than heroin or cocaine.

In a series of studies at the government's Brookhaven National Laboratory, the lead investigator, Dr. Nora Volkow, found that speed causes "significant changes" in the brain's dopamine transporters, and abusers still experienced reduced cognitive abilities, memory loss and slowed motor function one year after use.

"The drug's assault on the brain's dopamine [system] makes things slow down, just as aging makes things slow down," says Volkow. "Effectively, it accelerates the aging process of the brain."

Are the effects permanent? "We don't yet know, but we're doing the studies to find out," says Volkow. There is speculation that having used methamphetamine may predispose people to neuro-degenerative diseases like Parkinson's. So if you spent junior year whirling at 80 mph, share this news with your physician.

MARIJUANA: Marijuana is one of the most studied substances in science, yet the verdict on whether it's harmful or not is still quite inconclusive.

While one set of scientists is bent on proving marijuana's medical benefits (research suggests that the substance can stimulate appetite and relieve chronic pain), another is documenting its health risks. The studies pile up on both sides, but the jury is still out—especially on the long-term effects of smoking pot.

On the optimistic side, a study from the Biological Psychiatry Laboratory at McLean Hospital in Belmont, Massachusetts, found that when long-term marijuana tokers stopped toking—even after years of continued use—their mental acuity returned in full force. "In a full battery of neuro-psychological tests, our preliminary data showed that while smoking, all these activities were impaired," explains substance-abuse researcher Dr. Amanda Gruber. "But twenty-eight days later, the long-term smokers did as well on all the tests as non-smokers. There seemed to be no irreversible effects."

On the gloomy side, a study done by Dr. Zhang Zuofeng of UCLA's Jonsson Cancer Center found that past marijuana smoking could sharply increase the risk of developing head and neck cancers. Zhang puts the risk at 2.6 times higher for former occasional pot smokers than for nonsmokers, and 4.9 times greater for those who smoked more than once a day.

"In the sixties, we had very high numbers of people in their twenties smoking [marijuana]," says Zhang. "Our study suggests those people are just now getting to the ages at which they will get head and neck cancers."

And perhaps lung cancer, too. At the UCLA School of Medicine, Dr. Donald Tashkin is midway through a 2,400-person, five-year study investigating marijuana's long-term link to lung cancer.

"Can the microscopic, premalignant changes smoking [marijuana] causes in the lung be repaired? Is a former smoker's lung-cancer risk eventually eliminated?" asks Tashkin. "I suspect the answer will be no, not completely."

Importantly, those of us who still indulge should know that smoking pot causes a sharp increase in heart rate, and that could be dangerous for people over 50 with other health problems. In fact, one recent study found that people who smoke marijuana have a five times greater risk of heart attack during the first hour after use—the same degree of cardiac risk brought on by strenuous exercise. The short-term risk is considerable, especially for patients with other risk factors, such as high blood pressure or elevated cholesterol, says researcher Dr. Murray Mittleman, director of cardiovascular epidemiology at Boston's Beth Israel Deaconess Medical Center.

rock 'n roll:
You can almost hear Ted Nugent's mother saying, "I told you so." Unfortunately, Ted can't. He's nearly deaf in one ear, the archetypal victim of noise-induced hearing loss.

Yes, all that loud music damaged our eardrums. "We are beginning to see a lot of high-frequency hearing loss in forty- and fifty-year-olds," says Dr. Kenneth Einhorn, an Abington, Pennsylvania, otolaryngologist who treats many musicians for degrees of deafness. "Years ago, we didn't see these kinds of hearing problems till people entered their sixties or seventies." Noise-induced hearing loss happens gradually, as loud sounds blast the delicate cells of the inner ear and cause cumulative, irreparable damage.

After one loud concert, there may be a muffled quality to the ambient sound. After a few years of concerts, the muffle might not go away. By age 45, there may be some permanent high-frequency hearing loss—the kind that causes you to miss parts of conversations, particularly when there's competing background noise. Some people also develop tinnitus, or ringing in the ears.

There's no cure, but you can slow the damage and protect what hearing remains. Wear earplugs during any noisy activities, such as mowing the lawn, running an electric saw—or listening to loud music, recommends Einhorn.

If your hearing has been damaged, consider getting a hearing aid. Don't think they're just for fogies; Bill Clinton wears one. The latest models now use digital sound, a refinement that has noticeably improved their quality.

WHAT SHOULD WE MAKE OF ALL THIS INformation? Listed together, it makes for sobering reading. What it means, the professionals tell us, is that if we're still tempted to go home with strangers or to roll a joint when the kids are out, we shouldn't. There may be consequences we don't expect.

Although there's little we can do about the past, the most important prevention for the future, say medical researchers, is to give up (or limit) the two drugs we may have kept using all along: nicotine and alcohol. "These kill more people than all the illegal substances combined, particularly with prolonged use," says Seymour. Consider that about 434,000 people die of tobacco-related disease every year, and more than 100,000 are killed by alcohol.

Still, there's plenty of room for optimism. Sex and drug-taking—to the extent they went on in the '60s and '70s—are now just a distant memory to the boomer generation, says Rothenberg. "In fact, given all the healthy habits the baby-boomer generation has adopted, it's likely they'll achieve unparalleled longevity."

So forget the past, deal with the present and stop worrying. After all, Keith Richards is still alive and—despite any rumors to the contrary—doing remarkably well.

Improved **AIDS treatments** bring life and hope—at a cost

BY SUSAN BRINK

There is a generation of young people who learn about AIDS as a kind of history lesson. They were scarcely aware, or not yet born, when the epidemic stormed onto the scene in 1981 as a terrifying and highly visible slaughter. "I know a lot of older gay men in their 40s and 50s who lost not one or two friends, but dozens and dozens of friends. I listen, but I can't fully understand what that must have been like," says Jeffrey Timberlake, 28, of Boston, who is HIV positive. The danger, now, is that some people his age and younger may unwittingly be repeating history.

Clearly, much has changed. Not so very long ago, AIDS meant death within months or a few years. Patients would drown in their own fluids following pneumocystis carinii, a virulent form of pneumonia. Their lymph nodes would swell, they'd develop oral yeast infections, or salmonella would invade their intestines. Drenched in night sweats, their bodies would succumb to waves of infection, and they'd waste away. At first there was nothing but losing battles against one infection after another; then came a few drugs that could suppress the virus for a short time.

"AIDS is a different disease in 2001," says John Bartlett, chief of the division of infectious diseases at Johns Hopkins School of Medicine in Baltimore. "In 1995, we spent most of our time preparing people to die. By 1997, patients had at least a crack at a response. It was one of the most dramatic changes I've ever seen with an infection." What drove it was the intro-

duction, in late 1995, of a new class of drugs called protease inhibitors, which prevent the virus from being released from infected cells. In 1996, for the first time ever, deaths from AIDS in the United States dropped, by 25 percent. They've continued to fall, by an additional 18 percent in 1998 and 9 percent more in 1999.

Yet no one at the front lines is celebrating. Up to 900,000 people in the United States are HIV positive, and a third of them don't know it yet. With no cure in sight, they will spend years, even decades, on drugs that miraculously extend lives but carry a high price in side effects. And AIDS workers now worry that, in this epidemic, hope itself has a cost. Young people in the groups most at risk—gay men and IV drug users—no longer view HIV infection as a death sentence. The Centers for Disease Control and Prevention reports that sexually transmitted diseases are on the rise among some teenagers, a sign that they are taking sexual risks. And a 1999 study of 416 gay men found that the more optimistic they were about new treatments, the less likely they were to practice safe sex. "They think you just go and get some pills, and it's no big deal," says Valerie Stone, director of the AIDS clinic at Memorial Hospital in Pawtucket, R.I.

It's easy to see why. The transformation of the world's latest plague in America is nothing short of miraculous. In Boston, for example, the Hospice at Mission Hill, which opened in 1989 to care for dying AIDS patients, closed its doors in 1997 be-

cause it couldn't fill its beds. At a clinic run by Fenway Community Health, "We used to have 10 or 12 patients in the hospital at any one time," says Jerry Feuer, a physician's assistant. "Now, we go weeks without a single patient in the hospital."

Drug arsenal. The turnaround began with the introduction of saquinivir, the first of the protease inhibitors. But the real breakthrough came some months later when researchers found that using the new drugs together with older drugs led to rapid reductions in the amount of virus in the blood. Since then, another class of drugs called nonnucleoside reverse transcriptase inhibitors (NNRTIs) has been added to the arsenal, bringing the total number of HIV drugs to 16. Patients mix and match them in complicated, individually tailored combinations.

Taking these medicines has gotten easier, too. Combination therapy once meant swallowing 30 to 50 AIDS pills or more a day in highly structured regimens—some pills with food, some on an empty stomach, some in the middle of the night. Today the routine for many patients is far simpler. Timberlake, for instance, takes one pill in the morning and four at night. The newest AIDS pill, Trizivir, available since December, combines three drugs and means, for some patients, taking only two pills, one in the morning and one at night, with or without food.

In America, at least, most of those who need this kind of treatment, costing $10,000 to $12,000 a year for drugs alone, can get it through standard insurance or special federal funding for AIDs. Yet it remains a disease that dissects society largely along lines of haves and have-nots, increasingly affecting minorities and the poor, through both homosexual sex and IV drug use or sex with an IV drug user. But perhaps the most troubling aspect of the epidemic in 2001 is that despite a decline in disease and death, the rate of new HIV infections has held steady. Some young people are still taking risks with their lives, almost as though it were still that more forgiving sexual time before 1980.

WHERE TO LEARN MORE

• **Risks**. Take an online quiz to see if you're putting yourself at risk of HIV infection, at *www.aac.org/*.
• **Advice**. A question-and-answer page with an AIDS expert can be found at *www.hopkins-aids.edu/*.
• **Treatment**. Search the government site *www.niaid.nih.gov/* for information including HIV treatment guidelines for both adults and children.

Knowledge is not always protective. "I knew what was safe sex and what wasn't. Why was I taking risks?" Timberlake asks. Part of the answer, for him, was partying. "I was floundering. It only takes one time, and when you get drunk, you don't care." Those who try to educate teens about prevention report another factor: Youngsters often wrongly assume that people like Magic Johnson, who are successfully living with an undetectable viral load, have been cured.

Far from it. The new drugs are more like cancer treatments than allergy or blood pressure pills: toxic substances that attack the body even as they keep the disease in check. Their long-term consequences are unknown, but some early indications are unsettling. Effects like lipodystrophy, which redistributes body fat in bizarre configurations, or osteonecrosis, a crippling bone disease, appear out of nowhere. Some patients are becoming diabetic. The latest fear is a spike in cases of AIDS dementia, leading to fears that although the new drugs protect the body, they do not protect the mind.

No matter how harsh the side effects, patients cannot safely skip doses or go off the drugs. Studies show that patients who take 95 percent of their pills do better than those who take only 90 percent. No other disease demands such scrupulous compliance. If they miss even a pill or two a month, the virus can mutate, figuring out how to resist the drug and forcing patients to switch regimens. "The virus is still smarter than we are," says Kenneth Mayer, medical director of research and evaluation at Fenway Community Health.

Timberlake, diagnosed in 1997, was reluctant to take drugs at first. "There was always that gleaming hope that maybe I could fight this without medication. Maybe I would be one of those long-term nonresponders," he says, referring to the handful of people who have been HIV positive for years without developing symptoms of AIDS. But by last spring, he got a flu he couldn't shake. "I had a cough, fever. I would wake and the bedsheets would be drenched from night sweats. I got really scared. I knew I was playing with fire," he says. He prepared himself to take drugs.

Nightmares. He settled on a regimen of Sustiva, one of the new NNRTIs, and Combivir, which combines AZT and 3TC, two older AIDS drugs. He immediately ran into one of the more common, and disorienting, side effects of Sustiva. "I felt like I wasn't in my body. My heart rate felt like it was in slow motion. I would touch my skin and it would feel like it wasn't mine. I'd be taking a shower and it would feel like the shower floor dropped 6 feet. It was very, very bizarre," he says.

Most patients try to dodge these central-nervous-system effects by taking the pills at night. But the drug's effects can seep into a patient's unconscious. Eileen Ellis, 42, of Providence, R.I., and HIV positive since 1987, has chronic nightmares, rich in bright colors, towering shadows, and psychotic images. "I had this dream where one of my cats electrocuted the other cat," she says. People who take combinations of the 16 AIDS drugs suffer other side effects such as short-term nausea and chronic diarrhea. Some develop chronic fatigue, others depression. They worry about buffalo humps between their shoulders and bellies dubbed "protease paunch." "Ugly names for ugly symptoms," says

Maureen Cassidy of Boston, 46 and HIV positive since 1985.

The drugs still aren't easy to take. Each has its own demands. Some rule out alcohol, others are less effective with high-fat diets. Some cannot be taken with antacids. Some must be taken on an empty stomach, others with food. There are also unanticipated drug interactions. "I've had some problems with depression, so I started taking Saint-John's-wort [an herbal remedy for depression]," says Peter Rothschild, 41. "That's when my [viral load] numbers started inching up a little." Recent studies have shown that the herbal antidepressant diminishes the effect of a protease inhibitor. Even though that drug was not part of his regimen, Rothschild got worried.

When he stopped taking Saint-John's-wort, his numbers improved, though recently they've begun rising again. A doctoral student in counseling psychology and religion at Boston University, Rothschild knows he may have to switch to another drug regimen soon. "What I am facing now is the uncertainty of what's going to happen with all of this. Physically, right now things are OK. I know there are people who cycle through these drugs every two years. I may be one of those people," he says.

Yet people like Cassidy and Ellis, who have been through years of life-saving, yet very toxic drugs, realize that things today are better than ever. Patients once set alarms every four hours, day and night, to remember pills. They suffered through side effects that never subsided. For all their trouble, thousands died horrible deaths.

The terror has calmed, but there remains an undercurrent of fear among the people who will, the rest of their lives, be involved in a form of human experimentation. Cassidy, appalled at the disfiguring side effects she began to experience from protease inhibitors, has a prescription for a new drug regimen, including Sustiva. She knows she'll gather the courage to pick it up, but last week, it still sat unclaimed at the pharmacy. "I'm scared. It has [central nervous system] side effects. I am afraid of it because I don't want horror-movie nightmares. I also don't want uncontrollable diarrhea, I don't want a rash, I don't want buffalo hump, I don't want to be a diabetic," she says. "But I don't want to die. So what's my choice?"

---

too much of a good thing

Thanks to Bill Clinton, sex addiction is coming out of the closet. Thomas Beller visits the country's premier clinic for a firsthand dose of carnal knowledge

It was a bright Arizona day, and I was on my way to visit the sex addicts. The skies were blue, the vast desert was dotted with tumbleweed and cactus, and I was speeding down a narrow strip of pavement in a rented car, thinking about a particular kind of sex. Not good sex, or bad sex, but *overwhelming* sex. Sex: The Drug.

I was headed toward a private clinic called the Meadows, near Phoenix, that, under the direction of psychologist Patrick Carnes, has developed one of the leading programs in the country for the treatment of sex addiction. It was Carnes who initially coined the phrase, "sex addict" back in 1983, and who developed a system of treatment modeled after the twelve-step program of Alcoholics Anonymous. First, the patient has to admit he is powerless over his addiction. And then he has to appeal to a "higher power" for help.

So I was thinking, essentially, about sex and God. The vast desert around me didn't seem large enough to encompass all the possible variations on these two themes. Then, in the middle of nowhere (actually about forty miles south of a town called "Nowhere"), I saw a sign that made me smile.

It read: DETENTION CENTER. DO NOT PICK UP HITCHHIKERS.

I immediately imagined escaped sex addicts standing by the side of the road, next to a cactus, trying to wave down the passing cars. I should say very clearly that the sign didn't refer to the Meadows, which is *not* a detention center. People are there because their lives have spiraled out of control. They've lost their jobs or their marriages, been arrested, or come within a hair's breadth of those things hap-pening. They want to be there. (A thirty-five-day visit costs $35,000, so they have to *really* want to be there.) There is no chain-link fence. If you want to leave, you can take a cab.

But still, I liked imagining them lined up by the side of the road, and wondered what they might look like. Maybe they'd look like Kate Moss, whose recent rehabilitation for drink and drugs was rumored to include therapy for sex addiction. Or maybe like Michael Douglas, who reportedly sought treatment to avoid a divorce, or Aerosmith rocker Steven Tyler, a former Meadows patient. Or maybe they'd look like our president. You can't think about sex addiction for even a second without speculating about Bill Clinton, and vice versa. Now that the suspense of what will happen to him legally is over, we can return to the most fundamental question surrounding his behavior with Monica: why?

Carnes's books are laced with case histories. His simple prose has an almost incantatory quality: It's as though you are hiding behind the curtain in a doctor's office, or a confessional, a place where deep truths are laid bare. "Del was a lawyer. Brilliant, charming, and witty. His wife and three children were proud of his accomplishments. However, Del's public visibility was creating a problem because he was also a sexual addict. His double life included prostitution, porno bookstores, and affairs."

Or: "Chris... was an addict whose cruising was fused with her professional life as a consultant in urban planning. Her life was filled with seminars, conferences, and workshops. They served as a cover for her other life."

How about chocolate addiction? Golf addiction? People solemnly filing into Marx Brothers Anonymous declaring. "I am powerless to resist my desire to watch Zeppo"?

There is no question that there are men and women (according to Carnes, one of four sex addicts is female) whose relationship to sex has caused their lives to come undone. But then again, sex *addiction*? How about chocolate addiction? Golf addiction? People solemnly filing into Marx Brothers Anonymous declaring, "I am powerless to resist my desire to watch Zeppo"?

I imagined drivers anxiously speeding past the escaped sex addicts as they tried to hitch a ride. It made me laugh. Then I caught a glimpse of myself in the rearview mirror. I stopped laughing.

There are no meadows at the Meadows. The small cluster of bungalows and one-story buildings looks, at first glance, like a community-college campus, or a nursing home. There are a few patches of grass and a pine tree in its midst and from almost every vantage point there is a view of the desert. The very sight of it makes you feel meditative and small.

I'm greeted by John Ney, director of marketing. Although I don't ask him directly, I sense that, unlike all the other counselors here, he's not a reformed addict. He could well be marketing director for a consortium of podiatrists or a country club. But he has a sympathetic face, a sort of fixed expression of empathy that must be extremely useful as he spends his days among people who crave understanding.

The first thing we do is have lunch in the sunny cafeteria. The patients sit at tables chatting, a youngish bunch who are suffering from an assortment of ailments: drug addiction, alcohol addiction, sex addiction, eating disorders, with the odd gambling addict thrown in. I cast a longing gaze at them. I'd been told repeatedly that I would not be able to talk with them, and John seems quite jumpy to see me even looking in their direction.

After lunch, John takes me to meet Bob Fulton and Maureen Canning, the primary sex-addict counselors. While John goes to tell them I'm here, I wander over to a small, forlorn gazebo known as the "smoking hut." A guy with a bandanna asks if I'm in the Survivors' group. I tell him I'm not, and he walks away. But, in Meadows-speak, I *am* a survivor—because the thing that Survivors have survived is their childhoods.

The first thing I notice when I walk into Maureen's office is something that resembles a large red Wiffle-ball bat, though this one is made of foam rubber and canvas, and

seems designed more for bopping someone on the head (in a cathartic, constructive way) than for hitting a ball.

Bob was a Catholic priest for seventeen years. Maureen has a nice smile, but as we talk I notice that every now and then her blink is a little delayed, as though something she has just said has triggered a powerful memory and caused her momentarily to freeze, the eyelid paused at half mast. When I ask what their respective addictions were, Bob says he was an alcoholic, and Maureen says she was a sex addict.

Bob and Maureen are in charge of the process by which patients look to their past to discover the origins of their behavior—the central tenet of sex addiction being that sex addicts suffered abuse as children. "We look at the underlying trauma," says Maureen. "Each patient starts by writing an autobiography up to age seventeen." Part of me thinks this is only slightly better than going to a palm reader, and part of me likes the idea of taking a thirty-minute synopsis of my life and handing it over to a couple of experts who can discern where, exactly, I got screwed up.

"When the patients present their autobiographies," says Maureen, "what I'm listening for are the trauma bonds. What messages did they get as children, and how are they playing them out today? And then, throughout treatment, I'm constantly tying their current behaviors back to their original wounding."

Whereas Eve may have committed original sin, sex addicts are apparently victims of an "original wound." Sometimes this is an explicit wound, such as sexual molestation. At other times it is more "covert," but has a similarly corrosive effect, though less like a hurricane than a wave slowly eroding the rock that it crashes against. An example of this might be the way that a father looks at his daughter's breasts, or his repeated requests for a massage. Or a mother who shames her son for masturbating. (Hanging out at the Meadows, one comes to feel that parenting is a near futile enterprise.)

"Once the patients start to draw correlations between the past and present, they begin to heal the trauma," says Maureen. She makes it sound easy. You figure out your trauma, and then it goes away. But, she adds, "It's not something we're going to be able to heal in thirty-five days. What we *can* do is bring up the consciousness around those issues, and then start to give them tools to deal with the addiction as they continue to work on the trauma."

The Meadows has a capacity for seventy patients at a time, of whom maybe a quarter are being treated for sex addiction. At the moment, only one member of the sex-addict group is a woman. "Probably as few as 10 percent of our sex-addiction patients are female," says Maureen, "which is disheartening, because that means that women are not getting the treatment they need."

What type of destructive behavior do women engage in? I ask.

"They have affairs," Maureen replies. "We're seeing more and more women going on the Internet, having romantic exchanges, and then meeting people and having sexual affairs. Usually what brings a woman here are the consequences: facing a divorce, losing her job, depression, suicidal thoughts, being unable to get up out of bed or take care of the children."

What Bob and Maureen are saying seems to be a New Age version of Philip Larkin's line, "They f___ you up, your mum and dad." And he didn't get $35,000 for that poem.

Whether male or female, sex addicts make sex—and their own sexuality—central to their self-image. "At the very core of a sex addict's being, they feel worthless," says Bob. "The sense of who they are is not fully developed, because the parents haven't been there to give it to them. And so what will undo the shame is the trauma resolution around the abandonment wounds."

I begin to despair. On one hand, I find this interesting: People who were traumatized by their formative experiences with their parents (a group which includes, I think it's fair to say, *everybody*, but I'll leave that alone for now) need to constantly reaffirm their worth by having sex with other people. But what Bob and Maureen are saying seems to be a New Age version of Philip Larkin's famous line, "They f___ you up, your mum and dad." And he didn't get $35,000 for that poem. So, in this uncharitable mood, I ask about the rubber bat.

"It's called a Bataka," says Maureen. "We use it for anger work. Many times a patient has a lot of anger that they have never been able to express to the perpetrator. We have them sit across from an empty chair, raise the bat, and say, "I'm really *angry* with you," and then beat the empty chair. And then once they're moving the anger out, the sadness and the pain will start to come up, and then the tears. And when that happens, you're really getting down into the pain of that little kid and the healing can begin."

"Say you walk into an ice-cream store and there are a hundred flavors," I say. "Is it all right to taste a few different ones?"

For the sex addict, shame is both wound and medicine. Sex takes you out of your feelings, but it works like a drug, and when the effect has worn off, the only thing that can placate the ensuing guilt is more sex. "It's almost like the addict is a separate part of yourself," says Bob. This, then, is the central metaphor: Dr. Jekyll and Mr. Hyde. The addict feels shame about his secret life, goes to great lengths to

keep it a secret, yet has a strange, almost pathological desire to get caught. He doesn't so much engage in sex as enter it, as he would a secret chamber. But, I wondered, isn't this also an accurate description of the transformative power of sex itself? People lose themselves. They fall out of their own persona and enter into another self, more wild and voracious or tender or angry or mirthful than their normal, real, walking-around-the-office self. And that wild metamorphosis is half the delight of sex, isn't it?

At the end of our meeting pose the rather personal question that has been nagging at me throughout. It's the sort of question that is bound to creep into your thoughts if you're single and writing about sex addiction, namely: How much sex are you allowed to have before you have to start worrying about yourself?

"Say you walk into an ice-cream store and there are a hundred flavors," I say. "Is it all right to taste a few different ones?"

"Just because there are a hundred flavors doesn't mean you have to taste them all," responds Bob. "If you do, you've precluded the healthy intimacy that you get when you're not f___ the whole world. You can look at the one flavor that you have and get to know it in relationship to you."

"One?" I ask, somewhat grievously, suddenly feeling very literal-minded. "Should you marry the person you lose your virginity to?"

"I wouldn't press it into an absolute," says Bob.

"So what's the healthy area? Five flavors?"

"What's healthy is being in touch with one's own development; knowing what is motivating one's behavior. For me, it may be three flavors. For someone else, it may be twelve; for someone else, it may be one flavor."

"What about, say, twenty-five flavors?" I ask, apprehensively.

"For some people, twenty-five might be healthy. But if it's twenty-five, I would tend to think that there were things blocking—that many of those encounters were not a total engagement—that many of them were a way of self-medicating."

The one case study that I found truly persuasive did not appear in any of Carnes's books. It was a memoir by the poet Michael Ryan, called *Secret Life*. The only photograph of the author in the book appears on the back cover: a happy five-year-old boy sitting on the lawn. The picture was taken by a neighbor, a young man he calls "Bob Stoller," who abused Ryan regularly over the course of the following year. The bulk of the story is devoted to Ryan's youth and young adulthood—the bumbling but unremarkable path of a rebellious Catholic boy with a loving mother and an alcoholic father. Apart from the description of his molestation, it might be called charming, and yet in its details one can see an insidious pattern of deviant, unhealthy sexuality develop, like a photograph slowly materializing in a darkroom.

Describing his groping encounters with an early girl-friend who wouldn't sleep with him, Ryan writes, "I did not find this (rolling around) erotic, but sex was only erotic when it was bad, and this was love, and love was good." This relatively innocent revelation made me think, Well, so what? Good sex has always been, somehow, bad.

But it's a short leap to this chilling passage: "I was certainly a magnet for some women, as some women were for me—suicidal women for whom sex was both validation and self-annihilation, an intense temporary escape from being themselves. Their hunger made them sexy to me and, no doubt, vice versa. We always at least half hated each other, the half that was a mirror."

And not long after that, he begins engaging in absurdly compulsive sex, his marriage falls apart, he is fired from his professorial job at Princeton University, and only when he finds himself in the midst of a road trip to seduce a friend's fifteen-year-old daughter does he pull off to the side of the road and have the epiphany that leads him into recovery. Ryan's evocative book convinced me that Carnes is onto something in identifying certain patterns of sexual behavior, where they come from, and what might be done to stop them.

But then again, where do you draw the line? You can't help but look for echoes of your own experience among Carnes's case histories. And it's likely you'll find them. "The addict," he has written, "can transform even the most refined forms of nudity into his own particular fusion of loneliness and arousal." That's a nice phrase. As it happens, I'm prepared to admit that I can take many images—refined or nude or neither—and transform them into my own particular fusion of loneliness and arousal. But I don't know if that's such a bad thing. Sex is, by its very nature, a kind of counterattack on loneliness. That initial splitting of Adam and his rib, the ferocious desire to reconnect. It makes sense that the two are somehow entwined.

God, or its approximation, is a weird presence in twelve-step culture and, therefore, the Meadows. Joe Pack Arnold is the center's spiritual counselor, and his office is evidence of how a "higher power" could mean just about anything. The walls are festooned with a variety of religious objects: A cross hangs from a leather necklace, a brass menorah gleams in the afternoon light, a Buddha meditates in the corner, and there are quite a few Native American objects with feathers attached. His office is feathery.

"I try to get the patients in touch with their spirit, to help them experience intimacy as a spiritual experience," Arnold says in his Southern drawl. He has the strange transcendent vibe of someone whose concerns are more metaphysical than physical. Frizzy gray hair sprouts from beneath his fishing hat. He has sleepy, melancholy eyes—you could call them bedroom eyes, but given the setting, that might not be appropriate—that are enlarged by a pair of enormous glasses, and a face that reminds me (in a nice way) of a Cabbage Patch doll.

"If they're open to it, we talk a lot about a higher power outside the self, which is a source of energy beyond what we know in our mechanized society. God, if you will."

And what if you won't?

I ask about the President, whose aura is so strongly felt at The Meadows that they ought to have a portrait of him with a sign saying, THIS COULD BE YOU.

"Those are the patients I enjoy the most, because they don't bring a lot of baggage with them. We do simple things, like make eye contact with a mountain peak five minutes a day, something outside of ourselves. Or we take a walk—to listen, look, and smell, and see what happens. The desert is alive with a lot of things, and they become aware of that."

I ask about the President, whose aura is so strongly felt at the Meadows that they ought to have an oil portrait of him over the front door with a sign saying, THIS COULD BE YOU.

"Clinton is a textbook addict," says Arnold. "He grew up in a broken home, his father was an alcoholic, his mother practically raised him, he came from nothing. He's brilliant, which didn't work in his favor, because even though his sex addiction has been so obvious over the years, he's been able to rise above everything and there's been no intervention. I don't think he'll act out again while he's President… but I think he will act out again."

At long last I meet Patrick Carnes, PhD, the father, as it were, of sex addiction. He is a fine-looking man, with broad shoulders, a ruddy complexion, and a widow's peak that gives him a slightly roosterish aspect—he has the radiant good health of the early riser. His eyes are bright blue, slightly crossed, and gaze at me with a mixture of forbearance and suspicion. Journalists are not his favorite species.

For a long time, he and his speciality have suffered the slings and arrows of public ridicule. His books are littered with moments of frustration and exasperation with the media and the whole culture—sex addiction is his baby, and every snigger at its expense must have felt like a personal attack. So these post-Lewinsky days are a time of heady vindication for Patrick Carnes. The whole country has spent a solid year fixated on someone who does not seem in control of his sexual urges.

"Bill Clinton has helped a lot of people," he begins cautiously, "… inadvertently. Before the Monica Lewinsky stuff blew up, we were probably thirty years behind alcoholism in terms of public understanding. Now we're only fifteen years behind."

Throughout my readings of Carnes's books, I was always on the lookout for signs that he was, at heart, a kind of sex-negative scold; that the concept of sex addiction was really a way of turning the whole sexual revolution into a mental illness; that it was a cover for Puritanism. But whenever that seemed like the case, Carnes confounded my notion by advocating *more* sex, not less. "It is clear that sexual health should not be exploitative or judgmental or negative," he wrote. "Rather, the foundation for a healthy sexuality starts with acceptance, abundance, and exploration."

So how, I queried him now, is one to decipher where a healthy, lively sexuality ends, and an unhealthy, desperate, medicating sexuality begins?

"The question is whether the obsession is interfering with your life," Carnes replies.

"What about affairs?" I ask. "An affair will definitely interfere with your life. If there is an affair in a marriage, does that mean the unfaithful partner is a sex addict?"

"I would guess that 40 to 50 percent of relationships in this country end up with an affair somewhere," he says. "Asking how many affairs it takes to make a sex addict is like asking how many drinks it takes to make an alcoholic. It's more about a pattern of behavior over the long term, and about how you are living your life. Most people realize that they have a problem when they start making promises to themselves to stop their destructive behavior, and find that they can't. That's when people know they've crossed the line—when they can't stop having sex."

Sex is an instinct as fundamental to our existence as our appetite for food. I wondered how something necessary to our survival as a species could be the basis for an addiction.

For clarification, I call Chester W. Schmidt, Jr., MD, chairman of the department of Psychiatry and Behavioral Sciences at Johns Hopkins. He and his colleagues were part of a special task force that deliberated whether to list Sex Addiction in the DSM-IV, the psychiatrist's diagnostic manual. They decided against it.

"In terms of pop psychology," explains Dr. Schmidt, "the term 'sex addiction' is very appealing. It intuitively makes sense to a lay person that certain individuals have an appetite for sex that is greater than the norm. How better to explain that in today's psychological terms than to call it an addiction?"

"Carnes's method," he continues, "is to treat sex addiction with the same series of steps used for substance addiction: removal from stimulation, detox, a twelve-step program, and psychological support. But in medicine, the term *addiction* has a specific pharmacologic meaning, i.e., that substances taken into the body are active in the brain in such a manner that their removal causes a cascading effect of physiological symptoms known as withdrawal. We do not accept that excessive sexual activity is addictive, in the way we use that term."

The great mantra of the recovery movement is "whatever works." I ask Schmidt if he is being too pedantic, not seeing the forest for the trees.

"It's hard to say if Carnes's treatments are helpful, because he has never subjected his findings to a peer-review journal. He hasn't done controlled studies. Sex addiction is a facile explanation for an extraordinarily complex set of behaviors. If you can explain away certain disturbing acts with a 'diagnosis,' it literally catches your breath: 'I know my problem. I'm a sexual addict!'"

Of all our appetites, sex is the most anarchic. It's where we feel our keenest sense of sin.

But when I mention this to Carnes, he points out that there are difficult ethical considerations when it comes to applying scientific methods to the real world. "Doing a controlled experiment would mean taking certain people—whose behavior puts them in a life-or-death situation—and giving them virtually no treatment at all," he says. "What we do instead is follow the behaviors of people who recover, as well as the behavior of people who relapse. It's a different way of profiling what works."

A desert sunset is a sight that will have you believing in a higher power almost instantly, and it is against this backdrop that Carnes and I say goodbye. He is smiling at me with that expertly beneficent smile, the smile of a minister or a doctor or a hustler. He is not a hustler, but there is something in the "If you're hurting, come to us" embrace of the Meadows that I distrust.

In a way, my problem is similar to Schmidt's: It's a question of language. But my objection is not so clinically specific, it's rather that I can't abide the exhausting phenomenon by which the recovery movement colonizes every aspect of human experience and makes it something that needs to be cured.

Of all our appetites, it seems to me, sex is the most anarchic. It's where we feel our keenest sense of sin. The sexual impulse rides roughshod over our ethics and our desire to be just to other people. All over the world, people build these fragile structures called relationships, and the single biggest fault line that can destroy nearly all that hard-won trust is the issue of sexual wantonness, of infidelity—the idea that one of the partners will look outside the relationship to satiate a sexual appetite he or she cannot control.

Carnes's work is fascinating in its examination of the ways we misuse our sexuality—as a means of defining ourselves, of reliving childhood trauma, or simply as a narcotic to numb the discomforts of intimacy. The label "sex addiction," however, takes our lust and makes it something that needs *fixing*. It makes pathological that which is part of life. It makes, I suggest to Carnes, desire a disease.

"Sex addicts are not getting the sexual rewards they want," he responds. "They are not happy with what they are doing. If the only way for a woman to be orgasmic is for a man to hurt her, that is not a functional template. We want to help these people have more rewarding sex, encourage them to rewire themselves."

Standing against the distant mountains, Carnes has a kind of evangelical, John Wayne, last-good-man vibe. His voice is soothing. He just wants to help. He stands like a sexual Statute of Liberty amid an ocean of sand: give me your abused, your hurting, your sexually self-destructive bodies. We will rewire you. You won't have to hurt yourself anymore.

In truth, I'm lulled by his vision, comforted somehow. There is so much tumult, dissonance, fear, and despair out in the wide world of sex, but here the waters are calm. I have just one nagging qualm. "Couldn't you change the name?" I want to say. How about 'sex compulsion'? Sex obsession? Sex dependency?"

But I don't. Sex addiction by any other name just wouldn't be as sexy.

WHY ARE WE GAY?

Everybody has an idea: It's **genetics**—we're born that way. It's our mothers and **testosterone** in the womb. It's the **environment** as we were growing up. One thing we know for sure: The possible explanations raise as many questions as they answer, particularly: What would happen if we found the one true answer? and, Would we change if we could?

By Mubarak Dahir

Mark Stoner pins it on the clarinet.

Ever since Stoner, a 41-year-old creative director for an advertising agency in Lancaster, Pa., realized that three out of four of his childhood friends who played the clarinet grew up to be gay, he has taken note of who among his adult gay friends once played the instrument. What he calls an "exhaustive but unscientific" survey covering two decades indicates that "there is an extremely high correlation between playing the clarinet and being gay," he says.

> "THE QUESTION OF WHETHER OR NOT GAYNESS IS IMMUTABLE IS RATHER CRUCIAL IN THE POLITICAL ARENA. THE AMERICAN PUBLIC WILL HAVE A DIFFERENT ATTITUDE TOWARD GAY RIGHTS DEPENDING ON WHETHER THEY BELIEVE BEING GAY IS A MATTER OF CHOICE OR NOT."
> —*Neuroscientist Simon LeVay, who found differences in the brain*

"My theory is that most boys want to play the trumpet," the former woodwind player says, only partly in jest. "But the more sensitive boys wind up with the clarinet, and we're the ones who turn out gay."

Stoner's theory, of course, is offered tongue-in-cheek. But in the past decade or so, researchers from disparate fields spanning genetics, audiology, and behavioral science have amassed bits and pieces of evidence that they believe indicate what may determine sexual orientation. If they're right, our sexual orientation may well be fixed long before any maestro blows his first note.

But despite some compelling studies that indicate that the propensity to be gay or lesbian is determined before birth—either genetically or through biological processes in the womb—most researchers today agree a complex combination of genetics, biology, and environmental influences work together to make the determination. Just how much is predetermined by the forces of genes and how much is shaped by influences such as society and culture remain unclear—and hotly debated. So too does the corollary question of whether sexual orientation is somehow an innate trait and thus fixed for life or whether it is malleable and thus changeable over time.

More than scientific curiosity hangs in the balance. For years the gay and lesbian political establishment has leaned, at least to some degree, on the argument that sexual orientation is inborn and permanent and thus should not be a basis for discrimination. The tactic has proved incredibly successful. Polls repeatedly indicate that Americans who believe sexual orientation is either genetic or biological are much more likely to support gay and lesbian civil rights than those who believe it is determined primarily by environmental influences.

In a Gallup Poll conducted in May, half of those surveyed said they believe homosexuality is genetic, and half said it is environmental. In a 1977 Gallup Poll, respondents pointed to the environment over genetics by more than a 4-to-1 ratio. The poll calls this shift in perception "one of the more significant changes in American public opinion on gay and lesbian issues." It is clearly accompanied by increasing tolerance toward gays and lesbians. In May, 52% of Gallup respondents said homosexuality is an "acceptable alternative lifestyle," compared with 38% in 1977. And a majority, 54%, agreed that "homosexual relations between consenting adults should be legal," compared with 43% in 1977.

"The question of whether or not gayness is immutable is rather crucial in the political arena," says Simon LeVay, a neuroscientist who in 1991 found structural differences between the brains of gay men and heterosexual men. "The American public will have a different attitude toward gay rights depending on whether they believe being gay is a matter of choice or not. You can argue all you want that it shouldn't be that way, but that's the fact. If science can show sexual orientation is a deep aspect of a person's being, there is potential for immense good. But it does mean the science gets politicized."

ALL THE SCIENCE SO FAR

Here's what researchers have reported in their search for the "cause"

- Lesbians' ring fingers tend to be longer than their index fingers, whereas straight women's ring fingers tend to be the same length as their index fingers.

- Boys who show "pervasive and persistently" effeminate behavior have about a 75% chance of growing up gay.

- A person with a gay identical twin is at least 10 times more likely to be gay than a person without one.

- There is about a 2% chance that a firstborn male will grow up gay. That chance grows to at least 6% for males with four or more older brothers.

- Gay men and lesbians are more likely to be left-handed.

- Gay men have smaller hypothalamuses than straight men.

- A man is more likely to be gay if there are gay men on his mother's side of the family.

- Lesbians' inner ears tend to react to sounds more like men's inner ears than like straight women's.

- Gay men have more testosterone and larger genitalia than straight men.

IS IT GENETIC?

NICK VELASQUEZ

Stats: Student, 21, California native
Gay relatives: "My dad was gay. He died of AIDS in 1991 at 34 years old. Also on my dad's side I have two distant cousins, both lesbian."
Why are you gay? "I identify as bisexual, actually. I think it's very limiting, the notion that people can't love both [sexes], that it is one way or the other—it's on a continuum. I've always felt different, that there was something that separated me from other people, a different outlook on life; even when I was so young, [it was] in a nonsexual way."

DEBORAH REECE

Stats: Security guard and student, 45, California native

Gay relatives: "I have a gay grandmother, a bisexual aunt, and at least two gay nephews. Half my family is gay!"
Why are you gay? "That's the million-dollar question. And if I knew the answer, I'd be a millionaire! I am who I am. I've known since I was 4. It's natural to me. My mother told me [I was gay]. She used to tell me, 'Don't bother with those guys.'"

DANNY LEMOS

Stats: TV writer, 44, California native
Gay relatives: "Three gay brothers, including my twin, who died of AIDS."
Why are you gay? "Destiny. Some people are meant to be doctors, artists. I was meant to be gay, out, expressive. I served as a role model, especially to my younger brothers. If there's a God,

I think he picks it. If it's science, that's what picks it. I've never had a moment where I didn't know who I was."

KATE NIELSEN

Stats: Writer, 41, Colorado native
Gay relatives: None
Why are you gay? "I think you're born into it, just like some people are born left-handed. It's just what you're dealt. I was 6, I went to see *The Sound of Music*, and I wanted to be Christopher Plummer because I wanted to be with Julie Andrews."

Politics aside, scientists insist there is commanding research to show that sexual orientation is largely influenced by genetics. "There's no debate on that from any reasonable scientist. The evidence for it stands fast," says Dean Hamer, a molecular biologist at the National Insti-tutes of Health and an early pioneer in research linking sexual orientation to genes. In 1993, Hamer was the first to report finding a specific slice of DNA that could be linked to homosexuality.

He first studied the family histories of 114 gay men and discovered that many male relatives on the mother's side of the family were also gay. Since men always inherit an X chromosome from their mothers, the study suggested a genetic link between the X chromosome and homosexuality. Hamer then scrutinized the DNA for 40 pairs of gay brothers and found that

ADVOCATE READERS WEIGH IN

We asked out online visitors to tell us *their* stories about why they're gay.
Here are some of their responses.

GENETICS

No doubt about it in my family: God made us the way we are—genetically. I suspect that my grandfather was gay for many reasons. His second son, my uncle, came out to the entire family at my parents' 50th wedding anniversary party—he was 70 at the time! His son, my cousin, is gay. I am gay. Pretty sound evidence, considering we were all born in different decades, in different places, and were raised in totally different environments.

W.Z., Indianapolis, Ind.

I don't have a history of abuse, and I didn't just wake up one morning and decide to be lesbian. Also, I don't think it was anything my mom did while she was pregnant with me, as she often laments. I am this way. I must have been born this way. When I was growing up, The *Dukes of Hazard* was popular. I watched it every night, religiously. Daisy stirred something in me that I couldn't explain. I was 8 or 9 then.

T.M., Indiana

I am sure I was born gay. I used to steal dolls and jump ropes from girls then hide them, knowing that I would get into *big* trouble if I didn't like "boy things." Luckily I learned to "pass for a boy," so I didn't get bullied too often, but I did bear witness to the horrors bestowed upon more fey-type males.

A.S., via the Internet

Clearly genetic. No straight person I know can tell me the date, time, and even when they "decided" they were straight—so

this notion of "choice" is pure crap. It can't be a gift—it would be one that most people would return. But to where and to whom? Is there a customer service line for this? It's not a "choice" and it is not a "lifestyle"—it's a genetic "orientation." It was an initially unwelcome visitor... now [it] gives me comfort as well as challenges me every day.

E.B., Chicago, Ill.

ENVIRONMENT

I was raised in the archetypal situation for being a gay man: with a chronically overbearing, fiercely possessive mother; a weak, quiet, completely uncommunicative father; and a thorough disinterest in violent sports! I, like many, many thousands of other gay men of my generation (I was born in 1950, in a tiny town), went through absolute hell growing up "hiding." Growing up "gay" (never liked that word—there's nothing "gay" about being gay!) nearly destroyed my life! Frankly, I wish to God (or whoever or whatever is out there) that I had *never* been homosexual!

M.D., San Francisco, Calif.

I think genes are passed on with neutral sexual orientation. To me, homosexuality or heterosexuality is totally due to the environment in which we are raised. In a nutshell, I believe a male who stays bonded with his mother is usually homosexual. A female who bonds more strongly with the father is usually homosexual. A male and a female who bond about equally with the mother and the father are more likely to be bisexual.

My mother died when I was 8 months old. My father remarried

when I was 1 year old. His new wife did not want him to have much to do with his first children. I had five older brothers and three older sisters. My brothers did not want to have much to do with me. My three sisters adored me, so I spent most of my time with them. The sisters painted my deceased mother as being almost a saint. I think I naturally identified with my sisters' values and the values of my mother, which they told me about in detail. This included their sexual orientation.

We all inherit certain physical characteristics from our parents and we can inherit certain abstract characteristics such as temperament. I do not think that these genetically inherited qualities lead to homosexuality.

J.D., via the Internet

GOD

I personally believe I am gay because God made me such. I believe it is a gift and that he has a special reason for creating me as a lesbian. It doesn't matter if I was created this way biologically or if circumstances in my life molded me; this is who I am meant to be. I am proud to be a lesbian and at peace.

D.S., Poland, Ohio

I embrace the gift God gave me. I believe God chose each and every gay, lesbian, bi, and transgendered individual to teach others about love, tolerance, and acceptance. So I remind all my gay brothers and sisters: Don't worry. God did not make a mistake. He has a plan and a reason for your existence.

A.G., Oxnard, Calif.

Before I met Mary-love and fell in love with her, I never told myself I wanted to be a lesbian. The thought never crossed my mind. After a few bad relationships with guys, I guess falling in love with Mary-love after two years and four months of a friendship was bound to happen—it was a destiny I believe God gave to me.

E.D., via the Internet

IT'S A CHOICE

Although I have been married and have two sons, I was a late bloomer and decided in my late 20s or early 30s that being a lesbian was OK and that, for me, it is a choice.

J.L., via the Internet

As a graduate clinician in speech-language pathology, I find it difficult to deny that there is a genetic propensity to homosexuality, just as there is to stuttering. However, the choice to act upon the drive is entirely a symbol of our humanity. The degree to which we embrace our genetic predisposition is the degree to which we marry our understanding of our physical self and our identity.

T.A., Boston. Mass.

It is always a choice whether to be completely honest with yourself and admit you are not in the majority and are attracted to the same sex. I wasn't able to admit this to myself until a few weeks before my 28th birthday. The *choice* is to live your life as best as you can. The question "Why are you gay or lesbian?" is a small part of a much bigger question: "Why are you You?"

C.F., Louisville, Ky.

---

33 of them shared a specific region on a portion of the X chromosome.

His work supported earlier evidence pointing to a genetic link to homosexuality.

In 1991, J. Michael Bailey, a psychology professor at Northwestern University, and Richard Pillard, a psychiatrist at Boston University School of Medicine, examined

a group of gay men, 56 of whom had an identical twin, 54 of whom had a fraternal twin brother, and 57 of whom had a brother by adoption. Among those with an identical twin, in 52% of the cases the twin was also gay. Among fraternal twin bothers, in 22% of cases both twins were gay. Just 11% of those who had a brother by adoption reported that the brother was gay. Another study by Bailey and Pillard found similar patterns in lesbians.

WAS IT OUR PARENTS?

SUSAN DOST

Stats: Owner of an assisted-living company, 36, Michigan native
Gay relatives: "There seems to be a lineage of women in my family who end up 'single.'"
Why are you gay? "I believe that is the way the universe intended for me [to be]. I don't think I have a choice in the way I am. I think it's biological."

HAINES WILKERSON

Stats: Magazine creative director, 46, California native
Gay relatives: "One, but not out."
Why are you gay? "I didn't have any choice in the matter whatsoever. It's completely genetic. Environment modifies a gay person's behavior, but it doesn't cause it. I tried to impose straight attributes for my life. They never stuck."

CHUCK KIM

Stats: Reporter and comic book writer, 29, New York native
Gay relatives: None
Why are you gay? "I just remember always wanting to be around guys. I think being gay is a combination of environment and genetics—something that may act as a catalyst, activating that potential."

CLAUDIA SANCHEZ

Stats: Educator, personal chef, 26, California native
Gay relatives: None
Why are you gay? "All my physical and emotional attractions have been to women. It wasn't really a choice, just something I've always had. Men just never attracted me. Being a lesbian is my reality."

Overall, a person with a gay identical twin is at least 10 times more likely to be gay. A man with a gay brother is anywhere from three to seven times more likely to also be gay. And a woman with a lesbian sister is anywhere from four to eight times more likely to also be lesbian. "All this shows that sexual orientation is largely genetic," Pillard says.

Hamer says genes provide about 50% of the influence on sexual orientation. Pillard wouldn't give a fixed percentage, although he said he believes it is "substantially" greater than 50%. Other scientists have estimated the genetic contribution could be as high as 70%.

However strong the influence of genes, it is not 100%. "We're never going to find the 'gay gene'" Hamer says. "There's no switch that turns it on or off. It's not that simple."

He an other researchers agree that the remaining influences are a complex mixture of biological developments and environmental stimuli. But how much power each wields is as yet unknown.

Evidence is mounting, however, for the argument that much of the remaining influence comes from prenatal biological phenomena. LeVay, for example, found a size difference between gay men's and straight men's hypothalamuses—a part of the brain believed to affect sexual behavior. His "hunch," he says, is that gay men's brains develop differently than straight men's because they are exposed to higher levels of testosterone during pregnancy.

"There's a growing evidence to support the idea that biological and developmental factors before birth exert a strong influence on sexual orientation," LeVay says.

A host of biological indicators of homosexuality boost the theory. For example, research from the University of Liverpool in England has shown that gay men and lesbians are more likely than straights to be left-handed and that lesbians have hand patterns that resemble a man's more than a straight female's. Dennis McFadden, a scientist at the University of Texas at Austin, has reported that lesbians' auditory systems seem to develop somewhere between what is typical for heterosexual men and women. According to studies done by Marc Breedlove, a psychologist at the Uni-

---

versity of California, Berkeley, there is a direct correlation between the lengths of some fingers of the hand and gayness. An what gay man doesn't relish the study that found that gay men tend to be better endowed than their straight counterparts?

BY CHOICE?

JOHN STRAUSS

Stats: Retired motion picture music editor, 81, New York native
Gay relatives: None
Why are you gay? "Because I'm gay. I was an overprotected child, a sissy boy, and felt uncomfortable with my surroundings. My mother was very protective. My first awareness that I had a sexuality at all was when I was 12 or 13. It developed in an instance when I saw my roommate at camp undressed, and there was a voice in my head that said, *Oh, my God, I'm gay.* Only we didn't call it that at the time; we called it *homosexual.*"

TONY ROMAN

Stats: CyberCenter coordinator, Los Angeles Gay and Lesbian Center, 56, New York native
Gay relatives: "I had a gay cousin, who died of AIDS."
Why are you gay? "Nature and God just made me that way. At first I blamed my upbringing for it. I was raised by my mom and stepdad; my father died when I was young. It was a strict Catholic upbringing, [which] had a lot to do with the guilt and suppressing these feelings. I have no kind words for churches. I did a lot of drinking. After I sobered up, I realized I had no one to blame. I am who I am."
—Profiles reported by Alexander Cho

The common thread in many of these findings is the belief that differences in prenatal development are responsible for the variances in anatomy—and in sexual orientation as well. Like LeVay, Breedlove attributes his finding of finger-length differences between gay and straight men to the level of fetal exposure to testosterone. "There is a growing body of research to support the theory that differ-

WHY ARE WE GAY?

JESSICA MENDIETA

Stats: hairdresser, 31, Ohio native
Gay relatives: "I have a gay nephew and at least four gay cousins."
Why are you gay? "I was born gay. I was always attracted to women. My best friends all through junior high and high school were all women. I had my first lover when I was 19. When I met her it was like, *Bang! I definitely love women.*"

JOSHUA EWING

Stats: Student, 18, California native
Gay relatives: None
Why are you gay? "I think it's most definitely genetics. I grew up with my mom and step-dad, and in high school moved in with my biological father. My dad thinks it's a choice, but I knew all along that I wasn't like the other boys, chasing girls. I was doing it, but more to fit in, to conceal my true identity of being homosexual. There are people out there who say they choose, and that's OK. But I didn't have a choice. Everyone is different."

MICHAEL KING

Stats: Editor-designer, 28, West Virginia native
Gay relatives: "I don't know of any concretely, but there are a few that I suspect."
Why are you gay? "It's just who I am. I grew up in the Bible Belt; I played football. I am the perfect example of why environment *doesn't* cause you to be gay, because being gay in West Virginia is not even an option."

LIONEL FRIEDMAN

Stats: Retired from the entertainment industry, 69, Missouri native
Gay relatives: "My younger brother is gay."
Why are you gay? "It's always been there. I just like men. I absolutely feel like I was born with it. I came out at a very young age, 13. My dad was very supportive. My mother wasn't."

ALEXANDER CHO

Stats: Intern at *The Advocate*, 20, California native
Gay relatives: None

Why are you gay? "I have no clue. I grew up in a conventional home, and [being gay] has been with me as long as I can remember, so I'd probably say I was born with it. It was certainly not a choice, although I did choose to suppress it for a long time. I was filled with a lot of self-hate when I realized [I was gay], and it's something that I'm just now beginning the process of getting over."

MERCEDES SALAS

Stats: Waitress, 24, native of the Dominican Republic
Gay relatives: "I have two bisexual cousins, both female."
Why are you gay? "I just feel it. I feel no sexual attraction to men. Instead, I feel attraction to women. Even when I didn't know the concept, the feeling was always there. It was at age 16, when I was reading about it, I came to know that people were 'gay.' Women weren't as badly treated [as gay men], so that made me feel more comfortable asking questions."

---

ent hormone levels can cause the brain to differentiate one way or the other—to be straight or gay," LeVay adds.

> "THERE IS A SMALL MINORITY OF PEOPLE IN WHICH SEXUAL ORIENTATION IS MALLEABLE. IT WOULD SEEM THAT REPARATIVE THERAPY IS SOMETIMES SUCCESSFUL. I TALKED TO 200 PEOPLE ON THE PHONE. SOME MAY BE EXAGGERATING THEIR CHANGES, BUT I CAN'T BELIEVE THE WHOLE THING IS JUST MADE UP."
>
> —*Psychiatrist Robert Spitzer, who found that gay people can change their sexual orientation if they are "highly motivated"*

But it remains murky just how much and just how strongly these biological factors shape sexual orientation. "I honestly can't be sure how to interpret the differences I found in brain structure." LeVay says.

Which leaves open the final, and most controversial, possibility: How much is sexual orientation determined by a person's environment?

Even the most ardent geneticists and biologists aren't willing to discount a role for external stimuli. "I certainly wouldn't rule out that life experiences can play a role in sexual orientation." LeVay says.

Historically, determining the "causes" of homosexuality was left entirely to the domain of psychology, which attempted to explain homosexuality with theories of mental maladjustment. Perhaps ironically, today it is often psychologists and psychiatrists who argue most arduously against the environmental influence on gayness.

"I've spent 30 years studying psychology, and I don't see any environmental differences that affect a person's sexual orientation," says Richard Isay, a psychia-

try professor at Cornell University and author of the book *Becoming Gay*.

Psychiatrist Richard Pillard agrees. "I strongly believe that at birth the wiring in the brain tells us if we are gay or straight," he says.

Isay says that "all the tired old postulations"—that homosexuality is caused by, for instance, an overprotective mother, a distant father, or a sexual molestation or trauma in childhood—have been "completely discredited" by the mental health profession. What the environment affects, he says, is "how you express your sexuality. Very, very few mental health professionals hold on to the notion that environment molds sexual orientation, and there's just no real evidence to support that."

However, numerous researchers point to what LeVay categorizes as the "oodles of data" that sexuality appears to be more fluid in women than in men, suggesting that, for some people at least, sexual orientation may not be genetically or bio-

COMMENTARIES: "WHY?" IS THE WRONG QUESTION

BEING GAY OR LESBIAN IS A BLESSING, SAYS SPIRITUAL WRITER **CHRISTIAN DE LA HUERTA**. THE BEST USE OF THAT GIFT IS NOT TO SEEK ITS CAUSE OR TRY TO CHANGE IT BUT TO USE IT TO FIND OUR TRUE PURPOSE

Part of me would be fascinated to know what makes me gay. My earliest sexual fantasies—before I knew what sex was—were always about men. Interestingly, my earliest romantic fantasies—those involving kissing, holding hands, etc.—were about women. The heterosexist cultural conditioning had already begun.

Though we may never know for sure, I suspect that gayness results from a combination of genetic and environmental factors. Ultimately, however, does it really matter? Nature or nurture, genetics or the environment, choice or not, so what? Knowing what makes us gay might be interesting, might help take the discussion out of religious and moral arenas, but it won't change who we are or the fact that we are here and always have been.

Clearly, evolution, in its mysterious and inexorable wisdom, would long ago have handled the situation if queer folk did not serve some kind of purpose. It may be more useful, then, to ask a different question: What are we going to do with the reality of our existence? If, in fact, we serve a purpose, what might that be? What contributions do we make? How do we make a difference in the world?

In contrast to what "ex-gay" ad campaigns would have us believe, far from needing to "recover" from homosexuality in order to have spiritual grace, it appears that throughout history and across different cultures queer people have not only been spiritually inclined but have actually been respected and revered for assuming roles of spiritual leadership. Many enact those same roles today. Mediators, scouts of consciousness, keepers of beauty, healers, teachers, caregivers, sacred clowns, shamans, priests—these are roles to which we have gravitated, for which we have exhibited a propensity, and which we have filled in disproportionate numbers.

Our outsider status gives us a special sense of perspective—our ability to see the forest *and* the trees. Because we stand outside the mainstream in one area, we are not as rigidly bound by its rules in other areas. Although this may be stressful and cause pain, loneliness, and alienation at some points in our lives, it also creates the opportunity to live by our own rules. We are privy to a more honest process of enlightenment than blind acceptance of tired rules handed down to us by past generations.

Countless people have suppressed their sexual feelings—with varying degrees of success and failure—throughout history and continue to do so. But modifying or suppressing sexual behavior is one thing; changing a person's fundamental orientation is quite another. Far from being an effort to be more "natural," the attempt to change such a fundamental characteristic is an *affront* to what is natural.

One year after I came out to my father, a Catholic psychiatrist, I understood what is often meant by *choice*. After kindly reassuring me that I would always be his son and that he and my mother would always love me, my father proceeded to advise that I choose another lifestyle. He said that it is a very difficult life, that he knew because he had treated many homosexuals, even "curing" some. What my father didn't know, however, is that at least two of those he'd "cured" I'd slept with postcure. I know because after we did our thing, they asked if I was related to so-and-so. When I answered that he was my father, they said "Oh, I used to go to him."

Sexuality, like everything else, including matter, is a form of energy. Though it can be transmuted, energy cannot be destroyed. What is suppressed in one place will inevitably surface elsewhere. And when the suppressed energy of sexuality reemerges elsewhere, it too often does so in ugly and unhealthy forms.

For me, repressing such an intrinsic part of myself was no longer an option. It's been a very long and arduous journey, but I have come to such a profound place of acceptance that I actually live in a state of gratitude for being gay.

I look forward to the day when sexual orientation will be a nonissue, and perhaps all the energy now spent on trying to figure out why we're here could be redirected toward maximizing our unique potential. More and more people are beginning to realize that queers add value to our collective human existence, and given the desperate state of our world, we need all the help we can get—whatever the source.

Being gay is an advantage. It is a gift, a blessing, a privilege. In many ways it frees us up to discover who we really are. And who we are goes far beyond our sexual practices or the people with whom we tend to make romantic and emotional connections.

Had there been a way to alter my sexual orientation when I was growing up—and barely surviving the long, existential depression of my adolescence—what would I have done? I don't know, but now the answer is clear. To even consider the possibility of changing is ludicrous to me. Sure, life is still much easier for heteros. I still experience self-consciousness—truth be told, fear—in certain situations. Recently, at a national park, the guy I was with reached out and held my hand while a group of tourists approached. I felt tension. I felt fear. I pulled my hand away.

But would I change? Not a chance! I love being who I am and what I am. I love being gay. I love the sense of perspective, the freedom from societal rules, the generally more fun and open outlook on life. These blessings don't tell me *why* I'm gay, but they make me understand that "Why?" is not a question I need to ask.

De la Huerta is the founder of QSpirit and the author of Coming Out Spiritually *and* Coming Out Spiritually: The Next Step.

logically predetermined but heavily influenced by factors such as culture, customs, politics, and religion.

It's no secret why the long-standing debate over environmental influences is so critical and so contentious: If environmental stimuli can "make" us gay, can't other stimuli then "make" us straight?

COMMENTARIES "WHY?" IS THE WRONG QUESTION: (CONTINUED)

AS A GAY RIGHTS BATTLE CRY, "IT'S NOT OUR FAULT" SHORTCHANGES OUR HUMANITY, ARGUES **REBECCA ISAACS**. WHAT'S MORE, THE FLUIDITY OF SEXUALITY MAKES HARD-AND-FAST DEFINITIONS POOR POLITICAL TOOLS

Whatever we know about the origins of sexual orientation, we know that it is a complex and fascinating topic that will remain unresolved and controversial for the foreseeable future. Many discussions of sexual orientation's causes have subtext of the search for responsibility, even blame. But we need to attach blame only if we accept our opponents' premise that homosexuality is bad. The major point for me as we continue this discussion of the interplay between nature and nurture is that we need to affirm a basic premise: *Gay is good.* As a parent of a 6-year-old daughter, imparting a sense of pride in her family is critical to her well-being. Vanessa, my partner of 11 years, and I want Rachel to know that the most important value of our family is that we love and care for each other. She has learned from an early age about the importance of validating and believing in herself and her family.

From my perspective, the question is not so much "Where does homosexuality come from?" but "Why are we so concerned about knowing the 'cause'?" In the political arena, as in our daily lives, we need to assert the validity of our sexuality and our humanity as lesbian, gay, bisexual, and transgendered people *without* the need for caveats or explanations. After all, there is little discussion about the origins of *hetero*sexuality.

It's ironic that while heterosexuality is so entrenched and unquestioned, the right wing continues to paint marriage and heterosexuality as being in a constant state of instability and crisis, with alternative sexualities as a principal threat. Right-wing ideology puts forward the premise that homosexuality is an enticing disease that people will catch if exposed, that it's a choice or temporary mental condition that must be overcome by counseling, prayer, coercion, abstinence, repression or electroshock therapy.

The counterassertion, that sexual orientation is a fixed and immutable characteristic, has also long been a part of the legal and political arguments we make for equal rights. If sexual orientation is fixed, the argument goes, then we are not responsible for being gay and are therefore worthy of protection from discrimination. Yet a definitive answer to "Why are we gay?"—even if it were found—would not resolve our quest for equal rights, because those who would block our rights would continue to oppose us on other grounds.

I think that most people extrapolate a universal homosexual-origin story from their own personal experience. If they remember feeling different, feeling attraction to the same sex at an early age, they tend to think that sexual orientation is fixed from birth. Yet many people, women in particular, experience sexual orientation as more fluid than fixed. We need to be open to the range of personal, scientific, and social science theories that analyze sexuality in all its manifestations. Sexual orientation is not fixed in the same way for all people.

We know, for example, that there is a range to when people identify their sexual orientation. Many recognize same-sex attraction from an early age, but others come out later in life, in a particular context, with a particular person. Because we must embrace these differences, it also becomes more difficult to embrace a unified theory of sexuality's origins.

It is very hard to know what sexuality would look like freed from the dominance of heterosexuality. What if there were no stigma attached to being gay, lesbian, or bisexual? What if being gay didn't correlate to isolation, violence, rejection, and limited horizons for many teens? What if the strong arm of normative heterosexuality didn't force all of us into a separate and unequal box? What if sexual orientation truly were a part of each person's journey of self-discovery?

In my own experience I came to lesbianism through feminism, both personally and politically. Ti-Grace Atkinson said, "Feminism is the theory, lesbianism is the practice." I truly believed that, and I was in college in the 1970s at a time and in an environment where the heavy curtain of heterosexuality was mo-

mentarily lifted. My friends and I came out during that time of openness. Life after the lesbian nirvana, when we left our created community, was not so open. The pressures of dominant structures like heterosexual marriage reappeared. Today, some of us are still lesbians, some became straight-identified, and some identify as bisexual. I don't believe we each followed our one true, essential path or that there was only one path for each of us. A confluence of societal and personal experiences shaped our identities. Explaining that away with a scientific theory of sexual orientation seems unnecessary and indeed impossible.

I really do believe that for many people, sexuality involves acting on a range of feelings, behaviors, and opportunities. And I also believe that in a society that exacts a toll on people open to same-sex desire, options are more limited than they should be. We have learned from the bisexual movement that there is a range of sexual orientations and that desire is much more complicated than the identity categories we have set up. We box ourselves into a corner when we let others set the agenda and narrow the possibilities of expression.

Those who oppose our equal status politically and socially do so to deny our validity as human beings. Proving a biological or genetic basis will now sway them from that goal. The burden of equal treatment is on a society that discriminates, not on those who experience discrimination, coercion, and physical violence. We must show that the toll on a society that tolerates homophobia is great, that all of us suffer when any one group is targeted for discrimination and harassment. Each of us has a unique origin story that must be embraced. Our rights and freedoms depend not on what causes our sexuality but on our common humanity.

Isaacs is a director of policy and public affairs at the Los Angeles Gay and Lesbian Center.

The latest firebomb thrown into this discussion is the now highly contested report by Columbia University psychiatrist Robert Spitzer, who in May disclosed results of a study in which he claimed that 66% of the gay male partic-

It's all about choices

notes from a blond bruce vilanch

You can't blame straight people for being confused. Not only do we want to get married, have children, and serve in the military—three things they would cheerfully be rid of, given the chance—but just when they have decided that we are fundamentally OK, a doctor comes along on CNN and tells them that a lot of us would rather be straight. And it wasn't even Dr. Laura. His name is Spitzer, and he's gotten some mileage recently out of a survey he did that seemed to say it is easy for gays to convert. His subjects turned out mostly to be the product of "ex-gay" ministries, so his entire study would appear to be statistically flawed, but that didn't stop the networks from pouncing on him as catnip for the evening news.

Hot on the heels of this pronouncement, the folks at the Gallup Poll revealed that, at long last, a majority of Americans seem to accept homosexuality as "an alternative lifestyle" and don't register any major disapproval of us per se, even though we appear to register it about ourselves. Gallup probably didn't use the same phone book as Spitzer.

But straight people, who want to know as much about us as they want to know about plumbing, can be forgiven for shaking their heads in disbelief. If a straight majority thinks homosexuality is OK, why are homosexuals turning away from it? If homosexuality is as wicked as it is painted, why are so many gay people at KFC buying the family pack? Why do so many gay men spend so much time making women look pretty? How can people decide their sexuality anyway, and at so many different times of life? Is the closet we come out of stacked full of discarded ballots with dimpled chads from previous votes when we decided *not* to come out?

Just get me a beer and the remote and let somebody else work on it.

THAT'S WHEN YOU BEGIN TO UNDERSTAND WHAT CHOICE IS ABOUT. IT'S DENIAL. WE COME OUT WHEN WE ARE FINISHED DENYING OUR TRUE NATURES.

Part of the confusion stems from the notion of choice, of choosing to be gay. Since one thing science won't agree on is the genetic explanation of sexuality and since people keep tromping onto *Jenny* and *Jerry* and *Oprah* and *Ricki* to announce they have decided they are gay, it's difficult for the unknowing to dismiss the idea of choice.

It always amazes me when people who see me on *Hollywood Squares* ask me if I am really gay, as casually as they ask if I'm really blond. Why would I make this up? I like being blond because I like the look, but that's not why I'm gay. "Well," they say, "it works so well for you. It's your shtick, you know, like Dean Martin was drunk." But guess what? Dean Martin *was* drunk. I drank with Dean Martin. He didn't knock back a pitcher of lemonade before he staggered onto the stage. It was part of who he was. Cheech and Chong didn't hire a roomful of stoners and take notes. Besides, if I were going to choose a comic shtick, why would I choose one that would leave me open to so much potential hostility? Couldn't I just be a jovial fat guy?

The fact that sexuality is a part of who you are has been a very difficult concept for Americans to swallow, from Kinsey on down. Even prominent black civil rights leaders have had a difficult time when we try to position ourselves as an oppressed minority like theirs. We have a choice, they say. They have to be black, but we can be invisible. And that's when you begin to understand what choice is about. It's denial. We come out when we are finished denying our true natures. When we have had enough of paying the emotional price of passing for, I don't know, call it white. No one suddenly chooses to be gay. Even Anne Heche, at the height of her whirlwind ride on the gay roller coaster, didn't claim to be a lesbian. She just claimed to be in love.

No one chooses to be gay. But they do choose to be straight. They are comfortable enough in their lives, if not in their skin. They choose not to jeopardize their lives and instead do damage to their souls. Eventually, the gnawing within becomes too painful, and they can't stand it. They no longer have a choice. And that, the right wing will tell you, is when we choose to be gay. But we know different. It's when we choose to be free.

---

ipants and 44% of the lesbians who were "highly motivated" could change not just their sexual behavior but their sexual orientation. The study has come under harsh criticism from psychologists and psychiatrists for its methodology, particularly for relying on data provided solely by phone-interviewed subjects recruited primarily from religiously biased "ex-gay" organizations.

"There's no question in my mind that what Spitzer reported was not a change in sexual orientation but simply a change in sexual behavior," Isay says.

But Spitzer is sticking to his guns. While he admits that "the kinds of changes my subjects reported are highly unlikely to be available to the vast majority" of gay men and lesbians, "there is a small minority of people in which sexual orientation is malleable." He estimates that perhaps 3% of gays and lesbians can change their sexual orientation. "It would seem that reparative therapy is sometimes successful," he says. He brushes aside questions about his methodology of relying too heavily on the self-reporting of obviously self-interested parties. "I talked to 200 people on the phone. Some may be exaggerating [their changes], but I can't believe the whole thing is just made up."

Spitzer, who was among those who worked to get homosexuality removed as a mental disorder from the American Psychiatric Association in 1973 and who has long been a supporter of gay rights, says his work has come under attack "because it challenges both the mental health professionals and the gay activists on their party line. I would hope my work causes people in both camps to rethink their dogma."

Spitzer also acknowledges that his research is being "twisted by the Christian right" for political purposes and says that was never the intention of his work. But science, he says, "will always be manipulated by people on both sides of the political debate."

Spitzer's study notwithstanding, gay and lesbian activists applaud the mounting scientific evidence regarding the origins of sexual orientation. But even though most results would likely be considered favorable to the gay and lesbian political agenda, activists remain cautious about basing too much political strategy on scientific findings.

"We welcome research that helps us understand who we are," says David Smith, a spokesman for the Human Rights Campaign, a gay lobbying group based in Washington, D.C. "And we've seen a growing body of evidence to indicate there are genetic and biological in-

fluences on sexual orientation. But we believe the studies shouldn't have a bearing on public policy. Gay, lesbian, bisexual, and transgendered people should have equal rights regardless of the origins of sexual orientation."

And Shannon Minter, a senior staff attorney at the National Center for Lesbian Rights in San Francisco, is "skeptical that science can ever fully answer the questions to something as humanly complex as sexual orientation. Sure, it's interesting and worth studying, but I'd be careful about jumping to too many conclusions either way."

Mark Stoner shares Minter's ambivalence about finding "the answer" and her wariness that human sexuality can be easily tabulated and measured in the lab.

"It's interesting cocktail chatter, but I don't particularly care what made me

gay," says Stoner, who has two older brothers and thus may be a personal example of one theory that links having older brothers with higher levels of prenatal testosterone and thus a greater chance of being gay. "I don't think we'll ever be able to boil it down to a finite set of variables. It's probably genetic and biological and environmental and cultural and social and a whole lot more that we can't squeeze into comfortable definitions. There are always going to be exceptions to whatever rules the scientists discover."

As if to underscore his point, Stoner adds a footnote to his clarinet theory: "Over all the years of doing my survey, I did find one gay trumpet player."

Dahir, who writes for a number of publications, played the clarinet from age 8 to 17.

The Five Sexes, Revisited

The emerging recognition that people come in bewildering
sexual varieties is testing medical values and social norms

By Anne Fausto-Sterling

As Cheryl Chase stepped to the front of the packed meeting room in the Sheraton Boston Hotel, nervous coughs made the tension audible. Chase, an activist for intersexual rights, had been invited to address the May 2000 meeting of the Lawson Wilkins Pediatric Endocrine Society (LWPES), the largest organization in the United States for specialists in children's hormones. Her talk would be the grand finale to a four-hour symposium on the treatment of genital ambiguity in newborns, infants born with a mixture of both male and female anatomy, or genitals that appear to differ from their chromosomal sex. The topic was hardly a novel one to the assembled physicians.

Yet Chase's appearance before the group was remarkable. Three and a half years earlier, the American Academy of Pediatrics had refused her request for a chance to present the patients' viewpoint on the treatment of genital ambiguity, dismissing Chase and her supporters as "zealots." About two dozen intersex people had responded by throwing up a picket line. The Intersex Society of North America (ISNA) even issued a press release: "Hermaphrodites Target Kiddie Docs."

It had done my 1960s street-activist heart good. In the short run, I said to Chase at the time, the picketing would make people angry. But eventually, I assured her, the doors then closed would

open. Now, as Chase began to address the physicians at their own convention, that prediction was coming true. Her talk, titled "Sexual Ambiguity: The Patient-Centered Approach," was a measured critique of the near-universal practice of performing immediate, "corrective" surgery on thousands of infants born each year with ambiguous genitalia. Chase herself lives with the consequences of such surgery. Yet her audience, the very endocrinologists and surgeons Chase was accusing of reacting with "surgery and shame," received her with respect. Even more remarkably, many of the speakers who preceded her at the session had already spoken of the need to scrap current practices in favor of treatments more centered on psychological counseling.

Much has changed since 1993. Intersexuals have materialized before our very eyes.

What led to such a dramatic reversal of fortune? Certainly, Chase's talk at the LWPES symposium was a vindication of her persistence in seeking attention for her cause. But her invitation to speak was also a watershed in the evolving discussion about how to treat children with

ambiguous genitalia. And that discussion, in turn, is the tip of a biocultural iceberg—the gender iceberg—that continues to rock both medicine and our culture at large.

Chase made her first national appearance in 1993, in these very pages, announcing the formation of ISNA in a letter responding to an essay I had written for *The Sciences*, titled "The Five Sexes" [March/April 1993]. In that article I argued that the two-sex system embedded in our society is not adequate to encompass the full spectrum of human sexuality. In its place, I suggested a five-sex system. In addition to males and females, I included "herms" (named after true hermaphrodites, people born with both a testis and an ovary); "merms" (male pseudohermaphrodites, who are born with testes and some aspect of female genitalia); and "ferms" (female pseudohermaphrodites, who have ovaries combined with some aspect of male genitalia).

I had intended to be provocative, but I had also written with tongue firmly in cheek. So I was surprised by the extent of the controversy the article unleashed. Right-wing Christians were outraged, and connected my idea of five sexes with the United Nations–sponsored Fourth World Conference on Women, held in Beijing in September 1995. At the same time, the article delighted others who felt constrained by the current sex and gender system.

Clearly, I had struck a nerve. The fact that so many people could get riled up by my proposal to revamp our sex and gender system suggested that change—as well as resistance to it—might be in the offing. Indeed, a lot has changed since 1993, and I like to think that my article was an important stimulus. As if from nowhere, intersexuals are materializing before our very eyes. Like Chase, many have become political organizers, who lobby physicians and politicians to change current treatment practices. But more generally, though perhaps no less provocatively, the boundaries separating masculine and feminine seem harder than ever to define.

Some find the changes under way deeply disturbing. Others find them liberating.

W HO IS AN INTERSEXUAL—AND how many intersexuals are there? the concept of intersexuality is rooted in the very ideas of male and female. In the idealized, Platonic, biological world, human beings are divided into two kinds: a perfectly dimorphic species. Males have an X and a Y chromosome, testes, a penis and all of the appropriate internal plumbing for delivering urine and semen to the outside world. They also have well-known secondary sexual characteristics, including a muscular build and facial hair. Women have two X chromosomes, ovaries, all of the internal plumbing to transport urine and ova to the outside world, a system to support pregnancy and fetal development, as well as a variety of recognizable secondary sexual characteristics.

That idealized story papers over many obvious caveats: some women have facial hair, some men have none; some women speak with deep voices, some men veritably squeak. Less well known is the fact that, on close inspection, absolute dimorphism disintegrates even at the level of basic biology. Chromosomes, hormones, the internal sex structures, the gonads and the external genitalia all vary more than most people realize. Those born outside of the Platonic dimorphic mold are called intersexuals.

In "The Five Sexes" I reported an estimate by a psychologist expert in the treatment of intersexuals, suggesting that some 4 percent of all live births are intersexual. Then, together with a group of Brown University undergraduates, I set out to conduct the first systematic assessment of the available data on intersexual birthrates. We scoured the medical literature for estimates of the frequency of various categories of intersexuality, from additional chromosomes to mixed gonads, hormones and genitalia. For some conditions we could find only anecdotal evidence; for most, however, numbers exist. On the basis of that evidence, we calculated that for every 1,000 children born, seventeen are intersexual in some form. That number—1.7 percent—is a ballpark estimate, not a precise count, though we believe it is more accurate than the 4 percent I reported.

Our figure represents all chromosomal, anatomical and hormonal exceptions to the dimorphic ideal; the number of intersexuals who might, potentially, be subject to surgery as infants is smaller—probably between one in 1,000 and one in 2,000 live births. Furthermore, because some populations possess the relevant genes at high frequency, the intersexual birthrate is not uniform throughout the world.

Consider, for instance, the gene for congenital adrenal hyperplasia (CAH). When the CAH gene is inherited from both parents, it leads to a baby with masculinized external genitalia who possesses two X chromosomes and the internal reproductive organs of a potentially fertile woman. The frequency of the gene varies widely around the world: in New Zealand it occurs in only forty-three children per million; among the Yupik Eskimo of southwestern Alaska, its frequency is 3,500 per million.

I NTERSEXUALITY HAS ALWAYS BEEN TO some extent a matter of definition, and in the past century physicians have been the ones who defined children as intersexual—and provided the remedies. When only the chromosomes are unusual, but the external genitalia and gonads clearly indicate either a male or a female, physicians do not advocate intervention. In-

deed, it is not clear what kind of intervention could be advocated in such cases. But the story is quite different when infants are born with mixed genitalia, or with external genitals that seem at odds with the baby's gonads.

Most clinics now specializing in the treatment of intersex babies rely on case-management principles developed in the 1950s by the psychologist John Money and the psychiatrists Joan G. Hampson and John L. Hampson, all of Johns Hopkins University in Baltimore, Maryland. Money believed that gender identity is completely malleable for about eighteen months after birth. Thus, he argued, when a treatment team is presented with an infant who has ambiguous genitalia, the team could make a gender assignment solely on the basis of what made the best surgical sense. The physicians could then simply encourage the parents to raise the child according to the surgically assigned gender. Following that course, most physicians maintained, would eliminate psychological distress for both the patient and the parents. Indeed, treatment teams were never to use such words as "intersex" or "hermaphrodite"; instead, they were to tell parents that nature intended the baby to be the boy or the girl that the physicians had determined it was. Through surgery, the physicians were merely completing nature's intention.

Although Money and the Hampsons published detailed case studies of intersex children who they said had adjusted well to their gender assignments, Money thought one case in particular proved his theory. It was a dramatic example, inasmuch as it did not involve intersexuality at all: one of a pair of identical twin boys lost his penis as a result of a circumcision accident. Money recommended that "John" (as he came to be known in a later case study) be surgically turned into "Joan" and raised as a girl. In time, Joan grew to love wearing dresses and having her hair done. Money proudly proclaimed the sex reassignment a success.

But as recently chronicled by John Colapinto, in his book *As Nature Made Him*, Joan—now known to be an adult male named David Reimer—eventually rejected his female assignment. Even without a functioning penis and testes (which had been removed as part of the reassignment) John/Joan sought masculinizing medication, and married a woman with children (whom he adopted).

Since the full conclusion to the John/Joan story came to light, other individuals who were reassigned as males or females shortly after birth but who later rejected their early assignments have come forward. So, too, have cases in which the reassignment has worked—at least into the subject's mid-twenties. But even then the aftermath of the surgery can be problematic. Genital surgery often leaves scars that reduce sexual sensitivity. Chase herself had a complete clitoridectomy, a procedure that is less frequently performed on intersexuals today. But the newer surgeries, which reduce the size of the clitoral shaft, still greatly reduce sensitivity.

THE REVELATION OF CASES OF FAILED reassignments and the emergence of intersex activism have led an increasing number of pediatric endocrinologists, urologists and psychologists to reexamine the wisdom of early genital surgery. For example, in a talk that preceded Chase's at the LWPES meeting, the medical ethicist Laurence B. McCullough of the Center for Medical Ethics and Health Policy at Baylor College of Medicine in Houston, Texas, introduced an ethical framework for the treatment of children with ambiguous genitalia. Because sex phenotype (the manifestation of genetically and embryologically determined sexual characteristics) and gender presentation (the sex role projected by the individual in society) are highly variable, McCullough argues, the various forms of intersexuality should be defined as normal. All of them fall within the statistically expected variability of sex and gender. Furthermore, though certain disease states may accompany some forms of intersexuality, and may require medical intervention, intersexual conditions are not themselves diseases.

McCullough also contends that in the process of assigning gender, physicians should minimize what he calls irreversible assignments: taking steps such as the surgical removal or modification of go-

nads or genitalia that the patient may one day want to have reversed. Finally, McCullough urges physicians to abandon their practice of treating the birth of a child with genital ambiguity as a medical or social emergency. Instead, they should take the time to perform a thorough medical workup and should disclose everything to the parents, including the uncertainties about the final outcome. The treatment mantra, in other words, should be therapy, not surgery.

I believe a new treatment protocol for intersex infants, similar to the one outlined by McCullough, is close at hand. Treatment should combine some basic medical and ethical principles with a practical but less drastic approach to the birth of a mixed-sex child. As a first step, surgery on infants should be performed only to save the child's life or to substantially improve the child's physical well-being. Physicians may assign a sex—male or female—to an intersex infant on the basis of the probability that the child's particular condition will lead to the formation of a particular gender identity. At the same time, though, practitioners ought to be humble enough to recognize that as the child grows, he or she may reject the assignment—and they should be wise enough to listen to what the child has to say. Most important, parents should have access to the full range of information and options available to them.

Sex assignments made shortly after birth are only the beginning of a long journey. Consider, for instance, the life of Max Beck: Born intersexual, Max was surgically assigned as a female and consistently raised as such. Had her medical team followed her into her early twenties, they would have deemed her assignment a success because she was married to a man. (It should be noted that success in gender assignment has traditionally been defined as living in that gender as a heterosexual.) Within a few years, however, Beck had come out as a butch lesbian; now in her mid-thirties, Beck has become a man and married his lesbian partner, who (through the miracles of modern reproductive technology) recently gave birth to a girl.

Transsexuals, people who have an emotional gender at odds with their physical sex, once described themselves

in terms of dimorphic absolutes—males trapped in female bodies, or vice versa. As such, they sought psychological relief through surgery. Although many still do, some so-called transgendered people today are content to inhabit a more ambiguous zone. A male-to-female transsexual, for instance, may come out as a lesbian. Jane, born a physiological male, is now in her late thirties and living with her wife, whom she married when her name was still John. Jane takes hormones to feminize herself, but they have not yet interfered with her ability to engage in intercourse as a man. In her mind Jane has a lesbian relationship with her wife, though she views their intimate moments as a cross between lesbian and heterosexual sex.

> A person who projects a social gender at odds with his or her genitals may die for the transgression.

It might seem natural to regard intersexuals and transgendered people as living midway between the poles of male and female. But male and female, masculine and feminine, cannot be parsed as some kind of continuum. Rather, sex and gender are best conceptualized as points in a multidimensional space. For some time, experts on gender development have distinguished between sex at the genetic level and at the cellular level (sex-specific gene expression, X and Y chromosomes); at the hormonal level (in the fetus, during childhood and after puberty); and at the anatomical level (genitals and secondary sexual characteristics). Gender identity presumably emerges from all of those corporeal aspects via some poorly understood interaction with environment and experience. What has become increasingly clear is that one can find levels of masculinity and femininity in almost every possible permutation. A chromosomal, hormonal and genital male (or female) may emerge with a female (or male) gender identity. Or a chromosomal female with male fetal hormones and masculinized genitalia—but with female pubertal hormones—may develop a female gender identity.

THE MEDICAL AND SCIENTIFIC COMmunities have yet to adopt a language that is capable of describing such diversity. In her book *Hermaphrodites and the Medical Invention of Sex*, the historian and medical ethicist Alice Domurat Dreger of Michigan State University in East Lansing documents the emergence of current medical systems for classifying gender ambiguity. The current usage remains rooted in the Victorian approach to sex. The logical structure of the commonly used terms "true hermaphrodite," "male pseudohermaphrodite" and "female pseudohermaphrodite" indicates that only the so-called true hermaphrodite is a genuine mix of male and female. The others, no matter how confusing their body parts, are really hidden males or females. Because true hermaphrodites are rare—possibly only one in 100,000—such a classification system supports the idea that human beings are an absolutely dimorphic species.

At the dawn of the twenty-first century, when the variability of gender seems so visible, such a position is hard to maintain. And here, too, the old medical consensus has begun to crumble. Last fall the pediatric urologist Ian A. Aaronson of the Medical University of South Carolina in Charleston organized the North American Task Force on Intersexuality (NATFI) to review the clinical responses to genital ambiguity in infants. Key medical associations, such as the American Academy of Pediatrics, have endorsed NATFI. Specialists in surgery, endocrinology, psychology, ethics, psychiatry, genetics and public health, as well as intersex patient-advocate groups, have joined its ranks.

One of the goals of NATFI is to establish a new sex nomenclature. One proposal under consideration replaces the current system with emotionally neutral terminology that emphasizes developmental processes rather than preconceived gender categories. For example,

Type I intersexes develop out of anomalous virilizing influences; Type II result from some interruption of virilization; and in Type III intersexes the gonads themselves may not have developed in the expected fashion.

WHAT IS CLEAR IS THAT SINCE 1993, modern society has moved beyond five sexes to a recognition that gender variation is normal and, for some people, an arena for playful exploration. Discussing my "five sexes" proposal in her book *Lessons from the Intersexed*, the psychologist Suzanne J. Kessler of the State University of New York at Purchase drives this point home with great effect:

> The limitation with Fausto-Sterling's proposal is that… [it] still gives genitals… primary signifying status and ignores the fact that in the everyday world gender attributions are made without access to genital inspection.… What has primacy in everyday life is the gender that is performed, regardless of the flesh's configuration under the clothes.

I now agree with Kessler's assessment. It would be better for intersexuals and their supporters to turn everyone's focus away from genitals. Instead, as she suggests, one should acknowledge that people come in an even wider assortment of sexual identities and characteristics than mere genitals can distinguish. Some women may have "large clitorises or fused labia," whereas some men may have "small penises or misshapen scrota," as Kessler puts it, "phenotypes with no particular clinical or identity meaning."

As clearheaded as Kessler's program is—and despite the progress made in the 1990s—our society is still far from that ideal. The intersexual or transgendered person who projects a social gender—what Kessler calls "cultural genitals"—that conflicts with his or her physical genitals still may die for the transgression. Hence legal protection for people

whose cultural and physical genitals do not match is needed during the current transition to a more gender-diverse world. One easy step would be to eliminate the category of "gender" from official documents, such as driver's licenses and passports. Surely attributes both more visible (such as height, build and eye color) and less visible (fingerprints and genetic profiles) would be more expedient.

A more far-ranging agenda is presented in the International Bill of Gender Rights, adopted in 1995 at the fourth annual International Conference on Transgender Law and Employment Policy in Houston, Texas. It lists ten "gender rights," including the right to define one's own gender, the right to change one's physical gender if one so chooses and the right to marry whomever one wishes. The legal bases for such rights are being hammered out in the courts as I write and, most recently, through the establishment, in the state of Vermont, of legal same-sex domestic partnerships.

NO ONE COULD HAVE FORESEEN SUCH changes in 1993. And the idea that I played some role, however small, in reducing the pressure—from the medical community as well as from society at large—to flatten the diversity of human sexes into two diametrically opposed camps gives me pleasure.

Sometimes people suggest to me, with not a little horror, that I am arguing for a pastel world in which androgyny reigns and men and women are boringly the same. In my vision, however, strong colors coexist with pastels. There are and will continue to be highly masculine people out there; it's just that some of them are women. And some of the most feminine people I know happen to be men.

Anne Fausto-Sterling is a professor of biology and women's studies at Brown University. Portions of this article were adapted from her recent book SEXING THE BODY *(Basic Books, 2000).*

This article is reprinted by permission of *The Sciences* and is from the July/August 2000 issue, pp. 19–23. Individual subscriptions are $28 per year. Write to: The Sciences, 2 East 63rd Street, New York, NY 10021.

UNIT 3
Interpersonal Relationships

Unit Selections

Key Points to Consider

- What makes male-female intimacy difficult to achieve? Have you learned any lessons about yourself and the opposite sex "the hard way"?

- Do we as a society focus too little or too much on sexual mechanics—sexual parts and acts? List at least six adjectives you find synonymous with *great* sex.

- How do you feel about flirting? What would be different about establishing contact and relationships if people spoke directly and objectively to one another instead of flirting? How well do you think you know the "rules" of flirting?

- If you had to lose one of your senses *for sex only*, which would it be and why? Is this the same sense you would choose to do without if it were all-encompassing? Why or why not?

- Which do you think is harder—finding a partner or keeping a relationship strong? Why?

- Why does intimacy seem more difficult to achieve now than in previous generations? If you had a time machine, would you prefer to go back in time, forward in time, or stay where you are as you search for intimacy? Explain your reasons.

 **Links: www.dushkin.com/online/**
These sites are annotated in the World Wide Web pages.

American Psychological Association
http://www.apa.org/psychnet/

Bonobos Sex and Society
http://songweaver.com/info/bonobos.html

The Celibate FAQ
http://mail.bris.ac.uk/~plmlp/celibate.html

Go Ask Alice
http://www.goaskalice.columbia.edu

Sex and Gender
http://www.bioanth.cam.ac.uk/pip4amod3.html

Most people are familiar with the term "sexual relationship." It denotes an important dimension of sexuality—interpersonal sexuality, or sexual interactions occurring between two (and sometimes more) individuals. This unit focuses attention on these types of relationships.

No woman is an island. No man is an island. Interpersonal contact forms the basis for self-esteem and meaningful living. Conversely, isolation results in loneliness and depression for most human beings. People seek and cultivate friendships for the warmth, affection, supportiveness, and sense of trust and loyalty that such relationships can provide.

Long-term friendships may develop into intimate relationships. The qualifying word in the previous sentence is "may." Today many people, single as well as married, yearn for close or intimate interpersonal relationships but fail to find them. Despite developments in communication and technology that past generations could never fathom, discovering how and where to find potential friends, partners, lovers, and soul mates is reported to be more difficult today than in times past. Fear of rejection causes some to avoid interpersonal relationships, others to present a false front or illusory self that they think is more acceptable or socially desirable. This sets the stage for a game of intimacy that is counterproductive to genuine intimacy. For others a major dilemma may exist—the problem of balancing closeness with the preservation of individual identity in a manner that satisfies the need for both personal and interpersonal growth and integrity. In either case, partners in a relationship should be advised that the development of interpersonal awareness (the mutual recognition and knowledge of others as they really are) rests upon trust and self-disclosure—letting the other person know who you really are and how you truly feel. In American society this has never been easy, and today some fear it may be more difficult than ever.

These considerations in regard to interpersonal relationships apply equally well to achieving meaningful and satisfying sexual relationships. Three basic ingredients lay the foundation for quality sexual interaction: self-awareness, understanding and acceptance of the partner's needs and desires, and mutual efforts to accommodate both partners' needs and desires. Without these, misunderstandings may arise, bringing anxiety, frustration, dissatisfaction, and/or resentment into the relationship. There may also be a heightened risk of contracting AIDS or another STD (sexually transmitted disease), experiencing an unplanned pregnancy, or experiencing sexual dysfunction by one or both partners. On the other hand, experience and research show that ongoing attention to these three ingredients by intimate partners contributes not only to sexual responsibility, but also to true emotional and sexual intimacy and a longer and happier life.

As might already be apparent, there is much more to quality sexual relationships than our popular culture recognizes. Such relationships are not established by means of sexual techniques or beautiful/handsome features. Rather, it is the quality of the interaction that makes sex a celebration of our sexuality. A person-oriented (as opposed to genitally oriented) sexual awareness, coupled with a whole-body/mind sexuality and an

open, relaxed, even playful, attitude toward exploration make for equality in sexuality.

The subsection *Establishing Sexual Relationships* opens with "The New Flirting Game," which discusses the conscious, playful side of flirting, with examples of the rules of today's flirting game for men, women, heterosexuals, gays, and lesbians, as well as what happens when one is unaware of or violates the rules. Finally "Passion Flowers" provides an imaginative and inviting look at the role passion can play in our lives.

The subsection *Responsible Quality Sexual Relationships* opens with an article whose title is an intriguing question: "Are You Connecting on the Five Levels of Sex?" After studying the article, readers will understand erotic, sensual, intimate, push-the-envelope, and spiritual sex and how to add or enhance any missing levels. "Explosive Sex: The Surprising Turn-On You Can't Ignore" addresses the emotion-laden issues of conflict in relationships and the meaning and role of "make-up sex." Next, "Satori in the Bedroom" opens readers' eyes to the potential impact of memories, fears, beliefs, and expectations on intimacy. Finally, "How to Rediscover Desire" explains how counseling or therapy can help couples who are experiencing functioning or intimacy difficulties. Readers are encouraged to use the articles in this unit as a backdrop of perspectives and experiences that can assist all of us in considering, comparing, and improving our interpersonal and/or sexual relationships.

THE NEW
Flirting Game

IT MAY BE AN AGES-OLD, BIOLOGICALLY-DRIVEN ACTIVITY, BUT TODAY IT'S ALSO PLAYED WITH ARTFUL SELF-AWARENESS AND EVEN CONSCIOUS CALCULATION.

By Deborah A. Lott

To hear the evolutionary determinists tell it, we human beings flirt to propagate our genes and to display our genetic worth. Men are constitutionally predisposed to flirt with the healthiest, most fertile women, recognizable by their biologically correct waist-hip ratios. Women favor the guys with dominant demeanors, throbbing muscles and the most resources to invest in them and their offspring.

Looked at up close, human psychology is more diverse and perverse than the evolutionary determinists would have it. We flirt as thinking individuals in a particular culture at a particular time. Yes, we may express a repertoire of hardwired nonverbal expressions and behaviors—staring eyes, flashing brows, opened palms—that resemble those of other animals, but unlike other animals, we also flirt with conscious calculation. We have been known to practice our techniques in front of the mirror. In other words, flirting

among human beings is culturally modulated as well as biologically driven, as much art as instinct.

In our culture today, it's clear that we do not always choose as the object of our desire those people the evolutionists might deem the most biologically desirable. After all, many young women today find the pale, androgynous, scarcely muscled yet emotionally expressive Leonardo DiCaprio more appealing than the burly Tarzans (Arnold Schwartzenegger, Bruce Willis, etc.) of action movies. Woody Allen may look nerdy but he's had no trouble winning women—and that's not just because he has material resources, but because humor is also a precious cultural commodity. Though she has no breasts or hips to speak of, Ally McBeal still attracts because there's ample evidence of a quick and quirky mind.

In short, we flirt with the intent of assessing potential lifetime partners, we flirt to have easy, no-strings-

attached sex, and we flirt when we are not looking for either. We flirt because, most simply, flirtation can be a liberating form of play, a game with suspense and ambiguities that brings joys of its own. As Philadelphia-based social psychologist Tim Perper says, "Some flirters appear to want to prolong the interaction because it's pleasurable and erotic in its own right, regardless of where it might lead."

Here are some of the ways the game is currently being played.

TAKING The Lead

When it comes to flirting today, women aren't waiting around for men to make the advances. They're taking the lead. Psychologist Monica Moore, Ph.D. of Webster University in St. Louis, Missouri, has spent more than 2000 hours observing women's flirting maneuvers in restaurants, singles bars and at parties. According to her findings, women give non-verbal cues that get a flirtation rolling fully two-thirds of the time. A man may think he's making the first move because he is the one to literally move from wherever he is to the woman's side, but usually he has been summoned.

By the standards set out by evolutionary psychologists, the women who attract the most men would most likely be those with the most symmetrical features or the best hip-to-waist ratios. Not so, says Moore. In her studies, the women who draw the most response are the ones who send the most signals. "Those who performed more than 35 displays per hour elicited greater than four approaches per hour," she notes, "and the more variety the woman used in her techniques, the more likely she was to be successful."

SEXUAL Semaphores

Moore tallied a total of 52 different nonverbal courtship behaviors used by women, including glancing, gazing (short and sustained), primping, preening, smiling, lip licking, pouting, giggling, laughing and nodding, as if to nonverbally indicate, "Yes! yes!" A woman would often begin with a room-encompassing glance, in actuality a casing-the-joint scan to seek out prospects. When she'd zeroed in on a target she'd exhibit the short darting glance—looking at a man, quickly looking away, looking back and then away again. There was something shy and indirect in this initial eye contact.

But women countered their shy moves with other, more aggressive and overt tactics. Those who liked to live dangerously took a round robin approach, alternately flirting with several different men at once until one responded in an unequivocal fashion. A few women hiked their skirts up to bring more leg into a particular man's field of vision. When they inadvertently drew the attention of other admirers, they quickly

pulled their skirts down. If a man failed to get the message, a woman might parade, walking across the room towards him, hips swaying, breasts pushed out, head held high.

WHO'S Submissive?

Moore observed some of the same nonverbal behaviors that Eibl-Eibesfeldt and other ethologists had deemed universal among women: the eyebrow flash (an exaggerated raising of the eyebrows of both eyes, followed by a rapid lowering), the coy smile (a tilting of the head downward, with partial averting of the eyes and, at the end, covering of the mouth), and the exposed neck (turning the head so that the side of the neck is bared).

> *Who determined that baring the neck is a sign of female submissiveness? It may have a lot more to do with the neck being an erogenous zone.*

But while many ethologists interpret these signs as conveying female submissiveness, Moore has an altogether different take. "If these behaviors serve to orchestrate courtship, which they do, then how can they be anything but powerful?" she observes. "Who determined that to cover your mouth is a submissive gesture? Baring the neck may have a lot more to do with the neck being an erogenous zone than its being a submissive posture." Though women in Moore's sample used the coy smile, they also maintained direct eye contact for long periods and smiled fully and unabashedly.

Like Moore, Perper believes that ethologists have overemphasized certain behaviors and misinterpreted them as signifying either dominance or submission. For instance, says Perper, among flirting American heterosexual men and women as well as homosexual men,

the coy smile is less frequent than direct eye contact and sustained smiling. He suggests that some cultures may use the coy smile more than others, and that it is not always a sign of deference.

In watching a flirtatious couple, Perper finds that a male will perform gestures and movements that an ethologist might consider dominant, such as sticking out his chest and strutting around, but he'll also give signs that could be read as submissive, such as bowing his head lower than the woman's. The woman may also do both. "She may drop her head, turn slightly, bare her neck, but then she'll lift her eyes and lean forward with her breasts held out, and that doesn't look submissive at all," Perper notes.

Men involved in these encounters, says Perper, don't describe themselves as "feeling powerful." In fact, he and Moore agree, neither party wholly dominates in a flirtation. Instead, there is a subtle, rhythmical and playful back and forth that culminates in a kind of physical synchronization between two people. She turns, he turns; she picks up her drink, he picks up his drink.

> *Men are able to recite in enormous detail what they do once they are in bed with a woman, but it is women who remember each and every step in the flirtation game that got them there.*

Still, by escalating and de-escalating the flirtation's progression, the woman controls the pace. To slow down a flirtation, a woman might orient her body away slightly or cross her arms across her chest, or avoid meeting the man's eyes. To stop the dance in its tracks, she can yawn, frown, sneer, shake her head from side to side as if to say "No," pocket her hands, hold her trunk rigidly, avoid the man's gaze, stare over his head, or resume flirting with other men. If a man is really dense, she might hold a strand of hair up to her eyes as if to examine her split ends or even pick her teeth.

PLANNING It Out

Do women make these moves consciously? You bet. "I do these things *incidentally* but not *accidentally*," one adept female flirter told Perper. She wanted her movements and gestures to look fluid and spontaneous but they were at least partly planned. In general, says Perper, women are more aware than are men of exactly what they do, why they do it and the effect it has. A man might simply say that he saw a woman he was attracted to and struck up a conversation; a woman would remember all the steps in the flirtation dance. "Men can tell you in enormous detail what they do once they are in bed with a woman," declares Perper. But it is the women who know how they got there.

LEARNING The Steps

If flirting today is often a conscious activity, it is also a learned one. Women pick up the moves early. In observations of 100 girls between the ages of 13 and 16 at shopping malls, ice skating rinks and other places adolescents congregate, Moore found the teens exhibiting 31 of the 52 courtship signals deployed by adult women. (The only signals missing were those at the more overt end of the spectrum, such as actual caressing.) Overall, the teens' gestures looked less natural than ones made by mature females: they laughed more boisterously and preened more obviously, and their moves were broader and rougher.

The girls clearly modeled their behavior on the leader of the pack. When the alpha female stroked her hair or swayed her hips, her companions copied quickly. "You never

see this in adult women," says Moore. "Indeed, women go to great lengths to stand out from their female companions."

Compared with adults, the teens signaled less frequently—7.6 signs per hour per girl, as opposed to 44.6 per woman—but their maneuvers, though clumsy, were equally effective at attracting the objects of their desire, in this case, teen boys.

BEYOND The Straight and Narrow

Flirting's basic purpose may be to lure males and females into procreating, but it's also an activity indulged in by gays as well as straights. How do flirting rituals compare?

Marny Hall, a San Francisco-area psychologist who's been an observer and participant in lesbian courtship, recalls that in the 1950s, gay women adhered to rigid gender-role models. Butches did what men were supposed to do: held their bodies tight, lit cigarettes with a dominating flourish, bought drinks, opened doors and otherwise demonstrated strength and gallantry. "Butches would swagger and wear chinos and stand around with one hip cocked and be bold in their gazes," she observes. "Femmes would sashay and wiggle their hips and use indirect feminine wiles."

Beginning in the late 1960s, such fixed role-playing began to dissolve. Lesbians meeting in consciousness-raising groups rejected gender assumptions. It was considered sexually attractive, says Hall, to "put yourself out without artifice, without deception." In the 90s, however, the butch-femme distinction has returned.

But with a difference. Today's lesbians have a sense of irony and wit about the whole charade that would do Mae West proud. "A butch today might flirt by saying to a femme, 'Can I borrow your lipstick? I'm trying to liberate the woman within,'" she says with a laugh. "The gender

roles are more scrambled, with 'dominant femmes' and 'soft butches.' There's more plurality and less polarization."

Male homosexuals also exhibit a wide range of flirting behaviors. In his studies, Perper has observed two gay men locked in a stalemate of sustained eye contact for 45 minutes before either made the next move. At the other end of the spectrum, he's seen gay dyads go through the entire flirtation cycle—"gaze, approach, talk, turn, touch, synchronize"—and be out the door on the way to one or the other's abode within two minutes.

In San Francisco, gay men are learning the flirting repertoire used by straight women.

The advent of AIDS and the greater societal acceptance of long-term gay attachments are changing flirtation rituals in the gay community. A sign of the times may be a courtship and dating course currently offered at Harvey Milk Institute in San Francisco. It instructs gay men in the repertoire of gestures long used by straight women seeking partners—ways of slowing down the flirtation, forestalling physical contact and assessing the other's suitability as a long-term mate. In short, it teaches homosexuals how to employ what the ethologists call a "long-term strategy."

FLIRTING Bi-Ways

When you're a crossdresser, all possibilities are open to you," says a male heterosexual who goes by the name Stephanie Montana when in female garb. In feminine persona, says Montana, "I can be more vulnerable, more animated and use more intermittent eye contact."

On one occasion Montana discovered what women seem to learn early on. A man was flirting with her, and, giddy with the attention, Montana sustained eye contact for a bit too long, gave too many overt sexual signals. In response, the man started acting in a proprietary fashion, frightening Montana with "those voracious male stares." Montana had learned the courtship signals but not the rejection repertoire. She didn't yet know how to put on the brakes.

Bisexuals have access to the entire panoply of male and female gestures. Loree Thomas of Seattle, who refers to herself as a bisexual non-op transsexual (born male, she is taking female hormones and living as a woman, but will not have a sex-change operation), has flirted *four* ways: dressed as a man interacting with men or with women, and dressed as a woman in encounters with women or men.

As a man flirting with a woman, Thomas found it most effective to maintain eye contact, smile, lean close, talk in a low voice and offer sincere compliments about the woman's best features. Man to man, says Thomas, the progression to direct physical contact accelerates. As

a woman with a woman, Thomas' flirting has been "more shy, less direct than a man would be." As a woman with a man, she's played the stereotypical female role, "asking the man questions about himself, and listening as if totally fascinated." In all cases, eye contact and smiling are universal flirtation currency.

What the experience of cross-dressers reinforces is the degree to which all flirtation is a game, a careful charade that involves some degree of deception and role-playing. Evolutionists talk about this deception in terms of men's tendency to exaggerate their wealth, success and access to resources, and women's strategic use of cosmetics and clothing to enhance their physical allure.

Some of the exhilaration of flirting, of course, lies in what is hidden, the tension between what is felt and what is revealed. Flirting pairs volley back and forth, putting out am-

biguous signals, neither willing to disclose more than the other, neither wanting to appear more desirous to the other.

To observers like Moore and Perper, flirtation often seems to most resemble the antics of children on the playground or even perhaps the ritual peek-a-boo that babies play with their caregivers. Flirters jostle, tease and tickle, even sometimes stick out a tongue at their partner or reach around from behind to cover up their eyes. As Daniel Stern, researcher, psychiatrist, and author of *The Interpersonal World of the Infant* (Karnac, 1998), has pointed out, the two groups in our culture that engage in the most sustained eye contact are mothers and infants, and lovers.

And thus in a way, the cycle of flirting takes us full circle. If flirting sets us off on the road to producing babies, it also whisks us back to the pleasures of infancy.

Reprinted with permission from *Psychology Today*, January/February 1999, pp. 42–45, 72. © 1999 by Sussex Publishers, Inc.

PASSION FLOWERS

Five extraordinary women consider the many ways in which passion has marked their lives

Be who you are and who you will be
learn to cherish that boisterous Black Angel that drives you
up one day and down another
protecting the place where your power rises running like hot blood

AUDRE LORDE

SWEET STILLNESS

By Diane McKinney-Whetstone

There is a certain shade of pink that is a bold mix of brown and red and cream. This color stops me whenever I see it, whether it's in a string of the sky at dawn or a luxurious cashmere shawl or most recently, to my husband and children's near horror, on my living-room walls. Everything about me responds to this color with a rush of movement inside that feels like thunder getting ready to roll—without the sound though, just the deep, deep sensation. Except I now know that what I'm actually feeling is a rush of stillness about to descend. And after years of spinning my wheels in the mud, I've come to realize that, for me, much passion resides in stillness.

I spent decades skirting that simple truth. I once believed that motion heaped upon motion was an indicator of how passionate I was, that I needed to be in a perpetual state of expending frenetic energy, kicking up much dust around me to prove that I was passionate about my relationships with family and friends, work, community, wherever my interests took me. But instead of experiencing the intensity of burning passion, I mostly ended up striking matches in the wind, garnering more fatigue than passion because I hadn't given myself the necessary prerequisite of having my fire lit.

For me passion is a collective response, the climactic mix of intellect and desire, mind and body that can often feel erotic, except that to relegate it only to the sexual realm misses the point. Those things we respond to with a gush of intense feeling are often fickle, impulsive. But they can still lead us to sources of contentment that become our mainstays when passion's onslaught has come and gone.

I wasn't even aware that I was about to change my life the first time I peeled myself from the warmth of my bed one predawn morning almost a decade ago and pushed through the darkness to make it downstairs without waking anybody else in the house. I just knew that everything about me from my very core responded to the velvety stillness of that morning. I wrapped myself in a flannel robe and stared out the window to witness the silent blending of night into day, and there was that perfect mix of pink edging across the back of the sky. In that moment, maybe for the first time ever, I was dripping with stillness on the inside too, meditative. And the stillness transformed me. I became open. I gathered the confidence from my response to this new absence of movement to begin to do the very thing my perpetual motion had prevented me from doing. Finally the match was lit, and I was on fire. Finally I began to do what I believed I was really meant to do, spurred on by my response to the stillness. That morning I began to write. And I wrote using all of me, using all those deep, deep sensations.

Most of my passionate responses are not as transforming. There's the first touch of chocolate-covered coconut against the tip of my tongue, the fringed lamp shade I spotted at a thrift store that is perfect against my pink living-room walls; there's the feel of a good pen between my fingers, or the rare times I've done a truly charitable thing and managed to keep it to myself. All give me that sensation of thunder about to roll, though I know that instead a stillness will descend, because for me there is so much passion in stillness, getting me ready to feel.

Diane McKinney-Whetstone is the author of three novels. Her most recent is **Blues Dancing**.

THE KISS

By Shay Youngblood

As kisses go, it was one of the longest and most illuminating. I sat on the front porch of Miss Stanley's house (where I rented a room) at dusk behind the hedge of thick shrubbery outside her bedroom window, kissing a boy I'd just met.

This is how it started. It was the first week of sophomore year, the first day of my work-study job in the college library. He was a good-looking premed student, with honey-colored eyes and a sweet smile. I'd helped him find a book. He offered to walk me home. I couldn't invite him into my room, so we sat on the front porch. We talked for a long time, whispering so our voices wouldn't carry, about where we were born and what our majors were, our favorite books, music and what foods we liked to eat. He said something that made me laugh from deep down inside, and because I was shy about the small gap in the middle of my smile, I brought my hand up to my mouth. He reached for the hand covering my mouth and stroked it, brought it up to his face and closed his eyes. He tasted the inside of my wrist as if he were hungry. I was barely breathing. He, however, took a deep breath and rubbed his face into my hand as if it were a velvet glove. This hand dance made me shiver, though it was a warm, early fall evening in the South. It was the first time so much attention had been paid to my hand. He massaged my palms, stroked each finger firmly between his thumb and forefinger. He looked into my eyes not speaking, stroking my hands as if to soothe me. As my hands relaxed, so went my arms, my shoulders—my whole body became a puddle, a lake, a river.

Night was falling around us. With his fingers he studied my face slowly, gingerly, thoroughly, as if he were having a final exam in anatomy. He wrapped his arms around me and pushed his face into my neck, planting deep kisses as if roses would grow. I was a little afraid. *What if Miss Stanley looks out her window? What if he thinks I'm fast? What if...* I pushed away every doubt or fear as quickly as it came. I let myself go, never imagining how far he would take me. He knew I was ready. He leaned in toward me and pressed his dense, buttery lips to my yielding mouth. The instant we touched there was a powerful current that connected us. My mouth was moist and receptive. At first we were waltzing—one, two, three, one, two, three—but then our passion transformed into a fiery flamenco. We kissed nonstop for an hour and 15 minutes.

This sweet, delicious pleasure was what I've come to know as a soul kiss. The entire 75 minutes were not totally focused on the sensory experience. By the time the streetlights came on, my mind began to drift. I started to think about how coming to Atlanta was a new beginning for me. I had grown up in a public-housing project and was the first person in my immediate family to graduate from high school. It had taken all my family's meager resources, a government-sponsored grant, an academic scholarship and a work-study job in the school's library to make it possible for me to attend college. I wanted to be a television journalist or an entertainment lawyer. All the desire I felt for a full, rich and happy future I put into that kiss. All my hopes for a better life had me married to this unsuspecting premed student who would be a doctor in private practice within ten years. I would be the mother of his children, and we'd live in a house in the suburbs and spend vacations in the Caribbean. I kissed him as if all my happiness were contained in that moment in the porch swing. I kissed him as if all I had was this single moment of joy. If Miss Stanley hadn't come to the front door and cleared her throat, we might still be kissing. My lips raw, my body tingling, I could still feel his hands on my face hours later as I drifted to sleep, into dreams in which I was invincible.

I did not see much of my young man in the days following our big kiss. He was absorbed with his studies, and I became interested in pursuing more creative passions. By the end of the semester I had discovered the power of poetry, other kinds of kisses, new passions that would come to consume me and make me feel as fearless as I did when I chose the longest kiss.

Author and playwright Shay Youngblood's most recent novel is **Black Girl in Paris**. *She lives in New York.*

JAGGED EDGES

By dream hampton

My love for him is wide. My soul reached out and chose him. It holds on even when I want to be free. When we come together, it is all the things I'm told are dangerous to seek. It's perfect. Every moment is a dream. It transcends who we are, the other lovers we might know. It's all things made possible. It's utterly distracting. When we make love, it feels as if he is trying to disappear inside me, as if he wants to climb inside and make me his home. When we collaborate, I can see our future, a full life of love and art and purpose. Our conversations are marked by both kindness and a deep desire to understand.

Our connectedness feels many lifetimes old, and easy. When we part, and we do, for years at a time, I have private conversations with him in my mind. I need to know if he thinks my absurd thoughts might be brilliant. I want to know if he read the same book I did, if he knows to see the movie I just loved. Walking down the street I find myself laughing aloud at some quirky observation he made nearly 18 months before. I imagine him in his apartment with his imported vinyl, or on his farm with his children. I conjure in my mind his long fingers, his light touch, his comfort with silence, his bizarre sense of humor. I keep him near me in this parallel reality because to banish him altogether would be for me a virtual death. Loving him, I've learned my passion is a boundless place, impossible to map or contain.

Unchecked, I worry: Is my passion no different than romantic obsession? Is this lover, unable to totally commit no matter how complete our love, merely living proof of my own woundedness? Can my passion weather his moodiness? I am afraid that my hunger for him is matched only by his for other women. And now I understand blues women who cut their men. Or burned them with grits. But because I know this man, because I have held his heart in my hands, I find it impossible to truly judge or be angry with him. I'm disappointed, certainly, at the reckless way he sometimes moves through life. But no more so than I am with the many ways I have betrayed and hurt the ones I truly love.

He calls my love a pretty pressure, and concedes to failure before he even gives us a chance. I accuse him of cowardice, because crippling a giant love like ours is a way to do less living. So I punish him with my absence, create distance between the nape of my neck and his kisses, as if wind could be bottled. I don't want passion that is measured by fits. I don't want to be so damn Billie. I try so hard to get it right. I try, as my therapist friends recommend, to "disentangle," and where I can manage, I do. I visualize the mature, whole relationships I'm told to want. I even make attempts at them, but it is our love, burdened by the irreversible pain we have caused each other, that occupies, as if in protest, the seat of my heart. This stormy love, this makes-me-feel-alive love, this private, nameless love, this hold-on-my-soul love.

dream hampton leads an enviably romantic life in Harlem.

THE TROUBLE WITH PASSION

By Jeannine Amber

Even when I was a kid, I was always a little *extra*. Like when I was in fourth grade and found out that my teacher, Mrs. Murakami, was returning to school after having her baby. I was so happy when I told my mother that I started to cry. Not many 8-year-olds shed tears of joy, but I couldn't help myself. No more than I could hold back from overturning the pitcher of orange juice on the kitchen table because my baby-sitter was getting on my last nerve. Or sobbing in my room for hours because my father was mad at me. Or beating my little brother over the head with the remote because I didn't like his program selection. Even as a young girl my emotions ran high, and my responses were immediate, often violent, and with complete disregard for the consequences. I was a passionate child.

As a teenager it only got worse. There were months of inconsolable sadness and reckless sex punctuated by books and telephones and ashtrays being slammed into my bedroom wall. But by then I had convinced myself it was okay, because by acting on every impulse I was simply being true to myself. I possessed a certain integrity, I was sure, that other, more repressed girls lacked.

And despite my having no particular artistic talent, I considered myself kin of every passionate painter, poet and writer. We were all loose cannons, wildly intense and, I thought, far more special than everybody else. *I can't help it*, I told myself, *if I feel too much*. On those grounds alone, I reasoned, my behavior would be absolved. So after my boyfriend suddenly got up and walked out in the middle of one of my teary monologues, I opened the kitchen cupboard and smashed every single dish in his house. And when a motorcycle-riding boy from school sent me love notes in envelopes filled with tiny dried flowers and feathers, I gave him my heart, never mind that he had a girlfriend and a baby on the way.

That's how I lived for years. From temper tantrum to love affair to broken heart to utter joy to complete collapse. But I didn't have a problem living my life guided by impulse. The problem, to paraphrase Jean Paul Sartre, was other people.

Had I been a man, it would have been different. I might have been considered sexy or a rebel or a go-getter or frightening or even powerful. And the girls would whisper, "Oh, he's so *passionate*" and try to get a date. But as a woman I was labeled crazy. *Cra-zy*. As in not sane. As in out of her mind. And crazy was one of the nicer words.

As far as I can tell, people use *crazy* as a catchall for any impassioned behavior that makes them uncomfortable: too much crying, too much yelling, too much flying off the handle, too much falling in love too quickly or carrying on with more exuberance than others think the occasion requires. Sometimes, even the ones who know me the best can barely stand it. After one particularly emotive episode, my best friend locked herself in the bathroom and then didn't speak to me for months.

I've tried to accommodate people's sensitivities, and change. I've been to half a dozen therapists, including one who charged me $175 an hour to tell me that I'm "too impulsive." I've been prescribed various "mood regulators," one of which flattened me out so much that I couldn't cry even when something really, really sad happened. I've tried to fake it, spending the whole day at work with a smile plastered on my face only to burst into tears the minute I stepped into a cab just from the sheer exhaustion of it.

But none of this really worked. And besides, who was I really doing it for anyway? Coworkers I never liked to begin with? Men who (in my view) were too uptight for words? After years of trying to temper my impassioned responses to life, I've decided that the best approach is to simply surround myself with people who feel the world as I do: men who cry over a failed relationship, women who yell when something isn't going their way. Every one of these passionate, emotional, slightly bruised and damaged souls exists on the wrong side of appropriate behavior, where no one is in a position to judge. Instead, we grant each other immunity for the hysterical 3:00 A.M. phone call, listen patiently to every last detail of some painful interaction, celebrate with great fanfare any happy occasion. But sometimes I wonder what it would be like on the other side, where life is calm and emotions are kept in check. Boring, I imagine. And to me *that* would be crazy.

Jeannine Amber is a contributing writer for ESSENCE.

I PASS ON

By Edwidge Danticat

I have often heard people say that they have a passion for life. I always wonder, if we can have such a passion for life, then why can't our life itself be our passion: the routine melody of our breath; the thump of our beating hearts; the swing of our steps; what Maya Angelou brilliantly calls our "phenomenal woman-ness"; our abilities to think, create, make decisions for ourselves and even to choose what to let go of as much as what to hold on to.

I have had to sacrifice many destructive passions to make room for other positive and lasting ones. Indeed, when I unscramble the word *Pass-I-On*, I find, among other phrases, "I pass on." Thus my passions have as much to do with the things I let go as well as those I maintain in my life.

Most days I pass on my favorite Haitian coconut-and-peanut confections in order to maintain something of a waistline. I pass on meat and shellfish, which my body in its own wisdom violently rejects in order to keep some of the density in the fragile bones I have had since adolescence. I pass on body- and spirit-breaking relationships in order to know what it is like to truly and honestly love other human beings. Unlike years ago when I pursued the friendship of people who disliked me hoping to win them over, I now concentrate my energies on the people *I* love. I would rather hear my infant niece and nephew singsong baby talk, than sit and listen to someone tear me or others down.

I pass on crippling perfectionism and simply try to do the best I can in every situation. I pass on procrastination and try to accomplish my tasks, plain and difficult ones alike, one step at a time. I pass on parties and social calls and nights out in order to write in solitude, because I find myself more at ease in imaginary landscapes. I pass on saying things I don't mean, so at least I can trust my own voice.

I never fret too much about what I am forsaking, however, because somewhere on the other side is something fundamentally life-enhancing and instructive. Even if I am momentarily leaving a true passion behind, I know that another path will return me there, for authentic passions must, and will, stand the test of time. And if I am blessed, my passion will ignite such a flame that I will ultimately, in some direct or indirect way, pass it on to others. And they, too, will do what they can and give what they have and make their own passions a loving task.

Award-winning author Edwidge Danticat's most recent novel is **The Farming of Bones**.

From *Essence*, May 2001, pp. 152-154, 156, 158, 160. © 2001 by Essence Communications, Inc. Reprinted by permission.

ARE YOU CONNECTING ON THE FIVE LEVELS OF SEX?

YOU MAY THINK YOU'RE REACHING SEXUAL PEAKS OF PLEASURE, BUT HAS YOUR BEDROOM BONDING SCORED A HIGH-FIVE? PUT YOUR RELATIONSHIP TO THE TEST TO SEE IF YOUR ACTS OF AMOUR GO TO ALL LIMITS. AFTER ALL, WHY EXPERIENCE JUST A FRACTION OF THE FUN?

BY LESLIE YAZEL

HOW ADORABLE. Now that you're solidly with your boyfriend, who everyone—including you!—agrees is amazing, all your friends feel perfectly free to tell you what they really thought of your past sex partners "Ugh, White Bread Boy?" says one. "No one had ever told him that women could have orgasms!" They all shriek with laughter. "Then there was the New Agey yoga guy who meditated to the goddess of virility," recalls another. "And don't forget that macho bartender who could only get off if he called you Mommy!" Aren't you glad you were so open with your girlfriends?

Thankfully, those days are over. You, sister, are currently creating mattress magic with a stunningly normal—yet totally sexy—man who completely adores you. The lovemaking is as amazing as he is. But now's your chance to make it even better. Since you're in such a solid and exciting matchup, you can push your sexual ticket to make your bedtime the most spontaneous, orgasmic, fantasy-fulfilling, explosively intimate sex you've ever had.

How? By exploring all five levels of sex. Experts now believe that incorporating five dimensions—erotic, sensual, intimate, daring and spiritual—into your sexual menu can make a huge difference in your relationship. "Hitting all five levels not only keeps sex feeling fresh and new, it makes you feel more emotionally connected," explains Tracey Cox, author of *Hot Relationships: How to Know What You Want, Get What You Want, and Keep It Red Hot* (Bantam Doubleday Dell) "With a little effort, all couples have the capacity to reach all five."

To score a sexual high-five with your man, read on to identify which levels you're currently connecting on and which ones need a little buffing up. Then try our suggestions to help take your lovemaking from pretty good to peel-me-off-the-ceiling status.

SEX LEVEL 1 EROTIC SEX

The last time you watched a movie lovemaking scene where a couple knocks over lamps, breaks museum-caliber Ming vases and rips expensive underwear off each other's body just to get carnal quickly, you thought (a) Looks like my sex life, or (b) Uh-oh, I hope they have a replacement bag for their Dirt Devil Hand Vac.

If you picked (b), it's probably been awhile since you had real-life erotic sex—obstacle-free horizontal hula to enjoy simply for pleasure's sake. "When I'm with my boyfriend, I feel this hunger for him that's so strong, I have to go wherever my instincts take me: I'll lick his neck or dig my fingers into his back," says Julie, 29, a sales rep in Tulsa. "The best part of this feeling is that I never worry about anything; I'm too far gone on sexual autopilot."

Julie's primal passion bubbled to the surface once she was able to ditch her inhibitions about how she might look, sound or even smell during sex. "But too many women still have their deepest instincts blocked by superficial fears—they think, If I do that, I'll look fat," observes Cox. "Others are afraid that their man will think they're dirty or sleazy, so they hold back in bed."

To unleash your erotic side, Cox recommends taking a sex sabbatical for a week or two. During that time, you and your man should agree not to have any physical contact, but you should seek out daily sex-you-up triggers, like steamy movies, flirty gestures, even racy e-mails hinting at a torrid get-together in the very near future. "After a week or two of building up sexual tension without providing for a release, your desire will be so strong, it'll overcome any self-consciousness that may be holding you back," assures Cox.

SEX LEVEL 2 SENSUAL SEX

Ask yourself: Each time you get busy, do you get naked, kiss kiss, fondle fondle, and then move on to the actual act? Or is your bedroom experience a sonic boom of sensory overload that has you practically speaking in tongues? "Sensual sex is the latter—it's lovemaking that incorporates all five senses, during which you slowly and steadily stimulate each other to intense peaks of sexual pleasure," says Cox. The advantage to your relationship? Since all that sensual exploration leads you to know his body as intimately as you know your own (and vice versa), you learn new ways to send him to Ecstasy-ville while becoming emotionally closer, too.

But before you automatically do unto him what you would like him to do to you, bear in mind that sensual sex is the one level where gender differences matter. "Ongoing research shows that women become aroused with their ears and men with their eyes," asserts Linda Banner, Ph.D., a sex therapist in San Jose, California.

That's not to say all guys only get aroused by images of Pamela Anderson Lee leaking out over her bustier, but visual stimulation is a surefire route to getting his mind off the Yankees game and on to, well, your playing field. In addition to doing the tried-and-true eye-candy tricks like undressing slowly with the lights on and giving him a show when you're on top, you might want to try a more offbeat approach like the flashlight game. Turn out all the lights, take off your clothes, then shine your flashlight on his private parts—and he'll do the same to you. Or take both flashlights and shine them on yourself. The close-up view of your body illuminated by the light will make him think he's being treated to his own private peep show.

And when it comes to the aural aspect of sex, you don't need him to imitate Barry White on Viagra to reap the benefits—many women get turned on by tuning in to their own moans and groans, says Banner. This is how Rachel, a 26-year-old researcher from Indianapolis, encourages herself to have bigger, better orgasms while making love with her live-in boyfriend. "The first time we were together, I couldn't help but let out these throaty *oohs* and *ahhs*," recalls Rachel. "Now whenever I hear myself moaning like that, I'm turned on in an almost out-

of-body way—it's as if I'm listening to some other, totally uninhibited woman getting closer and closer to orgasm—plus, it reminds me of that first night."

CELEBRITY SEX MATCH

We rate the carnal chemistry of five film couples on a scale from 1 to 10. **by Sarah Copeland**

FROM HERE TO ETERNITY

Deborah Kerr and Burt Lancaster turn a deserted beach into a steamy, slippery, full-sensory playground. EROTIC: **1**; SENSUAL: **9**; INTIMATE: **8**; PUSH-THE-ENVELOPE: **2**; SPIRITUAL: **6**

GHOST

Nothing could stop the clay-smeared passion of Demi Moore and Patrick Swayze—not even his death. EROTIC: **6**; SENSUAL: **7**; INTIMATE: **8**; PUSH-THE-ENVELOPE: **3**; SPIRITUAL: **9**

THE ENGLISH PATIENT

Ralph Fiennes and Kristin Scott Thomas have a love affair steamier than the desert backdrop on their mapmaking expedition. EROTIC: **7**; SENSUAL: **4**; INTIMATE: **9**; PUSH-THE-ENVELOPE: **7**; SPIRITUAL: **8**

REINDEER GAMES

Ben Affleck's caged-up desire is finally freed when he and Charlize Theron engage in some fall-out-of-bed savage shagging. EROTIC: **10**; SENSUAL: **6**; INTIMATE: **5**; PUSH-THE-ENVELOPE: **7**; SPIRITUAL: **0**

COMMITTED

The sensual synergy of Goran Visnjic's hands-only approach leaves Heather Graham shivering in the front seat of her car. EROTIC: **3**; SENSUAL: **9**; INTIMATE: **4**; PUSH-THE-ENVELOPE: **2**; SPIRITUAL: **8**

SEX LEVEL 3 INTIMATE SEX

The word *intimate* has gotten a bad rap. It now implies being so comfortable that he'll show you that nasty boil on his back, and you'll go to bed with zit medicine on. And the words *intimate sex* are couple code for same-old sex, the kind that long-term sweethearts gripe about and brand-new daters pray that they can avoid like an incurable STD. "But preconceptions aside, intimate sex is actually one of the most passionate types two people can experience, since it's all about deep connection and trust," explains Cox. And this dimension of lovemaking does not have to depend on how long you've been together. "My current boyfriend and I have only known each other for six months, but we're incredibly close in bed—a kind of closeness I now realize I never achieved with the live-in boyfriend I had all through my twenties," remarks Juliette, 30, a paralegal from Washington, D.C.

Although adding an intimate facet to your sex life doesn't require a long-term bond, it does take a fairly unguarded heart. To get emotions to rise to the surface, think of things only the two of you share, like relationship rituals or goofy jokes. Or concentrate on the character quirks that made you fall for him in the first place. "Before my boyfriend and I began dating, he would come into the ice cream store where I worked and order cup after cup of ice cream, never getting up the nerve to ask me out," recalls Heather, a 24-year-old M.B.A. student. "Every time I remember his shy, geeky way of getting to know me, I feel this intense rush of love for him and a need to be physically close."

But just because you're craving physical contact doesn't mean you should drag him straight to the bedroom and jump his bones. Instead, translate your feelings into touches with small, simple gestures—brushing his hair with your fingertips while you two are entwined on the couch; holding him in bed as he blows off steam about his ogre of a boss. Once you've fully connected—and your libidos are ready for lift-off—try sex positions that closely align your bodies, like missionary or spooning. Cox also suggests licking hands and pausing midpassion just to hug and kiss. It may seem kind of corny, but it'll keep you on the same "I'm so glad we're together" wavelength.

SEX LEVEL 4 PUSH-THE-ENVELOPE SEX

If you don't remember the last time you giggled to yourself in the heat of the horizontal moment thinking, I can't believe we're doing this crazy thing, you may lack a little envelope-pushing in your love life. But that doesn't mean one of you has to don a rubber suit while the other swings from the ceiling trying to press record on the video camera. Push-the-envelope sex is about pushing your own sexual boundaries with a sense of playfulness and humor—not about acting out someone else's definition of kinky.

But even in this age of anything-goes-as-long-as-it's-legal loving, many women are afraid their partner will view them as weird if they propose a night of role-playing, sex in a public place or renting a softcore porno flick. "Women are still raised with this sense that 'good girls don't' when it comes to anything

outside what's considered 'normal' sex," explains Banner. "But guys love it when a woman suggests something new—he won't think you're weird, he'll be turned on by your boldness and sense of adventure."

Jamie, a 30-year-old writer from New Jersey, learned this firsthand when she finally gathered the courage to hint to her fiancé about her longtime silk-scarf fantasy. "I'd always thought that the most sexually thrilling thing would be to be blindfolded with a silk scarf and then slowly licked and teased to orgasm," recalls Jamie. "Finally, I'd met a man I trusted enough to indulge in that fantasy with me. So I brought it up one day by musing, 'You won't believe the crazy dream I had last night....' Then I described exactly what I wanted him to do to me. He got the hint—and later that night, I got my fantasy fulfilled."

SEX LEVEL 5 SPIRITUAL SEX

If you're like most women, you associate the word *spiritual* more with receiving communion than with tireless carnality. But spiritual sex has nothing to do with organized religion or even New Agey things like chanting or creating a shrine at the foot of your bed. "Incorporating spirituality into your sex life means you transcend concerns and worries about your physical selves to focus on the mingling of your inner selves, your souls," explains Rabbi Shmuley Boteach, author of *Dating Secrets of the Ten Commandments* (Doubleday).

"I know this sounds kind of hokey, but right before I reach orgasm, my body begins to open up in such a way that I feel like it's uniting with my husband's body," marvels Kelly, 32, a nurse in New York City. "Joined to him for a few moments like that, I feel this sense of blissful inner peace—as if everything is right with the world. I'm not a religious person, but I would definitely describe this feeling as otherworldly."

To prime your bodies for this divine type of passion, first clear your mind of nagging, day-to-day clutter. Next, Boteach recommends having sex in positions that afford plenty of eye contact—like missionary and girl-on-top. "Our eyes are the windows to our souls," he says, "so locking them with your lover's is critical to spiritually connecting." Boteach also advises lots of kissing: "Kissing is an opening up of one person's body to another's, a sharing of life breath." Finally, settle into one or two or three lovemaking positions that press your bodies close together—like missionary—so that as your passion grows, your bodies truly begin to feel as if they're melding into one, he says.

Explosive SEX:
The surprising TURN-ON
You can't ignore

EVEN HAPPILY MARRIED COUPLES FIGHT.
BUT REALLY HAPPY COUPLES KNOW HOW TO KISS AND MAKE UP AFTERWARD.
HERE, (ARE) 7 WAYS TO HAVE THE BEST MAKE-UP SEX OF YOUR LIFE.

By Susan Crain Bakos

The two of you have had an argument. You're still mad, but he's not—and he wants to make up by making love. Fat chance: You cross your arms in front of your chest and stand firm, unmoved by the tender kisses he attempts to plant on the back of your neck. "How could he think he's getting sex *now*?" you wonder. You're not alone: In a poll on *Redbook*'s website, 72 percent of female respondents said they withhold sex from their husbands when they fight.

Maybe you should open your arms and embrace your man instead of pushing him away. Making love is not an admission that you're wrong and he's right. It's an acknowledgment and a celebration of the love you share even in times of discord. "If you can be angry at your partner one minute and aroused by him the next," says Diane Andoscia Urso, a couples therapist in New York, "you've got a vital and healthy relationship."

I know, I know: You're worried that if you make love after a fight, he'll think he's won—that in his mind make-up sex means never having to work things out. Not so, say the experts. If he's thinking about the argument at all, he's probably thinking, "If we're making love, it means she still loves me," not "I win, she loses."

"He's not using sex to distract you," says Urso. "He's reaching for you out of love and a need for acceptance. Ten minutes after the shouting, he's already past the argument. Women hold on to anger longer than men do. We could learn from them how to let it go."

Besides, what earthly good does it do you to withhold sex? You don't get your own sexual needs met, you cut yourself off from intimacy with your partner, and you perpetuate a climate of ill will that encourages more fighting. Lovemaking is a way for the two of you to reconnect on an intimate level, whether or not you've resolved your dispute.

One important caveat: Fights over infidelity, alcohol or drug abuse, one partner's extreme financial irresponsibility, or other serious issues aren't likely to lead to great sex and an afterglow of warm feelings. "If the fighting has escalated into verbal or physical abuse, or you only have sex after a pitched battle, your marriage needs professional help," cautions Urso.

For garden-variety fights, though—disputes over household chores, child care duties, budgeting, in-laws—make-up sex has the power to heal emotional wounds. "These ongoing issues may never be satisfactorily resolved," says Urso, "but good sex can really take the edge off them."

Here, [are] seven make-up-sex strategies that have worked for wives who've found that it's better to give (and receive!) than to withhold.

1. LET YOUR ANGER AROUSE YOU

For many couples an argument is verbal foreplay; they're sexually aroused by debate. This isn't surprising. The adrenaline rush accompanying mild anger creates a response in the brain that is similar to sexual arousal. To use that rush to your advantage, avoid uttering the harsh words and accusations that turn a little fight into a big standoff. Don't be cruel to each other. Instead, feel the erotic possibilities in the energy pulsing through your angry body.

"He'll stop in the middle of a sentence and say, 'Your skin glows when you're angry' or 'Your nipples are hard under that shirt.' It turns me on. The adrenaline is pumping, and so are the sex hormones. I like knowing I can completely break his concentration by putting my hands on my hips and thrusting my chest out."

—Gina, 33

"When we fight we have to stand toe-to-toe and stage-whisper so we won't wake the baby. His lowered voice and the proximity of his body to mine is exciting. I can't help myself. I want to kiss his Adam's apple."

—Andrea, 29

2. TAKE A LAUGH BREAK

Laughter is healing. It can also be erotic, like champagne bubbles bursting in the brain. So laugh with each other—but not *at* each other.

"After a fight he'll say something funny, usually at his own expense. He can tell how ready I am to forgive and forget by whether I give him a thin smile or a real laugh. If I laugh he'll pull me into his arms and nuzzle my neck. Then he licks inside my ear with the tip of his tongue. That always makes me shiver and giggle. If he only gets a smile, he'll make another joke to loosen me up. He could be a stand-up comic."

—Jenna, 31

"Mark is more inclined to pout after a fight than I am. I'm the one who wants to make up with sex. I tickle him. He pushes my hand away, but not too forcefully. I tickle him again. He tickles back. We play like kids until one of us reaches inside the other's clothing to tickle bare skin. That does it! Once our hands are on each other's bodies, we can't stay mad about anything."

—Christine, 37

3. CLOSE WITHOUT CLOTHES

Some women need to make a closing "anger statement" before they can move on to lovemaking. Keep it brief. Give him encouragement with your eyes as you express your feelings. End by saying in a suggestive tone of voice, "But we can talk about it another time"—a sentence men always love to hear.

"I always have to get the last word in (I'm a lawyer). That doesn't mean I'll get my way. The last word is my summary statement, my last chance to clinch an argument. He might find this behavior obnoxious if I didn't undress him with my eyes while I'm talking."

—Deborah, 34

"I tell him, 'I want to make love to you, but I need a few minutes to speak my mind without interruption.' I stand across the room from him so he has to watch but can't reach out and touch. And I start undressing while I speak. He doesn't interrupt; I shut up when I'm naked. I feel a little bit exhibitionistic—but I have the power again."

—Kim, 32

4. ESTABLISH A MAKE-UP RITUAL

The make-up ritual, a bridge between anger and loving, is a way of calling a truce. It can be as simple as taking a shower together or exchanging shoulder rubs. Both of you recognize that it also means no more arguing.

"Rob does something for me without being asked—even if I'm the one who's more at fault. He makes tea or pours a glass of wine. Maybe he'll go out into the garden and pick a rose. His offering signals a cease-fire, and my gracious acceptance of his gift says, 'Me, too.' Recently he brought me the last dish of chocolate ice cream, significant because we'd been fighting about doing the shopping. We shared the ice cream, feeding each other with the same spoon. Afterward we kissed, and his mouth was sweet and cold. I asked him to suck my nipples before he warmed up."

—Tracey, 29

"Before we were married, we ended an argument about our wedding plans by taking a nude midnight swim in the pool at his apartment building. He dared me, and I did it. We had sex in the pool. After the wedding we moved to California, and we ended our first big argument by taking another nude swim—in the ocean this time—and having sex on the beach. Now we have little kids and can't throw our clothes off to go out and play. But we still have a water-

therapy ritual: We take a cool shower or bath together, and I cuddle against him until we generate some heat."

—Carolyn, 38

5. TAKE A TIME-OUT

Many angry women need a time-out after a fight. Take 15 or 30 minutes, even an hour alone to take a walk, exercise, bathe, or read—any activity that restores your equilibrium. Don't promise sex when the break is over, but let him know you're receptive to affection by being the one to give the first hug.

"I need more time to get over a fight than he does. He takes the kids; I get on the treadmill. Working up a good sweat gets rid of my residual anger and makes me feel sexy at the same time."

—Jeanette, 35

"I've learned from experience that we'll both feel better if we have sex soon after a fight. When he starts making up to me, I tell him I need a bubble bath if I'm not feeling warm toward him yet. I lock the bathroom door and soak. When I get out of the tub, I rub expensive perfumed cream into my skin. I only use the good stuff at times like this, and I take my time applying it to my breasts and thighs—almost like masturbating, but not quite."

—Angie, 39

6. GIVE A VIRTUOSO LOVEMAKING PERFORMANCE

Sex, especially make-up sex, isn't always an emotionally intense experience. Use the distance you feel between you to practice virtuoso lovemaking, the kind of performance that improves with a certain degree of distance. Pull out all the stops and remind him of what he could miss if he ever makes you *really* mad.

"After one big fight, I gave him the best blow job he ever had. I used all the strokes I learned from books, keeping my mouth in constant motion. He was so knocked out, he sent flowers to my office the next day and brought roses home, too."

—Annette, 34

"I hate to admit it when I'm wrong. I'd much rather come on like a courtesan than apologize. I do the things he really loves but doesn't get very often, like masturbating for him while he watches, playing bondage games with him, or dressing up in a bustier, stockings, and a garter belt. Putting on an outfit is good for make-up sex when I'm having trouble getting past the

fight. I pretend I'm someone else, a woman who isn't annoyed at him. It works for both of us."

—Lisa, 37

7. MAKE HIM WORSHIP YOU

If make-up sex still seems like something you're doing for *him*, turn lovemaking into your special-request session. Ask him for extended foreplay, an erotic massage—whatever you want, you can probably get it now. Assume the goddess position and expect worship.

"If I'm still a little mad at him, he knows what he has to do to get me hot. He gives me long, slow kisses, without too much tongue. When I'm ready for him to move down my body, I take his head in my hands and guide him to a breast. After he's sucked and licked my nipples to my satisfaction, I tweak his ears. On that signal he kisses his way down to my inner thighs and licks, strokes, and sucks. One intense orgasm, and I'm not mad at him anymore."

—Tiffany, 33

"He knows he has to come to me and make me want it. One night I went to bed still irritated with him. After I lay down, I turned my back on him. In a little while I felt him duck under the sheet. Then he parted my legs with his head. I pretended to ignore him, but I didn't push him away—or smash his head between my thighs. For a long time he just used the tip of his tongue and his fingers. He had me begging for it."

—Dana, 32

"He worships me, sometimes by doing something kinky, like sucking my toes. This is very effective because most of the time we're each pretty determined to keep the equality in our marriage. Once, after we'd yelled at each other, I was sitting in a chair, pretending to read. He crawled over to me and, on his knees, began to massage my legs, starting with the calves. Then he asked permission to take off my slacks. I gave it to him."

—Abby, 35

Satori IN THE BEDROOM

TANTRA AND THE DILEMMA OF WESTERN SEXUALITY

by Katy Butler

Freud once said that four people—two mothers, two fathers—lie in bed with every couple making love. If only that were all. Hugh Hefner is under the covers with us, and Carl Djerassi, who invented the birth control pill, and Alex Comfort, who wrote *The Joy of Sex*. Shere Hite is there taking notes, and a doctor from the Centers for Disease Control, and Pope John Paul II and Kenneth Starr. Cindy Crawford's perfect body may float in space above us, or Long Dong Silver's, daring us to turn on the light and look at how we don't measure up.

• When a man sleeps with a woman, he sleeps with her past as well, including her memories of pregnancy, date rape, abandonment or shame. When a woman sleeps with a man, she sleeps with the young boy caught reading his father's *Playboy* magazines and the teenager in the back seat, expected to know everything without being shown. Each of us in the industrialized West carries into the bedroom not only personal memories, but collective ones: we are layered with exhortations, like sedimentary rock. Sex, the Victorians told our great-grandmothers, is dirty: Save it for the one you love. The mature female orgasm, said Freud, is the vaginal orgasm: That comes only to women who resolve their penis envy. Women's sexuality, said the marriage manuals of the 1950s, is problematic, like the delicate wiring of an old MG: Husbands must be master mechanics. Vaginal orgasm is a myth, said the feminist theorists of the 1980s. Find the clitoris. Now.

Sleeping around will ruin your reputation, we were told in the fifties: Why buy the cow when you can get the milk through the fence? Sleeping around will free you, we were told in the sixties: Smash monogamy. Men and women are pretty much alike, we were told in the seventies. Men are from Mars, women are from Venus, we are told today.

Many of us enter the bedroom now as if we have been told we are about to play a high-stakes game. There is no rule book, or else it's been hidden. Everyone else, we think, knows how to play. We charge down the field. We pass the ball. A whistle blows. The rules have changed. The teams are being shuffled. We'll be playing with a shuttlecock now instead of a ball, and the goalposts have been moved to the other end of the field. We start running and the crowd roars, but we're not sure what we did right. Now we are on the bottom of a pile of bodies. We are given five different rule books and told to choose one that suits us. (We have no idea what book the other team is playing from.) Bleeding from the shin, we strap on our battered equipment again and once more run down the field.

We lie down with all of this, and more, when we lie down in bed with each other. We sleep with the war between men and women fueled by patriarchy and differences in physiology, and with the uneasy cease-fire in the erogenous zone that followed the feminist and sexual revolutions. We sleep with the legacy of the 1970s, when you could find, on many a middle-class nightstand, the dry,

clinical bestsellers of William Masters and Virginia Johnson, the pioneers of behavioral sex therapy. The bright lights of their science were supposed to banish our fears and superstitions, like crucifixes held before a vampire. Yet the fear of pleasure, and of being discovered having pleasure, still runs beneath our bedroom floors like an underground river.

For most of us, our first sexual act was also an act of secret rebellion against our parents. The memory of this defiant split lives on in our cells in the disembodied, suppressed yet obsessed way our culture approaches sex today. Few of our fathers talked to their sons about how to enhance a woman's pleasure or prolong their own; few of our mothers ever told their daughters about the delights or even the location of the clitoris. We found out anyway, and paid the price.

> **W**hen a woman lies down in bed with a man, a light show of images plays over her body without her knowing it. When a man lies down with a woman, she wonders how he will look as a hero.

In the dark recesses of our mental closets lies a negative cultural dowry—the muumuus that missionaries gave the naked Polynesians; the *penitentes'* cat-o'-nine-tails; the chastity belt; and the confessional—all the trappings of the

Augustinian Catholic tradition that declared sex a dirty distraction on the path to God and the source of original sin. ("As the caterpillar chooses the fairest leaves to lay her eggs on," wrote the poet William Blake two centuries ago, "so the priest lays his curse on the fairest joys.") All of this we bring into the bedroom.

W*e lie in bed with each other, reaching for pleasure, tenderness and connection, with both too much and too little to guide us. Yet sometimes we do get it right.*

When we sleep with each other, we sleep with images we've absorbed and, without knowing it, those our lovers have absorbed as well. Like fast food, images of other people's orgasms, stripped of context and connection, are now available 24 hours a day and consumed alone and on the cheap. They demand of us a bravado we rarely feel. They lurk eternally on the Internet and in the phone-sex banks, at the corner video store and in the *Congressional Record.* Our bedrooms are colonized by them. When a woman lies down in bed with a man, a light show of images plays over her body without her knowing it: red-satin garter belts, perhaps, or beaver shots or Marilyn Chambers or Monica Lewinsky or the *Penthouse* Pet of the Month. When a man lies down with a woman, images of imaginary men play over his face without his knowing it—the hero of Tristan and Iseult, perhaps, or a Tammy Wynette song or a romance novel. No wonder we feel split within ourselves and from each other. We expect sexualized romantic love to carry a greater psychological burden than does any other culture on earth while we simultaneously denigrate the sexual. And so we reverberate between sexual obsession and sexual shame.

Last September, we found on our doorsteps newspapers full of the details of the president's intimacies with Monica Lewinsky—the thong underwear, the cigar, the joke sunglasses, the rejected girl crying in the rain. It didn't matter what the details were or the context in which they occurred. All that mattered was the telling of them. Opening the paper, some of us imagined how our own intimacies would read some morning, printed in black and white and dumped on our neighbors' doorsteps.

What we read in the papers that day reflected the impoverished language we bring to sex. In 1931, the English novelist Virginia Woolf wrote in *The Waves,* "I need a little language such as lovers speak, words of one syllable." But we can speak of lovemaking everywhere except the bedroom. For the delicate skin that touches our lover's most tender places, we have no words except the pornographic, the childlike and the scientific. We speak of vaginas, labiae, clitorises, cunts, hair pies and "down there." We call it a prick, a dick, a sledgehammer, a penis, a pee pee or Mr. Happy. Our worst insults are sexual: *cunt, slut, whore, dickhead, pussy-whipped, cocksucker.*

And so we lie in bed with each other, reaching for pleasure, tenderness and connection, with both too much and too little to guide us: *Hustler* on the newsstand, Dr. Ruth or Dr. Laura on the radio and *Debbie Does Dallas* on the VCR. "You do not have to be good," wrote the poet Mary Oliver. "You do not have to walk on your knees for a hundred miles through the desert, repenting. You only have to let the soft animal of your body love what it loves." But that's a big *only.* No wonder we are sure that someone, somewhere, is having better sex than we are. No wonder someone, somewhere is pretending to have better sex than we are. No wonder we fear we will never get it right.

Y ET SOMETIMES WE DO GET IT RIGHT— or it gets us right. Many of us have experienced something in bed that the languages of pornography, sex therapy, feminism and the double standard could not contain. It might have been the afternoon we washed our partner from head to toe in the shower, kneeling under the spray to scrub even the soles of her feet, until washing became a ritual of tenderness and awareness. It might have been a dawn when we woke from a dream experiencing what the radical psychoanalyst Wilhelm Reich called a "full-body orgasm," in which we were the wave and also a body drifting at the water's edge, pulsating to our fingertips as the wave broke on the shore. It might have been a night a man looked into our eyes and stroked our nipples for hours until we gave in to our own responses rather than following what we imagined to be his timetable. Or a night a woman looked into our eyes while we were coming and we felt safe, seen and known.

In these moments, lovemaking is sensed as healing, wholesome and holy. Our focus broadens out beyond orgasm. Our small selves are no longer in command, and we give ourselves over, little boats on a deep river. The fear of not performing well disappears, the ghosts are banished from the bedroom and the present moment absorbs us. The West's self-created divisions—between sacred and profane, heart and pelvis, male and female, victim and predator, body and soul—are temporarily healed. We understand what Walt Whitman meant when he wrote, "If anything is sacred, the human body is sacred," and what the 16th-century Anglican marriage ceremony meant when it included among its vows, "With my body, I thee worship." Our bedroom is no longer hostage to the porn palace, the sex lab or the unfinished war between men and women. For a moment, the bedroom becomes a ritual space where we enter trance and forget time.

For most of us, such moments are rare and random, despite the mixed sexual blessings of the past three decades. The sexual revolution rightly told us that sex could be a domain of pleasure and self-expression. But its prescription—quantity over quality—did not free us. The feminist revolution challenged the practice of sex as a ritual of loving female submission and encouraged women to speak of their sexual desires and sexual violations. It lit up ancient chasms between the genders, but did not bridge them.

Modern sex therapy helped thousands with simple, effective behavioral techniques, usually focused narrowly on achieving erection, intercourse or orgasm. Yet few of us have much of a clue about continuing to create the more profound joys of sexuality—especially after the first six months to two years of a relationship, when hormones subside and desire fades. We may move from arousal to contentment or indifference or contempt. We may not know how to contend with softer, slower erections and other changes related to aging. A surprising number of stable couples stop making love much, or altogether. The ghosts return to the bedroom. We may lie down in resignation in the bed we've made together, or walk once more out the door.

O R NOT. SOME OF US WILL EMBARK instead on a quest for a fuller experience of intimate sexuality. We will use whatever tools we can, depending on who we are and the decade in which we set out. We may enter Reichian therapy, wrap ourselves in Saran wrap, read Nancy Friday, follow The Rules, or repeat phrases from *Men Are From Mars, Women Are From Venus*, but we will not give up. We want to banish the bedroom's ghosts or at least replace them with more benign presences. Risking the humiliation our culture visits on those who speak of their own sex lives rather than other people's, we will try to decolonize the bedroom. We sense that this quest requires not "more of the same"—not more sexual perfectionism or ever-more-exotic partners or positions—but a broader context, a change at the metalevel. If we embark on this quest today, we may buy a book, watch a video or go to a weekend workshop on Tantrism, which is now the West's most popular form of adult sex education.

Presaged by the popularity in the 1960s of the *Kama Sutra* of Vatsyayana, a 3rd-century Indian sex manual, Tantra has become a postmodern hybrid. On the most prosaic level, it is nothing more than a pastiche of positive sexual attitudes and techniques drawn from Western humanistic psychology, Chinese Taoist sexology and classical Indian Tantrism—a wild sexual and religious tradition that influenced both Buddhism and Hinduism and flourished in India about 500 A.D.

This esoteric system used breath, visualization and other yogas to arouse, channel and transform energy throughout the body. Its meditations often took the form of visualizing gods and goddesses in sexual union. In India, adherents of the tiny sect of "left-handed" Tantra took things a

step further: in secret rituals, they broke all the rules of their caste-bound society, consuming taboo foods, such as alcohol and meat, sounding yogic *bijas* or sacred syllables and coupling with one partner after another. In contrast to monastic traditions that suppressed sexuality and avoided women, *Tantrikas* welcomed the energies of aggression and sexuality and transformed them. Men did not ejaculate, and the goal was to move arousal up the spine to the brain in an explosion of enlightenment and bliss. Sex was not a dirty detour from the path to God, it was the path.

Today, Tantra's esoteric practices are being pressed into the service of goals that are tamer, more domestic and less religious: uniting sexuality and intimacy, and enhancing sexual pleasure for long-term couples. It's not the techniques that count so much as Tantra's enlargement of the context in which sex is held—as pleasurable, inclusive, healing, and holy. This widening of the lens was apparent as soon as modern Tantrism first registered on the American cultural radar in 1989, when a 450-page book called *The Art of Sexual Ecstasy: The Path of Sacred Sexuality for Western Lovers* tried to sweep the clutter of negative sexual images out of the Western bedroom. Written by Margo Anand, a writer and sex workshop leader who had studied psychology at the Sorbonne and meditation in India, it was like no sex manual the West had ever seen. She spent eight pages alone describing how to prepare a bedroom as a "sacred place," Anand wrote. Vacuum the bedroom and take out the newspapers and coffee cups. Bring in plants, flowers and candles. Drape a scarf over the bedside lamp to create soft lighting. Walk three times around the room with your partner, misting the air with a plant sprayer of scented water while saying "As I purify this space, I purify my heart." This, Anand implied, was as much a part of sex as kissing.

The suggestions might seem impossibly precious. But ceremonially cleaning the bedroom and bringing in flowers and soft light contained a metamessage: You do not have to go somewhere else or become a sliver of yourself to have sex. You don't have to "do the nasty" while hiding in the dark from your disapproving parents. When you bring flowers into the bedroom, you bring in more of yourself as

well, and that can make you realize how much you had previously left outside the bedroom door. And if the bedroom is already inhabited by ghosts, why not bring in flowers as well?

In the place of pornographic slang and Latin words, Anand suggested Taoist phrases that were free of negative Western sexual connotations. Try saying "jade stalk" or "wand of light" for penis, she suggested; for vagina, substitute "cinnabar cave" or "valley of bliss." Or call them "yonis" and "lingams," after the Sanskrit words used to describe the stone sculptures of sexual organs that are still bedecked with flowers and worshiped in rural temples in India. "Behold the Shiva Lingam, beautiful as molten gold, firm as the Himalaya Mountain," she quoted the "Linga Purana," a Hindu ode to the penis of the god Shiva, Lord of the Dance. "Tender as a folded leaf, life-giving like the solar orb; behold the charm of his sparkling jewels!" It was heady stuff for a culture where "testosterone poisoning" is a running joke and the only goddess worshiped is a virgin mother. And it cleared the decks for something new.

Anand and other teachers of modern Tantra suggested that sex could involve all of us, including the warring inner parts we think we've transcended but have merely avoided: the lustful and soulful; the wounded and voracious; the slutpuppy in her Victoria's Secret lingerie and the good girl in her flannel nightie; the sensitive postfeminist man and the crude teenage boy.

Last October, at a five-day, $795-a-person workshop for couples at the Esalen Institute, yoga and Tantra teacher Charles Muir wove these warring inner and outer sexual worlds together. On the first night, he spoke about his own sexual upbringing to 23 couples sitting before him in a circle. His listeners ranged in age from 22 to 73. Among them were two Latin American academics, four lawyers, a black woman doctor, two construction managers, two women who worked in television, several massage therapists from the Esalen staff and an Irish farmer. Some sat as entwined with their partners as trailing vines, while others betrayed, in their gestures and body language, uneasiness with each other and an inequality of love or desire.

Muir, who is now separated from his wife and coteacher, Caroline (she wanted sexual fidelity; he didn't), runs the Source School of Tantra in Maui, Hawaii, and leads frequent workshops around the country. He was wearing a silk shirt and an amethyst pendant. He was slim, in his early fifties, with brown hair, protuberant eyes and spatulate fingers that gave him the look of an elongated frog. His language was closer to New York street than Hindu temple.

By emphasizing energy and context, the workshop provided something usually missing from standard-issue sex—love, sensuous touching and intimacy.

He had come of age in the Bronx, he said, during "The Great F— Drought of the Fifties." Everything he knew about sex, he said, he had learned from Johnny Patanella, the leader of his childhood street gang: *Get it up, get it in, and get it off. F— 'em hard and f— 'em deep.* Muir said that before he discovered Tantra, he was a yogi on the mat and a "sleaze-bucket" in bed. He said that men give nicknames to their penises because they want to be on a first-name basis with the one who makes all their important decisions.

There were shocked laughs, a snigger. The men thought they were long past this. The women didn't want to think their men had ever thought this way.

But there was a method to his crudeness. Once Muir bonded with the part of the men that had eternally remained the teenage boy, he gently, without emasculating them, brought them into the sexual realm of context, emotion, feeling and intimacy traditionally defined as female. "In lovemaking, women lead with their hearts," he went on more softly. "Men lead with their second chakra [their groins]. We hurt each other."

Tantra, Muir said, could help them make love stay. "The average couple makes love 2.3 times a week for the first two years," he said. "After two years, the average couple makes love once a week—

and making love can be a well of energy and healing.

"Chemistry is temporary. You're going to learn to base love not on chemistry—which lasts six months or two years, if you're lucky—but on alchemy. When the chemistry is no longer there, alchemy says you take what is there and you change it. Become a master alchemist."

EASIER SAID THAN DONE, GIVEN SOME of the histories that the couples revealed in private conversations. One couple came to Esalen to put the "pizzazz" back in their marriage; later they acknowledged they'd hardly made love in the nine years since the birth of their son.

Paula, a Mexican American academic in her fifties who was there with Carlos, the professor with whom she lived, had not had an orgasm in the year since her hysterectomy. She had been raised a Catholic and was date raped in college. She still couldn't shake off a notion her mother had given her—that only bad girls are good at giving men sexual pleasure; at night, she still put on her pajamas behind the bathroom door. Carlos was in his forties; he had been divorced twice and had been raped and tortured a decade earlier in a South American prison.

Russ Solomon, a retired San Diego real estate developer, had raised four children with his wife, Liz, during 40 years of marriage. They looked as comfortable together as old shoes and clearly liked and respected each other. But sex, they said, had been disappointing on their wedding night when they'd both been virgins and disappointing ever since. "All I knew," Russ told me one day, "was that I was to get my penis in her vagina and that was it." He had lain back, expecting Liz to arouse and satisfy him.

She said nothing that night, and nothing for many nights to come. She had no language then, no woman had language then for what she felt or wanted. "When you were born in 1937," she says, "it wasn't your place to show him."

Since then, they had rarely taken more than 15 minutes to make love. She spoke frequently, in front of Russ, of "40 years of shit and disappointment in the bedroom." Russ didn't treat her like a woman, didn't measure up. "I would love a flower on the pillow or a note,"

she said one day. "But Russ cuts articles out of the newspaper that he thinks I would be interested in. And I am. But it's not the intimacy I long for."

Couples like these could have taken their "sexual dysfunctions" and marital issues into the private confines of a sex therapist's office. But they were seeking something that Western sex therapy, for all its strengths, does not provide. Sex therapy's pioneers, Masters and Johnson, had brought thermometers, charts and transparent vaginal probes mounted with tiny video cameras to the study of sex. Sexual problems, they argued, weren't usually rooted in intractable intrapsychic or interpersonal conflict; they could often be solved by learning new behaviors. They, and those who followed them, taught women to masturbate to orgasm and men to squeeze their penises just below the coronal ridge, before they reached the "point of no return," to resolve premature ejaculation. Their techniques often worked with amazing ease, and they drained sex of some of its shaming power by making things seem as brisk, practical and scientific as a good recipe for apple pie.

But they also drained sex of magic. If their governing metaphor was the bedroom-as-medical-lab and sexual practice an antiseptic medical-behavioral prescription, Muir's guiding metaphor at Esalen was the bedroom as temple and sexual practice as worship. And if sex therapy was predicated on healing people so that they could have sex with each other, Muir suggested that sexual pleasure itself could be healing.

In the course of the week, Muir gasped, held his breath, bugged out his eyes to demonstrate how men could use yogic breathing, pauses in lovemaking and finger pressure on their perineums to delay or forgo ejaculation. He and his coteacher, yoga practitioner Diane Greenberg showed women how to take a man's "soft-on" and "use it like a paintbrush" to stimulate their clitorises and outer lips, or stuff it softly into the vagina. And he extolled the sensual pleasures of the half-erect penis. Referring to the *Kama Sutra*, he talked of varying strokes, pressure and speed. "If we go straight down the fairway—deep deep deep—we'll only be stimulating one area, guys," he said one afternoon, strok-

THE EVOLUTION OF **MODERN Sex Therapy**

TWENTY YEARS AFTER THE SEXUAL revolution, in the most sexually explicit culture in the world, a surprisingly large number of people continue to have difficulties with the sexual basics. *The Social Organization of Sexuality*, a statistically balanced 1994 survey of the sexual habits of 3,432 Americans, found that 24 percent of the women questioned had been unable to have an orgasm for at least several months of the previous year. Another 18.8 percent of the women (24 percent of those over 55) reported trouble lubricating; 14 percent had had physical pain during intercourse; and 11 percent were anxious about their sexual performance. Equally high proportions of men reported interlocking difficulties: 28 percent said they climaxed too quickly, 17 percent had performance anxiety and 10.4 percent (20 percent of those over 50) said they'd had trouble maintaining an erection.

Before the 1950s, people with these sorts of problems were given pejorative labels like "impotent" and "frigid." Psychoanalytic therapy had little to offer them beyond symbolic explorations of their upbringings and "Oedipal" conflicts. Things got slightly better in the 1950s, when Joseph Wolpe and other behaviorists taught people to reduce their fear by breathing deeply and relaxing while imagining sexual situations that had made them tense. This was of some help, but things only really changed in the 1970s, after gy-

necologist William Masters and his research associate Virginia Johnson began studying the physiology of human sexual response in the laboratory.

Modern sex therapy—a repertoire of precise physical techniques that teach the body new responses and habits, lower anxiety and increase focus on the here-and-now—builds on Masters and Johnson's work. Therapy consists mainly of counseling and "homework" in which new experiences are tried and new skills practiced. If clients are too tense or reluctant to try something new, systems approaches, couples therapy, drugs and psychodynamic therapy may be tried as well.

Modern sex therapy often begins with instruction in "sensate focus." The pressure to have an orgasm, keep a firm erection or prolong intercourse is taken away. Instead, individuals or partners are told to set aside time to caress themselves or each other in a relaxed environment, without trying to achieve any sexual goal. Once anxiety is lowered, sex therapy often proceeds successfully especially in treating the following common problems:

Vaginismus. Vaginismus is the spastic tightening of the vaginal muscles and can make intercourse impossibly painful. It can be so severe that not even a Q-tip can be inserted in the vagina, and some women with vaginismus have never, or rarely, completed sexual intercourse in the course of years of marriage. Often the re-

sult of physically painful experiences like childbirth, painful intercourse, rape or molestation, it is a learned fear response. Therapy involves teaching the woman to relax and breathe while gently inserting the first of a graduated series of lubricated rods, starting with one as small as is necessary for comfort. In ensuing weeks, the woman uses incrementally thicker rods and then inserts her partner's finger and finally his penis into her vagina. Nothing is forced, and insertion is always under the control of the woman.

Premature ejaculation in men. Treatment involves lowering anxiety and teaching the man to become aware of his arousal during lovemaking, until he recognizes the sensations that precede his "point of no return." Then he practices what sex therapist Barbara Keesling, author of *Sexual Healing*, calls "peaking"—pausing before the point of no return and relaxing, breathing and stopping movement until his arousal subsides. After a few minutes' rest, the man returns to movement, stimulation and arousal. The "peak and pause" routine is repeated five or six times per homework session. The exercise can be done by a man masturbating alone, while his partner is giving him oral sex or during intercourse. Men can squeeze their pubococcygeal or PC muscles during the pause to dampen arousal, or the man's partner can squeeze on the coronal ridge just below the head of the penis.

(continued)

ing a Plexiglass wand inside an anatomically correct, purple velvet and pink-silk "yoni puppet" from San Francisco's House of Chicks. "Try shallow, shallow, shallow, deep! The more variety, the more information floods the brain, and the more you wake up."

A sex therapist, or in a more enlightened society, a sex educator, could have said the identical words, but the context—playful, normalized and semi-public—would not have been the same. A miniature culture, as transient and self-contained as a dewdrop, was being formed. For a handful of days, as the couples strolled the Esalen grounds above the Pacific, moving from cabin to hot tub to class, nobody was too busy or

too tired to have sex. Nobody read anything about Kenneth Starr, or looked at the *Sports Illustrated* swimsuit issue or downloaded pornography from the Internet. Every night, in their TV-free, phone-free cabins, they looked at and touched each other's flesh-and-blood bodies rather than electronic images and paper dreams.

In class, Muir held out to them the possibility that sex could be more than a source of pleasure: it could be a source of intimate bonding as well. He taught them how to lie together spoon-fashion and breathe in unison. Sex, he said, could be more even than emotional intimacy: it could be an interplay of invisible energies that coursed through each lover's body and radiated beyond it. Every day,

he led participants in yogic breathing and stretching, and then asked them whether they could feel an "energy hand" the size of an oven mitt growing beyond their flesh-and-blood hands. He had them fluff and clean their "auras" by sweeping their hands in circles a few inches from the body.

He acted not only as sex educator and yoga teacher, but priest. He taught them to chant one-syllable Sanskrit mantras designed to activate each of the body's seven *chakras* or energy centers that are believed to ascend the body's core. And he formed them into slow Tantric circle dances in which the men and women stared into the eyes of partner after part-

THE EVOLUTION OF **MODERN Sex Therapy**

Erectile difficulties in men. A common problem among older men, erectile failure is often caused by an interaction of physical and psychological factors. Smoking, diabetes, blood pressure drugs, alcoholism, neurological injury and normal aging can all worsen erectile problems. Treatment has been revolutionized since the introduction of Viagra, which not only helps men with primarily physical problems, but can also jump-start those suffering primarily from anxiety.

Men who awaken with erections or have them while masturbating can probably blame anxiety if they have trouble during intercourse: muscular tightness and breath-holding can send blood out of the penis, causing it to wilt. Sex therapy requires slowly disarming anxiety and performance pressure, and learning to enjoy sex with and without an erection. Therapy often begins with declaring intercourse off-limits and encouraging the couple to enjoy each other orally and manually, without demanding that the penis perform.

In the next "stop-start" phase, the man's partner stimulates him to the point of erection, stops until his penis becomes totally soft and then stimulates him again, repeating the process up to three times if the erection returns. Other exercises include "stuffing," which allows the man to become familiar with the sensation of being in the vagina without having to perform sexually. The female partner gently folds his flaccid penis into her vagina, using her fingers as a splint while lying in a scissors position, at right angles to the man, with one of his thighs between her legs. The couple then lies together for 15 to 30 minutes without moving. In subsequent sessions, as anxiety lessens, the man practices moving slowly while breathing evenly and staying relaxed.

Orgasmic difficulties in women. Therapy with "pre-orgasmic" women was pioneered by psychologists Lonnie Barbach of San Francisco, author of *For Yourself: The Fulfillment of Female Sexuality*, and Joseph LoPiccolo, a coauthor, with Julia Heiman, of *Becoming Orgasmic*. It has extraordinarily high success rates with women once written off as frigid. In group and individual programs lasting 6 to 10 weeks, women are given basic information about female sexual response and are encouraged to spend one hour a day on self-pleasure "homework," familiarizing themselves with their own anatomies and sexual responses, examining their vulvas with a mirror and speculum, massaging themselves, perhaps reading Nancy Friday's collections of sexual fantasies and masturbating. Most of the women soon learn to give themselves orgasms, and then gradually transfer their new skills to lovemaking. First they masturbate to orgasm in front of their partners, then learn to come while touching themselves during intercourse, and then teach their partners to pleasure them to orgasm using their fingers or penis.

Most women successfully transfer their new responsiveness to partnered sex. The exceptions tend to be women who have learned to reach orgasm by squeezing their thighs tightly together—a position that makes it virtually impossible for them to have an orgasm with a penis inside them. In LoPiccolo's clinic at the University of Missouri in Columbia, such women relearn a more fluid orgasmic response by deconstructing their masturbation rituals step-by-step and gradually learning to have orgasms without clenching their thighs. They may begin by simply uncrossing their ankles while masturbating and then slowly change their patterns until they can have orgasms with their legs apart.

If a woman can reach orgasm with digital stimulation from her partner, LoPiccolo considers the therapeutic goals have been met. Women respond orgasmically to a wide variety of stimuli—some to dreams and fantasies; others to the rubbing of an earlobe or breast; others to digital caressing of the clitoris or G-spot; and still others to intercourse. All are considered normal human variations. At an American Association of Marriage and Family Therapy conference last year, LoPiccolo said that when couples come to him saying they'd like the woman to have an orgasm during intercourse, he doesn't consider this a therapy goal so much as a growth goal, like learning to dance. "If you want to learn the tango," he said by way of analogy, "You get tango lessons, not therapy."

KATY BUTLER

ner while visualizing sending love and healing to virtual strangers.

If the West has defined male sexuality as the norm and female sexuality as the problem, Tantra glorifies the female: a woman's orgasms are said to increase her capacity to act as a channel for the flow of *shakti*, the universal female energy that powers the universe. And by deemphasizing the moment of ejaculation and emphasizing energy and context, the workshop provided the women with more of what they often complain is missing from standard-issue sex—love, sensuous touching and intimacy.

Under Muir's tutelage, lovemaking was not, as some feminists put it, a recapitulation of the power inequalities of rape, but a worship of the female and a reenactment of the drama of Shiva and Shakti, the Hindu god and goddess whose lovemaking created the universe. Partners were to see in themselves the flow of divine fundamental energies; the act of love as reproducing the first stages of the creation of the world.

Women, Muir declared, could and should have multiple orgasms, while men were depleted by ejaculation and should sometimes try the "valley orgasm"—orgasm without ejaculation. And he transcended the no-win squabble Freud started over the virtues of clitoral versus vaginal orgasms by teaching effective techniques for vaginal stimulation of the G-spot; he declared that women, too, could ejaculate when sufficiently stimulated.

This is a tall order of a culture in which 24 percent of women surveyed say that they, like Paula, have not had an orgasm during the previous year. A complex history lies behind this statistic. If the sexual lives of many men begin with repeated sexual rejection and shame, the sexual lives of many women begin in choicelessness: breasts stroked in a laundry room by a best friend's father; the struggle lost in a back seat; the unwanted kiss from uncle, teacher, boss or neighbor. When women sleep with men they sleep as well with their fear or memory of the peeper, the flasher, the child molester, the rapist, the Don Juan, the womanizer, the sexual predator, the horrible first husband and the just plain jerk. Women, too, have a double standard: we divide men not into virgins and whores, but into predators and marriage material. In a reverse of the fairy tale, we fear that while we lie in bed, our lovers will metamorphose from Beauty to the Beast.

Such memories and fears, Muir suggested, are embedded not only in the brain, but in the cells of the body. His cure was a sexual ceremony to be held in the privacy of each couple's bedroom on the third night of the workshop. In a men-only meeting beforehand, he showed videotapes and coached each man on how to do for his lover what no therapist or body worker could do—massage her "Sacred Spot," the G-spot inside her vagina.

> **T**hrough Tantra, lovemaking becomes a form of worship and partners see in themselves the flow of divine fundamental energies.

The G-spot, Muir said, is a little known and widely misunderstood area of sexual sensitivity—a raised, furrowed area of tissue about the size of a quarter, an inch and a half inside the front wall of the vagina, against the pubic bone. When stroked, it can become erect, firm and responsive and can trigger vaginal orgasms and ejaculation of a clear liquid. But it is also the dark closet in which old sexual pain is stored. "Sacred Spot" massage, he said, might release ecstatic sexual pleasure. It might also release old memories: the women might complain of numbness or bruising, or explode in fear, sobbing or rage. "This is Tantra kindergarten," he said, coaching the men to simply be loving and to be there, no matter what. "You get an A just for showing up."

After supper, before the ceremony began, the men fanned out to their cabins all over Esalen to take on the traditionally female task of "preparing the space" for the ceremony. While Liz and the other women relaxed and giggled in the Esalen hot tubs, Russ cleaned their cabin, combed his white hair and took a shower. In another cabin, one of the construction managers lit incense and paced his room. On the other side of the garden, one of the lawyers scattered rose petals on the sheets. Carlos, the Latin American academic, arranged a vase full of flowers he had cut from the Esalen garden, cued up a CD on his laptop, lit candles, put on a formal Mexican shirt called a *guayabera*, turned back the sheets and waited for Paula.

When the couples shared their experiences in the group the next day, it was almost as though the sexes had exchanged roles. "Carlos massaged me so gently so tenderly," Paula said. "The other times he had massaged me it was like, let's hurry up and get this over with." After an hour or so, she said, Carlos had turned her over and asked permission to stroke her "sacred spot" with his finger. Not long afterward, she had her first orgasm in a year. "I just had a whole strand of pearls full of climaxes," she said. "It kept going on and on, the pleasure."

One woman—whose husband had left her for another woman 14 months earlier—was floored by the tide of anger and fear the exercise released. It was, she said, "like a bad acid trip." Other women came close to bragging about having multiple orgasms and ejaculations (one woman had 22 over an hour and a half), while their men were quiet, tearful and open. The men had taken on the traditionally feminine role of focusing wholeheartedly on the pleasure of another, and it had changed them. The construction manager cried, describing how he'd waited nervously for his girlfriend, terrified that he wouldn't measure up. Another man told the group that whenever he'd made love before, his consciousness had zigzagged back and forth, first checking in on his own erection and then checking in on his partner. "Last night, my presence was so totally focused on Andrea that I didn't have to worry about myself at all," he said. "When she came, I was wailing with her like I was having the biggest orgasm of my life, and I was totally limp."

Here, in a context where differences between men and women were not only acknowledged but glorified and mythologized, and where men's performance fears were out in the open, women were getting what they wanted.

THE NEXT EVENING CAME THE TURNabout. After supper, Muir took off his amethyst crystal pendant, blue silk shirt and oatmeal jeans. He lay on pillows on the floor in his boxer shorts, holding a clear black plastic wand from a magic store at his groin like a surrogate penis. One man pushed his girlfriend to the front of the crowd. "I don't want you to miss any of this," he said.

Diane Greenberg knelt between Muir's legs and showed the women an unbelievable range of ways to pleasure a man's penis. She was competent and sure. She twirled her fingers around the wand like a feathery screw. She squeezed in at both at the top and the bottom, explaining that this way the blood wouldn't be forced out. She slapped it and tapped it and pretended to use it like a microphone. She clasped her fingers and encircled the wand, running her thumbs in circles up and down the frenulum as though winding a bobbin.

She was leading the women into the dangerous territory of the slut goddess. If some women's sexual lives begin in choicelessness, others begin with an inner war: lying on a blanket on a hill on a warm night, grabbing at the hands that give such pleasure and pulling them away, worrying what the owner of these hands will call her to his friends the next day—*slut, pig, whore*. There are years of this, and then the rings are exchanged, the rice is thrown, the church doors open and the woman is expected to become as sexy and free as the bad girl she struggled for years not to be. Fear of taking on the slut archetype can persist through years of financial independence and supposed liberation, narrowing the range of pleasure a woman dares to give a man in the bedroom. By way of antidote, Muir and Greenberg spoke of Uma, a Hindu female divinity who "wears her sexuality on the outside." They lauded Hindu temple dancers and sacred prostitutes, and urged the women to try on this aspect of the powerful divine feminine. They encouraged the couples to let loose with noise—Esalen had heard lots of it, they said, and if couples got too self-con-

Tantra AT HOME

Modern Tantric techniques to improve anyone's sex life

Heighten Awareness of All the Senses
William Masters and Virginia Johnson introduced to the West a technique called "sensate focus," in which the receiving partner focused on his or her own sensations while being slowly and nonsexually caressed.

Tantric versions are more playful and aesthetic: Tantric teacher Margo Anand of Mill Valley, California, for instance, recommends that the receiving partner sit blindfolded on the bed, while the nurturing partner wafts a variety of smells, such as peppermint, licorice, gardenia, or even Chanel No. 5, under his nose. Next he is treated to sounds—bells, gongs, even crackling paper. Then he is fed distinctive-tasting foods—almonds, grapes dipped in liqueur, whipped cream, fruit or bittersweet chocolate. Finally, the nurturing partner strokes the receiving partner's body with pleasant textures—silk scarves, fur mittens or feathers. The ritual closes gently and formally. "With utmost gentleness, as if you had never touched him before, let your hand rest on his heart," writes Anand. "Allow your hands to radiate warmth, tenderness, and love."

Create Intimacy Through Gentle Contact Modern Tantrism focuses strongly on the subtle physical harmony between partners. In *Tantra: the Art of Conscious Loving*, yoga teachers Charles and Caroline Muir of the Source School of Tantra in Maui, Hawaii, recommend spoon meditation:

Lovers lie together spoon-fashion on their left sides and gently synchronize their breathing. The outer person, the nurturer, rests his right hand on the heart of his partner. Placing his left hand on her forehead, he visualizes sending love and energy from his heart down his arm and into her heart on his out-breath. On the in-breath, he draws energy back from her forehead and into his body in an endless circle.

The Muirs also recommend that partners do yogic breathing in unison: inhaling, holding the breath for a few seconds, exhaling and holding the breath out for a few more seconds. While breathing out, one partner visualizes accepting energy while the other visualizes projecting it. Couples can also inhale and exhale in counterpoint, visualizing "shooting out" energy on the out-breath through heart, head or groin and receiving it on the in-breath.

Focus on Connection Rather Than Orgasm Much of conventional sex therapy has focused on orgasm. Many previously unsatisfied women were liberated in the process, but it also turned intercourse into a big project, made orgasm the be-all and end-all of being together sexually, and defined any other sexual interaction as "the failure to achieve orgasm." Tantrism extols the joys of brief sexual connections without orgasm. In *The Tao of Sexology*, for example, Taoist teacher Stephen Chang recommends that couples practice the "Morning and Evening Prayer" for at least 2 to 10 minutes, twice a day. Every morning and evening, partners are to lie together in the missionary position, lips touching, with arms and legs wrapped around each others' bodies and the man inside the woman. The couple breathes together in a peaceful, relaxed state, with the man moving only enough to maintain his erection. "The couple enjoys and shares the feelings derived from such closeness or stillness for as long as they desire," writes Chang, who notes that orgasm sometimes follows without any movement. "Man and woman melt together, laying aside their egos to exchange energies to heal each other."

Enhance Sexual Pleasure Ancient and modern Tantric and Taoist sex manuals are full of sophisticated physical techniques designed to enhance the pleasure of both partners, stimulate orgasm in the woman and delay orgasm in the man. Chang, for example, recommends a Taoist practice called "Sets of Nine." The man slowly penetrates the first inch or so of his lover's vagina with the head of his penis only. He repeats this shallow stroke slowly nine times, followed by one slow stroke deep into the vagina. The next "set" consists of eight shallow strokes and two deep strokes, followed by seven shallow strokes and three deep strokes and so on until a final set of one shallow stroke and nine deep strokes. The "sets" help men prolong intercourse by balancing intense and less intense forms of stimulation and arouse women by stimulating the G-spot and numerous nerve endings in the neck of the vagina.

Separate Orgasm From Ejaculation In its most signal departure from Western sex therapy, modern and ancient Tantrism recommend that men, especially older men, frequently enjoy what it calls a "valley orgasm"—orgasm without ejaculation. Chang recommends that as the man senses himself approaching the "point of no return," both partners stop all movement while the man clenches his pubococcygeal or PC muscle (the urination-stopping muscle known to many women from the Kegel exercises they were taught to strengthen uterine and bladder muscles after giving birth). The man also slows and deepens his breathing, looks into his partner's eyes, connects with her heart and channels energy upward from his groin toward his heart and the crown of the head. Orgasm without ejaculation often follows. Ejaculation can also be reserved, without stopping the experience of orgasm, by pressing on what Chang calls "The Million Dollar Point," in a small hollow between anus and scrotum.

Honor Sex, But Keep It in Perspective "When sex is good," Charles Muir said at a recent workshop, "It's 10 percent of the relationship. When it's bad, it's 90 percent."

—KATY BUTLER

scious, they could shout or wail into a pillow.

Then Greenberg coached the woman on the coming evening's ceremony. This time, the women would "honor" the men, first massaging their bodies and their penises. ("First get him hard, ladies," Muir interjected. "Then he'll agree to any-thing.") Next, Greenberg said, the women were to insert one finger into their man's anus and stroke and stimulate the exquisitely sensitive "sweet little hollow" at the base of the prostate. This, she cautioned, was a delicate business. "Rather than me entering him, I'll have him sit on my finger," she explained.

Then Greenberg turned to the men. "You're going to be penetrated, guys" she said, "as we are penetrated."

As Greenberg pulled the women into new territory, Muir took the men into the unknown as well. "Every man has gone through a war of his own that has robbed him of his *yin* [female aspect]," he said.

"Each young boy is taught that men don't cry, don't feel. The job of reclaiming your yin is sweet. You won't wake up the same guy in the morning. Tonight, you get to be the illogical one. You get to have feelings tonight. Ladies, I want you to show up big. He may test you, he may be irrational. He may become terrified.

"You give and you're strong and you fix things" he said, turning to the men. "You're gigantic. How much can you let yourself be small and feel? Allow yourself to be penetrable and vulnerable? Five million homosexuals can't be wrong. There must be something up there that's good."

When Carlos and Paula described their night's experience in the group the next morning, Carlos was in tears—deep, strong tears. During the ceremony, he had reexperienced being raped and tortured in a South American prison and had not "left his body," as he had when having flashbacks before. He had also experienced something beyond the personal as though a great wind were blowing through him and breathing his body for him. And Paula had faced something she'd once held at arms' length. "Being raised Mexican Catholic, women who do that are sluts," she said, referring to the way she'd stroked Carlos' penis and penetrated his anus. "I gave myself permission not just to touch it with my eyes closed, but to look at it and be there in all my glory, and I felt pure."

On THE LAST DAY OF THE WORKshop, Muir urged the couples to try a "10-day test drive"—to connect somehow sexually, physically and emotionally for at least 10 minutes every day. By the time the couples were packing their bags, few of the men displayed the sexual bravado they'd come in with—the bravado this culture trains them for. One man, a lawyer, had told the group the first night that he'd come to the workshop because he wanted to experience a 30-minute orgasm. He left muttering about "Tantra kindergarten."

His desires had become simpler and more ambitious: to only connect with his wife of 22 years. One busy day he left work, met his wife at their son's soccer game and drove with her to the far end of the field, where they kissed and held each other for 10 minutes in the car.

Some couples—like the pair who told me brightly that they wanted to put the "pizzazz" back in their marriage—left with little. Others took away all the bells and whistles you'd expect from a sex workshop: sobbing, wailing, energy releases, multiple orgasms, female ejaculations. Others left with something perhaps more precious: the understanding that good sex—wholesome, healing and holy—is an accumulation of small mercies, beginning with whatever mercy you need right now. Like being able to take off all your clothes in front of your lover, and touch his penis in all your glory and feel pure.

They went home—to San Diego and Cleveland and Denver, to the impeachment hearings and football games and a larger culture reverberating, more publicly than usual, between sexual obsession and sexual shame. Ghosts inevitably reentered their bedrooms. Old marital squabbles reared their ugly heads again. But sometimes old disappointments were held in a new way.

If anyone had come to understand the meaning of small mercies, it was Liz and Russ. On the night that Russ had pleasured her, Liz had come to their cabin door and found him still in the shower. Something about that melted her heart. "I brought to last night 40 years of lack of trust and feeling I'm not seen as a woman," she had said in the group next day. "I've stayed in the relationship oftentimes with doubt."

"I was so touched Russ was washing his body for me, that he would even be late to do this," she said. "All the resentment and fear was gone. I felt like a woman. It was enough."

"He put on a Japanese robe," she told the group, turning to her husband. "You looked very manly in it. I wore a white silk Dior nightgown and felt like a bride. When we slipped it off, I loved the look of my body. If we had only done this on our honeymoon, what a difference it would have made."

"She could have said, 'This is your obligation,'" said Russ. "But she dismissed all that. We didn't shout and cover our faces with pillows, but it's nice to know that it's possible. We take away the hopes and stories we've been told. I pray that we will remember."

"It was enough," said Liz. "Russ was willing, after 40 years of marriage, to try something. That was enough."

When they returned home, they followed Muir's suggestions for the "10-day test drive." Every day, she and Russ lay down with each other in the morning and the evening, and snuggled and held each other. "It's been wonderful," Liz told me. "There's been no anxiety, no repulsion. It's not about making love. It's about breathing together, holding hands, the eye contact, touching the heart, the forehead. We are doing our homework. But I'm not sure we're doing it right."

In her last sentence, I heard the reverberations of our culture's sexual perfectionism. She and Russ had returned to a society with bigger work to do than any person or couple can do alone. Yet they had grasped the essence of classical Tantra as practiced in India nearly two thousand years ago, and that essence is not purely sexual. At its base, it involves welcoming and transforming all energetic and powerful states, even negative and difficult ones, by holding them in a different context.

That context involves knowing that Saint Augustine and all his intellectual and spiritual heirs, including our parents and Larry Flynt and Kenneth Starr, were wrong: Sex is neither a nasty secret pleasure nor a sin, but a part of the pattern of the universe. To put it one way, the desire to make love, connect, procreate and survive has been programmed, along with pleasure, into our genes and dreams. To put it another: Sex is sacred—intricate and dangerous and pleasurable and utterly ungraspable.

Networker *associate editor Katy Butler, a former reporter for* The San Francisco Chronicle, *has contributed to* The Los Angeles Times, The New Yorker, The New York Times Book Review *and* The Washington Post. *For more information on Charles Muir, write to P.O. Box 69, Paia, HI 96779. Correspondence to Katy Butler may be sent to the* Networker.

How to rediscover desire

The *last* thing you want to do is discuss your love life with a stranger.
But sex therapists can help you reconnect with your spouse in bed—and in life.

By Michael Castleman

alan and Diane had what is known as a desire discrepancy: In other words, he wanted to make love twice as often as she did. The couple had been married 12 years and had two sons when they first consulted a sex therapist. For the next 18 months, Alan and Diane, both 41, discussed their sex life—and a lot of other things. It turned out that their problem involved more than different sexual appetites. Diane came from a family with fundamentalist religious beliefs and was raised to view sex—especially oral sex—as dirty. The couple also discussed Alan's desire for more cuddling and hand holding, and Diane's tendency to criticize her husband's abilities as a wage earner.

After Alan and Diane aired these concerns, they came to understand each other better—and to realize the impact marital problems were having on their sex life. In the end, Diane still didn't want sex as often as Alan did, but it became less of an issue between them. They learned how to enjoy each other more, and to enjoy their sex life more as well.

"Good sex is one of life's greatest pleasures," says sex therapist Dennis Sugrue, Ph.D., a clinical associate professor of psychiatry at the University of Michigan Medical School in Ann Arbor and president of the American Association of Sex Educators, Counselors, and Therapists. "If you're not enjoying it as much as you'd like, there's no reason to feel inadequate, embarrassed, ashamed, or resentful of your partner. That's where sex therapy can help. It not only improves the quality of your sex, but it also deepens the trust, security, and intimacy in your relationship."

Yet sex therapy, which was created by William Masters, M.D., and Virginia Johnson in the 1960s, has been vastly misunderstood. Over the years, misconceptions have included the idea that patients have intercourse in front of their therapists or are asked to make love with someone other than their spouse (a surrogate). Neither was true of legitimate sex therapy then—and it's not true now.

Sex therapy is basically talk therapy, during which couples sit down with a qualified professional to discuss problems that are primarily sexual in nature. Although marriage counselors and sex therapists are both psychotherapists, sex therapists have additional training. "Couples counseling often deals with issues of communication and control, but it may not deal with sex at all," says Janet Hyde, Ph.D., a professor of psychology and women's studies at the University of Wisconsin in Madison and current president of the Society for the Scientific Study of Sex. "However, when couples consult a sex therapist, sex is definitely on the agenda."

The process

Sex therapy usually takes four to six months of weekly, one-hour sessions. Depending on where couples live, each session costs between $75 and $175 per hour. Some health insurers will cover it, though they may place limits on the

talking sex... and solutions

Escaping stress

Larry, 37, and Janet, 34, had been married seven years when they decided to consult Allen Elkin, Ph.D., a certified sex therapist and director of the Stress Management and Counseling Center in New York City. They were arguing over Larry's lack of interest in sex, which was causing him to have performance problems. Larry had begun avoiding intimacy altogether—to his wife's dismay. The first thing Elkin did was get Larry to see that job stress was playing a major role in his sexual difficulties.

Next Elkin focused on Janet, who felt so rejected by Larry's lack of attention that she frequently lashed out at him. She was convinced that her husband found her unattractive. At Elkin's prompting, Larry reassured his wife. Once Janet realized that Larry's problem wasn't about her, she was able to be less angry and demanding—and to help her husband more.

Larry then learned breathing and muscle-relaxation techniques to relieve his physical tension. Elkin helped him identify his stress triggers, so Larry could catch himself before having an anxiety attack, and they discussed how Larry could function better on the job.

Elkin finally addressed the couple's sex problems directly. He advised them to do sensate focus, in which each partner massages the other, revealing how they like to be touched. Larry had to learn to concentrate on the process and not on his overall performance. Now, five months later, the couple has gone from having sex once very two months to once a week.

More tender time

Suki Hanfling, MSW, AASECT-certified sex therapist, and founder and director of the McLean Hospital Human Sexuality Program in Belmont, Massachusetts, first started seeing Steven, 42, and Catherine, 40, about five months ago. Catherine didn't enjoy the way Steven made love but was convinced that he was the "expert" in such matters and something must be wrong with her. During their ten years of marriage, she never spoke up about her desires or preferences. When her anger and discomfort grew unbearable, she started avoiding her husband's advances.

Steven, wounded by her withdrawal, began sulking and cooling off to her as well. Hanfling identified the problem quickly: Steven didn't realize how important romance and connection could be in a relationship. Catherine wanted tender time with her husband, in bed and out.

But Catherine also had to learn to communicate. After working on this in a separate session, she was able to discuss her preferences more easily with her husband. Then Hanfling addressed some practical matters: Because making love right before bedtime could be rushed, she advised the couple to save sex for mornings or weekends. Husband and wife decided to send their four-year-old daughter to her grandparents every other Saturday night so they could enjoy each other's company. And Steven learned to approach Catherine in a softer, less demanding way that made her feel less pressured. This change also allowed for more cuddling—which both of them had been missing. By the end of their therapy, the couple was back on track, having sex regularly.

Less pressure

Jack and Pamela had been married for 23 years and had a healthy sex life. Then Jack, 56, started having difficulty ejaculating. The couple went to see Norman S. Fertel, M.D., an AASECT-certified sex therapist in Brooklyn. Dr. Fertel first sent Jack for a urology exam to make sure the condition wasn't caused by an enlarged prostate or other medical problem.

After the tests came back normal, Dr. Fertel sat down with Pamela, 45, and Jack and explained that aging causes delayed ejaculation and that older men need more stimulation to get aroused. Then he talked the couple through their relationship history, helping them rediscover what attracted them to each other, identify what had changed over the years, and pinpoint what kept them close.

Once Pamela understood the physical component of Jack's problem and heard him tell her why he still loved her, she immediately felt better. Jack, realizing his problem was common, felt less pressure. Dr. Fertel then suggested a few techniques they could try to vary their routine. Pamela and Jack both learned not to worry if everything didn't always go as planned, and their sex life began to improve.

number of sessions. (See "Finding a Qualified Therapist.")

Most therapists use the first session to ease their clients into the process, because so many feel uncomfortable talking about sex. They start by reviewing the couples' medical histories. "Sexuality can be affected by chronic illness, medications, substance abuse, and de-

pression," explains Michael Plaut, Ph.D., an associate professor of psychiatry at the University of Maryland School of Medicine in Baltimore and president of the Society for Sex Therapy and Research, "so we need to understand if outside factors are involved." Next, they discuss the clients' family backgrounds and their relationship history.

Usually toward the end of the initial meeting, the questions begin to center around sex. Therapists ask the basics. Why are you here? How long has the problem been going on? When does it occur? How are each of you reacting? "Then I make it clear," Plaut says, "that I have no agenda for what the sexual relationship 'ought' to be in terms of what they do together, when they do it, or how often. That's up to them. I see my job as helping them work out a sexual relationship they can both live with comfortably."

Subsequent sessions focus on the sexual and nonsexual issues that factor into the relationship. "Couples often come in resenting each other," says Louanne Cole Weston, Ph.D., a sex therapist in Fair Oaks, California. "They don't see the other person's perspective. I try to help them make peace with each other."

Unlike most couples counseling, sex therapy involves various types of homework. In addition to reading, assignments may include practicing sensual, but nonsexual, intimacy—for example, hugging more often, cuddling, or trading massages. "Sensual massage without genital contact," Sugrue says, "can be a great way for couples to rediscover the power of touch without getting caught up in performance concerns."

Adds Weston, "If I'm dealing with a man who has premature ejaculation or a woman who can't have orgasms, then the homework involves some type of self-stimulation."

Weston recently worked with Ted, 37, and his wife, Susan, a 33-year-old teacher who had never had an orgasm. The therapy not only involved Susan's problem but also her guilt about faking

---

finding a qualified therapist

•Ask your family doctor or gynecologist for a recommendation.

•Call local or state psychological or social work organizations for referrals. (Don't pick the sex therapist closest to you only because it's convenient.)

•Write to the American Association of Sex Educators, Counselors, and Therapists, P.O. Box 238, Mount Vernon, IA 52314-0238. If you include a self-addressed, stamped, business-size envelope, the organization will send a list of AASECT-certified sex therapists in your area. Some of the therapists are listed on the organization's Web site: www.aasect.org.

•Interview all the candidates by phone, and ask about their experience dealing with your problem, their credentials, their approach, when you might arrange sessions, and fees. Then select the one with whom you feel the best rapport.

•Don't be afraid to change therapists if the one you've chosen isn't meeting your needs.

---

orgasms with Ted and his anger about her deception. After a lot of discussion, experimentation, and support from Ted, Susan learned how to have orgasms.

The proof

Studies support the effectiveness of sex therapy. Researchers at the University of Pennsylvania School of Medicine in Philadelphia tracked 365 married couples who sought sex therapy for a variety of problems. Sixty-five perfect reported that their problem was resolved. Those who *didn't* find the therapy effective usually had an illness that impaired sexual functioning.

"Although husbands and wives occasionally seek individual sex therapy, it is most helpful in a cooperative relationship where both people are equally committed to working together," Plaut says.

Sex is perfectly natural, but often not naturally perfect. "You have to pay attention to your own pleasure, while simultaneously paying attention to the other person's," Weston explains. "Some people don't pay enough attention to themselves. Some don't pay enough to the other. But with a little time and energy, sex therapy can help couples in loving relationships overcome their problems and enjoy themselves again."

UNIT 4
Reproduction

Unit Selections

Key Points to Consider

- In your opinion, what are the most important characteristics of a contraceptive? Why?

- What personal feelings or expectations make you more likely to use contraception regularly?

- Under what circumstances might a person not use contraception and risk an unintentional pregnancy?

- Should contraceptive responsibilities be assigned to one gender or be shared between men and women? Defend your answer.

- Have you found a fairly comfortable way to talk about contraception and/or pregnancy risk and prevention with your partner? If so, what is it? If not, what do you do?

- In the situation of an unplanned pregnancy, what should be the role of the female and the male with respect to decision making? What if they do not agree?

- Should there be some kind of proficiency test or license required in order to be a parent? Why or why not? If you had the responsibility for setting forth the requirements—age, marital status, knowledge of child development, emotional stability, income level, or anything you choose—what would they be and why?

- How do you feel about the prospect of human cloning? Are there circumstances in which you believe it should be undertaken? Why?

 **Links: www.dushkin.com/online/**
These sites are annotated in the World Wide Web pages.

Ask NOAH About Pregnancy: Fertility & Infertility
http://www.noah-health.org/english/pregnancy/fertility.html
Childbirth.Org
http://www.childbirth.org
Medically Induced Abortion
http://content.nejm.org/cgi/content/short/333/9/537
Planned Parenthood
http://www.plannedparenthood.org

While human reproduction is as old as humanity, many aspects of it are changing in today's society. Not only have new technologies of conception and childbirth affected the *how* of reproduction, but personal, social, and cultural forces have also affected the *who*, the *when*, and the *when not*. Abortion remains a fiercely debated topic, and legislative efforts for and against it abound. Unplanned pregnancies and parenthood in the United States and worldwide continue to present significant, sometimes devastating, problems for parents, children, families, and society.

In light of the change of attitude toward sex for pleasure, birth control has become a matter of prime importance. Even in our age of sexual enlightenment, some individuals, possibly in the height of passion, fail to correlate "having sex" with pregnancy. In addition, even in our age of astounding medical technology, there is no 100 percent effective, safe, or aesthetically acceptable method of birth control. Before sex can become safe as well as enjoyable, people must receive thorough and accurate information regarding conception and contraception, birth, and birth control. However, we have learned that information about, or even access to, birth control is not enough. We still have some distance to go to make every child one who is planned for and wanted.

Despite the relative simplicity of the above assertion, abortion and birth control remain emotionally charged issues in American society. While opinion surveys indicate that most of the public supports family planning and abortion, at least in some circumstances, there are certain individuals and groups strongly opposed to some forms of birth control and to abortion. Within the past few years, voices for and against birth control and abortion have grown louder, and, on a growing number of occasions, overt behaviors, including protests and violence, have occurred. Some Supreme Court and legislative efforts have added restrictions to the right to abortion. Others have mandated freer access to abortion and reproductive choice and have restricted the activities of antiabortion demonstrators. Voices on both sides are raised in emotional and political debate between "we must never go back to the old days" (of illegal and unsafe back-alley abortions) and "the baby has no choice."

The nature and scope of the questions raised about the new technologies of reproduction from contraception and abortion through treatments for infertility, known as "assisted reproduction," to the possibility of human cloning, have become very complex and far-reaching. Medical, religious, political, and legal experts, as well as concerned everyday people, are debating basic definitions of human life as well as the rights and responsibilities not only of men, women, and society, but of eggs, sperm donors, and surrogates. The very foundations of our pluralistic society are being challenged. We will have to await the outcome.

The three articles in the *Birth Control and Abortion* subsection cover a wide range. "What's New in Contraception? Understanding the Options" looks at the most recent additions to the birth control options available to couples. "What You Need to Know

About RU-486" removes the considerable secrecy from this "medical" abortion method and provides an easy-to-understand comparison to other methods. Finally "Childless by Choice" deals with voluntary sterilization and raises some interesting questions about whether it is really okay to choose not to parent.

The second subsection opens with "How Old Is Too Old to Have a Baby?" an article that suggests that in the not-too-distant-future there may be no scientific upper limit to fertility. "Birth of a Father: Becoming Dad" visits with five regular and one celebrity father to expose the feelings, fears, and experiences that were part of their "becoming dads." The last two articles focus on human cloning with the first covering the objective and scientific realities and possibilities. "Which Babies?" addresses the not-so-objective issues and questions involved in the purpose and process of cloning.

What's New in Contraception?

UNDERSTANDING THE OPTIONS

Kristen Kennedy, Ph.D., and Paul Insel, Ph.D.

Since the fourth century b.c., humans have used anything from crocodile dung to lemon juice to seaweeds—to suspend the unwanted union of sperm and egg. While we've certainly come a long way since the days of lemon juice, the search for the ideal contraceptive continues—and it is, indeed, a much needed exploration. Consider that 50% of all pregnancies are unplanned, and that the U.S. boasts one of the highest teen pregnancies rates of all industrialized nations. These facts alone point to some problems with our current options for and the effectiveness of birth control methods, not to mention the lack of reliable, comprehensive information available to people looking for answers. Add to this the many unreliable representations of sexuality and sexual responsibility broadcast in popular culture as well as our general difficulty discussing sexual matters in a frank and honest way, and the need for consistent and careful information about birth control is clear.

The advent of HIV and AIDS in both the cultural and medical worlds opened some dialogue about—among many other things—the limits of contraceptives that do not protect against STDs as well as the need for ones that do. However, confusion still surrounds newer methods, how they work, and how effective they really are. In addition, the recent FDA approval of the emergency contraceptive Preven has raised questions about how this method differs from RU-486, which has also received tentative approval in the U.S. In response, we want to report on some of the newer methods available, how they work, and their effectiveness. Of course, any discussion of contraception can only be partial when it excludes the parties who are considering their options. Ultimately, you have to decide which choices are best for you, your body, your wallet, and your values.

With an estimated 925,000 daily occurrences of curable STD transmission and 550,000 daily pregnancies worldwide, a con-

> **Consider that 50% of all pregnancies are unplanned, and that the U.S. boasts one of the highest teen pregnancy rates of all industrialized nations.**

traceptive that offers protection against both STDs and pregnancy would be optimal. At the moment, the most effective option to prevent STDs is still the latex male condom, but even this method doesn't protect against everything. Condoms must be applied before sexual intercourse occurs and only act as a barrier over the areas the condom covers. Norplant implants, male sterilization or vasectomy, and Depo-Provera injections are the three leading, and most reliable, ways to prevent pregnancy. Any of these methods in combination with condom use are the best ways to prevent pregnancy as well as the transmission of STDs. What's interesting, however, about hormonal therapies—therapies that use hormones to suppress ovulation—like Norplant and Depo-Provera—is that while they are the most effective at preventing pregnancy, less than 2% of women worldwide use them.

The most widely used hormonal method is, of course, the oral contraceptive or the pill. The pill works quite effectively to prevent pregnancy if it's taken properly: that's every day, at the same time. It suppresses ovulation by mimicking the hormonal behavior of pregnancy. During pregnancy, the body secretes progesterone and estrogen in amounts high enough to prevent pregnancy. The pill imitates this hormonal effect. Fertility is not affected by the pill either. Its health benefits include a decrease in benign breast disease, iron-deficiency anemia, PID or pelvic inflammatory disease, ectopic pregnancy, endometrial cancer, and ovarian cancer. For healthy, young, non-smoking women, the pill does not present any higher risk of stroke or heart attack.

The Norplant Implant and Depo-Provera

MANY OF US KNOW VERY LITTLE ABOUT THESE OTHER, LESS popular hormonal methods. We might hear about them in magazines or on the news, but have little direct experience with the method and how it works. Take, for example, the Norplant implant, which looks a little bit like an acupuncture kit. Norplant implant is made up of six flexible, match-stick-sized capsules, each containing progestin, a synthetic progesterone, which is released in steady doses for up to 5 years. The capsules are placed under the skin, usually on the inside of a woman's upper arm. The insertion procedure takes about 15 minutes under a local anesthetic and requires only a small incision. Similar to the birth control pill, Norplant works by inhibiting ovulation. Unlike the pill, however, Norplant does not use estrogens to do so. Its other contraceptive effects include thickening of the cervical mucus, which inhibits the movement of sperm, and protecting against pelvic inflammatory disease.

Like Norplant, Depo-Provera works by releasing a steady dose of progestin which prevents ovulation. Unlike Norplant, Depo-Provera injections are given every 12 weeks, rather than a one-time insertion. None of the hormonal methods alone protect against STD and HIV infection and both Depo-Provera and Norplant can have similar side effects: irregular menstrual periods, headaches, weight gain, breast tenderness, and acne, not unlike those side effects associated with oral contraceptives. Norplant, in particular, has also received some negative press since lawsuits claimed the manufacturer did not disclose difficulties with capsule removal and warnings about side effects. Nevertheless, for women who are not able to take oral contraceptives—and the estrogen that comes with them—injection and implant methods may be viable options.

Preven Emergency Contraception

DERIVED FROM THE BIRTH CONTROL PILL, THE PREVEN Emergency Contraception Kit was approved by the FDA in 1998 for use as emergency contraception. The Kit contains four pills and a pregnancy test. If a woman fears she might be pregnant shortly after unprotected sex, say when a birth control method has failed, she takes two of the pills within 72 hours of last intercourse. The second two pills follow 12 hours later. Preven works just like the birth control pill by preventing ovulation, and a doctor must prescribe it. Side effects include nausea, vomiting, and breast tenderness. While there is some debate about how emergency contraception works and how it differs from an abortifacient, Preven is not the same as the so-called "abortion pill." Preven can only prevent pregnancy, it is not designed to end one.

RU-486

THE LATEST NEWS ON THE LEGALITY AND APPROVAL OF RU-486 is that the FDA has given tentative approval for the drug to be marketed in the U.S. However, legal, political, and manufacturing difficulties have delayed its introduction. RU-486 or Mifepristone works in two doses. The first works by preventing uterine absorption of progesterone, which in turn causes the uterine lining and any fertilized egg to shed. Progesterone is a necessary hormone for pregnancy, so when RU-486 prevents it from working the way it should, the uterus sheds its lining, just like it does during a menstrual period. Two days after the first dose of the drug, a woman takes a second drug, a prostaglandin that induces contractions.

RU-486 has a 95% success rate, and has been approved for use in the first 7 weeks of pregnancy. The downside of this method is that it generally takes longer than surgical abortion—anywhere from 4 to 24 hours. Mild side effects include abdominal pain, nausea, and vomiting, while more serious side-effects include vaginal bleeding, which generally lasts longer than that associated with surgical abortion.

Sterilization

IN ADDITION TO ORAL AND INJECTION CONTRACEPTIVE, BARRIER methods such as the diaphragm, the cervical cap, and the female condom are also available, but have higher failure rates. More permanent solutions to the question of contraception is, of course, sterilization. Surprisingly, sterilization is the most popular contraceptive choice in both the U.S. and the world. For men, a vasectomy is easier, less costly, and can be performed in a doctor's office. For women, sterilization presents more risks of complication and infection than vasectomy, but the risks are quite low. Tubal sterilization for women involves blocking or cutting the fallopian tubes, a process that prevents the egg from reaching the uterus. Hysterectomy also results in sterilization, but it is not a recommended or preferred method of contraception. Most hysterectomies are performed only in the presence of disease or damage to the uterus.

New Methods

RESEARCHERS ARE CURRENTLY TESTING IMPROVEMENTS AND new designs for both male and female contraception. Most of this work involves improving upon or developing variations of existing contraceptives. Some of those in the works include the following.

Biodegradable Implants Like Norplant, these progestin-filled implants reside under the skin, providing uninterrupted, long-term contraception. Unlike Norplant, they dissolve over time rather than requiring surgical removal.

Vaginal Ring Similar to the ring of a diaphragm, the vaginal ring emits progestin and estrogen which prevent ovulation and is worn internally for three weeks at a time. After three weeks, the ring is removed and a menstrual period begins. Another ring can then be inserted.

Contraceptives for Men Weekly injections of the hormone testosterone enanthate have proven to prevent pregnancy. However, weekly injection is hardly an advantage of this method. Researchers hope to develop a pill or implant for men.

Hormone Injection A solution containing tiny clusters of molecules, each filled with hormones, is injected into the body. Over several months, doses of hormones are released at a steady level. This method is being studied for use by both men and women.

Contraceptive Immunization By sensitizing them to their own sperm or egg cells, a man or woman would produce antibodies that inactivate the sperm or egg cells as if they were a disease. One immunocontraceptive currently under study targets just the protein covering of the egg cell, which would prevent sperm from penetrating the egg without affecting normal egg development.

Reversible sterilization Current methods of sterilization are 50–70% reversible, but researchers would like to make the process more reliable. Techniques such as injecting liquid silicone into the fallopian tubes where it forms a plug, and placing various type of clips on the vas deferens to block sperm flow are two ideas currently in the works.

Prostaglandins These are chemicals that exist naturally in the body and that stimulate muscle contractions, like cramping. Via pill or tampon, prostaglandins induce a menstrual period, regardless of whether conception has occurred.

Evolving approaches to contraception insure that more—and hopefully better—options remain in the future. At the moment, that future promises a steady increase in world population, especially in developing countries. There as well as here, issues of access, affordability, culture, and religion are but a few factors that affect contraceptive use. Medicine can only provide the means of controlling when or if conception will occur. Ultimately, the decision about which method is right for you comes from having the most timely and helpful information at hand.

Paul Insel is Clinical Associate Professor of Psychiatry and Behavioral Sciences at Stanford University School of Medicine. Kristen Kennedy is Managing Editor of HEALTHLINE and SICKBAY TODAY.

What you need to know about
RU-486

BY MOLLY M. GINTY

MIFEPRISTONE (aka RU-486, aka the "abortion pill") is like no other medication on the market today. Women who want it may never get to take it, because their doctors are unwilling or unable to provide it. Women who try it may never learn the name of its manufacturer, the address of its distributor, or the identities of government experts who approved it—facts concealed from the public for fear of anti-abortion violence. The secrecy that surrounds mifepristone may frustrate its many supporters, but it illustrates a crucial point: the decision to take mifepristone—like the decision to try any method of abortion—is as fiercely political as it is personal.

After a decade of successful use in Europe and a protracted tug-of-war here, mifepristone is at long last available to women in the U.S. On the surface, this option seems straightforward enough—a way to end early pregnancy by taking two drugs over the course of three days. It will provide women and girls with an alternative to surgery for the approximately 1.4 million abortions that occur in the U.S. every year.

Nevertheless, mifepristone's arrival has fueled fervor on both sides of the abortion debate. Already fettered by existing waiting-period and parental-consent laws, it has also inspired new anti-choice legislation. Requiring extensive medical protocols, the drug is too expensive for many women to afford. But despite its drawbacks, many women's health advocates are applauding mifepristone's arrival. The drug has the potential to improve access to abortion, boosting the number of doctors who offer it and frustrating the efforts of anti-choice militants. As Gloria Feldt, president of Planned Parenthood Federation of America, says, "This is the first truly major technological breakthrough for women's reproductive health care since the birth control pill was introduced in 1960."

Abortion Rx

Originally called RU-486 (for Roussel Uclaf, the French company that developed it, and the catalog number assigned to it), mifepristone was synthesized in 1980 and has been available in Europe since 1988. Since then, 620,000 women have used the drug in Europe, and it now accounts for 20 percent of all abortions in France. In the U.S., it has been sold since November 2000 under the brand name Mifeprex. Although it can be used to treat everything from breast cancer to brain tumors, it is prescribed primarily as an abortion drug. Taken fewer than 49 days after a woman's last menstrual period, mifepristone helps terminate pregnancy in its earliest stages.

Many women who have TRIED MEDICAL ABORTION say it feels more natural than standard surgical abortion and that they APPRECIATE THE PRIVACY it affords.

To have a "medical abortion," as nonsurgical abortion is sometimes called, a woman visits her health care provider and is given three pills totaling 600 milligrams of mifepristone, which blocks the action of the hormone progesterone, causing a fertilized egg to detach from the uterine wall and the uterine lining to break down. Two days after taking the first drug, the woman returns and takes 400 micrograms of misoprostol (brand name Cytotec), which causes uterine contractions and helps

Mifepristone: A Chronology

1980
Researchers at Roussel Uclaf in France develop mifepristone, a drug that blocks the action of stress hormones. While testing it, they discover that it also blocks hormones needed to sustain pregnancy.

1982
Clinical trials of mifepristone as an abortion drug begin in France and, a year later, in the U.S.

1985
The National Institutes of Health begins research on other uses of mifepristone.

1988
Women in France and China gain access to mifepristone.

1989
Roussel Uclaf announces it will not market or distribute mifepristone outside of France, and the FDA bans importation "for personal use."

1990
Feminist Majority Foundation members travel to France to urge Roussel Uclaf to bring the drug to the U.S.

1991–1992
The United Kingdom and Sweden approve mifepristone.

1992–1993
U.S. customs officials seize mifepristone from a woman who tries to enter the country with it. *The New England Journal of Medicine* publishes studies showing it is effective, and the National Institute of Medicine reports that it can help fight a range of diseases. President Clinton asks the FDA to lift the importation ban and urges the Department of Health and Human Services to promote mifepristone.

1994–95
Roussel Uclaf gives U.S. patent rights to the Population Council, which conducts clinical trials of mifepristone on 2,121 women. Abortion Rights Mobilization, an activist group, produces a copy of the drug and distributes it to researchers and patients seeking abortions.

1996
The FDA determines that mifepristone is "approvable," but requests additional information.

1997
Gedeon Richter, the Hungarian company that pledged to produce mifepristone in the U.S., backs out of its agreement to do so.

1999
The Feminist Majority Foundation begins distributing the drug for "compassionate use" in treating diseases like breast cancer, Mifepristone becomes available in ten more countries.

2000
The FDA approves the use of mifepristone for abortion on September 28.

expel the fertilized egg. Afterward, bleeding or spotting occurs for 9 to 16 days. The patient returns to her doctor 12 days after her second appointment and has an exam to ensure that she is no longer pregnant. Doctors can make slight variations on these FDA-approved protocols: they can prescribe a slightly lower or higher dosage of mifepristone or misoprostol; they can administer misoprostol orally or vaginally; or they can allow patients to take misoprostol at home, resulting in fewer office visits and a lower cost.

Many women who have tried medical abortion say it feels more natural—more like a miscarriage or heavy period—than a standard surgical abortion. "The cramping wasn't worse than anything I'd have with a normal period, which surprised me because I was expecting more pain," says Sara*, a hospital administrative assistant from Maryland who took misoprostol to complete a spontaneous miscarriage. "Having this option gave me a lot more control," says Sara. "I don't like anesthesia. I don't like not being able to actively participate in what's going on with my body. To be knocked out with my legs in stirrups would be absolutely terrifying to me." Women also say they appreciate the privacy nonsurgical abortion affords and the ability to go home and rest while the abortion is still occurring, either alone or with a partner or friend close by. In a study by associates at the Pacific Institute for Women's Health, 63 percent of patients who took the abortion pill said they wanted to avoid surgery; 56 percent believed it was safer; 41 percent believed it

EMERGENCY CONTRACEPTION

Medical abortion should not be confused with emergency contraception (EC), which prevents a pregnancy before it starts, instead of terminating one already in progress. The most common method of EC involves taking a series of birth control pills, as prescribed by a health care provider. There are also two FDA-approved EC kits available: Preven (progestin and estrogen) and Plan B (progestin only). These methods are 75 to 90 percent effective at preventing pregnancy if used within 72 hours of unprotected intercourse. A woman can also be fitted with an IUD within five days after intercourse, a method that is 99 percent effective. For more information, call the Emergency Contraception Hotline at (888) Not-2-Late or visit www.not-2-late.com.

was more natural; 35 percent wanted to lower their risk of infection; and 27 percent wanted to end their pregnancies as early as possible. Most patients had a positive experience: 94 percent would recommend the procedure to others and 87 percent would choose it again.

But some women have had slightly more negative experiences with medical abortion. "It was painful," says Lynn*, who used the drugs during clinical trials in 1999. "There were sharp, vigorous contractions, and it took three hours to expel most of the clotted tissue." Physical reactions to the drugs vary with each woman's body chemistry and the length of her pregnancy. And mental reactions vary as well: some patients say medical abortion requires more emotional involvement than traditional surgical abortion, because surgery shields a woman from the sight of the embryo. And mifepristone also takes a lot longer— two weeks as opposed to a few hours for a standard abortion. "If you want abortion over and done with in a short period of time, then medical abortion is not for you," says Amy Allina, program director for the National Women's Health Network.

It took 18 years, A STRING OF LAWSUITS, and a reported $50 million in nonprofit funding to bring MIFEPRISTONE to the U.S. And now it appears the uproar is only beginning.

The drug is also not appropriate for women who have bleeding disorders, adrenal gland problems, use IUDs, or take corticosteriods or blood thinners. The most common side effect is cramping, followed by nausea, vomiting, and diarrhea. In 8 percent of cases, bleeding or spotting lasts for 30 days or more. Also in 8 percent of cases, surgical intervention is required to complete the abortion, or more rarely, to stop excessive bleeding. Within a month of taking abortion drugs, most women can conceive again. Overall, the earlier a pregnant woman uses mifepristone, the gentler and safer it appears to be.

Women who want to try mifepristone can turn first to their regular doctors. Surveys by the Kaiser Family Foundation conducted before FDA approval indicated that more than half of obstetricians and gynecologists would likely prescribe mifepristone at some point in the future—including some who don't already do surgical abortions. About 45 percent of family physicians expressed interest in prescribing the drug regimen, as well. But in a country where seven doctors or other clinic workers have been murdered since 1993, providers have cause to worry about their safety and may decide to steer clear of mifepristone.

FDA protocols that apply to mifepristone may also turn doctors away, especially those who aren't already set up to provide surgical abortions. Before taking the drug, a woman must read a medication guide and sign a "patient agreement" verifying that she has discussed mifepristone with her doctor and decided to terminate her pregnancy. "Doctors say mifepristone is 90 percent counseling, so it takes more time than surgical abortion," says Planned Parenthood's Feldt. Physicians must be able to peg the precise duration of a patient's pregnancy—a protocol that could mean investing in a $20,000 ultrasound machine. If doctors don't have surgical expertise, they must find a qualified surgeon to help in the event of an emergency. Because of the extra counseling, malpractice insurance, and staff training that

mifepristone can involve, many physicians are now taking a wait-and-see approach. "I don't think many doctors will jump up and say 'I want to do this!'" predicts Allina. "They will watch. They will listen. And as it becomes more common, more of them will include it in their practice."

If a woman discovers that her regular doctor is not willing or able to offer mifepristone, there are still ways to find qualified providers. By the end of this year, all of the National Abortion Federation's 360 members—along with 180 Planned Parenthood affiliates—plan to prescribe mifepristone to patients who request it.

Doctors can order mifepristone from Danco Laboratories, the pharmaceutical company that distributes it in the U.S. Danco will ship mifepristone only to licensed M.D.'s who sign and return a prescriber's agreement. It will not sell the drug in pharmacies or on the Internet. Danco is charging physicians $270 for each dose of mifepristone—bringing the cost for women to anywhere from $300 to $700 or more.

At press time, many of the nation's major insurers had pledged to cover mifepristone. Health maintenance organizations will likely cover it in two thirds of cases, as they do for surgical abortions. For women who must rely on public health care, some government assistance may be available: the federal Medicaid program covers abortion in cases of rape, incest, or threats to a woman's life, and sixteen states cover abortion for poor women in all cases. Planned Parenthood will likely offer the regimen on a sliding scale, as it does for surgical abortion.

The Maelstrom

Some patients who choose mifepristone over surgery do so in part because of politics. "If a doctor gives me a pill and I am taking that pill, my doctor is less likely to be putting his or her life on the line," says Lynn. "It brings the pro-choice argument right back where it belongs, which is with me. I'm taking full responsibility for my actions by not putting somebody else in jeopardy."

Politics and mifepristone have been all but inseparable since French researchers first used the drug in 1982 to induce abortion. It took 18 years, a string of lawsuits, and a reported $50 million in nonprofit funding to bring it to the U.S. But now that the drug has arrived, it seems that the uproar is only beginning.

First there is the flap over mifepristone's price—it will be as expensive, if not more, than a standard surgical abortion. "We priced this drug to be a viable option in the marketplace," says Heather O'Neill, a spokesperson for Danco. "We also have to recoup the costs associated with bringing it to the U.S." The high price of mifepristone came as a surprise to health activists who hoped the drug would cost at least $100 less than it does." There is nothing we would love more than for the price of this drug to be lower," says Planned Parenthood's Feldt. "But we have to recognize the reality that bringing mifepristone to the U.S. took more than the usual amount of time, money, and courage." While some activists are shrugging off the high cost as inevitable, others are seething. "They should justify this or explain it," says Barbara Seaman, vice president of Abortion

Other Methods of Abortion

NAME	PROCEDURE	TIMING	COST	OF NOTE
DILATION AND CURETTAGE (D&C)	The cervix is dilated, and the contents of the uterus are removed with forceps and a curette (a surgical instrument with a scoop, ring, or loop at the tip).	4 to 12 weeks after a woman's last menstrual period (LMP)	$250 to $1,000	Although this is the procedure that many people associate with abortion, it is considered outdated by many gynecologists and is rarely used today.
DILATION AND EVACUATION (D&E)	The cervix is dilated, and a combination of suction and forceps are used to remove the fetus and placenta.	14 to 24 weeks after LMP	$400 to $5,000	Considered the safest way to terminate second-trimester pregnancy, this method is used for later abortion in the event of an emergency.
ELECTRICAL VACUUM ASPIRATION (SUCTION CURETTAGE)	The cervix is dilated if necessary, and an electric vacuum aspirator removes the contents of the uterus. Often a curette is used to complete the procedure.	4 to 14 weeks after LMP	$250 to $1,000	This first-trimester method is the most common type of abortion performed in the U.S. and is 97 to 99 percent effective. It is sometimes referred to as a D&C.
HYSTEROTOMY	In this surgical procedure, the fetus and placenta are removed through an incision in the uterus, similar to cesarean section.	16 to 30 weeks after LMP	$1,000 to $4,000	Generally used only in cases where the mother's health is endangered and no other method is possible. This procedure carries a higher-than-average risk of complication but is very rare.
MANUAL VACUUM ASPIRATION (MVA OR MENSTRUAL EXTRACTION)	The cervix is dilated if necessary, and the contents of the uterus are removed through a tube into a handheld vacuum syringe.	4 to 12 weeks after LMP	$250 to $1,000	Performed by pioneering feminists before abortion was legal in the U.S., this procedure is still popular in countries where electric vacuum methods are not yet available. It is 97 to 99 percent effective.
PROSTAGLANDINS (INDUCTION)	Drugs are administered orally or vaginally to induce contractions that eventually expel the fetus.	12 to 26 weeks after LMP	$500 to $2,000	Misoprostol, the second drug in the mifepristone regimen, is used this way. Although not as effective as other methods used in the first trimester, prostaglandins are very effective in the second trimester.
METHOTREXATE	An alternate form of medical abortion, also used in combination with misoprostol. It detaches the fetus from the uterine wall by interfering with cells' ability to multiply and divide, thus halting embryonic development.	4 to 7 weeks after LMP	$250 to $500	Methotrexate is approved in the U.S. to treat cancer and arthritis, and is prescribed "off-label" as an abortion drug, particularly in ectopic pregnancies. But methotrexate has several drawbacks: it takes longer to work than mifepristone and triggers bleeding that is less predictable.

Rights Mobilization and a contributing editor for *Ms*. "They should also be able to do this for much less."

The FDA's handling of the drug is just as controversial as mifepristone's price. Some health advocates claim the agency dragged its feet by taking four years to review mifepristone's application, making its approval agonizingly slow compared to that of other medications reviewed simultaneously. Activists also claim extra protocols were slapped on the drug for political reasons. These protocols, while safeguarding patients, make

mifepristone more time-consuming for doctors and thus boost its price.

Countering activists' criticisms of the FDA are spokespeople from Danco and the Population Council, the health research firm that ran clinical trials of mifepristone in the U.S. Both insist that the FDA acted in a timely manner. "We don't believe it was politics that held it up at the FDA," says Sandra Waldman, director of public information at the Population Council. But neither side can deny that the FDA took special precautions with mifepristone, carefully hiding the names and addresses of key players in the drug's approval and production. Danco has taken its own precautions, refusing to release the names of its executives and investors. "We're not exactly handing out our address on street corners," says O'Neill. But safety measures didn't stop vandals from locating the car of Danco's medical director, Dr. Richard Hausknecht, and doing $2,000 worth of damage to it. "At least they didn't shoot me," Hausknecht shrugs.

Some women's health advocates claim the FDA DRAGGED ITS FEET by taking four years to review mifepristone's APPLICATION, an agonizingly slow process compared to other drugs.

To avoid the controversy and violence that often surround abortion, other health professionals are distancing themselves from mifepristone. Several colleges across the country (including Boston University, Emory University, and the entire Florida public university system) have announced they will not offer it at their campus health centers. Searle—the pharmaceutical company that makes misoprostol, the second drug used in medical abortion—has fired off a strongly worded letter to health care providers saying that misoprostol (normally prescribed to prevent gastrointestinal ulcers) is "not approved for the induction of labor or abortion" and that its maker promotes it "only for its approved indication." The letter doesn't mention that misoprostol's use in abortion is perfectly legal because the FDA has approved its use in other regimens. And of course hospitals affiliated with the Roman Catholic Church (currently 10 percent of all hospitals and increasing, thanks to recent mergers) have proclaimed they will not carry the drug.

Then there are the antiabortion militants, who call mifepristone "baby poison" and are already threatening the doctors who provide it. One anti-choice group has even created an "RU-486 Registry," a Web site, which proclaims to be a "database of baby-butchering doctors and their closest blood cohorts." Before being temporarily shut down in December 2000, the site listed the names and states of nearly 500 abortion providers, politicians, and others who support a woman's right to choose. The names of those wounded by militants were printed in gray typeface. The names of those murdered had black lines slashed through them.

What scares some activists most are the legal assaults on mifepristone. Though surveys indicate that 55 to 65 percent of people in the U.S. believe the government should not bar a woman's access to abortion, government as it stands today may not support that majority. In recent years, state legislatures have passed a barrage of restrictions that speak of abortion in general terms and will thus apply to mifepristone. "These laws could put women [who want to try mifepristone] past the 49-day cutoff," says Bebe Anderson, a staff attorney for the Center for

MORE THAN AN ABORTION DRUG

In addition to terminating early pregnancy, mifepristone can help treat a host of health problems. Developed to block stress hormones, it has been used to treat brain tumors called meningiomas and a glandular condition called Cushing's syndrome. It is also able to block sex hormones and may be able to fight endometriosis, uterine fibroids, and breast and ovarian cancers. Scientists began investigating these applications in the mid-1990s, before politics and distribution delays intervened. "There has been some very basic work, but we haven't had access to this medication before," says Dr. Eric Schaff, a professor at the University of Rochester School of Medicine and a leading researcher on mifepristone. "Now that we do, we're very excited. This drug has tremendous potential for treating some very serious diseases."

Reproductive Law and Policy (CRLP). "Waiting periods enforced in 13 states require women to consult their doctors, then return 48 hours later to have an abortion. In areas where abortion doctors are only available one day a week, women may have to wait a full week between appointments. Parental involvement laws enforced in 32 states could make the delay even longer. It can take a minor several weeks to get permission to have an abortion without her parents' knowledge or consent."

Like conservative state legislatures, the Federal government also contains a significant antiabortion element. Between 1998 and 2000, Representative Tom Coburn (R.-Okla.) introduced measures to block access to the drug. None of this legislation passed, and Coburn retired in December, but his cohorts are still in Congress. "Someone else will step up," predicts Simon Heller, director of domestic programs for CRLP. "And every time anti-choice legislation is introduced, it gives [antiabortion activists] a chance to spread false propaganda about this drug."

The current House is 50 percent anti-choice, 32 percent pro-choice, and 18 percent mixed, while the Senate is 47 percent anti-choice, 35 percent pro-choice, and 18 percent mixed. On the Supreme Court, three justices consistently support *Roe v. Wade*, three consistently oppose it, and three support more restrictive abortion laws. It is crucial that abortion rights supporters keep the pressure on their senators and representatives to make sure that conservative justices are not placed on the high court, and that anti-choice laws do not make it to President George W. Bush's desk.

If mifepristone can weather the political maelstrom, it could potentially change the scope, scale, and nature of abortion in the U.S. If more doctors begin administering the drug, it could boost abortion access in the U.S., where the number of abortion providers has dropped 30 percent since 1982 and 86 percent of counties have no provider at all. Since mifepristone could hypothetically be administered by almost any physician with prescription-writing privileges, it could frustrate the efforts of anti-choice protestors—and spare women the pain of being called "baby killer" as they enter a clinic to carry out a decision that was for many already agonizing. If abortion moves into private offices, where will the militants stand with their placards, rosaries, and megaphones?

As they roll up their sleeves for the battles ahead, mifepristone's supporters take heart in the victories they've already won. They know this medication, unlike many "new" drugs, has been safely used by millions of women and has been researched by scientists for nearly two decades. They also know that mifepristone is gaining new ground every day. Planned Parenthood and the National Abortion Federation are training doctors to use it. Danco and the Population Council are conducting follow-up studies, as are independent scientists, in order to refine the medical abortion regimen. Proponents are preparing to bring mifepristone to new countries, where it could reduce the number of unsafe abortions now estimated at 20 million worldwide each year.

The decision to terminate an unwanted pregnancy is one that more than a million U.S. women make annually. Statistics show that 43 percent of us will have an abortion by the time we are 45. For women who don't want surgery, "mifepristone may make abortion physically easier," says Sharon*, a housewife and mother in Rochester, New York, who took the drug in January 2000. "But emotionally, I don't think anything can make the decision to terminate pregnancy easier. This is a gut-wrenching decision and not one that women take lightly." But it must be a choice that women make, not legislators or anti-choice crusaders. To help keep this choice in women's hands, activists must make their voices heard. "Women need to vocalize that they want their physicians and insurance providers to both offer and cover mifepristone," says Vicki Saporta, executive director of the National Abortion Federation. The battle plan is simple and straightforward. Talk to your friends about medical abortion. Join organizations that support it. Write letters to the editor of your local newspaper. Lobby your federal and state representatives. Urge the National Institutes of Health to fund more studies on mifepristone. Put pressure on the FDA to approve taking misoprostol at home. As Elizabeth Cavendish, legal director of the National Abortion and Reproductive Rights Action League, says, "This is a tremendously important development for women's reproductive health. It is also a fight that we can win."

* The names of the women who have had abortions have been changed at their request.

Molly M. Ginty is a writer in New York City.

Childless By Choice

One writer finds she can be fruitful without multiplying

BY CAROLYN E. MEGAN

I like the harshness of the language I hear when the message machine clicks on, "Hi, you've reached the sterilization clinic." It is as clean and precise as the moment when the tubes are cauterized. A possibility forever altered. And it begins at this moment, when I leave my name and number for a woman named Debbie, the sterilization nurse.

I come to the decision finally when kissing Richard, a man I have just started seeing. It isn't sudden decision; rather, it is finding myself wondering what I will use for birth control and sensing that none of my options give me the confidence of being in control of my body. I compiled the list as I do each time: pill— too many strokes and aneurysms clotting my family line; IUD—a low-grade infection in the uterus; diaphragm–pressing against the cervix for hours; Norplant, cervical cap, condoms. None of them seem like great options.

When the nurse calls back, we talk specifics. Laparoscope enters near the navel, carbon dioxide inflates the abdomen. "In hospitals," Debbie tells me, "they use several liters of gas to distend the abdomen, whereas we only use two or three liters. They use so much in the hospital that you almost look pregnant." Debbie describes the procedure; uterine elevator, IV, grasping rod, low voltage, dissolvable stitches. I am entering a new language. I am surprised by how calm I am, how the steps of the procedure mean nothing to me at this point, now that I've moved into the place of decision. When I hang up the phone, I feel excited. It isn't the idea of carefree sex; it is the feeling, at last, of what it is to have control over my body, to have a will.

There's a fairly well known picture in *Our Bodies, Ourselves* of a woman who has been left on a motel floor, dead from an illegal abortion. The picture shows the woman slumped over on her knees, naked, her buttocks to the camera, ripped sheets pulled from a stained mattress. There's blood everywhere.

When I look at the photo, I don't have a sense of her pain, nor do I feel rage about the laws that placed the woman in this situation. What I sense is shame. Shame for being caught, humiliation for being discovered by some chambermaid. It starts the reverse narrative: she shouldn't have had an abortion, she shouldn't have gotten pregnant, she should have used better birth control. She shouldn't have had sex. I land on this last and most difficult of conclusions; for literally what I am saying is that to be female means not having control over one's own body: she shouldn't have had sex. I am saying ultimately that she shouldn't even have a body; she shouldn't have desire.

It is one more layer to add to the sense that as a female, my body is unwieldy and out of control. For in the moment of sexual intercourse, there is always that place where, in order to completely let go, you need to believe that the thin piece of latex or the redirected hormones coursing through your bloodstream are enough. But birth control fails. And it is the woman who bears the brunt of that failure.

How long had I known that I didn't want to have kids? There was never a feeling when I was young of wanting a family, but it never occurred to me that I had a choice. Yet through my first marriage and into subsequent relationships, I've been a zealot about birth control, to the point of never being able to fully enjoy intimacy.

After I divorced my husband, friends and family told me, "You must have known that something wasn't right, that was why you decided no to have kids." Always, there is this sense of people looking for a way to explain my decision, looking for tortured paths, for some coldness or frigidity in me. In social situations, I hear myself saying, "I like children," as it that will help them to see me as a person making a decision.

Out of the blue he says to me, "So, do you want to have children?" "No," I say.

Richard and I haven't spoken about children; we haven't had sex. He did not have children in his first marriage, but I know that the last person he dated had two children and that he started to "get into the whole family scene," as he says. Why don't I tell him? There is a trace of me that thinks I will scare him off or imagines him talking me into not having the tubal ligation, like he is the right man to come along and make me want to have a child. It isn't an expression of my doubt but instead that desire, still, to fit into what society and what my culture expects or determines is the role of women. Sometimes I want it to be that simple. I want to believe that I can make myself into a mother, into a parent who wants to spend my time and life with a child.

I sit and watch a child on a mother's lap. The mother brushes a tendril of her daughter's hair away while the daughter plays with Barbie. With each slight pull of her heir, the daughter's head bobs back slightly and then down again. I need to create a story around this quiet gesture. I want to be the daughter who, for that moment, is touched by the constant presence of her mother. I want to be the mother who has that sort of freedom to enter her daughter's space, to be in her daughter's body. It is a gesture that I long to believe in, one that seems to me to be one of ownership. As if the mother is literally saying with this gesture, "I know you. I own you."

Sometimes I want to believe that the parent-child connection is the definitive story. Indeed, I think most parents have to believe it is–otherwise they could never undertake the continual challenge of parenting. Many of my friends who are parents talk about how they never understood responsibility or creativity until they had a child. They seem to suggest that I haven't considered these issues because I haven't had a child. There is a sense of omnipotence in their language that says they deserve a certain destiny, that being a parent suspends them from the sorrows and tragedies of everyday life and gives them greater vision of the world order. The writer in me knows that this isn't possible.

Only a few of my friends who have children can speak openly of the desire, at times, not to have them. Sarah talks about there being times when she wants to put her children to bed and drive away. Ann says her children are a "golden handcuff." They're not talking about the logistics of hectic schedules; rather, they are talking about the deeper binds of parenting. My mother used to say to me, "It's different when they are your own." I don't doubt this. I know that once the bond is made there is a continual wrestling with the desire to have that connection and to cut it off at the same time. I feel this tug-and-pull in creating my art. The unspoken uncomfortable truth is that the loving bind with one's children is what allows a person to keep parenting, but also prevents a person from growing in other areas.

Several years ago a woman named Susan Smith killed her two children. Initially, she said that she had been carjacked, that a man had pushed her out of the car and taken off with the children. Then slowly over the next several days, the truth began to unfold. In fact, she had killed her children. Not violently with strangling, but in a slow water suffocation, as if she were returning them to the womb. She parked near a lake, put the car in drive, and watched it roll into the water. Was there relief for her then? What was she trying to escape?

WE DON'T HAVE ROOM IN OUR CULTURE FOR parents to say, "Enough." Indeed, had Susan Smith given her children away, she would have been labeled unwomanlike. Perhaps it was that golden handcuff that prevented her from admitting she couldn't raise her children anymore and no longer wanted to. And so in her quiet, desperate logic, she saw only one alternative. I think about that moment when she let them go, when she watched the car sink into the water, and I wonder if she knew then that she could never leave them, that, really, she could never move on.

Fine parenting begins with the recognition that there are sacrifices and losses in having children, as there are sacrifices and losses in not having them. What surprises me is that the decision not to have children is given far more scrutiny in our culture than the decision to have them.

Richard and I walk into Harvard Square to have dinner. This is our fourth date. I'm thinking about the tubal ligation and that eventually I may need to tell him, particularly if I am ill afterward or slow to recover. Out of the blue he says to me, "So do you want to have children? No," I say. I see a flashing or rippling of feelings on Richards' face–he can't quite place the news, doesn't know where to put it. He says that he has always thought of having kids, that it seems to him part of what it is to be human. "You live," he says, "you reproduce, you die." He says he sees himself on this definitive path: marriage and children. I want to say that what makes us human is the ability to choose, to create in many different ways.

The conversation is stilted. Richard looks at me with a sense of distance, as if I had told him I have a fatal disease. I've left his world, and he is trying to create a way to bring me back, a way for me to fit. A few days later he tells me that he likes me a lot, except for one strike against me. I ask him what that is and he says quietly, "You know." When I finally tell Richard about the tubal ligation he asks, "Why would you do that? You've giving up the chance of growth, of possibility." I am struck by the words "growth" and "possibility." For the tubal ligation has always seemed to be a choice toward possibility.

In presurgery, I am brought into a room with posters of landscapes and am hooked up to an IV or sugar water. I am to wait here while they finish with the patient before me. This gives me time to reflect. I can leave if I want to. I picture the process: pull out the IV, open the door, shuffle down the hallway in my foam slippers, hold the back of my johnny shut, back through the maze to where I've left my clothes, change, leave, get in my car and drive. I imagine telling my friend Carla, who has accompanied me, that I've changed my mind. I imagine waiting for a call from Richard, who is out of town on business—how happy I could make him. But I don't move. I come back to my lack of birth control and my fear of getting pregnant. My moment of doubt is not about thinking maybe I want to have a child, it is about whether I need to do this to my body. I shut my eyes and listen to my breath. A few minutes later a door opens.

The decision not to have children is given far more scrutiny than the decision to have them.

I expect something to go wrong. The doctor inserts the laparoscope, tilts the table back, and puts the carbon dioxide in. Immediately something starts pulling in my right side and I think that this is the thing gone wrong. I glance over to the screen and can see my uterus, which is full and round, floating like a balloon losing its helium. I watch the cauterizing tool reach for my fallopian tubes, and then I stop looking; it hurts too much. It is a pulsating pain originating from deep inside of me, from a place that I've never felt before. It is how I learn that I indeed have fallopian tubes. I catch glimpses of my bobbing uterus and the tubes snaking around. The fallopian tube is pale pink but changes color completely when it is cauterized. A tendril of smoke rises from the tube, a black thread against the pink uterus. In and out of awareness, the anesthesia is taking effect.

In the days afterward, the carbon dioxide rises, and my shoulders feel as if the circulation had been cut off. I fall to the floor knowing that will disperse the gas. My belly button has been sewn shut, and I am swollen with a tightness that pushes into my lower back. I'm wondering now if, with the act of sterilization, I have brought a story to a definitive end. Have I hindered possibility? My emotions swing wildly: flashes that I'll never hold my own child leave me feeling weepy, flashes that I never wanted to hold my own child leave me laughing. I take showers with plastic wrap over the incision. The water beads on top or slips underneath, forming rivulets of water down my abdomen. I feel as though I've wrapped myself in plastic and am forever separated from the world. When I am able to have sex, when I can walk well, when I get my period, I tell myself, then I can decide whether I've made the right choice.

BUT AFTER THE SURGERY I AM PLAGUED. I KEEP imagining the fallopian tubes shirking away from the cauterizing tool, as if they have a life of their own–similar to how men refer to their penises as separate entities. It seems to me that I have mutilated myself on a very basic level, and I wonder if I've lost some essence of myself as a woman. It is as if I, too, am now defining womanhood in terms of my sexual organs. What is it to be female? What is it to be sexual? Is it my organs and my ability to procreate that make me female?

A week later I am at my mother's home. We are looking at a crib in her guest room. I wish I could tell her about the tubal ligation, but I would become pitiful in her eyes. People who have children assume they know what it's like not to have children. They don't. Living with the decision not to have children creates a different sense of the world and the future. It creates a different set of responsibilities that people who intend to have children never face. I tell my mother that my younger brother will be the last to give her grandchildren. "Well," she says to me, "you never know. You'll change your mind."

I am living into the decision of having had the tubal ligation. Sex is more enjoyable, freeing, and carefree; I feel more sexual and thus more womanly. The decision not to have children will probably pull at me for the rest of my life. It is an intimidating and difficult task to choose to live powerfully, to make decisions, and to define myself beyond the roles that society has deemed for women. Each time I write, I live the decision not to have a child. Each moment, each page, each paragraph, each sentence, each word, this word now, moves me further into what it means to be a powerful, fruitful woman. I am continually entering the language of possibility.

Carolyn E. Megan is a writer living in the Boston area.

From *Ms.* Magazine, October/November 2000, pp. 43-46. © 2000 by Ms. Magazine. Reprinted with permission of the author.

How Old Is Too Old to Have a Baby?

Fertility technology is advancing at such an astonishing pace that couples who fail to have children in their forties could realistically wait until their sixties to try again

BY JUDITH NEWMAN

TO BECOME A FATHER at 52 is unusual. To become a mother at 52 is to defy nature. Alan and Deirdre, both 52, don't want to let many of their friends and colleagues in on their secret yet, in case something goes wrong. But they are doing everything in their power to have a baby. They have the money, and they have the will. Deirdre, a trim, athletic researcher at a medical school in Connecticut, has three adult children from a previous marriage; Alan, a college English professor, has never had kids. "I always wanted children," he says. "Three years ago, when I found this woman I loved who was my own age, I thought, 'Well, that's one dream I'll have to relinquish.'"

Deirdre had already gone through menopause. By supplying the correct amounts of estrogen and progesterone via hormone therapy, it is relatively easy to make the uterus of a post-menopausal woman hospitable to a fetus. But even then, the chance of a woman Deirdre's age getting pregnant with her own eggs is nonexistent. So doctors suggested the couple consider implanting a donor egg fertilized with Alan's sperm. Egg donation is no longer considered cutting-edge medicine, but using the procedure to impregnate a woman over 50 is. Still, Alan and Deirdre

were overjoyed. "I thought, 'Isn't science great?'" Alan says.

In a few weeks, Machelle Seibel, a reproductive endocrinologist at the Fertility Center of New England, will mix the eggs of a much younger woman with Alan's sperm and introduce the resulting embryos to Deirdre's uterus. Her chances of giving birth will then rocket from less than 1 percent to 50 percent. "I would have considered doing this even if I hadn't remarried," Deirdre says with a lopsided grin. "The idea of having another child at this stage is compelling."

Not that Deirdre and Alan are unaware of the problems of being older parents. They worry about how they'll function with little sleep—"although I needed a lot of sleep even when I was in college," Alan says—and they are concerned that they might not be around to see their child come of age. If Deirdre gets pregnant, they plan to move to the Midwest to be near Alan's four brothers and sisters. "As a hedge against possible early death, we want our child to be surrounded by as much family as possible," Alan says.

Deirdre's three children, all in their twenties, are trying to be supportive. But they're skeptical. "Independently they came to me and said they thought it would be weird to be their age and have parents in

their late seventies," Deirdre says. "But I look at it like this: Our definition of 'family' has expanded. Now there are gay and adoptive and single-parent families who've used assisted technology. So although an 'older-parent family' is what we'll be, it's only one of several variations."

Twenty-two years after the world's first test-tube baby was conceived through in vitro fertilization, science is giving men and women—at least those who can afford the steep medical fees—increasing flexibility to alter the seasons of their lives. Infertility treatments once considered revolutionary are now commonplace: If a man has a low sperm count, sperm cells can be retrieved from a testicle for direct injection into an egg's cytoplasm. If the shell of an egg has hardened because of age, doctors can hatch it in the lab and then implant it on the uterine wall. If a woman has stopped producing eggs, she can avail herself of drugs to induce ovulation, as well as donor eggs or donor embryos. These days, the science of assisted reproductive technology is advancing at such a rapid rate that laboratory researchers say it will soon be medically possible for even a centenarian to give birth. But such tinkering with the biological clock begs a commonsense question: How old is too old to have a baby? And this seemingly straightforward question trickles into a cascade of other questions: How old is too old for parents? For children? For society?

When it comes to treating women for infertility, the American Society for Reproductive Medicine would like to draw its line in the sand at menopause. "Around 50, that's when reproductive processes have physiologically stopped, and therefore the intervention and treatment by physicians should also stop," says Robert Stillman, a former member of the society's board of directors. "Infertility is a medical disorder, affected by the reproductive life span. Just as we wouldn't consider inducing a prepubescent individual to conceive—although we could—we shouldn't induce pregnancy in someone who's gone through menopause."

In recent years, an increasing number of women have chosen to spend more time building a career, or looking for the right mate, before having children. Some have been shocked to belatedly discover there is no denying a fact of nature. Without any scientific intervention, childbearing is out of the question for most women by the time they reach their early forties. Between the ages of 35 and 40, fertility tapers off, and after 43 it pretty much plummets off the cliff. That is because something about the aging process upsets the process of meiosis, the nuclear division of the ovum or sperm in which chromosomes are reduced to half their original number. Sex cells do not divide properly, and there are too many or too few chromosomes in the egg or sperm. For women in their mid-forties, there is a dramatic increase in the risk that their eggs will have the wrong number of chromosomes after ovulation. Hence the difficulty in getting, and staying, pregnant. And unlike a man, whose sperm supply is constantly renewing itself, a woman is born with all the eggs she'll ever have. In fact, ovaries start aging before a woman's birth. A 20-week-old fetus has about 7 million eggs. Eighteen weeks later, at birth, that number has been decimated to less than 2 million. Even though the eggs remain unused throughout childhood, by puberty the egg supply has dropped to 400,000—less than 6 percent of what the child started with. By menopause, the egg larder is close to empty.

Even when an older mother manages to get pregnant, she and her baby face additional medical hurdles. With mothers over 35, there is a greater risk of hypertension and diabetes for themselves, and likely a greater risk of juvenile diabetes for the

children. A 1995 Swedish study found that women born to mothers age 45 or older had a slightly higher chance of developing breast cancer than women born to younger mothers. Most well known is the increased risk of certain chromosomal abnormalities such as Down's syndrome, in which there is an extra set of genes in each cell.

Studies suggest that being the child of an older father also carries risk. Because older sperm tend to have more chromosomal mutations—ranging in seriousness from harmless to lethal—there is among older fathers a higher rate of kids born with certain rare tumors, neural-tube defects, congenital cataracts, and upper limb defects. Curiously, there's also a higher rate of homosexual children born to older dads.

While men experience some decline in the number of sperm, motility, and morphology—the number of normal sperm—after age 40, it's generally not enough to prevent them from becoming fathers. There are typically 150 to 300 million sperm released in one ejaculation. Even if the number drops by 50 percent, there are still pretty good odds there will be some keepers.

And now, technology has advanced to the point where even men with extremely poor sperm quality can father children. With intracytoplasmic sperm injection, an embryologist can inject a single sperm into the cytoplasm of an egg with a microscopic needle while bypassing the normal cascade of chemical reactions necessary for fertilization. The procedure, which has only been around since 1992, is a primary reason for the speed-of-light development of fertility treatment for aging would-be parents—because it's not only sperm that can be injected into the egg. The processes of microinjection and micromanipulation of egg and sperm are making a wider array of new treatments possible.

For example, embryologist Jacques Cohen, scientific director at the Institute for Reproductive Medicine and Science of Saint Barnabas in Livingston, New Jersey, has developed a procedure called cytoplasmic transfer that shows promise for assisting women approaching their early forties who either can't get pregnant through in vitro fertilization or have embryos of such poor quality they don't survive. Doctors take the cytoplasm of a youthful and healthy egg—containing not the DNA but the proteins and enzymes for healthy cell growth—and inject it into the problematic egg to boost its quality. Possible health risks with the procedure have not yet been conclusively studied and there are trou-

bling ethical questions. (See box "Can a Baby Have Three Parents?") But out of 26 attempts, the technique has resulted in 12 live births.

Jamie Grifo, director of New York University's reproductive endocrinology unit, is further refining another technique to assist women between 42 and 45, whose chances of having a child with their own eggs hover around 5 percent. He takes an older woman's egg and extracts the nucleus, which contains the DNA. Then he removes the nucleus from the donor egg of a much younger woman and in its place microinjects the genetic material of the older woman. The procedure, attempted on two women last year, resulted in fertilized embryos but not babies. Grifo and his team went back to the lab, perfecting the process on mice. The result: baby mice.

Double Trouble

Since the advent of in vitro fertilization two decades ago, there has been an explosion in the number of multiple births, particularly among women over 40. Statistics released last September by the Centers for Disease Control reveal a 52 percent increase overall in twin births between 1980 and 1997. Among women between 40 and 44, the increase in the number of twins born was 63 percent, and among women between 45 and 49 it was a staggering 1,000 percent. The ages of the mothers had less effect on the health or survival of the infants than the pregnancy complications generally associated with multiple births. For example, the risk of a very low birth weight is eight times higher for twins than for single births. The ultimate impact of multiple births on the lives of older parents is immeasurable. "Keeping up with two kids instead of one is a real challenge," says Machelle Seibel. "The increase in energy required is exponential rather than additive."

Grifo's groundbreaking work could provide the answer women like Alison Carlson are looking for. Carlson is a golden girl: blond, sunny, a former professional tennis coach in San Francisco. When she got married last year to a younger man and started trying to get pregnant at 42, she assumed she'd succeed quickly. "I was an athlete," she says. "I felt

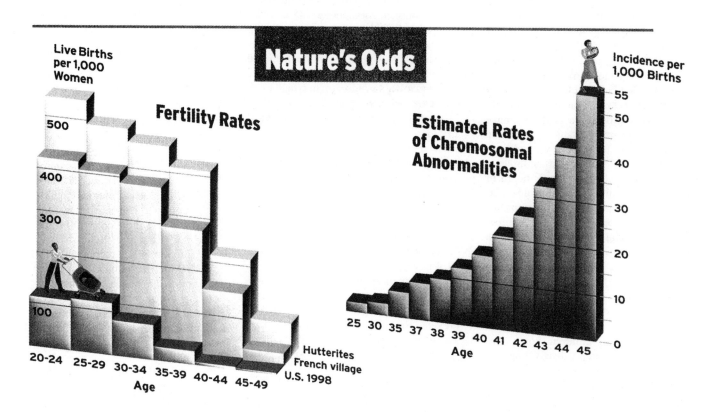

Dale Glasgand

LEFT: Contemporary birth records of the Hutterites, a religious sect in the western U.S. and Canada that does not practice birth control, and seventeenth-century birth records from a French village reveal a similar pattern: Natural fertility rates among women drop off precipitously around age 40. The latest available overall birthrates for U.S. women follow the same downward trend but are lower across the board because of the prevalence of birth control and a tendency of women to marry later in life. RIGHT: Statistics indicate that the risk of women having children with chromosomal abnormalities, including Down's syndrome, rises steadily from 2.1 per thousand births at age 25 to 53.7 per thousand births at age 45.

the normal rules wouldn't apply to me." At first it seemed she would be right. In her initial round of in vitro fertilization, Carlson produced an impressive 27 eggs, and 25 were fertilized: "I was a champ." She got pregnant but quickly miscarried. Forty-five percent of women over 40 do, usually because of chromosomal abnormalities in their eggs. "Suddenly I felt like I should buy one of these T-shirts that say 'I Can't Believe I Forgot to Have Children.'" Carlson says that when she tried again, she failed to get pregnant at all.

Intellectually, Carlson knows the problem is age, but emotionally she cannot accept it. Like so many men and women over 40 who begin fertility treatments, she feels pressure to keep trying. "I'm embarrassed because, first, I felt I was being so arrogant," she says. "Like, here we all are, a bunch of baby boomers who went to college in the second wave of feminism, dedicated to having important careers before having

babies, and then paying gobs of money so science can give us what we want. I'm appalled at my own sense of entitlement."

Given the anguish many aging baby boomers now experience trying to get pregnant, it's hard to fathom that the future holds no less than the end of infertility. Doctors recently discovered how to freeze a woman's eggs when she's young and then thaw them when she's ready to get pregnant. A woman could finish college and graduate school, launch a career, and then start a family with eggs she parked on ice at age 18.

Banking individual eggs is just the beginning. Recently Kutluk Oktay, the chief of reproductive endocrinology and infertility at New York Methodist Hospital in Brooklyn, has been experimenting with freezing and transplanting swatches of ovarian tissue. Each bit of tissue contains thousands of immature follicle eggs. While individual, already-developed eggs die

easily when frozen, immature follicle eggs embedded in the ovarian tissue fare a lot better. Oktay has already tried the technique on a 30-year-old dancer from Arizona who'd had her first ovary removed at 17 because of cysts but had the foresight to have her second ovary frozen. Last fall, Oktay sewed 80 small pieces of the tissue back into her pelvis and revived her menstrual cycle. The woman is not trying to conceive. But Oktay's colleague, Roger Gosden, now reproductive biology research director of McGill University's Royal Victoria Hospital in Montreal, has removed the ovaries of sheep, frozen them, thawed them, sutured them back in the sheep—and gotten lambs aplenty.

Of course cryopreservation will not help those whose eggs are already sitting on the porch in little rocking chairs. But researchers have found ways to keep old eggs alive. Jon Tilly, the director of the Vincent Center for Reproductive Biology at Massachusetts General Hospital in Boston, has been studying genetically altered mice to better understand the process of apoptosis, or natural cell death. Cells are programmed to die: Fifty or sixty genes, maybe more, regulate their expiration. One specifically involved in the death of immature eggs in the ovaries is known as the bax gene. When Tilly and his researchers studied mice that lacked the bax gene, they found that 24-month-old females—the equivalent of 80- to 100-year-old humans—still have functioning, estrogen-producing ovaries. "We were pretty amazed," says Tilly. "And the bax gene has a precise counterpart in humans that appears to be responsible for the decimation of eggs during menopause." Silencing of one of the "cell death" genes may be the first step in finding treatments to help woman delay menopause or avoid the health problems—osteoporosis, heart disease—associated with the cessation of estrogen production. Tilly also believes that in the not-wildly-distant future the ability to suppress the bax gene in women's ovaries may prolong their fertility too. He is quick to add, however, that even though the old female mice with newly viable eggs were allowed to cavort with young, studly mice, they did not produce offspring. This is because older mice lose the capacity to excrete adequate levels of two hormones: one that stimulates egg follicles to grow and mature and another that causes the ripened egg to be released from the ovary into the reproductive tract.

Another approach to ending infertility involves beating the numbers game. What if a woman had an unlimited number of eggs? This may someday be possible if researchers can get somatic cells—that is, cells from anywhere in the body—to act like sex cells. Normal cells are diploid, with 46 chromosomes—23 from one's father and 23 from one's mother. The gonads (testicles and ovaries) divide the chromosomes to create haploid cells, namely spermatozoa and eggs. As the eggs age, most suffer from aneuploidy, the uneven division of the chromosomes. Anything other than 23 sets of chromosomes makes the egg either entirely unviable, or viable but resulting in abnormalities like Down's syndrome. It is not that the eggs, in their undeveloped state, are abnormal; it's that something about the machinery of meiosis—the chromosomal division at ovulation—goes awry as women age. The key to fixing this problem is to make faux eggs—normal body cells that behave like eggs by undergoing meiosis. Thus, anyone 18 to 100 would have an unlimited supply of easily harvested "sex cells."

This is exactly what Cohen and some other researchers are working on now. Bioethicists balk, because the process sounds like a kissing cousin to cloning. But it's not. The resulting cell has half its mother's chromosomes and, when united with sperm, could be expected to create a bona fide, half-his, half-hers human. The catch is that the parents could theoretically be 100 or more years old. "This is going to involve some major discussions about what's clinically acceptable and what's socially acceptable," Cohen says.

Can a Baby Have Three Parents?

One new fertility treatment called cytoplasmic transfer involves taking a younger woman's "egg white," which contains the proteins and enzymes necessary for proper growth, and microinjecting it into the egg of an older woman. The idea is to restore healthy components to the older woman's egg, making fertilization and pregnancy more likely. The problem, says Machelle Seibel, is that mitochondria—tiny football-shaped structures in the cytoplasm that are the energy powerhouses of a cell—also contain some DNA. And scientists know that there are a number of inherited mitochondrial DNA diseases, resulting in health problems that range from the mild to the fatal. (Problems as varied as sudden infant death syndrome and Alzheimer's are thought to stem from genetic defects in the mitochondria.) Theoretically, the young woman giving her cytoplasm becomes the third parent, capable of passing along some genetic information, including her family diseases. "I don't think this component of the procedure is completely appreciated by the providers or the receivers," says Seibel. "Cytoplasmic transfer may be fine, but its safety is unproven. This makes me a little uncomfortable."

Of course, even if they have all the financial resources in the world, most couples past the age of retirement probably won't want to start raising children. "This won't be some huge public policy issue," says Arthur Caplan, director of the University of Pennsylvania's Center for Bioethics. "It's not like you'll see all these people running from nursing homes to birthing centers." But, Caplan adds, the very fact that 50-year-old mothers and fathers could become relatively commonplace raises another issue. "One of the ethical questions becomes: What's in the best interest of the child? And the answer is simple: It's good not to be an orphan. A good, loving environment requires one parent. So if a father is 20 and a mother 80, that's not a problem. If the father is 60 and the mother 40, well, one should think about the implications of depriving a child of grandparents. It's not morally reprehensible, but it's an issue. Now, if both parents are in their sixties"—as was the case in 1996 with Arceli Keh, the 63-year-old Filipino who gave birth after lying about her age to her fertility specialists in California—"that's a problem."

Contemplating their own untimely demise won't deter truly determined older parent wanna-bes, like Eileen and Charles Volz of Millbury, Massachusetts. Eileen, a certified public accountant, was 42 and had just married Charles, a digital commerce executive, in 1992 when she was diagnosed with breast cancer. Radiation and chemotherapy put her into immediate menopause, but she overcame the cancer. Four years passed before she and her husband heard about egg donation. "People thought we were a little nuts," says Charles Volz. "I mean, I already had three children, and she had survived breast cancer—why should we tempt fate?"

One look at their son, C.J., answers the question. On her first try at Machelle Seibel's clinic, she got pregnant with a donor egg and had C.J. at 48. "I never for a moment felt he wasn't mine," Eileen says. "Genetics is the smallest part of being a mother."

Eileen Volz is now 50; her husband is 48. They tried a second round of egg donation, which failed, but they are contemplating a third. Sure they'll be collecting Social Security by the time C.J. is ready to head off to college. But Charles Volz speaks for older parents everywhere when he offers this Pollyannaish view of his midlife adventure: "It's not a problem at all. Hey, I'm going to live forever."

Perhaps the biggest question for science and society will not be answered for a number of years, until the first generation of children born to older parents through assisted reproductive technology enters their teenage years: What happens when children nature did not intend to create become adults? Already there are some troubling questions about the 20,000 children conceived throughout the world by intracytoplasmic sperm injection. Aggressively injecting a sperm into an egg manually has been found to change a whole sequence of molecular events in fertilization; for example, the DNA packaged in the head of the sperm unravels more slowly than in normal fertilization, throwing off the timing of the process. Scientists worry that although there hasn't been an obvious increase in birth defects so far, sex chromosome abnormalities may show up when the children reach puberty. One 1998 study in Belgium showed that of 1,082 prenatal tests on intracytoplasmic sperm injection pregnancies, one in 120 had sex chromosome abnormalities, as compared to a general population figure of one in 500 pregnancies.

"Fertility is a unique field in some respects," says Massachusetts General's Jon Tilly. "In most fields of scientific inquiry, most of the problems are worked out in animal models. But here, technology is moving so fast, and people are so desperate for answers, that work on humans is paralleling work on animals. That may turn out to be good, because we are accelerating the application of our knowledge. But it may be bad, because we don't know what's safe. We don't know about unforeseen problems. There may be reasons the body is not designed to be reproducing after its early forties."

birth of a father:
BECOMING DAD

HOW DO MEN **REALLY** FEEL ABOUT MAKING THE TRANSITION FROM REGULAR GUY TO DEAR OL' DAD?

A group of men—some of them expecting fathers, some dads already—got together recently over pizza and beer to talk about what it's really like to be a parent. Once we edited out all the Monty Python jokes and references to that cute chick on *Survivor: The Australian Outback*, what was left were honest admissions, valuable advice and true tenderness. That, and a couple of veggie slices, which one dad-to-be took home for his pizza-craving wife.

The participants:

BILLY *37*, sound editor for television and film; wife is six months pregnant with first child.

KEVIN F. *29*, dot-com refugee; has one son, 4 months old.

KEVIN D. *45*, programmer; wife is eight months pregnant with first child.

DON *47*, engineer; 2-year-old son; wife is seven months pregnant.

KEITH *35*, boat captain; has three sons, ages 6, 5, and 20 months.

Fit Pregnancy: When you found out you were going to become a father, what was the first thing that went through your head?

BILLY We weren't trying, but we weren't *not* trying. My wife came out of the bathroom with this terrified look on her face, extremely upset, and that's when she told me. I said, "That's great! Cool!" But she thought she'd ruined all our plans—we had these financial goals that we wanted to reach before a baby came. But I was like, "Hey, we didn't get up there and say all those vows for nothing."

DON We were trying for a second baby, and she did the same thing—came out of

the bathroom and said, "Come check this out," and there's the little green line on the test. We were really happy, but we were much calmer the second time around. The first time, we were probably panic-stricken in terms of not knowing exactly what to do. Right after we found out, we ran out to the bookstore and bought about $100 worth of pregnancy books.

KEITH We took the test—she actually made me go buy it—and it was stressful. We weren't married at the time, and we didn't know what to expect. But we were happy about it.

KEVIN D. My wife had had a miscarriage before, and she was pretty sure she

WHY TESTOSTERONE IS LIKE THE NASDAQ

Fatherhood can tweak a man's hormones, too. Canadian researchers found that men's testosterone levels temporarily dropped by one-third after their babies were born. And the less testosterone the new dads had, the more protectively they behaved toward their newborns. Men who felt concerned after listening to a tape of a baby crying showed a bigger testosterone drop than less concerned men.

PRENATAL CARE: IT'S A MANLY JOB

Most men think their primary role during their wife's pregnancy is to provide her with love, affection and positive words, according to a North Carolina State University survey. While the men said that seeking information on prenatal care was their least important job, experts believe it's just as urgent as providing emotional support.

SMOKING IS BAD FOR SEX AND CONCEPTION

A man who smokes may take longer to impregnate his partner, perhaps due to changes in his sperm quality, says a report in *Fertility and Sterility*. And researchers at the Andrology Institute of America in Lexington, Ky., found that male smokers had sex 5.7 times per month on average, compared with 11.6 times per month for nonsmokers.

THE HYPERTENSIVE DAD-TO-BE

If a man has high blood pressure, the best place for it to be discovered may be the obstetrician's office, reports the *American Journal of Hypertension*. Twenty-one percent of men accompanying women to prenatal exams were found to have elevated blood pressure; almost none knew they had the condition.

WHEN DADS GET DOWN

Three percent of new fathers become depressed, a British study reported in the *American Journal of Psychiatry* found. Risk factors include a family that has stepchildren and a new mother who is also depressed. Solution: Get help from a mental-health professional.

TALK TO YOUR MOM

Men whose mothers developed the late-stage pregnancy complication known as preeclampsia are twice as likely to father a child whose birth is also complicated by the condition. To be prepared, a man should ask about his own birth.

—Shari Roan and Mary Ellen Strote

---

was pregnant—it was the first time since losing the baby that we'd tried. But the test said no. We were disappointed for about a week—until she took another pregnancy test and it came out positive. But it really didn't become real for me until we saw the first ultrasound. I was so surprised to see the baby moving around so much... I guess I'd thought that they mostly just sleep in there. But he was just sort of spinning around, and it was amazing.

KEVIN F. In the movies, you get the test results and there's this lightning bolt, but for me it was more surreal. Women can feel these things going on with their bodies, but for a guy, no matter how close you are as a couple, no matter how much you've planned it, the baby isn't growing inside *your* body or making *you* tired or nauseated.

Was that a problem for you and your wife?

KEVIN F. She was a little ahead of where I was in seeing the baby as real, as part of the family. We didn't have conflicts about

it, but I was thinking, "Shouldn't this be more real for me?" In some way, I don't think the reality sets in until you see that head coming out.

Has your lifestyle changed a whole lot during the pregnancy or when the baby came? Are you missing out on things that you used to enjoy?

DON We'd traveled a lot already and done a lot of things—what we were missing out on was having a family.

KEVIN F. I found myself thinking about things like money and investments, education IRAs. We'd go out for breakfast and I wouldn't order coffee, and I'd think, "All right! A dollar-fifty in the college fund!"

KEVIN D. With work and everything, it seems like I'm always fighting for free time now, and I wonder how much time there'll be once we have a baby. But as far as going out and partying or anything, that's not really us.

BILLY Yeah, our Friday and Saturday nights were usually Blockbuster videos and a pizza. We've never been party animals.

Hey, I've got another full pitcher here. Anyone for a refill? [Beer mugs are trust forward simultaneously.] What's the one thing you're looking forward to most about being a dad, or what were you looking forward to before you became one?

KEITH Being a kid again—playing catch, making snow angels, throwing snowballs, doing silly kid stuff.

KEVIN D. I know what you mean—like re-experiencing your childhood through your own child's eyes.

KEVIN F. Through your own father's eyes, too. Becoming a father really helps to clarify your relationship with your own dad.

SECOND ROUND
JUST SHOOT ME'S ENRICO COLANTONI ON BABY NO. 2

Enrico Colantoni may have found the secret to being the perfect dad: Don't try to be perfect. Colantoni, who plays Elliott DiMauro on the NBC sitcom *Just Shoot Me*, is the father of Madelyn Francesca, almost a year old, and Quintin, 4. During his busy movie-shooting summer, we asked him to give us his take on fatherhood and found him unafraid to voice some feelings that many men have but don't admit to.

Fit Pregnancy: Six weeks after you met, you found out your wife, Nancy, was pregnant. What was your reaction?
Enrico Colantoni: It felt like the powers that be had taken over. The romanticism kept me elated the whole nine months. Then Quintin just came out fighting and screaming. He wouldn't sleep, you couldn't put him down, and I was in the darkest place. My wife is giving all her attention to this little guy, and I am left out in the cold. I asked her, "What can we do?" and she said, "I don't know."

So what did you do?
Well, I left for a while. When I came back, I realized that I'd been trying to be Super Dad and work all day, then take over as Super Mom at night. I'd given up male companionship and having fun. So I went back to playing football and hanging out with other dads, guys who had grown children and who could give me some perspective.

How was having a second child different?
I know how to take care of myself. I can't lose sleep 'cause I have to go to work, so sometimes I go sleep in the back office. Nancy and I divided things up. I said, "You need to mother the baby, and I will

take care of Quintin." So now Quintin and I are spending a lot of time alone. And it's OK for me that Nancy is completely consumed with this new life. As for Madelyn, I know that someday she's probably going to end up with someone like me, so I better put my best foot forward.

Anything you would have done differently?
I would have let Quintin cry more instead of trying to pacify him so much. He had something he was trying to say, and I would have liked to just hold him, let him scream and not try to fix everything all the time.

Both babies were born at home. Was that scary?
The first time definitely was scary: Nancy had to push for five hours. Madelyn came out in 23 minutes. And that's the way it is with her; she doesn't cry unless she falls down or something.

Would you like more kids?
I don't think so. I like feeling that each of them has at least one parent around at all times. And I don't get babies—I want them to come out walking, the way baby horses do. But Quintin and I are really having fun now.

What would you like new dads to know?
Be yourself, and know that dads are different from moms. It exhausts me to try to do Nancy's work. Also, don't just hand kids everything—to me, it's most fun to allow them the lesson. I will always be there for my kids, but I want to let them figure things out.

—*Peg Moline*

How?

KEVIN F. In my earliest memories, my father seemed really old, but he was about the same age I am now. And to me, he was like a god. It's a humbling thought—how am I going to be worthy of the trust and affection my son puts in me?

BILLY It's a rite of passage, understanding your own place in the world.

What about your relationship with your wife? You're really close during the pregnancy and delivery, but all of a sudden, there's a baby with needs to be met.

KEVIN D. Actually, we're kind of gearing up for that, for a lot of our emotional energy and time being dedicated to taking care of the baby.

BILLY Our relationship changed at the end of the first trimester, when my wife went into premature labor and the doctor told us no more sex. There's a stress that comes with that, but I think that in some ways, my wife and I have become more intimate. Other couples can work out their stress in the bedroom, but we have to communicate in other ways.

DON'T EVER TELL YOUR WIFE SHE LOOKS BIG.

Let's talk a little bit more about sex. How do you cope with the changes in your physical relationship?

DON It's definitely more planned than spontaneous now, especially when she's feeling nauseated or fatigued. And with trying to not make her uncomfortable with

the weight and the pressure, it kind of becomes a Keystone Kops sort of thing.

KEITH It was great during pregnancy. She was still really sexy. Sex is a different story with three kids, though—there's no time or place to hide.

KEVIN F. Since the baby, we've been figuring out how to make our lives work. His needs are all-consuming, and ours, physical and emotional, have taken a back seat. We're both frayed, so I have to think twice and not say or do anything I'll regret.

Speaking of stuff you regret, is there anything you'd advise an expecting father to never say or do?

BILLY Don't ever say she looks big.

KEVIN D. Actually, my wife is very small, and the doctor keeps telling her to gain more weight, so I get to call her a hippopotamus with impunity.

DON My wife gets kind of a dopiness thing, but she takes it in stride if I kid her about it. I don't push it, though.

BILLY No matter how much she's worrying about something, don't ever tell her not to worry or try to stop her from expressing her emotions. She needs to do that; it's your job to listen.

KEITH You have to be more sensitive.

How about your ages? Do you think it makes a difference if you wait to become a dad?

DON Well, we've both had longer careers than many new parents, and money isn't as stressful as it could be. I also know that age and maturity have given me a lot more patience. The biggest negative is the concern that later, I won't be able to throw a baseball to my kids. I hope they help keep me going.

BILLY There's a certain amount of finesse required for being a parent. I think I have that now, but a few years ago I might not have.

KEITH And you've left the wild stuff behind you.

So out of all this, how has fatherhood, real or imminent, changed you?

KEVIN F. I think it's a sense of wonder at this unfolding relationship, of having him look into my eyes and know who I am.

DON More than anything else, the feeling that what's to come far exceeds anything I've given up.

BILLY There's a Zen saying about how it's better to want what you have than have what you want. I think that when you become a father, that's particularly true. Now if I can just do that in real life, it's gonna be great.

Jeff Lucia *and his wife, Carole, aren't officially trying for child no. 2, but they aren't not trying, either.*

From *Shape* magazine, August/September 2001, pp. 68-72, 74. © 2001 by Weider Publications.

BABY, IT'S YOU!

AND YOU, AND YOU...

Renegade scientists say they are ready to start applying the technology of cloning to human beings. Can they really do it, and how scary would that be?

BY NANCY GIBBS

BEFORE WE ASSUME THAT THE MARKET FOR human clones consists mainly of narcissists who think the world deserves more of them or neo-Nazis who dream of cloning Hitler or crackpots and mavericks and mischief makers of all kinds, it is worth taking a tour of the marketplace. We might just meet ourselves there.

Imagine for a moment that your daughter needs a bone-marrow transplant and no one can provide a match; that your wife's early menopause has made her infertile; or that your five-year-old has drowned in a lake and your grief has made it impossible to get your mind around the fact that he is gone forever. Would the news then really be so easy to dismiss that around the world, there are scientists in labs pressing ahead with plans to duplicate a human being, deploying the same technology that allowed Scottish scientists to clone Dolly the sheep four years ago?

All it took was that first headline about the astonishing ewe, and fertility experts began to hear the questions every day. Our two-year-old daughter died in a car crash; we saved a lock of her hair in a baby book. Can you clone her? Why does the law allow people more freedom to destroy fetuses than to create them? My husband had cancer and is sterile. Can you help us?

The inquiries are pouring in because some scientists are ever more willing to say yes, perhaps we can. Last month a well-known infertility specialist, Panayiotis Zavos of the University of Kentucky, announced that he and Italian researcher Severino Antinori, the man who almost seven years ago helped a 62-year-old woman give birth using donor eggs, were forming a consortium to produce the first human clone. Researchers in South Korea claim they have already created a cloned human embryo, though they destroyed it rather than implanting it in a surrogate mother to develop. Recent cover stories in *Wired* and the New York *Times* Magazine tracked the efforts of the Raelians, a religious group committed to, among other things, welcoming the first extraterrestrials when they appear. They intend to clone the cells of a dead 10-month-old boy whose devastated parents hope, in effect, to bring him back to life as a newborn. The Raelians say they have the lab and the scientists, and—most important, considering the amount of trial and error involved—they say they have 50 women lined up to act as surrogates to carry a cloned baby to term.

Given what researchers have learned since Dolly, no one thinks the mechanics of cloning are very hard: take a donor egg, suck out the nucleus, and hence the DNA, and fuse it with, say, a skin cell from the human being copied. Then, with the help of an electrical current, the reconstituted cell should begin growing into a genetic duplicate. "It's inevitable that someone will try and someone will succeed," predicts Delores Lamb, an infertility expert at Baylor University. The consensus among biotechnology specialists is that within a few years—some scientists believe a few months—the news will break of the birth of the first human clone.

At that moment, at least two things will happen—one private, one public. The meaning of what it is to be human—which until now has involved, at the very least, the mysterious melding of two different people's DNA—will shift forever, along with our understanding of the relationship between parents and children, means and ends, ends and beginnings. And as a result, the conversation that has occupied scientists and ethicists for years, about how much man should mess with nature when it comes to reproduction, will drop onto every kitchen table, every pulpit, every politician's desk. Our fierce national debate over issues like abortion and euthanasia will seem tame and transparent compared with the questions that human cloning raises.

That has many scientists scared to death. Because even if all these headlines are hype and we are actually far away from seeing the first human clone, the very fact that at this moment, the research is proceeding underground, unaccountable, poses a real threat. The risk lies not just with potential babies born deformed, as many animal clones are; not just with desperate couples and cancer patients and other potential "clients" whose hopes may be raised and hearts broken and life savings wiped out. The immediate risk is that a backlash against renegade science might strike at responsible science as well.

The more scared people are of some of this research, scientists worry, the less likely they are to tolerate any of it. Yet variations on cloning technology are already used in biotechnology labs all across the country. It is these techniques that will allow, among other things, the creation of cloned herds of sheep and cows that produce medicines in their milk. Researchers also hope that one day, the ability to clone adult human cells will make it possible to "grow" new hearts and livers and nerve cells.

WHAT IF. . . a child dies and one parent wants to clone but the other doesn't? Who owns the rights to a dead person's DNA?

But some of the same techniques could also be used to grow a baby. Trying to block one line of research could impede another and so reduce the chances of finding cures for ailments such as Alzheimer's and Parkinson's, cancer and heart disease. Were some shocking breakthrough in human cloning to cause "an overcompensatory response by legislators," says Rockefeller University cloning expert Tony Perry, "that could be disastrous. At some point, it will potentially cost lives." So we are left with choices and trade-offs and a need to think through whether it is this technology that alarms us or just certain ways of using it.

BY DAY, RANDOLFE WICKER, 63, RUNS A lighting shop in New York City. But in his spare time, as spokesman for the Human Cloning Foundation, he is the face of cloning fervor in the U.S. "I took one step in this adventure, and it took over me like quicksand," says Wicker. He is planning to have some of his skin cells stored for future cloning. "If I'm not cloned before I die, my estate will be set up so that I can be cloned after," he says, admitting, however, that he hasn't found a lawyer willing to help. "It's hard to write a will with all these uncertainties," he concedes. "A lot of lawyers will look at me crazy."

As a gay man, Wicker has long been frustrated that he cannot readily have children of his own; as he gets older, his desire to reproduce grows stronger. He knows that a clone would not be a photocopy of him but talks about the traits the boy might possess: "He will like the color blue, Middle Eastern food and romantic Spanish music that's out of fashion." And then he hints at the heart of his motive. "I can thumb my nose at Mr. Death and say, 'You might get me, but you're not going to get all of me,'" he says. "The special formula that is me will live on into another lifetime. It's a partial triumph over death. I would leave my imprint not in sand but in cement."

This kind of talk makes ethicists conclude that even people who think they know about cloning—let alone the rest of us—don't fully understand its implications. Cloning, notes ethicist Arthur Caplan of the University of Pennsylvania, "can't make you immortal because clearly the clone is a different person. If I take twins and shoot one of them, it will be faint consolation to the dead one that the other one is still running around, even though they are genetically identical. So the road to immortality is not through cloning."

Still, cloning is the kind of issue so confounding that you envy the purists at either end of the argument. For the Roman Catholic Church, the entire question is one of world view: whether life is a gift of love or just one more industrial product, a little more valuable than most. Those who believe that the soul enters the body at the moment of conception think it is fine for God to make clones; he does it about 4,000 times a day, when a fertilized egg splits into identical twins. But when it comes to massaging a human life, for the scientist to do mechanically what God does naturally is to interfere with his work, and no possible benefit can justify that presumption.

On the other end of the argument are the libertarians who don't like politicians or clerics or ethics boards interfering with what they believe should be purely individual decisions. Reproduction is a most fateful lottery; in their view, cloning allows you to hedge your bet. While grieving parents may be confused about the technology—cloning, even if it works, is not resurrection—their motives are their own business. As for infertile couples, "we are interested in giving people the gift of life," Zavos, the aspiring cloner, told TIME this week. "Ethics is a wonderful word, but we need to look beyond the ethical issues here. It's not an ethical issue. It's a medical issue. We have a duty here. Some people need this to complete the life cycle, to reproduce."

WHAT IF. . . people don't want to be cloned after they die? Will they be able to insert a do-not-clone clause in their will?

In the messy middle are the vast majority of people who view the prospect with a vague alarm, an uneasy sense that science is dragging us into dark woods with no paths and no easy way to turn back. Ian Wilmut, the scientist who cloned Dolly but has come out publicly against human cloning, was not trying to help sheep have genetically related children. "He was trying to help farmers produce genetically improved sheep," notes Hastings Center ethicist Erik Parens. "And surely that's how the technology will go with us too." Cloning, Parens says, "is not simply this isolated technique out there that a few deluded folks are going to avail themselves of, whether they think it is a key to immortality or a way to bring someone back from the dead. It's part of a much bigger project. Essentially the big-picture question is, To what extent do we want to go down the path of using reproductive technologies to genetically shape our children?"

AT THE MOMENT, THE AMERICAN PUBLIC IS plainly not ready to move quickly on cloning. In a TIME/CNN poll last week, 90% of respondents thought it was a bad idea to clone human beings. "Cloning right now looks like it's coming to us on a magic carpet, piloted by a cult leader, sold to whoever can afford it," says ethicist Caplan. "That makes people nervous."

And it helps explain why so much of the research is being done secretly. We may learn of the first human clone only months, even years, after he or she is

HOW TO CLONE A HUMAN

If it works in humans as it has in other mammals, cloning will be technically possible, but also terribly inefficient and risky.

According to experts, producing a single viable clone will require scores of volunteers to donate eggs and carry embryos—most of which will have major abnormalities and never come to term. The clones that do survive could suffer more subtle problems that might show up well after birth. Here's how it might be done.

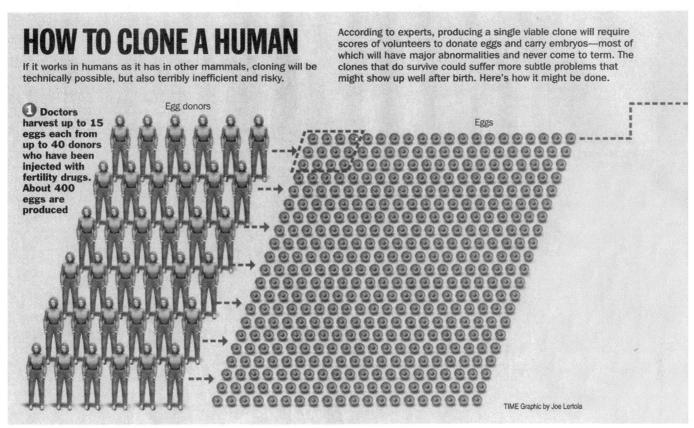

❶ Doctors harvest up to 15 eggs each from up to 40 donors who have been injected with fertility drugs. About 400 eggs are produced

Egg donors

Eggs

TIME Graphic by Joe Lertola

Graphic continued on next page.

born—if the event hasn't happened already, as some scientists speculate. The team that cloned Dolly waited until she was seven months old to announce her existence. Creating her took 277 tries, and right up until her birth, scientists around the world were saying that cloning a mammal from an adult cell was impossible. "There's a significant gap between what scientists are willing to talk about in public and their private aspirations," says British futurist Patrick Dixon. "The law of genetics is that the work is always significantly further ahead than the news. In the digital world, everything is hyped because there are no moral issues—there is just media excitement. Gene technology creates so many ethical issues that scientists are scared stiff of a public reaction if the end results of their research are known."

Of course, attitudes often change over time. In-vitro fertilization was effectively illegal in many states 20 years ago, and the idea of transplanting a heart was once considered horrifying. Public opinion on cloning will evolve just as it did on these issues, advocates predict. But in the meantime, the crusaders are mostly driven underground. Princeton biologist Lee Silver says fertility specialists have told him that they have no problem with cloning and

would be happy to provide it as a service to their clients who could afford it. But these same specialists would never tell inquiring reporters that, Silver says—it's too hot a topic right now. "I think what's happened is that all the mainstream doctors have taken a hands-off approach because of this huge public outcry. But I think what they are hoping is that some fringe group will pioneer it and that it will slowly come into the mainstream and then they will be able to provide it to their patients."

WHAT IF. . . it becomes acceptable to clone a person once? What about 10 times? One hundred?

All it will take, some predict, is that first snapshot. "Once you have a picture of a normal baby with 10 fingers and 10 toes, that changes everything," says San Mateo, Calif., attorney and cloning advocate Mark Eibert, who gets inquiries from infertile couples every day. "Once they put a child in front of the cameras, they've won." On the other hand, notes Gregory Pence, a pro-

fessor of philosophy at the University of Alabama at Birmingham and author of *Who's Afraid of Human Cloning?*, "if the first baby is defective, cloning will be banned for the next 100 years."

"I WOULDN'T MIND BEING THE FIRST PERson cloned if it were free. I don't mind being a guinea pig," says Doug Dorner, 35. He and his wife Nancy both work in health care. "We're not afraid of technology," he says. Dorner has known since he was 16 that he would never be able to have children the old-fashioned way. A battle with lymphoma left him sterile, so when he and Nancy started thinking of having children, he began following the scientific developments in cloning more closely. The more he read, the more excited he got. "Technology saved my life when I was 16," he says, but at the cost of his fertility. "I think technology should help me have a kid. That's a fair trade."

Talk to the Dorners, and you get a glimpse of choices that most parents can scarcely imagine having to make. Which parent, for instance, would they want to clone? Nancy feels she would be bonded to the child just from carrying him, so why not let the child have Doug's genetic material? Does it bother her to know she would,

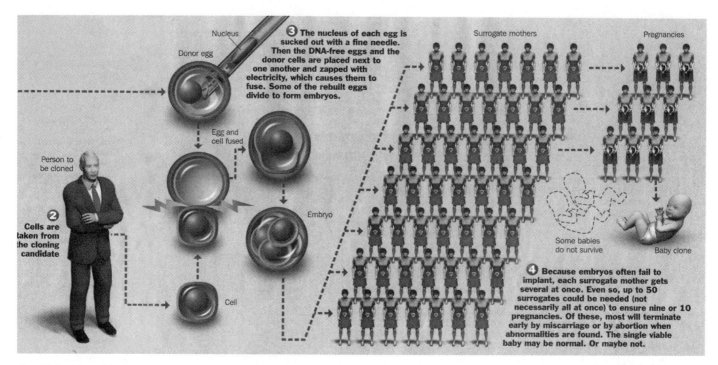

Graphic continued from previous page.

in effect, be raising her husband as a little boy? "It wouldn't be that different. He already acts like a five-year-old sometimes," she says with a laugh.

How do they imagine raising a cloned child, given the knowledge they would have going in? "I'd know exactly what his basic drives were," says Doug. The boy's dreams and aspirations, however, would be his own, Doug insists. "I used to dream of being a fighter pilot," he recalls, a dream lost when he got cancer. While they are at it, why not clone Doug twice? "Hmm. Two of the same kid," Doug ponders. "We'll cross that bridge when we come to it. But I know we'd never clone our clone to have a second child. Once you start copying something, who knows what the next copies will be like?"

In fact the risks involved with cloning mammals are so great that Wilmut, the premier cloner, calls it "criminally irresponsible" for scientists to be experimenting on humans today. Even after four years of practice with animal cloning, the failure rate is still overwhelming: 98% of embryos never implant or die off during gestation or soon after birth. Animals that survive can be nearly twice as big at birth as is normal, or have extra-large organs or heart trouble or poor immune systems. Dolly's

"mother" was six years old when *she* was cloned. That may explain why Dolly's cells show signs of being older than they actually are—scientists joked that she was really a sheep in lamb's clothing. This deviation raises the possibility that beings created by cloning adults will age abnormally fast.

"We had a cloned sheep born just before Christmas that was clearly not normal," says Wilmut. "We hoped for a few days it would improve and then, out of kindness, we euthanized it, because it obviously would never be healthy." Wilmut believes "it is almost a certainty" that cloned human children would be born with similar maladies. Of course, we don't euthanize babies. But these kids would probably die very prematurely anyway. Wilmut pauses to consider the genie he has released with Dolly and the hopes he has raised. "It seems such a profound irony," he says, "that in trying to make a copy of a child who has died tragically, one of the most likely outcomes is another dead child."

That does not seem to deter the scientists who work on the Clonaid project run by the Raelian sect. They say they are willing to try to clone a dead child. Though their outfit is easy to mock, they may be

even further along than the competition, in part because they have an advantage over other teams. A formidable obstacle to human cloning is that donor eggs are a rare commodity, as are potential surrogate mothers, and the Raelians claim to have a supply of both.

Earlier this month, according to Brigitte Boisselier, Clonaid's scientific director, somewhere in North America, a young woman walked into a Clonaid laboratory whose location is kept secret. Then, in a procedure that has been done thousands of times, a doctor inserted a probe, removed 15 eggs from the woman's ovaries and placed them in a chemical soup. Last week two other Clonaid scientists, according to the group, practiced the delicate art of removing the genetic material from each of the woman's eggs. Within the next few weeks, the Raelian scientific team plans to place another cell next to the enucleated egg.

This second cell, they say, comes from a 10-month-old boy who died during surgery. The two cells will be hit with an electrical charge, according to the scenario, and will fuse, forming a new hybrid cell that no longer has the genes of the young woman but now has the genes of the dead

MY SISTER, MY CLONE

I have a clone. She lives in Pittsburgh, Pa., and her name is Diana. She's my body double: blond hair, hazel eyes and fair skin. She's half an inch taller, but we have the same voices and the same mannerisms. We're both unmarried. We love to read, we relish Mexican food, and we get the same patches of dry skin in winter. We both play tennis and golf. O.K., she's funnier than I am—but just a little.

In the debate over the ethical, emotional and practical implications of human cloning, identical twins—distinct beings who share the same DNA—present the closest analogy. Identical twins are in fact more similar to each other than a clone would be to his or her original, since twins gestate simultaneously in the same womb and are raised in the same environment at the same time, usually by the same parents.

But even with our genes and backgrounds the same, my sister and I are very different people. Diana is a corporate lawyer; I'm a former magazine editor, now a literary agent. She studied classics at Bryn Mawr; I studied the history of religion at Vassar. She favors clothes that have actual colors in them; I opt for black. She's politically conservative; I'm more liberal. She's a pragmatist; I'm an optimist.

We're not the only twins with differences in our family. My father, a writer and former diplomat, had an identical twin brother, Francis, who was a right-brained banker. Francis, who died in 1992, also had identical twin daughters. My cousin Rose is an intense adventurist while her sister Peg is softer and more traditional.

Of course, there are ways in which identical twins are bound together that are more profound than the usual sibling links. When I walk into a room, it takes no more than a glance before I can sense my twin's mood—if she's happy or tense or upset. I know what it's about and why. It's something I suspect few people, maybe not even all twins, experience. Would clones? I suspect not, since their life experiences would be so different.

Other connections between Diana and me may be more related to our matching DNA and thus more applicable to clones. My twin and I filter information in much the same way, and we think, perceive and interpret things similarly. When we're together, we often respond simultaneously with the same word or sentence. We have put on the same T shirt on the same day in different cities. We have friends who are twins, both doctors, who have similar experiences. They took a pharmacy class together in medical school but sat across the classroom from each other and took separate notes. They studied separately for the exam. When it was returned, they had missed the same questions, for the same reasons.

Despite these shared propensities, people who hope they can create a duplicate of, say, a lost child may be setting up that clone for heartbreak. Imagine the expectations that would be created for such a person. Comparisons are tough enough on identical twins. Between Diana and me, there were issues such as who got the better grade, who scored more points in a basketball game, who had more friends. But neither of us had to live with the idea that she was created to match up to the other's best features. A cloned child might not play the piano as well as the original. Or be as smart.

Identical twins are living proof that identical DNA doesn't mean identical people. My sister and I may have the same hardwiring—and a wire that connects us. We have fun with our similarities, but at the end of the day, there's no confusion about who is who. Just as the fingerprints of all individuals, even identical twins, are unique, so are their souls. And you can't clone a soul.

—By Susan Reed

child. Once the single cell has developed into six to eight cells, the next step is to follow the existing, standard technology of assisted reproduction: gingerly insert the embryo into a woman's womb and hope it implants. Clonaid scientists expect to have implanted the first cloned human embryo in a surrogate mother by next month.

Even if the technology is basic, and even if it appeals to some infertile couples, should grieving parents really be pursuing this route? "It's a sign of our growing despotism over the next generation," argues University of Chicago bioethicist Leon Kass. Cloning introduces the possibility of parents' making choices for their children far more fundamental than whether to give them piano lessons or straighten their teeth. "It's not just that parents will have particular hopes for these children," says Kass. "They will have expectations based on a life that has already been lived. What a thing to do—to carry on the life of a person who has died."

The libertarians are ready with their answers. "I think we're hypercritical about people's reasons for having children," says Pence. "If they want to re-create their dead children, so what?" People have always had self-serving reasons for having children, he argues, whether to ensure there's someone to care for them in their old age or to relive their youth vicariously. Cloning is just another reproductive tool; the fact that it is not a perfect tool, in Pence's view, should not mean it should be outlawed altogether. "We know there are millions of girls who smoke and drink during pregnancy, and we know what the risks to the fetus are, but we don't do anything about it," he notes. "If we're going to regulate cloning, maybe we should regulate that too."

OLGA TOMUSYAK WAS TWO WEEKS SHY OF her seventh birthday when she fell out of the window of her family's apartment. Her parents could barely speak for a week after she died. "Life is empty without her," says her mother Tanya, a computer programmer in Sydney, Australia. "Other parents we have talked to who have lost children say it will never go away." Olga's parents cremated the child before thinking of the cloning option. All that remains are their memories, some strands of hair and three baby teeth, so they have begun investigating whether the teeth could yield the nuclei to clone her one day. While it is theoretically possible to extract DNA from the teeth, scientists say it is extremely unlikely.

"You can't expect the new baby will be exactly like her. We know that is not possible," says Tanya. "We think of the clone as her twin or at least a baby who will look like her." The parents would consider the new little girl as much Olga's baby as their own. "Anything that grows from her will remind us of her," says Tanya. Though she and her husband are young enough to have other children, for now, this is the child they want.

Once parents begin to entertain the option of holding on to some part of a child, why would the reverse not be true? "Bill" is a guidance counselor in Southern California, a fortysomething expectant father who has been learning everything he can about the process of cloning. But it is not a lost child he is looking to replicate. He is interested in cloning his mother, who is dying of pancreatic cancer. He has talked to her husband, his siblings, everyone except her doctor—and her, for fear that it will make her think they have given up hope on her. He confides, "We might end up making a decision without telling her."

WHAT IF . . . cloning becomes popular and supplants natural selection? Will that skew the course of human evolution?

His goal is to extract a tissue specimen from his mother while it's still possible and store it, to await the day when—if—cloning becomes technically safe and socially acceptable. Late last week, as his mother's health weakened, the family began considering bringing up the subject with her because they need her cooperation to take the sample. Meanwhile, Bill has already contacted two labs about tissue storage, one as a backup. "I'm in touch with a couple of different people who might be doing that," he says, adding that both are in the U.S. "It seems like a little bit of an underground movement, you know—people are a little reluctant that if they announce it, they might be targeted, like the abortion clinics."

If Bill's hopes were to materialize and the clone were born, who would that person be? "It wouldn't be my mother but a person who would be very similar to my mother, with certain traits. She has a lot of great traits: compassion and intelligence and looks," he says. And yet, perhaps inevitably, he talks as though this is a way to rewind and replay the life of someone he loves. "She really didn't have the opportunities we had in the baby-boom generation, because her parents experienced the Depression and the war," he says. "So the feeling is that maybe we could give her some opportunities that she didn't have. It would be sort of like we're taking care of her now. You know how when your par-

ents age and everything shifts, you start taking care of them? Well, this would be an extension of that."

TIME/CNN POLL

■ Is it a good or bad idea to clone animals such as sheep?

Good idea 29% Bad idea 67%

■ Is it a good idea to clone human beings?

Good idea 7% Bad idea 90%

■ What is the main reason you are against cloning humans?*

Religious beliefs	34%
Interferes with human distinctiveness/individuality	22%
Used for questionable purposes like breeding a superior race	22%
The technology is dangerous	14%

*Asked of the 914 people who think human cloning is a bad idea

■ Is it against God's will to clone humans?

Yes 69% No 23%

■ Do the following justify creating a human clone?

	YES	NO
To produce clones whose vital organs can be used to save others	28%	68%
To save the life of the person being cloned	21%	74%
To help infertile couples have children	20%	76%
To allow parents to have a twin child later	10%	88%
To allow parents to create clone of child they lost	10%	88%
To allow gay couples to have children	10%	86%
To create genetically superior human beings	6%	92%

■ Would a clone of a dead person have his or her same personality?

Yes 10% No 74%

■ If you had a chance, would you clone yourself?

Yes 5% No 93%

■ When will it be possible to create a human clone? In next:

10 years	45%	50+ years	10%
20 years	23%	Never	15%

From a telephone poll of 1,015 adult Americans taken for TIME/CNN on Feb. 7-8 by Yankelovich Partners Inc. Sampling error is ±3.1%. "Not sures" omitted.

A world in which cloning is commonplace confounds every human relationship, often in ways most potential clients haven't considered. For instance, if a woman gives birth to her own clone, is the child her daughter or her sister? Or, says bioethicist Kass, "let's say the child grows up to be the spitting image of its mother. What impact will that have on the relationship between the father and his child if that child looks exactly like the woman he fell in love with?" Or, he continues, "let's say the parents have a cloned son and then get divorced. How will the mother feel about seeing a copy of the person she hates most in the world every day? Everyone thinks about cloning from the point of view of the parents. No one looks at it from the point of view of the clone."

If infertile couples avoid the complications of choosing which of them to clone and instead look elsewhere for their DNA, what sorts of values govern that choice? Do they pick an uncle because he's musical, a willing neighbor because she's brilliant? Through that door lies the whole unsettling debate about designer babies, fueled already by the commercial sperm banks that promise genius DNA to prospective parents. Sperm banks give you a shot at passing along certain traits; cloning all but assures it.

Whatever the moral quandaries, the one-stop-shopping aspect of cloning is a plus to many gay couples. Lesbians would have the chance to give birth with no male involved at all; one woman could contribute the ovum, the other the DNA. Christine DeShazo and her partner Michele Thomas of Miramar, Fla., have been in touch with Zavos about producing a baby this way. Because they have already been ostracized as homosexuals, they aren't worried about the added social sting that would come with cloning. "Now [people] would say, 'Not only are you a lesbian, you are a cloning lesbian,'" says Thomas. As for potential health problems, "I would love our baby if its hand was attached to its head," she says. DeShazo adds, "If it came out green, I would love it. Our little alien… "

Just as women have long been able to have children without a male sexual partner, through artificial insemination, men could potentially become dads alone: replace the DNA from a donor egg with one's own and then recruit a surrogate mother to carry the child. Some gay-rights advocates even argue that should sexual preference prove to have a biological basis, and should genetic screening lead to terminations of gay embryos, homosexuals would have an obligation to produce gay children through cloning.

All sorts of people might be attracted to the idea of the ultimate experiment in single parenthood. Jack Barker, a marketing specialist for a corporate-relocation company in Minneapolis, is 36 and happily unmarried. "I've come to the conclusion that I don't need a partner but can still have a child," he says. "And a clone would be the perfect child to have because I know exactly what I'm getting." He understands that the child would not be a copy of him. "We'd be genetically identical," says Barker. "But he wouldn't be raised by my parents—he'd be raised by me." Cloning, he hopes, might even let him improve on the original: "I have bad allergies and asthma. It would be nice to have a kid like you but with those improvements."

Cloning advocates view the possibilities as a kind of liberation from travails assumed to be part of life: the danger that your baby will be born with a disease that will kill him or her, the risk that you may one day need a replacement organ and die waiting for it, the helplessness you feel when confronted with unbearable loss. The challenge facing cloning pioneers is to make the case convincingly that the technology itself is not immoral, however immorally it could be used.

One obvious way is to point to the broader benefits. Thus cloning proponents like to attach themselves to the whole arena of stem-cell research, the brave new world of inquiry into how the wonderfully pliable cells of seven-day-old embryos behave. Embryonic stem cells eventually turn into every kind of tissue, including brain, muscle, nerve and blood. If scientists could harness their powers, these cells could serve as the body's self-repair kit, providing cures for Parkinson's, diabetes, Alzheimer's and paralysis. Actors Christopher Reeve, paralyzed by a fall from a horse, and Michael J. Fox, who suffers from Parkinson's, are among those who have pushed Congress to overturn the government's restrictions on federal funding of embryonic-stem-cell research.

But if the cloners want to climb on this train in hopes of riding it to a public relations victory, the mainstream scientists want to push them off. Because researchers see the potential benefits of understanding embryonic stem cells as immense, they are intent on avoiding controversy over their use. Being linked with the human-cloning activists is their nightmare. Says Michael West, president of Massachusetts-based Advanced Cell Technology, a biotech

company that uses cloning technology to develop human medicines: "We're really concerned that if someone goes off and clones a Raelian, there could be an overreaction to this craziness—especially by regulators and Congress. We're desperately concerned—and it's a bad metaphor—about throwing the baby out with the bath water."

Scientists at ACT are leery of revealing too much about their animal-cloning research, much less their work on human embryos. "What we're doing is the first step toward cloning a human being, but we're not cloning a human being," says West. "The miracle of cloning isn't what people think it is. Cloning allows you to make a genetically identical copy of an animal, yes, but in the eyes of a biologist, the real miracle is seeing a skin cell being put back into the egg cell, taking it back in time to when it was an undifferentiated cell, which then can turn into any cell in the body." Which means that new, pristine tissue could be grown in labs to replace damaged or diseased parts of the body. And since these replacement parts would be produced using skin or other cells from the suffering patient, there would be no risk of rejection. "That means you've solved the age-old problem of transplantation," says West. "It's huge."

WHAT IF. . . a clone develops unforeseen abnormalities? Could he sue his parents—or the cloners—for wrongful birth?

So far, the main source of embryonic stem cells is "leftover" embryos from IVF clinics; cloning embryos could provide an almost unlimited source. Progress could come even faster if Congress were to lift the restrictions on federal funding—which might have the added safety benefit of the federal oversight that comes with federal dollars. "We're concerned about George W.'s position and whether he'll let existing guidelines stay in place," says West. "People are begging to work on those cells."

That impulse is enough to put the Roman Catholic Church in full revolt; the Vatican has long condemned any research that involves creating and experimenting with human embryos, the vast majority of which inevitably perish. The church believes that the soul is created at the mo-

ment of conception, and that the embryo is worthy of protection. It reportedly took 104 attempts before the first IVF baby, Louise Brown, was born; cloning Dolly took more than twice that. Imagine, say opponents, how many embryos would be lost in the effort to clone a human. This loss is mass murder, says David Byers, director of the National Conference of Catholic Bishops' commission on science and human values. "Each of the embryos is a human being simply by dint of its genetic makeup."

Last week 160 bishops and five Cardinals met for three days behind closed doors in Irving, Texas, to wrestle with the issues biotechnology presents. But the cloning debate does not break cleanly even along religious lines. "Rebecca," a thirtysomething San Francisco Bay Area resident, spent seven years trying to conceive a child with her husband. Having "been to hell and back" with IVF treatment, Rebecca is now as thoroughly committed to cloning as she is to Christianity. "It's in the Bible—be fruitful and multiply," she says. "People say, 'You're playing God.' But we're not. We're using the raw materials the good Lord gave us. What does the doctor do when the heart has stopped? They have to do direct massage of the heart. You could say the doctor is playing God. But we save a life. With human cloning, we're not so much saving a life as creating a new being by manipulation of the raw materials, DNA, the blueprint for life. You're simply using it in a more creative manner."

A field where emotions run so strong and hope runs so deep is fertile ground for profiteers and charlatans. In her effort to clone her daughter Olga, Tanya Tomusyak contacted an Australian firm, Southern Cross Genetics, which was founded three years ago by entrepreneur Graeme Sloan to preserve DNA for future cloning. In an e-mail, Sloan told the parents that Olga's teeth would provide more than enough DNA—even though that possibility is remote. "All DNA samples are placed into computer-controlled liquid-nitrogen tanks for long-term storage," he wrote. "The cost of doing a DNA fingerprint and genetic profile and placing the sample into storage would be $2,500. Please note that all of our fees are in U.S. dollars."

When contacted by TIME, Sloan admitted, "I don't have a scientific background. I'm pure business. I'd be lying if I said I wasn't here to make a dollar out of it. But I would like to see organ cloning become a reality." He was inspired to launch the

COPYDOG, COPYCAT

I've never met a human worth cloning," says cloning expert Mark Westhusin from the cramped confines of his lab at Texas A&M University. "It's a stupid endeavor." That's an interesting choice of adjective, coming from a man who has spent millions of dollars trying to clone a 13-year-old dog named Missy. So far, he and his team have not succeeded, though they have cloned two calves and expect to clone a cat soon. They just might succeed in cloning Missy this spring—or perhaps not for another five years. It seems the reproductive system of man's best friend is one of the mysteries of modern science.

Westhusin's experience with cloning animals leaves him vexed by all this talk of human cloning. In three years of work on the Missyplicity project, using hundreds upon hundreds of canine eggs, the A&M team has produced only a dozen or so embryos carrying Missy's DNA. None have survived the transfer to a surrogate mom. The wastage of eggs and the many spontaneously aborted fetuses may be acceptable when you're dealing with cats or bulls, he argues, but not with humans. "Cloning is incredibly inefficient, and also dangerous," he says.

Even so, dog cloning is a commercial opportunity, with a nice research payoff. Ever since Dolly the sheep was cloned in 1997, Westhusin's phone at A&M's College of Veterinary Medicine has been ring-ing with people calling in hopes of duplicating their cats and dogs, cattle and horses. "A lot of people want to clone pets. A lot of people. Especially if the price is right," says Westhusin, raising his eyebrows. "A lot." Cost is no obstacle for Missy's mysterious West Coast billionaire owner; he's plopped down $3.7 million so far to fund A&M's research.

Contrary to some media reports, Missy is not deceased. The owner, who wishes to remain anonymous to protect his privacy, wants a twin to carry on Missy's fine qualities after she does die. The prototype is, by all accounts, athletic, good-natured and supersmart. She's not a show dog, as one might expect, but a mongrel—collie and husky—rescued from a pound. Missy's master does not expect an exact copy of her. He knows her clone may not have her temperament. In a statement of purpose, Missy's owners and the A&M team say they are "both looking forward to studying the ways that her clones differ from Missy."

Besides cloning a great mutt, in other words, the project may contribute insight into the old question of nature vs. nurture. It could also lead to the cloning of special rescue dogs and endangered canids like the Ethiopian wolf and African wild dog. At the A&M labs, a picture of Missy's cheerful mug hangs over the micromanipulator, where technicians inject her genetic code into eggs from donors whose own DNA is of no particular interest to anyone. The biggest problem is getting eggs. Because dogs randomly go into heat only every six months to a year, there's a lot of waiting for one of the lab's 50 dogs to enter estrus. Last week a bitch named Betsy caused a flurry of activity when she did just that, but no one knows whether she will actually ovulate—or if another female will go into heat and thus be ready as a surrogate.

Despite the lack of canine breakthrough, dog owners are the biggest clients of Genetic Savings & Clone, a commercial spin-off of Missyplicity that offers to freeze pet DNA for future cloning for $895 plus $100 annual storage. A white canister—which looks like an Artoo Detoo unit—is already full of hundreds of trays containing genetic material from cats and dogs, with a few prized horses and cattle nestled in the whirling eddies of subzero liquid nitrogen.

The fate of the dog samples will depend on Westhusin's work. He knows that even if he gets a dog viably pregnant, the offspring, should they survive, will face the problems shown at birth by other cloned animals: abnormalities like immature lungs and cardiovascular and weight problems. "Why would you ever want to clone humans," Westhusin asks, "when we're not even close to getting it worked out in animals yet?"

—By Cathy Booth Thomas/College Station

business, he says, after a young cousin died of leukemia. "There's megadollars involved, and everyone is racing to be the first," he says. As for his own slice of the pie, Sloan says he just sold his firm to a French company, which he refuses to name, and he was heading for Hawaii last week. The Southern Cross factory address turns out to be his mother's house, and his "office" phone is answered by a man claiming to be his brother David—although his mother says she has no son by that name.

The more such peddlers proliferate, the more politicians will be tempted to invoke prohibitions. Four states—California, Louisiana, Michigan and Rhode Island—have already banned human cloning, and this spring Texas may become the fifth. Republican state senator Jane Nelson has introduced a bill in Austin that would impose a fine of as much as $1 million for researchers who use cloning technology to initiate pregnancy in humans. The proposed Texas law would permit embryonic-stem-cell research, but bills proposed in other states were so broadly written that they could have stopped those activities too.

"The short answer to the cloning question," says ethicist Caplan, "is that anybody who clones somebody today should be arrested. It would be barbaric human experimentation. It would be killing fetuses and embryos for no purpose, none, except for curiosity. But if you can't agree that that's wrong to do, and if the media can't agree to condemn rather than gawk, that's a condemnation of us all."

—*Reported by David Bjerklie and Andrea Dorfman/New York, Wendy Cole/Chicago, Jeanne DeQuine/Miami, Helen Gibson/London, David S. Jackson/Los Angeles, Leora Moldofsky/Sydney, Timothy Roche/Atlanta, Chris Taylor/San Francisco, Cathy Booth Thomas/Dallas and Dick Thompson/Washington, with other bureaus*

Which Babies?

Dilemmas of Genetic Testing

Shelley Burtt

What sort of life is worth living? Advances in medical technology have given Socrates' question a new, more poignant meaning. For the first time in history, we have the means to will the disappearance of those born disabled at the same time that we have the resources to enable these children to live better and longer lives than was ever possible before. How will we respond to these new cross-cutting possibilities? Genetic testing gives us the tools to choose in advance against certain sorts of lives. How are these tools to be used? What sort of lives are worth living?

As a bereaved parent of a child with Down syndrome, I am painfully aware that the life my son led for two and a half joyous years is a life that many individuals would cut short before it began. Although genetic testing is often presented as a service designed to reassure parents that their children-to-be are without congenital abnormalities, the practice in fact functions to prescreen "defective" fetuses for abortion. The assumption of most health care providers in the United States is that the successful diagnosis of a genetic anomaly provides an opportunity to "cure" a pathological condition. Once the arrival of a normally healthy baby is in doubt, the decision to abort is seen as rational and the opportunity to do so as fortunate.

For an anxious parent, genetic testing accompanied by the possibility of therapeutic abortion appears to enhance individual freedom by providing an additional measure of control over one's reproductive choices. But this perspective represents a woefully limited understanding of what it might mean to live as or with a person whose genetic makeup differs markedly from the general population and in a way that will to some extent impair his functioning. I'd like instead to explore what reasons we might have to resist the conclusion that a diagnosis of genetic abnormality is in itself a good reason to terminate a pregnancy and what cultural resources might be required to encourage this resistance.

My husband and I first welcomed Declan into our lives on a hot summer morning in July 1993. We had just come from the midwives' office where I had refused the genetic test (AFP) that screens for neural tube defects and would almost certainly have alerted us to our son's chromosomal abnormalities. Sitting on a bench outside Central Park, we asked ourselves, "What if there were a disability? What use would we make of the information the test promised to provide? Although we come from different religious traditions (my husband is Jewish; I am Christian), we shared the view that the decision to create another human being was not conditional on the sort of human being that child turned out to be. For both of us, the child I was carrying was best understood as a gift we were being asked to care for, not a good we had the responsibility or right to examine for defects before accepting. With a blissfully innocent optimism, or perhaps an eerie prescience, we affirmed that day that we would love this child for who he was, whatever that turned out to be.

Not every couple will willingly go through a pregnancy in ignorance of their fetus's health or future prospects, especially when the tests for a variety of disabling conditions are so readily available. What we can insist on, however, is a clear-eyed recognition of how genetic testing actually functions in our society and a greater commitment on the part of medical practitioners and prospective parents to fully reflect on the knowledge it provides. Whether or not to carry on with a pregnancy at all, let alone one which will result in the birth of a child with either moderate or profound disabilities, ought to be a decision made carefully and thoughtfully by the prospective parents of that child, not by strangers, legislators, or disability rights activists. But what does a good decision in these circumstances look like?

For many bioethicists, the watchword when it comes to difficult decision-making is individual autonomy. The role of the medical practitioner is not to prescribe a course of action but to provide the necessary information for the patient to decide what he or she truly wants to do. Yet, when a fetus is diagnosed as disabled or "defective" in some way, few parents are offered a truly informed choice about their options, as medical providers are rarely neutral when it comes to choosing between bringing an abnormal fetus to term or ending the pregnancy and "trying again." Because genetic abnormality is defined not as one characteristic with which a human being might be challenged but as a treatable medical problem, few parents faced with a positive diagnosis are invited to think beyond the now troubled pregnancy to the joy and rewards as well as the heartache and challenge that accepting and raising a child with special needs can bring.

More than this: to offer a therapeutic abortion as a "cure" for the diagnosed disability is deeply disingenuous. We do not cure cystic fibrosis and Down syndrome by ensuring that fetuses caring this trait do not come to term; we simply destroy the affected entity. The service health care providers offer in this regard is more truthfully characterized as a form of eugenics, either medical (if driven by physicians' preferences) or personal (if driven by parents'). Physicians genuinely committed to patient autonomy in the context of genetic testing would not prejudge the worth or desirability of bearing a child whose genetic makeup was in some way abnormal. Instead, they would seek to ensure that parents truly understood what it meant to care for a child with special needs. This would mean, at a minimum, encouraging parents to inform themselves about the diagnosed condition, giving them the opportunity to speak to pediatricians familiar with the problem, and enabling them to meet with families already caring for children with this condition.

Those who believe that the practice of genetic testing followed by selective abortion is an acceptable way of ensuring the birth of a healthy child often argue that the desire to parent a certain sort of child is not morally blameworthy. We can wish to be parents without wishing to be parents of a child with Fragile X syndrome or Tay-Sachs disease. Yet few who make this argument are willing to probe how our reproductive desires are constructed or at what point our desires become sufficiently self-reflective to be valid guides to action. On what basis do parents feel themselves "not ready" to parent a child with unexpectedly special needs? The picture they hold of a child's disabling trait and the effect it will have on the child and the family's life as a whole may be grounded in a volatile combination of fear and ignorance, not in some acquaintance with the actual life experiences of individuals already engaged in this task or deep reflection on the nature and purpose of parenting. It also seems likely that we cannot accurately assess in advance what challenges we are ready for. It is difficult to predict how we might grow and change in the face of seemingly adverse circumstances.

Certain parents might feel they cannot responsibly continue a pregnancy in which an abnormality has been diagnosed because they lack the financial or emotional resources to care for such a child. But this assessment is not made in a vacuum. What we feel we can manage depends in part on the level of social and political support families with disabled children can expect to receive, support which in turn depends on the degree to which such lives are valued or appreciated by our community.

The weight it is appropriate to give to parental desires in a reproductive context can perhaps be clarified by considering the internationally prevalent practice of sex-selective abortions. Parents around the world currently use the information derived from prenatal sonograms to advance their desire for a son by aborting female fetuses, a practice about which many physicians and most ethicists have grave moral reservations. Here, where parental desires are already considered suspect, the cultural construction of these desires and the appropriateness of resisting their expression is readily acknowledged. It is held to be an important part of making the world more just to change those cultural scripts which led parents to prefer a son over a daughter so strongly that they will end a pregnancy rather than have a girl. We need to think critically and courageously about why a similar revaluation of social attitudes towards congenital disabilities is not also considered necessary.

I believe it is possible for some parents, after profound and prayerful reflection, to make the difficult decision that, all things considered, it is best for a child that it never be born. Incapacitating physical or mental deformity or the certainty of a life destroyed by a wasting disease are conditions which might conceivably, but not necessarily, call forth such a conclusion. But a judgement of this sort cannot be made with any fairness when speaking of disabilities such as spina bifida or Down syndrome where the quality of life available to the afflicted person is relatively high. A commitment to truly informed choice would ensure that we do not dismiss the possibility of caring for children burdened by disease or disability without an effort to appreciate and understand their possible lives.

But we need more than a commitment to truly informed choice if we are to create a world in which the birth of a disabled child is not thought of primarily as a stroke of bad luck, readily avoidable by more aggressive prenatal testing. The lives of those whose capacities fall outside the normal range must be personally and socially recognized as independently valuable, not only worth living in themselves but worth living with.

As the parent of a disabled child, I have experienced first hand the transformed perspective on life possible when one is given the opportunity to live with those who confound our routine expectations, who have too much or too little of a range of expected human traits, who experience life in a way that much remain opaque to the majority of normally functional human beings. What my parents' generation would have called Declan's "mental retardation," we termed his "developmental disabilities." But what was neither retarded nor disabled was a infectious enthusiasm for life which illuminated any interaction with him, an ability to give and receive love that was uncomplicated by the egoism, self-awareness, or self-consciousness of a "typical" child. Parenting this child forced us to reconsider our conception of what qualities and capacities made life worth living; the joy my son clearly took in life and the joy he gave us compelled such a re-evaluation.

But it is not enough to catalog the ways in which life with "them" is valuable for what it brings "us." The respect due to all persons by virtue of their humanity is not dependent on possessing only that sort of genetic makeup which guarantees normal human functioning. Our religious and political traditions teach that each human life has independent and intrinsic value. What would the consequences be of taking this truth seriously when we contemplated becoming parents?

Such a commitment would have to call forth a profound re-assessment of the place of human will in the creation of human life. Both the cause of human freedom and of human equality have been admirably served by the ability, achieved only in this century, to choose to become parents. But we in the industrialized world now teeter on the brink of being able to choose what sort of children we want to become parents of. To some this capacity to control our destiny as parents is an almost unadulterated positive. One of the advantages of scientific progress is supposed to be the ability it gives humans to control their lives. Some make the point that being a good parent is hard enough without the additional burdens of severe or moderate disabilities to cope with. Other argue that it is cruel to bring a child into the world who will always be different, for whom the normal trials of life will be magnified hundreds of times. Why not, then, embrace the opportunity offered by advances in prenatal testing to discard those reproductive efforts we will experience as "disappointing," less than perfect, abnormal, or unhealthy? The most important reason is that sorting the results of the human reproductive process in this way ranks human beings according to their capacity to please their creators, fulfill their parents' dreams, or contribute to social productivity. This willingness to sit in judgement over the sorts of persons deserving a place in our moral communities closes down rather than enlarges the scope of human freedom. The ability to control one's destiny that science supposedly promotes turns out to be conditional on being the right sort of person.

As my younger sisters became pregnant in the wake of Declan's death, I hoped right along with them for a niece or nephew free from illness, defect, or developmental challenges. The question is not whether it is right to desire a "normal" child, but how one ought to respond when genetic testing reveals that desire has been thwarted. To take steps at that point to abort the fetus and "try again" is not just to decide against being pregnant or in favor of "controlling one's life." It is to decide in advance and for another that a certain sort of life (a female one, a physically handicapped one, a mentally retarded one) is not worth living. The moral scope and impact of this decision appears to me far more troubling than a decision for or against parenthood based solely on a positive pregnancy test. Postponing an abortion decision until one knows what sort of child has been created places relative weights on human beings: some are more worthy of living, of being cared for, of being cherished, than others.

Having cared, however briefly, for a special needs child, I do not belittle the level of care and commitment called forth by the opportunity to parent a child or adult with moderate to severe disabilities. But I remain deeply skeptical that the best response to these challenges is the one currently favored by the Western medical establishment: to treat congenital imperfections as we do infectious diseases and to seek their cure by their eradication. Rather we need, through a genuine encounter with those whose identities are shaped but never fully encompassed by their bodies' imperfections, to rethink our willingness not only to live with the disabled but to live with unchosen obligations. Our cultural assumptions to the contrary, living a good and rich life does not require and is not identical with complete control of its circumstances. In fact, the aspiration for such "freedom" dishonors a fundamental aspect of the human condition. To those willing to recognize the essential humanity of every possible child, sometimes to choose not to know—or not to act on what we do know—will be the best choice of all.

Shelley Burtt has taught at Yale University and the London School of Economics and Political Science. She is the author of Virtue Transformed (*Cambridge, 1992*).

From *Tikkun*, Vol. 16, No. 1, pp. 45-47. Reprinted with permission of the Institute for Labor & Mental Health.

UNIT 5

Sexuality Through the Life Cycle

Unit Selections

Key Points to Consider

- Do you remember trying to get answers about your body, sex, or similar topics as a young child? How did your parents respond? How did you feel? Do you hope your children will ask you questions about sex? Why or why not? Which topics or questions do you expect will be hardest for you to handle and answer?

- Would you like to be a junior or senior high school–aged young person today? Why or why not? In what ways is being a young teen easier than when you were that age? How is it more difficult? In what ways is being a young male different? A young female? A young person discovering that she or he is not heterosexual?

- How do you view sex and sexuality at your age? In what ways is it different from when you were younger? How do you perceive the changes—positively, negatively, not sure—and to what do you attribute them? Are there things you feel you have missed? What are they?

- Close your eyes and imagine a couple having a pleasurable sexual interlude. When you are finished, open your eyes. How old were they? If they were younger than middle age, can you replay your vision with middle-aged or older people? Why or why not? How does this relate to your expectations regarding your own romantic and/or sexual life a few decades from now?

- Do you ever think about your parents as sexual people? Your grandparents? Was considering these two questions upsetting for you? Embarrassing? Explain your answers as best you can.

 **Links: www.dushkin.com/online/**
These sites are annotated in the World Wide Web pages.

American Association of Retired Persons (AARP)
http://www.aarp.org
National Institute on Aging (NIA)
http://www.nih.gov/nia/
Teacher Talk
http://education.indiana.edu/cas/tt/tthmpg.html
World Association for Sexology
http://www.tc.umn.edu/nlhome/m201/colem001/was/wasindex.htm

Individual sexual development is a lifelong process that begins at birth and terminates at death. Contrary to popular notions of this process, there are no latent periods during which the individual is nonsexual or noncognizant of sexuality. The growing process of a sexual being does, however, reveal qualitative differences through various life stages. This section devotes attention to these stages of the life cycle and their relation to sexuality.

As children gain self-awareness, they naturally explore their own bodies, masturbate, display curiosity about the bodies of the opposite sex, and show interest in the bodies of mature individuals such as their parents. Exploration and curiosity are important and healthy aspects of human development. Yet it is often difficult for adults (who live in a society that is not comfortable with sexuality in general) to avoid making their children feel ashamed of being sexual or showing interest in sexuality. When adults impose their ambivalence upon a child's innocuous explorations into sexuality, fail to communicate with children about this real and important aspect of human life, or behave toward children in sexually inappropriate ways, distortion of an indispensable and formative stage of development occurs. This often leaves profound emotional scars that hinder full acceptance of self and sexuality later in the child's life.

Adolescence, the social stage accompanying puberty and the transition to adulthood, proves to be a very stressful period of life for many individuals as they attempt to develop an adult identity and forge relationships with others. Because of the physiological capacity of adolescents for reproduction, sexuality tends to be heavily censured by parents and society at this stage of life. Societal messages, however, are powerful, conflicting, and confusing: "Just Say No," "Just Do It"; billboards and magazine ads using adolescent bodies provocatively and partially undressed; "romance" novels, television shows, movies with torrid sex scenes; and Internet chat rooms. In addition, individual and societal attitudes place tremendous emphasis on sexual attractiveness (especially for females) and sexual competency (especially for males). These physical, emotional, and cultural pressures combine to create confusion and anxiety in adolescents and young adults about whether they are okay and normal. Information and assurances from adults can alleviate these stresses and facilitate positive and responsible sexual maturity if there is mutual trust and willingness in both generations.

Sexuality finally becomes socially acceptable in adulthood, at least within marriage. Yet routine, boredom, stress, pressures, the pace of life, work or parenting responsibilities, and/or lack of communication can exact heavy tolls on the quantity and quality of sexual interaction. Sexual misinformation, myths, and unanswered questions, especially about emotional and/or physiological changes in sexual arousal/response or functioning, can also undermine or hinder intimacy and sexual interaction in the middle years.

Sexuality in the later years of life has also been socially and culturally stigmatized because of the prevailing misconception that only young, attractive, or married people are sexual. Such an attitude has contributed significantly to the apparent decline in sexual interest and activity as one grows older. As population demographics have shifted and the baby boomer generation has

aged, these beliefs and attitudes have begun to change. Physiological changes in the aging process are not, in and of themselves, detrimental to sexual expression. A life history of experiences, good health, and growth can make sexual expression in the later years a most rewarding and fulfilling experience, and today's aging population is becoming more vocal in letting their children and grandchildren know that as we age we don't grow out of sex, but that, in fact, like fine wine, it can get better with age.

The three articles in the *Youth and Their Sexuality* section raise some unsettling questions about today's children and the world in which they are growing up. First, "Are Boys the Weaker Sex?" confronts the growing evidence that being a boy is a significant handicap with physical differences colliding with dysfunctional masculinity expectations. Next, "Too Sexy, Too Soon" addresses growing concerns about the impact of the extensive sexualization of American pop culture. Finally, "The Secret Lives of Kids" presents what is likely to be at least surprising, if not shocking, statistics about the sexual lives and experiences of today's young adolescents.

The two articles in the *Sexuality in the Adult Years* subsection look realistically at lifelong sexuality and sexual satisfaction as natural, desirable, but, at times, hard to manage life goals in today's world. "Sexual Passages" looks developmentally at the changes women experience that can affect their sexual feelings and satisfaction over the four decades from their 20s through 50s. "Married With Children" confronts the age-old dilemma faced by parents of young children—not having enough time or energy to have sex as often as they would like, but still wanting to maintain their intimacy and connection. It offers a wealth of expert advice and real-life experiences designed to help anyone, regardless of age or the particular dilemma facing them, to increase their capacity for a full, healthy, and satisfying sex life for each and every decade of their lives.

Are Boys the Weaker Sex?

Science says yes. But society is trying to deal with male handicaps

BY ANNA MULRINE

Sandy Descourouez worries about her sons. The eldest, 18-year-old Greg, was never the chatty type, but he became positively withdrawn following his parents' nasty divorce a decade ago. Last year, Greg's problems erupted into the open: He was arrested for stealing a golf cart and caught smoking marijuana. David, 13—loving, messy, and disorganized—struggles with borderline grades and attention deficit disorder. Sandy's baby, 2 1/2-year-old Luke, is a one-boy demolition derby. But his reckless energy isn't her main cause of concern. While the toddler strings together sound effects with reasonably good results, he rarely utters a word.

Sandy initially took Greg's silence for male reserve—that is, until she happened on his journal. The teenager's diary roiled with frustration and pain. Perhaps to positive effect: Greg wrote a letter to his absent father and reached out for help. "I don't know how to talk about these things," he wrote, "and I know you don't either, so maybe we can help each other."

Boys earn 70 percent of the D's and F's doled out by teachers.

Sandy's "boys will be boys" sighs gave way to bewilderment—and fear. The Aurora, Ill., real-estate broker realized that all three sons had problems very distinct from

those she had encountered in her daughter, a champion speller; problems that needed attention.

The travails of the Descourouez family mirror America's struggle with its sons. "We are experiencing a crisis of the boy next door," says William Pollack, a clinical psychologist at Harvard University and author of *Real Boys*. Across the country, boys have never been in more trouble: They earn 70 percent of the D's and F's that teachers dole out. They make up two thirds of students labeled "learning disabled." They are the culprits in a whopping 9 of 10 alcohol and drug violations and the suspected perpetrators in 4 out of 5 crimes that end up in juvenile court. They account for 80 percent of high school dropouts and attention deficit disorder diagnoses. And they are less likely to go to college than ever before. By 2007, universities are projected to enroll 9.2 million women to 6.9 million men.

Truth to power. That's not what America expects from its boys. "Maybe because men enjoy so much power and prestige in society, there is a tendency to see boys as shoo-ins for success," says child psychologist Michael Thompson, coauthor of *Raising Cain*. "So people see in boys signs of strength where there are none, and they ignore all of the evidence that they are in trouble."

But that evidence is getting tougher than ever to overlook. Today, scientists are discovering very real biological differences that can make boys more impulsive,

more vulnerable to benign neglect, less efficient classroom learners—in sum, the weaker sex. "The notion of male vulnerability is so novel, but the biological facts support it," says Sebastian Kraemer, a child psychiatrist in London and author of a recent *British Medical Journal* article on male fragility. "We're only just now beginning to understand the underlying weakness of men, for so many centuries almost universally projected onto women."

What's more, social pressure often compounds biological vulnerability. "Boys today are growing up with tremendous expectations but without adequate emotional fuel or the tools they need to succeed in school or sustain deep relationships," says Eli Newberger, a pediatrician at Boston Children's Hospital and author of *The Men They Will Become*. Girls now outnumber boys in student government, honor societies, school newspapers, and debating clubs. A recent study found girls ahead of boys in almost every measure of well-being: Girls feel closer to their families, have higher aspirations, and even boast better assertiveness skills. "I regularly see girls who are both valedictorian and captain of the soccer team, but I almost never see that in boys," says Leonard Sax, a family physician and psychologist in Poolesville, Md.

Schools are taking note, too—and they are beginning to act. Early childhood specialists, concerned with ever accelerating curriculum demands, are advocating delayed entrance of boys into kindergarten, to give them time to catch up with girls developmentally. Other districts are experimenting with single-sex classrooms within coed schools, in the hopes that all-boy classes will allow boys to improve standardized test scores in reading and writing, much the way girls have narrowed the gap in math and science. (Currently, the average 11th-grade boy writes with the proficiency of the average eighth-grade girl.) In response to charges of the "feminization" of the classroom—including, critics argue, female teachers with too little tolerance for the physicality of boys—schools are beginning to re-examine their attitudes toward male activity levels and even revamp disciplinary techniques.

Boys make up two thirds of learning-disabled students.

The measures aren't without skeptics. "Isn't it ironic that it's only been in the last two decades that we've really considered making schools equitable for girls," says David Sadker, an American University professor and pioneer in research on girls' treatment in the classroom. "And now people are already saying, 'Whoa, too much time on girls. Let's get back to boys.'"

Pole position. Yet the latest research not only documents boys' unexpected vulnerabilities but indicates that they can be traced back to the womb. While more boys than girls are conceived (the speculation is that sperm carrying the male's Y chromosomes swim faster than those carrying the larger X), this biological pole position doesn't last long, says Kraemer. Perhaps to offset the speed advantage, when mothers experience stress, male embryos are more likely to perish. The male fetus is at greater risk of peril from almost all obstetric complications, including brain damage, cerebral palsy, and premature birth. By the time a baby boy enters the world, he is trailing the average girl, developmentally, by six weeks.

Male newborns are also more emotionally demonstrative than females—a fact that has been shown experimentally despite the cultural stereotype to the contrary. When asked to rate photos for expressiveness, adults who had not been told the children's sex were far more likely to dub boys "more intensely expressive" than girls. And when researchers intentionally misidentified the boys as girls, adults gave the

boys presumed to be girls the highest expressiveness marks. In other words, their actual perceptions trumped the stereotypes.

What's particularly interesting, says Thompson, is that while there is evidence that boys may feel more stress in emotional situations, they routinely show less. When placed within earshot of a crying baby, boys have higher increases in heart rate and sweatier palms than girls. But their behavior belies their biological reaction: Their typical response is to turn off the speaker broadcasting the crying.

Judy Chu, a researcher at Harvard University, has also noted how boys' behavior often masks emotional inclinations. "Boys are a lot more attuned and a lot more sensitive than people give them credit for," she says. Chu spent two years having conversations with a group of boys in a preschool classroom outside Boston. At age 4, the boys candidly discussed their feelings about subjects that ranged from sharing toys to hurt feelings. "They were insightful in ways I hadn't expected—so articulate and attentive," says Chu. Over time, however, as the expectations of parents, teachers, and peers compounded, the boys' behavior changed. "They became inattentive, indirect, and inarticulate," says Chu, "and self-conscious about what other boys thought." Chu recalls one child who was friends with a preschool group of kids who had dubbed themselves "the mean team." "I'm friends with all of the girls," he told Chu. "But if Bill [the unofficial leader of the team] finds that out, he'll fire me from the team." As the result of these observations, Chu firmly believes that boys lose their voice, much as girls do in adolescence, and begin to camouflage feelings and behaviors that might put them in conflict with other boys.

Girls outnumber boys in student councils and debate clubs.

Their friendships also begin to change. "We associate girls with the sharing of secrets, the emotional intimacy, and boys with the sports and activity-oriented friendships," says Niobe Way, a professor of psychology at New York University. "But what's interesting is that these very tough boys talk about wanting friends to share their secrets with, to confide in."

She recalls Malcolm, great in sports, admired by the other boys. One day, Malcolm learned that one of his closest friends had been talking about him and began to cry. "The conventional wisdom is that gossip and arguments with friends don't affect boys or that they'll just 'fight it out,' then let it roll off their backs," says Way. But that's often a misconception. In Malcolm's case, he announced that he was giving up on his friends ("They won't keep your secrets, and they'll stab you in the back")—an attitude he maintained throughout high school.

When boys get emotional, parents and other adults often encourage them to tone it down. "People come to me time and time again saying, 'My son, he's so sensitive,'" says Thompson. "What they don't realize is that it's not the exception. It's the norm." And so, parents react differently to upset daughters and sons. "The actions can be as subtle as asking a girl what's wrong when she's crying but patting a boy on the head and saying, 'You're OK; now get back out there.'" The result can be emotional isolation that starts in boyhood and plagues men in middle age, often with emotional, and even physical, consequences. "Every now and then I catch myself saying things to my sons that I wouldn't say to my daughter—like 'Be tough, don't cry,'" worries Descourouez. "Now I'm trying not to say anything to them that I wouldn't say to my daughter. They can decide what they want to cry about."

Action figures. But despite the evidence of boys' sensitivity, not all of the old stereotypes are unfounded. As much as day care provider Marcy Shrage encourages sensitivity in her boys, she has noticed how they crave action. At her home in Lawrenceville, N.J., she cares for five boys under the age of 4. She piles them all into her minivan and takes them on drives. She'll stop for senior citizens in crosswalks to model good behavior and take them on long walks through the woods. But, the karate black belt admits, the boys do get most excited when she teaches them martial-arts moves. And though she doesn't allow toy weapons in the house, "There are plenty of days when they'll bite their sandwiches into the shape of guns and start firing away at each other."

It is the unexpected combination of physical aggressiveness and emotional vulnerability that now fascinates scientists at the University of Pennsylvania's Brain Behavior Laboratory, who are looking for explanations in the neurons. According to center director Ruben Gur, they have found some intriguing differences in brain structure—anatomical disparities that make it harder for boys to process information and even read faces but easier for them to excel at gross motor skills and visualize objects in three dimensions.

Women's brains are, on average, 11 percent smaller than men's, says Gur. And while there appears to be a subtle correlation between brain volume and IQ, he adds, there is no difference in the IQs of males and females. "So we have to ask how women manage to have the same IQ in a proportionally smaller brain." The answer is that female brains are not simply a smaller version of male brains. From a strictly evolutionary standpoint, the female brain is a bit more finely developed, says Gur. Brains are composed of gray matter (where information processing is done), white matter (long fibers covered in fat that, much like rubber-coated wire, transmit electrical impulses from brain to body), and spinal fluid (which acts as a buffer from the skull). The most recent research shows that males have less gray matter and more white matter than do females. And the right and left hemispheres of the brain are linked by a bundle of nerves that helps the two sides of the brain communicate. In women, this bundle—the corpus callosum—is thicker. It's the difference, researchers explain, between a narrow path in the woods and a two-lane highway.

As a result, says Gur, female brains tend to be more facile when it comes to verbal skills. This may explain why girls utter their first words earlier, string together complete sentences first, and generally surpass boys in tests that involve verbal fluency. "The female brain is an easier brain to teach," says Michael Gurian, a family therapist and author of *Boys and Girls Learn Differently*. "It's harder for the male brain to learn." It may also explain why, when Sandy Descourouez subscribed to a "developmental milestones" E-mail update from a babyfood site, she learned her son Luke was, like many boys, a "late talker."

Males do have more white matter, however—with longer, more complex nerve networks from their brains to the tips of their toes—allowing boys like Luke to excel at gross motor skills. And their greater volume of spinal fluid, says Gur, also means that male brains are built to sustain blows. "Thank goodness for that," says Descourouez, recalling Luke's penchant for spinning in circles near the fireplace.

Reptilian feelings? There appear to be brain-related differences in male and female emotions as well. The latest research suggests that the emotional brain is "more primitive" in men. Women make use of an emotional processing center adjacent to the speech areas of the brain, which makes it easier for them to link emotions to speech. The female brain is also "architecturally finer—a later arrival in evolution," says Gur. Men make use of an older limbic system "present in more primitive creatures," often known as the reptilian brain. Which means that male emotion is often more closely linked with action.

These are just the sort of details that the "Raising Sons" seminar participants at the Parenting Center in Fort Worth are gathering to learn. Moms and dads circle their chairs and share their fears, trying to come to some sort of agreement on what constitutes "normal" boy behavior: Why is their son struggling in school? Why won't he listen? Is he too sensitive? Too taken with guns and violent video games?

Boys are the culprits in 9 of 10 alcohol and drug violations.

Pam Young debates with fellow "Raising Sons" classmate Brian Rice about her sons' penchant for wrestling. "They seem to know what drives me crazy," she says, conceding that it's also their way of bonding with dad. Rice, by contrast, worries that *his* son doesn't wrestle enough.

Another parent wonders aloud where his son's high spiritedness ends and brattiness begins. "I'm curious about the back talk," he inquires. "I want my son to be an independent thinker, but I also want him to have respect." Young leans in, nodding in agreement. "Yes," she says. "My son is very independent, then very dependent for approval."

In class, parents learn about the selective "pruning" of brain cells that scientists believe can lead to impulsivity—and that is thought to occur more rigorously in adolescent boys than girls. "It would explain why my son acts like a windshield wiper sometimes," says Young. "He's on, then he's off. He gets it, then he doesn't."

Later, a facilitator asks, "What's the only emotion that it's OK for boys to have?" The class pauses for a moment, then answers virtually in unison: "anger." Maybe that's why we have so many angry boys, the facilitator suggests. And so the parents learn how to teach their sons to match words with feelings, to build a vocabulary for the emotions that they often have trouble expressing.

Boys are twice as likely as girls to be held back a grade in school.

Let's get physical. The teachers at Thomas Edison Elementary School in St. Joseph, Mo., have begun to put some of the brain science to the test. Three years ago, when third-grade teacher Denise Young asked the boys in her class a question, she would get frustrated if they didn't respond, and simply move on. Today, she gives them at least 60 seconds to "process" the question. "They need more time to stop, switch gears, and respond," says Young. "But they didn't have it, and I think that's why a lot of boys have gotten into trouble in the past." She also gives them "stress balls" to squeeze while they're reading or working out a problem. "It seems to help them engage when they're also doing something physical," she says.

For more information

- **Real Boys Workbook** by William Pollack. Outlines "Some Do's and Don'ts With Boys." Also specific tips for talking to sensitive sons.
- **Speaking of Boys** by Michael Thompson. *Raising Cain* coauthor answers "the most asked questions about raising sons," delving into topics such as male puberty and underage drinking.
- **The Men They Will Become** by Eli Newberger. A thoughtful look at the emotional tug-of-war within boys.
- **Boys and Girls Learn Differently!** by Michael Gurian. The latest on boys' and girls' thinking styles.

On a typical day, her children stand by their desks as they complete work sheets and work on projects. That's because there is now a greater understanding, says principal Debbie Murphy, of the activity level and physicality of their school's boys. "There was a child who just couldn't sit still in music class, and we decided, well, if it's not going to bother anyone, it's fine if he stands at the back of the room."

Murphy also tried something new during her disciplinary chats with the boys. "I will not make the children talk when they're angry, for starters. Boys, in particular, just have trouble verbalizing when they're upset." Once they've cooled down, Murphy takes them for a stroll. "I find boys have an easier time talking if they're walking, too—it seems to tap into something in their brains," she says. In three years, Edison Elementary has watched its test scores skyrocket from what Murphy calls "ghetto statistics" to among the top 10 percent in the state. Incidents of in-school suspension have decreased from 300 to 22 this year.

The controversial drugging of boys also appears related to fundamental temperamental differences. Family physician Sax became alarmed when, increasingly, he was asked to prescribe Ritalin to otherwise healthy boys who simply couldn't sit still through long lessons. But the fact that boys are prescribed medicines and still fail at twice the rate of girls has given him pause. One of his patients, Andrew Yost, was a bright 8-year-old but uninspired by school and constantly getting into spats with his teachers. Sax suspected ADD and suggested Andrew's family consult with a child psychiatrist from the National Institutes of Health. The specialist confirmed the diagnosis and prescribed Ritalin.

When Sax encountered Andrew again several years later, he had indeed shown dramatic improvement. But it was not the result of the drugs. The difference, according to Andrew's parents, was that they had enrolled him in an all-boys school. "The teachers just seem to understand boy behaviors," says his father, David. "We tried so much before that, but now, I think he's where he should be." Andrew no longer takes any medications and, he adds, "I don't worry as much about what girls think."

By 2007, girls may outnumber boys in college nearly 3 to 2.

Other school districts are experimenting with voluntary single-sex classrooms within coed schools. "Parents are showing up in droves to sign up for the classes," says Anthony Basanese, middle school principal in Pellston, Mich. This fall, fully half of the sixth-grade class will be enrolled in single-sex classes, meeting throughout the day for coed lunch periods and extracurricular activities. "Parents like it because they see their kids doing better in school."

While American University's Sadker worries about the declining presence of male teachers—"down from 20 percent when I was a boy to 15 percent of all elementary school teachers now"—he is also wary of single-sex education. "Why aren't we fixing coed classes instead of running away from them? If we want a democracy that lives and works together, don't we also want one that learns together?"

Too much too soon. But many boys may need a substantial boost in schooling, say Sax and other specialists advocating a later start in kindergarten for boys. "The early curriculum is more accelerated than ever before," says Sax. "Boys are expected to do too much too soon—their brains aren't ready for it." The result, he adds, is too often a lifelong struggle with school. "They begin their school careers in 'the dumb group.' They're frustrated with their lack of ability, they start disliking school, and they begin to avoid it. We're seeing that more than ever now."

The extra year before kindergarten would allow boys to catch up. "Not all girls are precocious, and not all boys are delayed," says Sax. "But I've come to the conclusion that later enrollment would solve 80 percent of the problems we see with boys and school today."

Descourouez is considering holding Luke back from kindergarten. "His speech isn't up to speed," she worries, "and I don't want school to be a miserable experience for him." School is no pleasure for her son David, but she's determined to nurture the tenderness she sees in him. "He designs computer screens that say, 'I love you.' I can't remember the last time Greg said that to me." And she vows not to disregard the silence of her sons. "When they can't find the words for their emotions, I try to help them," she says. As they find the words, she hopes they will break the old patterns—and become husbands and fathers who talk.

From *U.S. News & World Report*, July 30, 2001, pp. 40-47. © 2001 by U.S. News & World Report, L.P. Reprinted by permission.

TOO SEXY TOO SOON

Between sultry pop stars and suggestive prime-time TV, children encounter sexual language and images at very young ages. Here's how to protect your kids. A special must-read report.

By Dianne Hales

For many years, children at one Chicago nursery school have enjoyed playing with big cardboard boxes, transforming them into trucks, spaceships, castles, and forts. Lately, though, the preschool staff has been watching a little more closely when kids disappear into the cartons. The reason? Teachers recently found a 4-year-old boy lying on top of a female classmate, trying to kiss her.

In the past, educators would have thought such behavior was an indication that a child had been sexually abused. But these days, they're just as likely to suspect that kids are merely mimicking something they've seen on TV. "Children always react to what they're exposed to in the media," says Diane Levin, a former teacher and author of *Remote Control Childhood? Combating the Hazards of Media Culture* (National Association for the Education of Young Children, 1998). "Play often in-

volves issues children are trying to understand, and one of those issues is sex."

Although violence in the media has provoked major public controversy, concern is growing about the impact of exposure to sexualized language and situations, especially on the very young. There's no consensus among experts on the short- or long-term effects our sex-heavy pop culture has on kids. But parents of young children seem to agree that the media's obsession with sex is prodding kids to look and act precociously sexual. "My 3-year-old stands in front of the mirror and belts out words from a Britney Spears song—'I'm not that inn-o-cent,' " says Molly Gordy, a mother of two girls in New York City. "We sure hope that's not true."

What's coming out of the mouths of babes hardly *sounds* innocent—even though it usually is. Driving a car pool of 5-year-olds, a California mother was

dumbfounded when her daughter asked, "What's a blow job?"

Sex-saturated culture

The first response of startled parents is to wonder where their youngsters are picking up such words and ideas. But the answer is simple: everywhere. Long before they can read, today's kids are bombarded with sexual imagery—on magazine covers, in TV commercials, in movie trailers, and on billboards. "Advertisers increasingly use sex to capture a consumer's attention," says Gail Dines, Ph.D., a professor of sociology at Wheelock College, in Boston.

At home, television has turned up the sexual heat. More than half of all television programs—56 percent—contain some sexual material, according to a recent study by the Parents Television Council, a non-

152

partisan advocacy group. From 1989 to 1999, the frequency of sexual interactions, verbal and physical, more than tripled during prime-time viewing hours. References to genitalia occurred more than seven times as often, while foul language increased more than five and a half times.

Even movies geared toward young children aren't as tame as they were a generation ago. Pocahontas, with her strapless dress and exposed cleavage, is far sexier than Cinderella ever was. Remakes of *The Adventures of Rocky and Bullwinkle* and Dr. Seuss' *How the Grinch Stole Christmas*, unlike the originals, are sprinkled with double entendres and sexual references.

Many parents assume that sexual sizzle goes over the heads of kids barely old enough to tie their shoes. But that's not necessarily the case, says clinical psychologist Ben Allen, Psy.D., of Northbrook, Illinois. "Children are sponges," he says. "They don't respond to suggestive material by becoming sexually stimulated in the way that adults do, but they do find it intriguing."

Certainly, young children are curious and impressionable. "My 6-year-old picks up on everything he sees in ads, on billboards, and on magazine covers," says Mary Kay Turner, of San Ramon, California. "He'll ask questions like 'Why are they kissing that way?' I find myself having conversations that I don't think he's ready for." A Washington, D.C., mother, certain that her preschooler wasn't even paying attention to a commercial for Viagra that came on during a game show, said she was amazed when the 4-year-old asked her what *erectile dysfunction* meant. "I told him it was a medical problem, and that was enough information to keep him satisfied," she said. "I'm glad he wasn't watching television with his 12-year-old cousin. Who knows how he would have explained it."

Some experts say that the barrage of sexual material can be baffling to young children. "Kids have always been interested in each other's bodies, but now they're puzzled because they're seeing things that are far more complex than what they would naturally be curious about," says Levin. Worse, a precocious interest in sexuality may distract 4- and 5-year-olds from more important developmental tasks, such as learning to negotiate with friends, use language precisely, and play creatively.

Peering into the future, parents wonder where the bombardment of sexual messages and images will lead. "What parents fear most is the impact on later behavior and sexual experimentation," observes Debra Haffner, former president of the Sexuality Information and Education Council of the United States and author of *From Diapers to Dating: A Parent's Guide to Raising Sexually Healthy Children* (Newmarket, 2000). "But there's no evidence at all to suggest that learning to roll your hips to a music video at age 6 means you're more likely to have sex when you're in ninth grade," Haffner says.

Nonetheless, sexual experimentation is beginning at surprisingly early ages. According to the Alan Guttmacher Institute, a nonprofit reproductive-health research organization, two out of ten girls and three out of ten boys have had sexual experience by age 15. What's more, there are widespread reports of increased sexual activity, including oral sex, among middle-school students—although reliable statistics are hard to come by.

Talking About SEX

Here's advice on how to handle potentially awkward moments:

THINK AHEAD

Sexual attitudes and values are highly personal. What do you most want to communicate to your child about sex?

FOCUS ON HOW YOU SOUND

Tone is as important as content. Be straightforward and matter-of-fact. If you're nervous, make it clear that it's because you want to get everything right, not because sex is shameful.

CHOOSE A PRIVATE SETTING

If youngsters bring up something embarrassing in the supermarket line or a crowded restaurant, let them know that you will discuss it just as soon as you get to the car or arrive home—and be sure to do so.

Even at younger ages, though, children have an awareness of sexuality and sexual terms. One mom described taking her 5-year-old to a birthday party where little girls were gyrating their hips while lip-synching the lyrics of a suggestive song. "They looked like a bunch of little Lolitas," she says.

Fashion feeds into the trend as well. Though little girls have always delighted in dressing up in grown-up clothes, some kids' styles are even sexier than what's inside Mom's closet. Stores sell tube tops, belly-baring hip-hugger skirts, even bras and bikini panties for girls as young as 6 or 7. "They all want to look and dress just like the sexiest pop stars," one New York City mom complains.

How do the sexually charged images of pop music affect children? Experts disagree. "Young girls don't comprehend that people can view a pop singer as a sex symbol," says Dr. Allen. "But at the same time, they know that looking and acting like Christina Aguilera grabs attention. The danger is that girls may think they need to be like her to have a sense of self-worth."

However, others believe that children find harmless comfort in contemporary music. "Young kids get into a hypnotic state that's somewhat erotic when they watch music videos or listen to pop songs," says psychiatrist Lynn Ponton, M.D., of the University of California at San Francisco, an expert on child sexuality and author of *The Sex Lives of Teenagers* (Dutton, 2000). "It's one of the ways they feel safe having their first sexual feelings. The songs give them permission to feel excited in a harmless way."

Curbing the sleaze

Most parents say they can largely control what movies, television, and music their children are exposed to. Nonetheless, even the most vigilant parent can't completely shield a child from the sexual material that's so much a part of contemporary culture. Sooner or later, every youngster is going to see an inappropriate video or listen to a song with obscene lyrics. "We live in an age when sexuality is freely accepted and exposed," Dr. Allen says. "Trying to insulate a child from sexual material is like fighting a tornado. You need to think of it as junk food. Once in a while, it's not really a threat, but you want to avoid a steady diet."

Parents should make an effort to help a child understand what he'll inevitably encounter. The best way to do that is by talking openly with your child about sex and being available and willing to answer any questions that come up. For preschool kids, it's wise to teach correct anatomical terms for body parts and functions. If a child hears (or uses) slang, parents may want to explain that such words are inappropriate.

Opinions vary on when parents should talk to their children about the birds and the bees; some experts say that explaining sex to a child at about age 5 or 6 can help ensure that he'll get the message from you, not his friends. With kids this age, keep conversations simple and brief. Ask kids what they already know to gauge how much they've heard. Listen carefully to their responses, and clarify any mistaken impressions. Provide only the information they want at the moment.

When it comes to a child's using sexual language or mimicking sexual behavior, the way parents respond makes a lasting impression. It's important not to scold or punish a child or make him feel ashamed. "Remember that sexual curiosity and experimentation, like playing doctor, are normal for 4- and 5-year-olds," Haffner says. However, children who engage in behaviors such as oral-genital contact or simulated intercourse may well have been victims of sexual abuse, so that possibility should be investigated. It's also possible, however, that these kids may have come across inappropriate materials in the media.

If parents find that young children are venturing into adults-only territory, they should explain why the material isn't suitable for kids. "It's not fair for adults to make children feel bad for their fascination with material that we expose them to," says media expert Levin. "If you say,

'Don't do that' without explaining why, children conclude that they can't go to adults for help figuring this stuff out."

Rather, your goal should be to put what your children see and hear into context. Here are some ways to begin:

•**TAKE CHARGE**. In the same way that you wouldn't give preschoolers free rein over what they wear or eat, carefully choose the videos, CDs, and television shows that your youngsters listen to and watch. If your kids complain that their friends get to see other programs, explain that your family has made a different choice.

•**KEEP TVS AND COMPUTERS IN FAMILY SPACES** rather than in children's rooms. Whenever you can, watch with your child and discuss what you see. Monitor their Internet use, and use filtering software (available from most Internet service providers) to keep them away from inappropriate Websites.

•**MAKE SURE YOUR TELEVISION HAS A V-CHIP**, a device that prevents kids from accessing certain channels. Particularly useful if older siblings or baby-sitters may flip to inappropriate shows when you're not around, the V-chip will keep out explicit sexual language and behavior.

•**DON'T ASSUME ANYTHING GOES OVER A CHILD'S HEAD**. By ages 5 and 6, children pick up the sexual undercurrents in prime-time programs like *Friends* and *Will & Grace*. Some experts say that kids may actually pay closer attention than

adults, who have been desensitized to sexual innuendo in the media.

•**DON'T ENCOURAGE SEXUAL PRECOCIOUSNESS**. You may be sending your child the wrong messages if you buy skin-baring clothing or applaud sexy dancing as cute. Encourage children to appreciate their bodies for the many things they can do rather than for how they appear.

•**TAKE ADVANTAGE OF TEACHABLE MOMENTS**. When sexual subjects come up on a TV program that you're watching with your kids, ask open-ended questions, such as "What do you think about that?" or "How would you feel if someone treated you like that?" This is a good opportunity to communicate your values about sex and sexuality.

•**EMPHASIZE RESPECT FOR ONESELF AND OTHERS**. "Boys need to know that being a man is not about sexual conquests, which is what the media tell them," Dr. Dines says. "Girls should know that they weren't put on earth to please boys—which is what they see in the media—but to live a full, happy, and successful life."

•**KEEP THE CONVERSATION GOING**. Try to help make your child feel comfortable approaching you to discuss issues of sex and sexuality. Never dismiss his questions and concerns as silly or trite. Children who learn early on that they can talk with their parents about these subjects without fear of ridicule or rebuke develop a trust that can endure into adolescence and beyond.

The Secret Sex Lives of Kids

One in twelve children is no longer a virgin by his or her thirteenth birthday, and 21 percent of ninth-graders have slept with four or more partners. An alarming report every parent must read

By Lisa Collier Cool

Thirteen-year-old Ashley Robinson* began dating in fourth grade. At first, "it was movies, malls and making out," says the eighth-grader from Pleasantville, New York. These days, "about half of the people in my class are sexually experienced. Some have lost their virginity, but most have oral sex. It's popular because you can't get pregnant." Last July, she decided to try oral sex with a boy she'd been seeing for a month. "We did it to each other; it was fun. Now we do it at his house, my house, everywhere. Oral sex rules!"

Robinson and her friends are part of a horrifying trend. Increasingly, children barely past puberty are sexually active, says Sarah Brown, director of the National Campaign to Prevent Teen Pregnancy (NCPTP), in Washington, D.C. By the time kids turn fifteen, according to research from the National Center for Health Statistics, one third of girls have had sex (compared with less than 5 percent in 1970), as have 45 percent of boys (up from 20 percent in 1972).

But even those kids who remain virgins aren't necessarily innocent. In a recent survey by *Seventeen* magazine, 55 percent of teens, aged thirteen to nineteen, admitted to engaging in oral sex. Half of them felt it wasn't as big a deal as intercourse—a view Sarah Brown often hears from kids. "It didn't help that we had a president who said oral sex isn't sex," she says. Adds Robin Goodman, Web site director of New York University's Child Study Center, in New York City, "Oral sex is like the latest sport, an activity kids egg each other on to try. Parents may say, 'That's not my child,' but nearly half of them are wrong."

Recent scandals highlight the extent of the problem. In 1998, parents of as many as fifteen eighth-graders at Williamsburg Middle School, in Arlington, Virginia, were aghast when school

> "Oral sex is an activity kids egg each other on to try," says one expert. "Parents may say, 'That's not my child,' but many are wrong"

officials informed them that their kids were having oral sex at parties and in local parks. (Apparently, a child had confided in a school counselor.) Also that year, a twelve-year-old girl and thirteen-year-old boy were arrested for allegedly organizing an oral-sex-for-hire ring at Langston Hughes Middle School, in upper-middle-class Reston, Maryland. The boy was convicted and sent to a juvenile-detention center, and the girl was placed under house arrest. And in suburban Rockland County, Georgia, more than two hundred children—some as young as twelve—were exposed to syphilis through group sex in 1996. Local health officials were appalled by reports of fourte-year-olds with as many as fifty sex partners, and girls who engaged in sexual activities with three boys at once.

Deborah Roffman, author of *Sex and Sensibility: The Thinking Parent's Guide to Talking Sense About Sex* (Perseus Publishing, 2001) and a sex educator, has heard similar stories. "There have always been some middle-school students who talk about oral sex, but now there's a surge in kids who actually do it," she says. Meanwhile, schools are hearing from parents who worry that their kids aren't being taught enough about sexuality. In a recent Kaiser Family Foundation (KFF) survey, more than three quarters of parents of kids in seventh to twelfth grades said they wanted schools to offer more detailed information in sex-

155

The Dreaded "Talk"

Research shows that parents are the number-one influence on their children's sexual decisions, and that the more information you give a child, the more likely he or she is to abstain. Yet only 44 percent of moms and dads have discussed the topic with their preteen, according to a recent poll by the Kaiser Family Foundation. These tips can help you become more comfortable with the subject:

•**Start young.** Around age four, kids wonder where babies come from. This is a good time to teach them the words for female and male genitals, although you don't need to explain sex (it's best to say that babies come from Mom's belly). When your child is eight or nine, tell him about the bodily changes of puberty. Since kids often encounter sexual pressure during their preteen years (ages nine through twelve), educate your child on how to say "no" and about disease prevention. She needs basic information about vaginal and oral sex, as well as an explanation of the dangers. Make it clear that the best way to avoid STDs and pregnancy is abstinence, but that condoms and contraception can reduce these risks. Helpful tips are available online at: *www.pta.org, www.plannedparenthood.org, www.siecus.org* and *www.mvoices.org.* To initiate a discussion, use a situation from a book, newspaper article or TV show you've watched together. You might ask your child what he thinks of a character's actions, then offer your judgment.

•**Encourage questions.** Even if you're shocked by what your child asks—such as the meaning of a crude sexual expression—praise him for coming to you for answers. Ask him what he already knows about the topic, then give a sample explanation along with your views. If your child sees you watching a sex-filled TV show or even reading this article and asks if he can watch or read with you, explain that while you don't feel the information is appropriate for him, you'd like to discuss sex and answer any questions he might have.

•**Share your values.** Let your child know that it's natural to be curious about sex, but he can—and should—resist acting on impulses. Explain your beliefs about the appropriate time and circumstances for sex.

•**Set limits on your child's TV and computer time.** Reduce her exposure to inappropriate material by keeping close tabs on the TV shows and videos she watches. Better yet, watch the programs with her. Supervise your child when she's using the Internet.

•**Discourage early dating.** Going out with a group of friends—and an adult chaperone—is fine, but permitting one-on-one dating in middle school is asking for trouble. Make sure that adults will be chaperoning the parties and events your child attends, and talk to other parents about reasonable curfews. In addition, discourage your child from dating older boys or girls, because it can raise the risk of an exploitative sexual relationship.   —L.C.C.

education classes. They want their kids to learn how to obtain and use birth control and deal with the pressure to have intercourse.

The Price of Preteen Intimacy

Not surprisingly, children often regret having sex too soon. In a recent NCPTP survey, 73 percent of twelve- to fourteen-year-olds who had lost their virginity said they wished they'd waited. That sentiment is shared by 58 percent of sexually experienced fifteen- to seventeen-year olds. When *Ladies' Home Journal* conducted a survey of kids on the NCPTP Web site last June, many described their first sexual experience the way fifteen-year-old Jennifer Jacobson* does: "It was the stupidest mistake I ever made." At age twelve, "I snuck out of my house to have sex with a fifteen-year-old guy I'd known for only about a week," she says. "Now I'm going to have to spend the rest of my life trying to forgive myself."

Judy Kuriansky, Ph.D., host of a call-in radio show for teens and author of *Generation Sex: America's Hottest Sex Therapist Answers the Hottest Questions About Sex* (HarperCollins, 1995), sees even more serious repercussions. "Often, a lack of self-esteem makes kids experiment with sex," she says. "Frequently, the result is guilt and shame. As adults, they may punish themselves for their past by not letting themselves enjoy sex. Or they may have trouble establishing meaningful relationships because they've disconnected sex and love."

Girls are especially at risk. Tara Thrutchley, eighteen, a volunteer peer educator for AID Gwinnett, a nonprofit HIV awareness group in Lawrenceville, Georgia, has noticed that girls tend to give oral sex more than they receive it. "A lot of eighth-grade girls engage in this activity with high-school boys," she says. "They see it as a way to please a guy without losing their virginity." The consequences can be dire. "Girls may become vulnerable to exploitative relationships, especially when they're involved with older boys," says Michael Resnick, Ph.D., professor of pediatrics and director of the National Teen Pregnancy Prevention Research Center, at the University of Minnesota in Minneapolis. "They expect emotional intimacy but don't necessarily get it. That can lead to emotional distress, as well as substance abuse."

Surrounded by Sex

What's behind this alarming trend? Virginia Navarro, Ph.D., assistant professor of educational psychology at the University of Missouri, in Columbia, says our sex-saturated culture pushes kids to grow up too fast. "Children's stores and catalogs sell junior versions of sexy styles," she explains. "You see silky bras and panties for five-year-olds and skintight Lycra tops and slit skirts that make prepubescent girls look provocative."

Adding fuel to the fire are racy TV shows like *Dawson's Creek* and *Popular,* which depict teen sex as exciting and normal. More than half of all TV shows include sexual content, with the average prime-time program featuring five or more sexual references per hour, according to a recent study by KFF. Only 9 percent of these widely watched shows ever mention responsible behavior, such as abstinence or using contraception.

The Internet is also swarming with sex. In a recent survey of fifteen hundred kids by the National Center for Missing and Exploited Children, in Alexandria, Virginia, one quarter reported having accidentally stumbled upon pornography while Web surfing or opening e-mails.

But the media is only half the problem, says Resnick. "The majority of parents are squeamish about discussing contraception and doubly squeamish about oral sex," he says. "So, at puberty, young people with natural curiosity about sex encounter uncomfortable silence from their parents instead of guidance."

Megan Ruggiero,* thirteen, an eighth-grader from Armonk, New York, and Kim Abrams,* sixteen, of New York City, say sex and its risks were never discussed in their homes. In Ruggiero's case, suggestive material on the Internet and sex scenes on Dawson's Creek "made me think about doing it." Curious, she performed oral sex on her date at a New Year's Eve party last year, an act she says she regrets.

Abrams engaged in oral sex—an activity she now calls disgusting—two years ago, then intercourse, which was also unpleasant. "I started doing things I shouldn't have been doing," she says.

Beth Risacher, a program coordinator at a state agency, in Indianapolis, understands parents' reluctance to discuss sex with their children. "Kids at this age are so sensitive that if you don't take the right approach, they don't listen or they think you're accusing them of something," she says. She waited until her daughter, Elizabeth, was fourteen before discussing AIDS, contraception and sex. Soon afterward, Elizabeth asked for birth control pills, says Risacher. "That's when I found out she'd been having sex since she was only thirteen."

Fifteen-year-old Adam Dennison,* of Brooklyn, New York, says his parents would be shocked if they knew that he started having oral sex two years ago. About 75 percent of his friends also do it, he estimates, adding "I learned most of what I know from my older brother and *Sex and the City*."

While some parents buy into the myth that talking about sex encourages experimentation, the opposite is true, says Debra Haffner, author of *From Diapers to Dating: A Parent's Guide to Raising Sexually Healthy Children* (Newmarket Press, 2000)

and past president of the Sexuality Information and Education Council of the U.S., in New York City. "The research is clear: Giving preteens accurate information and sharing your values makes them more likely to abstain."

Leaving children in the dark can promote risky behavior, says Resnick. "Most kids think oral sex is safe because they aren't told that it can lead to sexually transmitted diseases [STDs]," such as gonorrhea, syphilis, chlamydia, HIV, human papilloma virus and possibly hepatitis C, he explains. Nearly all of the kids with whom *Ladies' Home Journal* spoke believed the practice posed little danger. Meanwhile, four million teens contract an STD each year; some from oral sex.

Sex Ed: Too Little, Too Late?

Although the U.S. has among the highest rates of STDs and teen pregnancy of any modern country, 7 percent of schools offer no sex education at all and 35 percent limit teachers from discussing contraception and safe sex. "Abstinence until marriage" courses have become common since the government launched a $250 million program in 1996 to pay for them. A Centers for Disease Control and Prevention study shows that only 17 percent of teachers inform junior-high students about the proper use of condoms and just 37 percent do so in senior high.

This trend alarms Susan N. Wilson, executive coordinator of Network for Family Life Education at Rutgers University's School of Social Work, in Piscataway, New Jersey. "It's dangerous in a world where STDs kill young people," she says. A recent study by the Alan Guttmacher Institute, in New York City, shows that nearly three out of ten teachers nationwide work in schools that don't offer sex-ed classes to fifth- and sixth-grade students. Among schools that do, subjects tend to be limited to puberty, the transmission of HIV and abstinence.

Wilson believes that schools should introduce sex ed at the beginning of middle school and expand the range of topics covered. "Our silence is creating dangerous myths," she says. "There should be a wake-up call—withholding crucial information about sexual risk doesn't make our kids safer. Telling them the truth does."

---

* Names have been changed to protect privacy.

From *Ladies' Home Journal*, March 2001, pp. 156-159. © 2001 by Ladies Home Journal with permission of the author Lisa Coolier Cool.

sexual passages

Experts are finally unlocking the mysteries of the female libido. What every woman should know about her sex drive—in all the stages of her life

By Lauren Picker

Not long ago, my friend Jean and I were talking, when the conversation turned to sex. She had just finished reading a book when in which one of the characters was an adolescent girl in hormonal overdrive. "I used to feel that way, too, and, wow, have things changed," said Jean, a 37-year-old mother of two in Connecticut. "I thought women were supposed to reach their sexual peak in their mid-thirties. What happened?"

In an age that celebrates women who enjoy a very healthy libido (consider the popularity of the HBO series *Sex and the City*), the ups and downs of female desire still remain something of a mystery. But that's changing. With pharmaceutical companies in hot pursuit of a pill that could do for women's sexual fulfillment what Viagra has done for men's, experts are busy investigating what's responsible for female passion.

Researchers are finding that the sex experts Masters and Johnson were wrong when they claimed that female and male desire were alike. New studies suggest that women need to be aroused physically or psychologically to get in the mood for sex. Unlike men, who can get aroused by the sight of a buxom babe in a beer commercial, women rely on different—and subtler—cues. A woman may be responsive to intimate conversation—or a caring gesture by her husband.

Of course, you can't have a healthy sexual appetite without the hormones estrogen and testosterone. Genetics may also play a role. "The characteristics of sex drive appear to be innate early on," says Steven Petak, M.D., J.D., an endocrinologist in Houston. "But psychological factors are probably more important [than genetics]."

That helps explain why women's libidos vary. This diversity is evident not only among women, but within individuals. Like my friend Jean, you may have a strong sex drive during one stage of your life only to have your interest flag during another. Here, experts explain the hormonal, psychological and social factors that affect a woman's libido from her 20s through her 50s.

20s— Sex and the Single Girl

By the time women enter their 20s, the majority have regular menstrual periods—and a sex drive that ebbs and flows with their cycle. "Around ovulation"—not coincidentally, the time of peak fertility—"women have more interest in sex and are better able to have an orgasm than women who are just about to get their period," says Anita H. Clayton, M.D., associate professor and vice chair of the department of psychiatric medicine at the University of Virginia Health System, in Charlottesville.

• *Finding their way* Contrary to popular belief, the 20s are not necessarily a time of sexual voraciousness. Many young women are grappling with identity and body-image problems at the same time that they're trying to establish themselves professionally and find a mate. According to the National Health and Social Life Survey (NHSLS), conducted at the University of Chicago, unmarried women are nearly twice as likely as married women to have anxiety about their sexual performance and have difficulty climaxing. "A woman's sexual interest is greatest when she's in a stable relationship," says Sheryl Kingsberg, Ph.D., assistant professor of reproductive biology and psychiatry at Case Western Reserve University, in Cleveland.

• *Use it or lose it* If a woman in her 20s doesn't have frequent sex, her desire may wane, according to Clayton. Studies have shown that women who engage in sexual activity less than once a week are more likely to have irregular menstrual cycles and ovulation problems than those who do so weekly.

• *The fear of disease* Two thirds of sexually transmitted diseases (STDs) occur in people 25 and younger, and women are more likely to be infected than men, according to the National Institute of Allergy and Infectious Diseases. Those who have contracted an STD may experience shame and be less interested in sex. And women who want to protect themselves must negotiate condom use with their partner, which may dampen desire.

• *Birth control and the blues* The most popular form of contraception for twentysomething women is the birth control pill. But because it suppresses testosterone production, some women find that the Pill actually undercuts desire. Others, however, find the Pill's convenience—and its reassuringly high success rate—helps promote passion. Another factor influencing sex drive: Up to 20 percent of women in their 20s struggle with clinical depression, a condition that diminishes desire. While antidepressants may boost a woman's mood, some may lower her libido.

30s— Married with Children

By the time women have hit their 30s, most have acquired some level of self-understanding. They're also likely to have established a stable relationship. Having a husband can be an aphrodisiac for women; the libido flourishes in the security of a committed relationship. But the stresses of child rearing and a career can diminish desire.

• *Practice makes perfect* Women get better at achieving orgasm in their 30s, which may stimulate desire—hence the popular notion that women reach their sexual peak in their 30s. "During the first few years of marriage, before children, women have, on average, the fewest sexual complaints of their lives," says Louann Brizendine, M.D., co-director of the program in sexual health at the University of California, San Francisco. That testosterone levels begin to decline at around 35 is not necessarily meaningful.

• *The power of pregnancy* For many women, the 30s are the reproductive years. During the second trimester of pregnancy, when you are no longer struggling with nausea but are not yet so big that sex feels like an elaborate game of Twister, many women find they have a surge in desire. This can be attributed, in part, to a sense of connection to your partner, but hormones also play a role. During pregnancy, there is a thousandfold increase in progesterone and a hundredfold increase in estrogen, which causes the vaginal lips to engorge and become more lubricated. The pressure of the growing baby on the genitals may also be a turn-on. In their book, *For Women Only: A Revolutionary Guide to Overcoming Sexual Dysfunction and Reclaiming Your Sex Life* (Henry Holt, 2001), sex therapist Laura Berman and her sister, Jennifer Berman, M.D., a urologist, say that during the second trimester, "Some women feel they are constantly in a state of mild sexual arousal." Being pregnant with a boy can further

heighten desire; during the second trimester, the male fetus starts producing testosterone, which may boost Mom's libido.

THE KEYS TO HIS DESIRE

Men and women may be made for each other, but the design sure could use a little tweaking. On average, men have five to 10 times the level of testosterone and three times the sexual interest that women have. And unlike women, for whom sex drive is highly individual, there is little variation among men. Among happily married couples under age 40, about 31 percent of women report a lack of sexual desire, while only 16 percent of men have (or admit to) that complaint. Research shows that the majority of men have one or more sexual fantasies every day, compared to only 25 percent of women.

Psychological factors play a role in male desire, but hormones are the key. That is, until men reach middle age. As testosterone levels gradually decline, usually beginning in the 40s, many men become more dependent on physical stimulation for arousal than, say, the sight of an attractive woman.

Still, the testosterone well runs deep. Although a 45-year-old man typically has a lower testosterone level than a 25-year-old, many men have normal testosterone levels throughout their lives. They will, however, probably initiate sex less frequently in midlife. About 5 percent of men in their 40s start to experience arousal problems; a decade later, that number doubles to 10 percent.

As with women, stress also figures in any discussion of the male libido. Says Sheryl Kingsberg, Ph.D., assistant professor of reproductive biology and psychiatry at Case Western Reserve University, in Cleveland, "One of life's little ironies is that women need to be relaxed to want to have sex, while for men, sex is a stress-reliever."

• *Post-baby burnout* Many women find that after the baby comes, sex has all the appeal of a root canal. This fall-off in desire can be attributed, in part, to exhaustion, but hormones are also implicated. Testosterone levels drop by about half after childbirth, though they quickly return to normal. "It's common for couples to have only one or two sexual encounters up to four months after the baby is born," says Brizendine. For Margo, a 33-year-old mother of one, those few encounters were memorable if only because of the pain, a problem that affects 70 percent of women in the first six months postpartum. "We kept trying, but it took a few months—and a bottle of Astroglide," she recalls.

Nursing mothers may be particularly uninterested in sex. Breastfeeding causes the release of the hormone prolactin, which can suppress ovulation and estrogen production, as well as testosterone. "Nursing mothers are experiencing the equivalent of menopause," says Mary Lake Polan, M. D., Ph.D., professor and chair of the department of gynecology and obstetrics at Stanford University School of Medicine, in Palo Alto, California.

But you don't have to be nursing to find your interest in sex waning. The Berman sisters observe that about 60 percent of the women in their practice have low levels of testosterone—a key to desire—after the birth of their second or third child. While the reason is unclear, Jennifer Berman believes this may be due to decreased production of testosterone by the ovaries or an acquired enzyme deficiency that hinders testosterone production.

• **Stressed to the max** Even if your hormone levels are normal, the advent of parenthood can throw a bucket of ice water on desire. Between the demands of work, young children and housekeeping, women in their 30s are under tremendous pressure. Often, they're angry at their husbands, who don't seem to take on an equal share of the new demands. "Women hit their stress peak in their thirties," says Peter Kanaris, Ph.D., a psychologist and sex therapist in Smithtown, New York. "And stress is a killer of desire."

40s— The (Mostly) Fabulous 40s

Hormone levels are starting to decline, but midlife can be a time of sexual reawakening. Many women find that they're less burdened by the stressors—children, financial uncertainty—that can undermine desire in the 30s.

• **The new sexual peak?** According to the NHSLS, the prevalence of sexual problems in women tends to decrease with advancing age. Like women in their 30s, fortysomethings are at ease with their sexual selves, but now they have the time and energy to enjoy this aspect of their life. Even if you experience a decline in interest, you may find that you can achieve new heights of sexual satisfaction. "Women [at this age] know what they want sexually and are not afraid to ask for it," says Sheryl Kingsberg. (The sad irony is that, with the passage of time, sexual problems become more prevalent in men; see "The Keys to His Desire.")

• **Hormones gone haywire** This is also the decade when women enter perimenopause, the period preceding menopause, when production of estrogen and testosterone begins dropping off. Perimenopause typically kicks in at age 46. About half of all women over 45 experience some symptoms, including irregular periods, lower li-bido and vaginal dryness. But a decline in sex drive doesn't mean sex can't be great. "You might not have the spontaneous interest, but your ability to achieve orgasm doesn't change in your forties," says Kingsberg.

• **The Pill for perimenopause** Many perimenopausal women are prescribed birth control pills to help stabilize hormonal fluctuations and ease symptoms. Of course, the Pill also protects against unwanted pregnancy, which can occur during this transition. Although the Pill may interfere with desire, it may also help a perimenopausal woman feel like herself again—and perhaps more in the mood for sex.

• **Thyroid trouble** Disorders of the thyroid gland, which produces hormones that stimulate body functions, are common in women over 40. By age 40, 1 in 15 women have thyroid problems; by age 50, 1 in 10 women do. Hypothyroidism, in which the gland secretes too little hormones, is a major cause of low libido. Women with the condition also experience fatigue, weight gain and depression. Fortunately, treatment with synthetic thyroid hormone helps relieve symptoms.

50s— A New Beginning

Although the 50s heralds menopause—and a dramatic change in sexual desire—many women discover that this decade offers some libido-boosting benefits.

• **Good-bye hormones** When women enter menopause, typically at age 51, about 40 percent begin to experience an even more significant drop-off in sexual interest or report some kind of dysfunction, says Mary Lake Polan. Small wonder: With menopause, there's a dramatic decrease in the ovaries' production of estrogen, the hormone that helps lubricate the vagina and increases blood flow to the genitals. Testosterone also declines.

• **The bright side of menopause** Many women are thrilled to put the hassles of menstruation and contraception behind them. And even though you can't count on your hormones to rev up your libido, you don't have to kiss your sex life good-bye. New medications, including Viagra, are currently being tested.

• **Getting a handle on HRT** Many postmenopausal women take hormone replacement therapy (HRT), which usually involves a combination of estrogen and a synthetic version of progesterone. While HRT is effective in treating symptoms of menopause, such as vaginal dryness and hot flashes, it can lower testosterone levels, dampening libido, according to Laura and Jennifer Berman. As a result, some physicians are starting to prescribe testosterone in addition to HRT.

Married with Children

A husband and wife on what happens to passion when kids enter the picture.

by Mark Harris and Theresa Dougal

MARK: It's daybreak, a school morning. Both girls are in the family room, simultaneously scarfing down a plate of waffles, watching an Arthur video they could recite by heart, and drawing pictures in old bluebooks. At the moment it seems they're deepest in their flow. Theresa and I make our break. With freshly poured coffees in hand, we sneak up the stairs behind them and settle back into bed for fifteen minutes of peace before the day's activities are launched.

It's often our most—and sometimes only—intimate moment of the day. Though there are no guarantees. More mornings than not, Sylvie, age seven, and three-year-old Linnea trail us into the bedroom before we've even had a chance to readjust the pillows. And with an alacrity that's noticeably absent when, say, they've been asked to pick up their bedroom, both girls have wedged themselves between us, sometimes snuggling in quietly, but more often burrowing into the covers to play House, Whining Baby, or the highly interactive Pretend You're This, I'll be That.

In my better moods, when the girls haven't bumped my coffee mug, sloshing java into the bedcovers, or kneed me once again below the bathrobe belt, I embrace what's a truly beautiful family moment. At other times, I see it as just another intrusion into

what's left of the intimacy Theresa and I share.

Kids. They've come between us, in bed and otherwise. That's been true from the beginning, of course. From the moment Theresa was first pregnant we naturally began to focus less on each other and more on the growing bulge that was Sylvie, the family we were becoming. So, willingly, we took in stride the changes in intimacy that followed—massages that once eased into lovemaking were now begged to ease the lower back ache of a third trimester: candle-lit table talk now turned on such romantic themes as diapering systems and the mechanics of breastfeeding.

When the kids came on, and with a vengeance it seemed, they tugged us further apart. The sheer effort and time it takes to keep them fed, clothed, marginally well groomed, happily engaged, and out of the emergency room draws straight from time in which we could connect, lend an ear, offer a hug. And when bedtime stories have been read, last potty parades marched, and the girls are finally asleep, our first impulse is to turn not to each other but to our other pressing needs. Which are legion, from unfinished writing assignments and ungraded student essays to grocery shopping and the ritual shoveling out of the family room.

Some nights we're so wiped from it all that we've been known to check the clock and calculate the value of sex with all the passion of a government economist. And when it's well past midnight, we're deep in sleep deficit, and Linnea's cough medicine is sure to wear off just when we're slipping into R.E.M., we've easily chosen more Z's over Big O's.

This won't always be so (I'm hoping); at least the parenting lit says these early childhood years are among the hardest on moms and dads. I'm certainly planning on some of our labor lessening when Linnea walks into that first-grade classroom (1,247 days from this date, but who's counting?). Our choice to live away from family members who could take the kids for a Sunday afternoon, or to limit our in-home day care, hasn't helped our cause either.

We could do more to close the gap between us that the kids have opened. But that would require a closer meeting of the minds than Theresa and I have arrived at. I'd be more willing than she to take the advice of the marriage counselors who extol the value of the weekly parents' night out, and I'm the one who attempts to set more of the kinds of limits between parent and child my own mother and father established.

By her own admission, Theresa, a full-time professor at the local college, isn't inclined to part with the girls for an evening date after she's been in the classroom and office all day. It's the working mother's guilt, I know, and I wouldn't deny her the bonding that's so vital to her, even if I could. To the extent I'm able, I understand—and accept—her need to mother.

But I'm not always happily resigned to it. I often nudge Theresa to carve out more time for us—and for herself. Like the kids, I want some of her attention too. An involved father, I've been home half the day with the kids, and when she walks in the door, I'm ready to disengage from them and connect with her. And I'll admit that when Theresa chooses them over me, I sometimes resent it and withdraw, taking refuge in the diversions of my bachelorhood, the movies, beers out with friends, my own work. Some days I feel I'm just waiting for the kids to get older, for them to need her less, to make her more available for us.

Our solid past has helped us weather this lean period, for sure. We'd been together eight years before Sylvie arrived, time to forge a strong marriage well before we created a family. And while we may connect less often, less deeply than we used to, we still do make time for us. We just squeeze more from less to do it. Before kids, connecting meant birthdays that would take days to celebrate, a Friday night out that would take in dinner, a movie, and a late morning rising. Today, intimacy is a ritualistic glass of wine we share in bed every night, or the odd twenty minutes of snuggling on the couch while the kids are lost in play up in their bedroom. These doses of intimacy are smaller, sure, but still meaningful, powerful, and restorative.

I'm just now beginning to accept the fact that Theresa and I, both together and alone, will forever struggle for more intimacy, to balance the incessant demands of the family life with those of the husband and the wife who created it. We accepted that challenge, knowingly or not, at that heart-stopping moment on a sunny May afternoon seven years ago when Sylvie was first laid in our arms.

Still, the struggle to balance the needs of the lovers with the needs of the parents has not been without its unexpected rewards. Like how watching Theresa as a mother—the woman who jumps out of a deep slumber to comfort a crying child, who at midnight can be found icing a birthday cake for Sylvie she's fashioned into a magic kingdom, and then marches into a classroom at 9:00 the next morning to lead a discussion of Thoreau—has only increased, not diminished, my love for her. Or how our kids have drawn Theresa and me closer together. They're our joint creation, after all. Because of them, we spend even more time together, struggle and enthuse even more, and talk more than ever, even if it is about Linnea's disinclination to ever comb her hair, or how to get Sylvie to tell off the school chum who's stealing her morning snack. For that and a million other reasons, this husband, this father, is willing—if not always happy—to move over when little girls arrive to turn our marital bed into a raucous playhouse.

THERESA: The scene was both cute and annoying. Sylvie, then age three and enthralled with dress-up play, had come downstairs to parade her latest ensemble. She sported something new yet vaguely familiar—long and pink, silky, and embroidered with flowers. It was my sole surviving wedding-shower negligee, which Sylvie had rooted out of my pajama drawer. I opened my mouth to protest—"Hey, wait a minute, that's not yours!"—and then I sighed and succumbed. "Oh well. I don't use it anyway."

The significance of Sylvie's triumph was not lost on me. The child of our dreams, she had become much the center of our lives, a place of honor she would soon share with her little sister Linnea. Her contentment was paramount to me, and the negligee incident underscored that fact. But the symbolism nagged at me and forced me to address an important question: Could there be room in my life for children, with their myriad physical and emotional needs and desires, and for a loving, intimate relationship with my husband? What happens to the passion when a twosome becomes a threesome?

The years Mark and I shared before Sylvie was born were full of excitement and the sheer enjoyment of being together. We had a wealth of leisure time, and we made the most of it. Our favorite pastimes revolved mostly around talk—watching a movie and then hashing it out, discussing books, taking long walks in our neighborhood, lounging in bed while ruminating over a morning cup of coffee or an evening glass of wine. We have come to know each other so well through these self-revelatory conversations, creating a deep and intimate bond.

With the arrival of Sylvie, the tectonic plates of our existence shifted. Sylvie, so welcome and so loved, bonded us, but she also demanded most of our time and attention, as babies do. While we willingly and happily cared for her, we couldn't help but notice how little time we had left to focus on each other. We still laugh ruefully over a particularly telling incident. Mark was holding the baby, and from another room I heard a thump and a groan. "What happened!?" I cried. "I bumped my head," Mark said. "Oh, good," I replied in sincere relief. "I was afraid it was the baby." "Thanks a lot," he muttered.

If Sylvie's infancy challenged our previous absorption in one another, how much more so does our busier life now. Mark and I both have fulfilling careers, and we also take almost sole care of our two children. We've worked hard at "having it all," but in the process we've stretched ourselves thin. Something has to go, and often it's the time we devote to each other. If we can barely make it through a chock-full day, how on earth are we going to have the energy at night to light the candles, warm the massage oil, dwell on each other the way we used to do?

While we both bemoan this state of affairs, reminding each other on particularly hard days, as we sneak a hug, that "I'm still in here," it's clear that we come at the issue from somewhat different perspectives. I easily yield to the demands of my daughters. Sometimes, their needs get in the way of my closeness with Mark, especially when I let myself become just too tired to devote real energy to our intimacy. This problem frustrates me, but I have a hard time getting around it. Sometimes Mark encourages me to "set more limits"—to preserve a little more space for myself and for "us," but I am torn.

Fortunately, though, Mark and I have begun to find ways to carve out more moments for ourselves. The girls play together more now, which gives us a little more time to reconnect. And at night we make time—even if it comes out of our sleep—to sit in bed together and talk. This evening ritual has been a constant in our relationship, making our bedroom the locus of an intimacy that is still deep and multi-faceted. When we turn out the lights, we still turn to each other with love and desire, whether we act on it or not.

Still, I have been longing to return ourselves to the center stage a little more often, so two weeks ago I secretly orchestrated our very first, luxurious night away alone together since Sylvie was born. Mark's birthday called for something special, so I planned an outing to approximate the "old days" of life before kids. I could have predicted that Mark would enjoy himself—once he got over the shock—but I wasn't quite prepared for the eagerness with which I embraced the opportunity to feed a flame that has admittedly been serving somewhat as a pilot light. When Mark asked me if I wanted to make a checkup call home, I declined. I didn't want to alter the tender mood that had been deepening in us since the moment we entered the hotel. I knew perfectly well that the girls were fine. I also knew that I liked what was happening between Mark and me; I liked our intensifying and prolonged awareness and enjoyment, both emotionally and physically, only of each other.

I guess our time away crystallized for me what I had long sensed but not fully acknowledged—that although motherhood reaps many rewards, the kind of passion that brings and keeps two people together is not necessarily one of them. If I want to have such intimacy, I must create it with Mark alone, and that's what this night was all about. Our little second honeymoon was so gratifying, in so many ways, that we won't wait another seven years to try it again. And in the end, we had no use for that pink negligee; Sylvie and Linnea can keep it. Such props are for newlyweds.

Mark Harris is a frequent contributor to Hope. Theresa Dougal is a professor of English at Moravian College in Bethlehem, Pennsylvania.

UNIT 6
Old/New Sexual Concerns

Unit Selections

35. **Christy's Crusade**, Patrick Tracey
36. **Silent No More**, Robin D. Stone
37. **The Last Sexual Taboo**, Judith Newman
38. **Lust and Revenge on Wall Street**, Allison Glock
39. **Pregnant? You're Fired!** Stephanie B. Goldberg
40. **Is It Cool to Be a Virgin?** Sara Glassman
41. **Naked Capitalists**, Frank Rich
42. **Carnal Knowledge**, Michelle Burford
43. **A Disembodied 'Theology of the Body': John Paul II on Love, Sex & Pleasure**, Luke Timothy Johnson

Key Points to Consider

- What does your college or university do about date or acquaintance rape? Are there education or prevention programs? How is a report of an assault handled? How do you think these issues should be handled on campuses?

- Are birth control (contraceptive prescriptions, emergency contraception, and sterilization) abortion, and infertility services available at the clinics and hospitals in your community? If not, why and how far would someone have to travel to get them?

- Have you ever had a discussion about masturbation? Did it include discussion of techniques or sex aids? Do you agree that this topic is the last sexual taboo? Why or why not?

- Have you ever watched an "adult" video or logged onto an "adult" Internet site. What purpose do you believe these products serve?

- How do you feel about laws restricting sexual behaviors (for example, age limits, marital requirements for engaging in sex, or laws making specific sexual behaviors illegal)? Which laws would you add or change that relate to sexual issues or behaviors?

- Where do you believe "personal freedom" or "choice" about sexually related behaviors begins to collide with the "greater good" of society? How about sex online?

- If you had a magic wand, what would you change about sexuality and how American society affects it? (Go ahead and dream; you're not being asked to identify if and how it could really happen.)

 **Links: www.dushkin.com/online/**
These sites are annotated in the World Wide Web pages.

Abortion Law Homepage
http://members.aol.com/_ht_a/abtrbng/index.htm

Infertility Resources
http://www.ihr.com/infertility/index.html

Men's Health Resource Guide
http://www.menshealth.com/new/guide/index.html

Other Sexual Violence Resources on the Web
http://www.witserv.com/org/ocrcc/resource/resource.htm

Sexual Assault Information Page
http://www.cs.utk.edu/~bartley/saInfoPage.html

Third Age: Love and Sex
http://www.thirdage.com/romance/

Women's Studies Resources
http://www.inform.umd.edu/EdRes/Topic/WomensStudies/

This final unit deals with several topics that are of interest or concern for different reasons. Also, as the title suggests, it combines "old" or ongoing topics and concerns with "new" or emerging ones. In one respect, however, these topics have a common denominator—they have all taken positions of prominence in the public's awareness as social issues.

Tragically, sexual abuse and violence are long-standing occurrences in society and in some relationships. For centuries, a strong code of silence surrounded these occurrences and, many now agree, increased not only the likelihood of sexual abuse and violence, but the harm to victims of these acts. Beginning in the middle of this century, two societal movements helped to begin eroding this code of silence. The child welfare/child rights movement exposed child abuse and mistreatment and sought to improve the lives of children and families. Soon after, and to a large extent fueled by the emerging women's movement, primarily "grass-roots" organizations that became known as "rape crisis" groups or centers became catalysts for altering the way we looked at (or avoided looking at) rape and sexual abuse.

Research today suggests that these movements have accomplished many of their initial goals and brought about significant social change. The existence and prevalence of rape and other sexual abuse is much more accurately known. Many of the myths previously believed (rapists are strangers that jump out of bushes, sexual abuse only occurs in poor families, all rapists are male and all victims are female, and so on) have been replaced with more accurate information. The code of silence has been recognized for the harm it can cause, and millions of friends, parents, teachers, counselors, and others have learned how to be approachable, supportive listeners to victims disclosing their abuse experiences. Finally, we have come to recognize the role that power, especially unequal power, plays in rape, sexual abuse, sexual violence, and, a term coined more recently, sexual harassment.

As we as a society have sought to expose and reduce abusive sex, it has become increasingly clear that all of society and each of us as individuals/potential partners must grapple with the broader issue of what constitutes consent: What is nonabusive sexual interaction? How can people communicate interest, arousal, desire, and/or propose sexual interaction, when remnants of unequal power, ignorance, misinformation, fear, adversarial sex roles, and inadequate communication skills still exist? Finally, another layer of perplexing questions that confront the proactive/reactive dilemma: What is, or should be, the role of employers, school personnel, or simply any of us who may be seen as contributing on some level due to awareness or complicity to an environment that allows uncomfortable, abusive, or inappropriate sexual interaction? Is it possible that we are so "sensitive" to the potential for abuse that combined with our discomfort, anger, and fear we have become hysterical vigilantes pushing an eager legal system to indict "offenders" who have not committed abuse or harassment?

The articles in the first subsection, *Sexual Abuse and Harassment,* seek to highlight ongoing and emerging issues with respect to sexual abuse, violence, and harassment. Despite some progress, such abuse still occurs, and the damage to victims can be compounded when they are not believed or, worse yet, they, rather than the perpetrator are blamed. "Christy's Crusade" follows the courageous fight—all the way to the Supreme Court—for justice by a college student rape victim. The next article focuses on emerging complexities surrounding sexual abuse, and, in turn, all sexual behavior. "Silent No More" personalizes the harm done when abuse is kept secret and the process of healing from victim to survivor.

The second subsection, *Legal and Ethical Issues Related to Sex,* delves into some current legal and ethical dilemmas associated with sexuality and sexual behavior. All societies have struggled with the apparent dichotomy of freedom versus protection when it comes to enacting laws about human behavior. In addition, the pace of technological advances (infertility treatment, AIDS, and nonsurgical abortion methods, to name just a few) has far outstripped society's attempts to grapple with the legal, ethical, and moral issues involved. At the present time, a variety of laws about sexual behaviors exist. Some are outdated, apparently in conflict with evolving social norms, even majority behaviors. Some laws are permissive, seeking to protect individual freedoms. Others are restrictive, seeking to protect society and allowing the intrusion of legal representatives into the private, even consensual, sexual behaviors of otherwise law-abiding citizens. "The Last Sexual Taboo" covers a law some readers may be surprised exists: outlawing the sale of personal sex aids or vibrators. "Lust and Revenge on Wall Street" recounts the affair of two Wall Street traders, their subsequent firing, and the lawsuit filed against the employer. The next article, "Pregnant? You're Fired!" addresses pregnancy and reproduction-related rights, laws, and services.

Each year *Annual Editions: Human Sexuality* closes with a final *Focus* section that is designed to give readers "food for thought" and/or fuel for discussion with classmates, friends, and/or family. Sometimes the focus identifies an emerging trend or timely issue in the "big picture" of sexuality. Other times the focus section raises one or more very broad questions that defy simple answers. This year's focus is one of the latter and it brings together four articles from quite varied sources on topics ranging from virginity to fidelity, to sex as business, to the role and purpose of personal sexuality and behavior in a spiritual or religious context, in order to raise the complicated issues of sexual decision making and morality. As with each previous focus section, readers are challenged to confront, consider, and discuss these complex personal and societal issues in order to conceptualize a better future for all of us—a future where humankind's quest for joyful, healthy, and fulfilling sexuality can be realized.

CHRISTY'S CRUSADE

WHEN WOMEN VICTIMS OF VIOLENT crimes do not find justice in state courts, do they have the right to sue for damages in federal court? For one young woman, attempting to gain that right took her all the way to the United States Supreme Court.

by Patrick Tracey

IN SEPTEMBER OF 1994, THE CONFLUENCE OF TWO EVENTS—one in the United States Congress and one in a college dorm room—would provide the backdrop for a U.S. Supreme Court case of crucial importance to women. On September 13 of that year, Congress passed the Violence Against Women Act (VAWA). The law, which women's groups had lobbied Congress to pass, was created to provide federal protections for women on the grounds that states were not vigorously pursuing cases involving violence against women. In addition to the equal protection component, Congress inserted an economic component to the law, based on evidence that violence against women impairs their ability to earn a living. Among other things, VAWA put federal muscle into prosecuting abusers who cross state lines or violate orders of protection. Under its civil rights remedy, it also allowed victims of gender-motivated violence to sue their attackers for damages. It was this last provision that brought the case of then 19-year-old Christy Brzonkala (pronounced bron-KA-la) before the U.S. Supreme Court.

Just one week after the passage of VAWA, Brzonkala was allegedly raped in a dorm room at Virginia Polytechnic Institute, in Blacksburg, Virginia, by two university football players. After two university disciplinary hearings failed to adequately address the charges, Brzonkala sued her attackers for damages in federal court under the still untested Violence Against Women Act. This prompted state prosecutors to open an investigation. A grand jury was called but refused to indict Brzonkala's alleged attackers. The case wound its way through the federal court system until March of 1999, when the U.S. Fourth Circuit Court of Appeals, in Richmond, ruled against Brzonkala, finding that Congress exceeded its constitutional au-

thority when, in enacting VAWA, it claimed that violence against women affected interstate commerce. The court also ruled against Brzonkala on the equal protection front, finding that VAWA was not an appropriate response to the failure of state criminal courts to treat female and male victims of violence equally. VAWA supporters countered both points, arguing that violence against women does affect commerce by undermining a woman's ability to get and keep a job. (The Bureau of National Affairs found that domestic violence costs U.S. employers $3–$5 billion annually. And according to the Department of Justice, the cost of rape to society is $127 billion annually.) Supporters also argued that the civil rights remedy was an appropriate response to bias in the state courts because it gave women another option for redress—the chance to litigate their claims in federal court. After the Richmond appeals court rejection, Brzonkala's attorneys took the case to the U.S. Supreme Court, where it was heard on January 11 of this year. A decision is expected by June.

—The Editors

THE 23-YEAR-OLD PLAINTIFF IS SUFFERING FROM BATTLE FATIGUE. For five years, she has shunned the media spotlight. But on this blustery January morning, at the foot of the wide marble steps of the United States Supreme Court, it isn't easy. Christy Brzonkala lowers her head, running the gauntlet to the back entrance of the courthouse. Hordes of reporters staked out to film her arrival have missed her completely.

Brzonkala v. *Morrison; Crawford; and Virginia Polytechnic Institute and State University* began as a university disciplinary hearing at Virginia Tech in Blacksburg, a rural town nestled in the New River Valley of the Blue Ridge Mountains. One of the football players whom Brzonkala had accused of rape, James Crawford, was acquitted by the disciplinary panel. The other, Antonio Morrison, after initially being found guilty of sexual assault then later acquitted, was only required to attend a one-hour session with a university affirmative-action counselor. "It was obvious," Brzonkala says, "that rape victims weren't going to get any justice on campus, so I decided to get my own attorney."

> # "It was obvious that rape victims weren't going to get any justice on campus."

Eileen Wagner, an English professor turned lawyer, had close ties to the academic world. She was a member of the American Association of University Women (AAUW), an organization to which Brzonkala's mother also happened to belong. Mary Ellen Brzonkala was referred to Wagner by an AAUW member who assured her that Wagner was not afraid to take on a large university and was well-equipped to handle her daughter's case.

Wagner told her young client that she didn't stand much of a chance in criminal court because rape cases were not always vigorously pushed by state police and prosecutors. Not only that, there was no physical evidence. And indeed, a state grand jury later failed to indict, partly because, as in the vast majority of rape cases in the U.S., Brzonkala's physical evidence had literally swirled down the drain when she bathed that night. However, Wagner told her client that there was one possibility: Congress had passed VAWA just one week before Brzonkala was allegedly raped, and she could be one of the first to sue under it. She could file a suit in federal civil court even without physical evidence because there is a lower burden of proof there than in criminal courts.

Brzonkala recalls Wagner saying to her that no one had yet sued for damages under VAWA and "we might get some justice from it." Brzonkala says, "[Wagner] and I talked for about five hours that day. Three days later, I said I'd do it." What tipped the balance for Brzonkala was the fact that Wagner had represented other students in disputes with universities.

For her part, Wagner says, "We knew she had the right case to test the law." The "right case" meant, first, that the perpetrators and victim didn't know each other. "Getting court sympathy when they do know each other is difficult," Wagner says. Second, statements made by Morrison could reflect "gender animus." Third, Brzonkala had already gone public. "If you're going to change policy," Wagner explains, "it's much better to have a real live person," rather than a Jane Doe. And finally, VAWA requires that the perpetrators' behavior be felony level, which in this case it was.

Nevertheless, Brzonkala and Wagner hit a brick wall in federal court, with a majority of judges ruling that VAWA was un-constitutional. This outcome actually bolstered Wagner's initial predictions. "We knew that some people were concerned with the constitutionality of the law, so we thought from the beginning that this would go to the Supreme Court," she says.

Today Brzonkala is just where Wagner expected her to be—at the High Court, swinging for the fences on behalf of all women. But it isn't going to be easy. Throughout the 1990s, the Rehnquist Court has steadily curtailed federal power, and Brzonkala's case represents a direct challenge to this effort. Chief Justice Rehnquist has already tipped his hand, having previously singled out VAWA as an example of Congress intruding on the traditional power of the states to prosecute rape.

When Congress passed the law, it declared that "[all] persons within the United States shall have the right to be free from crimes of violence motivated by gender." Paradoxically, many states welcomed the new federal law. In fact, attorneys general from 36 states have signed briefs arguing that Brzonkala deserves the right to have her case reheard by the first judge who ruled VAWA unconstitutional.

AS THE NINE ROBED SUPREME COURT JUSTICES enter the courtroom, Brzonkala rises with a capacity crowd of 350 spectators. The justices will spend the next 90 minutes prying apart legal arguments that hinge on the question of whether victims of gender-based violence can sue their attackers for damages in federal court.

Seth Waxman, the U.S. Solicitor General, representing the U.S. government, and Julie Goldscheid, an attorney for the National Organization for Women (NOW) Legal Defense and Education Fund, representing Brzonkala, attempt to show the need for a "federal remedy" to the problem of states not giving women equal protection.

Goldscheid tells the Court, "The states agreed that they needed federal help." The Supreme Court now has an opportunity to "further the legacy of civil rights legislation" by recognizing that women "have a right to recover damages when their civil rights are damaged through gender-based violence." The justices grapple with the question of whether gender-based violence affects interstate commerce.

Legal experts speculate that four justices will vote to uphold VAWA and three will dissent. All eyes are on Justice Sandra Day O'Connor, one of the two crucial swing votes and the likely author of the Court's decision. As the Court weighs up a host of federal statutes, O'Connor, who has been a staunch defender of women's rights, now questions the wisdom of treading on the traditional right of the states to prosecute rape charges.

Ruth Bader Ginsburg, the only other woman on the Court, seems to like the law. Peering over her glasses, Ginsburg says Congress's goal was not to displace state authority but "to provide an alternate forum. Why can't Congress do that?"

"Because this is not commerce," replies Michael Rosman, representing the two football players on behalf of the Center for Individual Rights, a conservative Washington, D.C.-based legal think tank. "This is violence, interpersonal violence, the kind of thing states have had as their exclusive province ever since the start of our country."

For Brzonkala, the link between rape and commerce is not an academic one.

For Brzonkala, the link between rape and commerce is not an academic one. She says that for her own safety, she was forced to drop out of college—a circumstance that will affect her ability to earn a decent wage—while the men she charges with rape were initially allowed to stay on campus and maintain their football scholarships. The alleged rape took place just three weeks after she'd entered the university to begin her freshman year. She hung in for the rest of that year, went home for summer vacation, and then never returned to Tech.

As the courtroom empties, she allows as how she could tell the Court a thing or two about intrusions—and not the feds intruding on the states. "It's called rape," she says, her heels clicking down the marble stairs. "Rape is the real quote-unquote 'intrusion.' "

The plaintiff strides down the sidewalk as a scrum of reporters catches up to her, wielding notepads and video cameras and poking microphones in her face. She addresses them briefly and then strolls around the corner for a post-argument reception sponsored by NOW. Senator Joseph Biden (D.-Del.), who sponsored the VAWA law, is on hand to thank Brzonkala "on behalf of my daughter, my granddaughter, and every other woman I love."

BRZONKALA, WHO HAD NURTURED DREAMS OF becoming a nutritionist, makes her living these days as an assistant manager at Madam's Organ, a blues club in the trendy Adams Morgan neighborhood of Washington, D.C. At the long pine bar, Brzonkala is having a few laughs with her best friends, who also happen to be her coworkers. "This bar is staffed by strong, independent women—people who kept me sane and allowed me to ease into independence," she says.

There is a stark contrast between the woman relaxing with friends and the pensive plaintiff listening to dry legal arguments. Deep down, she says, lies a desire to shield herself from pain. As evidence, she points to her willingness to tell new acquaintances her history: "They tend to treat me with kid gloves if I tell them. And that's how I like to be treated. Plus, if they know, they might be careful about how they use the word 'rape.' It's not a word to be taken lightly."

The biggest step in her recovery came, she says, when she moved into her own place downtown: "I needed to know that I could stand on my own two feet."

Brzonkala's first chance to stand on her own two feet came in the fall of 1994, when she left her suburban home on a quiet little cul-de-sac in Fairfax, Virginia. Heading off to Virginia Tech, four hours south, she waved good-bye to her father, Kenneth, a civil servant with the Federal Emergency Management Agency and her mother, Mary Ellen, an optician. She was also leaving behind several touchstones of her past. In her bedroom were swimming, softball, and basketball trophies. On one wall was a collage of smiling classmates at her senior prom. On another, an aerial photo of the Tech campus.

If the trophies would remind her parents of where she had been, the picture of Tech's campus would tell them where she was going: to a safe rural university that would midwife their daughter's passage to adulthood.

"Everything was going fine," Brzonkala recalls about her first few weeks at school. "I loved my classes." She had already made friends and probably could have played basketball for Tech but decided to forgo athletics to concentrate on her studies.

One night several friends from the women's soccer team invited her to a party off-campus. They were there for "three, four, or five hours," she says, and during that time she had "three, four, or five beers. I was by no means loaded."

After the party, Brzonkala and her friend Hope Handley walked back to their dorm, Cochrane Hall. As they approached, two guys whistled at them from a third-floor window, inviting them up for a nightcap.

"So we just go up," says Brzonkala. "We're going up to Hope's room, which is on the same floor, and we decide to drop in on these guys, just to say hello, nothing more. We go down the hall and they say, 'Oh, I'm so-and-so and so-and-so, and we're football players.' I almost cracked up, because I was a jock in high school, so it did not impress me."

What began as small talk soon degenerated into blatant come-ons, at which point Handley left the room. Handley remembered that she'd said good-bye when she left, but Brzonkala says, "It was my impression that she had gone to the bathroom. After a few minutes, she didn't come back. I got up to go, and that's when it all happened."

Morrison, a six-foot-one-inch defensive linebacker, weighing over 200 pounds, barred her from leaving and asked her for sex. "I am not that kind of person. I said 'No.' No is no, and that's all you need to hear."

After she refused a second time, he stopped asking, a point upon which she and Morrison both later agreed, with one major distinction. He says that he asked twice and then they fell into each other's arms. She says he pushed her onto his bed, forcefully removed her clothes, pinned her arms and legs, and pushed himself into her.

As soon as Morrison finished, Brzonkala says, his friend Crawford raped her. For about 15 minutes, she says, it was Morrison, then Crawford, then Morrison again.

"I was in shock, and I blanked out. When Morrison got off me, Crawford came in. Then Crawford left, and Morrison did the same thing again. The only thing I remembered was [Morrison] saying, 'You better not have any fucking diseases.'"

For those who have questioned her judgment in going to the dorm room of two big jocks in the wee hours of the morning, Brzonkala has an answer: "We never learned about rape in high school. They thought they were protecting us. Do you know what my senior quote in my yearbook was? It says, 'I will trust you until you do something to make me not trust you.' I was just so naive."

Afterwards, Brzonkala walked down the long hallway to the stairwell. She says Morrison followed her. "I just walked ahead

> ## "I'm not that kind of person, I said 'No.' No is No, and that's all you need to hear."

of him," she recalls. "It was weird. He said, 'Oh, maybe I can call you sometime?' And I just remember feeling disgust. I went back to my suite and just sat in the tub for hours. I put it somewhere way in the back of my head. Of course the next day I knew what happened, but..." Her voice trails off.

BRZONKALA SANK INTO A PARALYZING DEPRES-sion. She rarely left her room for fear of running into Morrison or Crawford. To keep from being recognized by her assailants, she cut her hair into a bob and wore baggy clothes. Even sunshine seemed sinister. She slept all day, skipping classes. Her failing grades seemed a trivial matter. "At that point, I sort of felt that I'd lost my college life. I was terrified of everything."

Uncharacteristically, she started smoking and drinking every day. Alcohol was the easiest way to blot it all out. "She had a tight-knit group of friends before," her roommate Charlotte

LEGAL EAGLES

BRZONKALA V. *MORRISON* will profoundly affect the way violence against women is treated in the United States. *Ms.* reporter Amy Aronson asked feminist law experts to comment on the case.

MARTHA DAVIS, legal director of the NOW Legal Defense and Education Fund

The Court is really deciding how far Congress can go in protecting civil rights. We thought this was resolved in the '60s, but the Court has gone so far to the right that the question is up for grabs. This is also an opportunity to educate the Court and the country about the fundamental impact that violence toward women has on the economy. We are hopeful that *Brzonkala* will prevail. Congress was so careful in drafting the statute. They sifted through tons of evidence from state courts about the economic impact of violence against women. For the Court to ignore the considered opinion of Congress would be shocking. One possibility is a narrow ruling, in which case we'd go back to Congress to reenact the law with slightly different provisions.

CATHARINE A. MACKINNON, Elizabeth A. Long Professor of Law at the University of Michigan and visiting professor at the University of Chicago Law School

This case is women's Civil War—the war over women's rights in civil society and women's full citizenship in the federal union. Sex-based violence with impunity denies women equal protection under the law and sex equality in society. The Fourteenth Amendment authorizes federal equality legislation. The antiequality side, as they did with race, argues that federal civil rights legislation violates states' rights. But the states are overwhelmed by male violence against women. VAWA does not take away state power; it gives women a law to take into our own hands. It recognizes that violence against us because we are women violates our civil rights, and the Constitution backs us up. Concretely, women can sue their abusers, and hold them responsible, without having to involve police or beg prosecutors. It shifts the balance of power toward sex equality. If Christy Brzonkala does not prevail it will be a staggering setback for human rights and an affirmation of the systemic nature of male dominance.

MARI MATSUDA, professor of law at Georgetown University Law Center and coauthor of *We Won't Go Back: Making the Case for Affirmative Action* (Houghton Mifflin)

The right has supported efforts to prosecute crime, and this Court has been aggressive in dismantling the Bill of Rights when it comes to protections for people accused of crimes. The fact that this Court has been dismantling these protections at the same time that

it has been making it harder to prosecute violence against women says something about who it does and does not care about. When the Republicans had the appointment power, they sought out antifeminist High Court judges and made antifeminist principles a litmus test. The Democrats have not been equally aggressive. This shows that judicial appointments should be a critical focus for feminist activism.

Representative ELEANOR HOLMES NORTON (D.-D.C.)

VAWA gives women what blacks have had since the Civil War—civil protection. There is still plenty of racial violence in this country, but there is less because those laws are on the books and are invoked. I'm concerned because of the skepticism I heard from the justices. Justice O'Connor, who has tended to understand women's issues, said, in effect, 'Your approach would justify a federal remedy for child support and alimony cases.' Nonsense. We had great debate in the House and Senate that led to a very narrowly written statute. Under VAWA, a woman has to prove more than a crime itself. She has to show that words said or actions taken prove a special animus was directed toward her because she's a woman. That's a very high burden to meet.

JUDITH RESNIK, Arthur Liman Professor of Law at Yale Law School

This statute is about how to enable women to be fully authorized economic actors, free from the threat of violence. VAWA continues a process started in the '60s when Congress enacted civil rights statutes, many of them through its commerce-clause powers. State attorneys general told Congress they wanted help in correcting patterns of discrimination in state criminal justice systems. I'm struck that when some people talk about VAWA, they describe it as intrusive of state power over families. The fact that violence against women is seen primarily through the lens of family life is the result of a long history of discrimination that did not protect women from violence in the home.

DEBORAH RHODE, professor of law and former director of the Institute for Research on Women and Gender at Stanford University

I'm guardedly optimistic that *Brzonkala* will prevail. There is ample precedent. The facts in this case are as good as you get. This reminds me of the struggle over the Equal Rights Amendment. In that instance, too, people said "The states can handle this." I remember one feminist attorney saying, "Yes, but that's like fighting the battle against slavery plantation by plantation." If the Court goes the wrong way, we'll be back to fighting things out one at a time.

Wachter recalls. "And then, she never really left the room after that."

Three weeks after the alleged rape, Brzonkala swallowed a vial of pills she'd been taking for a hypothyroid condition. "She was trying to keep me from getting anyone to help her," Wachter says. "But I woke up the girl in the room next to ours, and we tricked her so I could go get help."

Brzonkala was treated at Montgomery Regional Hospital in Blacksburg and released. The suicide attempt had been a cry for help, but Brzonkala's parents were never notified, and she didn't tell Wachter what had happened to her. As the Virginia Tech Hokies went on to win the Big East Championship, Brzonkala bottled up her rage. When she went home for Christmas break, her parents were still in the dark and mystified by her abysmal academic performance.

Says Brzonkala, "I know that I can never understand, because I'm not a parent, what it's like having to see your child go through something like that. So I didn't really want to talk to them about it."

With football season over, avoiding her attackers was getting harder. "I was seeing them coming out of the dining hall," Brzonkala says. "And that was starting to freak me out."

One March night, she was hanging out in her dorm room when Wachter, who worked in the dining hall downstairs, casually mentioned that she'd overheard some football players boasting about how they liked to "get girls drunk and fuck the shit out of them." Wachter told Brzonkala that she didn't appreciate the comment because she had a friend who always regretted not having pressed charges after she'd been raped.

It was this story that finally gave Brzonkala the courage to speak. "I was raped," she said softly, then started to cry.

Suddenly, Brzonkala's bizarre behavior made sense. The baggy clothes. The short haircut. The hapless suicide attempt.

Wachter says Brzonkala did not know the names of her alleged assailants, so Wachter returned to Cochrane Hall the next day with a Hokies media guide. When she opened the glossy brochure, there they were. "That's him," Brzonkala said. "That's Crawford, the cornerback. And that's Morrison, the defensive linebacker."

Brzonkala was finally out of the closet. At the suggestion of her resident assistant at Cochrane Hall, she sought help at the women's center. The modest white clapboard house on the edge of the Tech campus is carpeted and cozy, with framed photos of women basketball, soccer, and softball players lining the walls. After opening up to rape-crisis counselor Donna Lisker, Brzonkala says, "I stopped crying for the first time in months."

Later, Brzonkala's attorney Eileen Wagner would uncover a startling fact: a number of other campus rapes had been reported that fall. (Wagner and her client will probably never know if charges were brought because that information is confidential.) Brzonkala soon confided in a small circle of friends, including a few women soccer players who in turn met with Tech's sports psychologist on Brzonkala's behalf. They also arranged for Brzonkala to meet with Tech football coach Frank Beamer, who quickly punted the idea of punishing his players. "He said his job was to protect his boys," Brzonkala says.

Beamer had been hired eight years earlier to restore pride in a team tarnished by scandals. He was now on his way to the Sugar Bowl with a ragtag roster of players nobody else wanted. With his eye on a Top Ten finish, the last thing he needed was to lose Morrison, his highly recruited starting linebacker.

It was time, Brzonkala knew, to level with her parents. Fortified with a drink, she dialed their number. "Mom," she said, "I have something to tell you."

Mary Ellen Brzonkala says she dropped the receiver when she heard the news. Kenneth Brzonkala, wringing his large hands, says he "just wanted to kill the two bastards."

The next day Brzonkala and her parents met in Lisker's office. "We talked about the judicial options," says Lisker. "There was the criminal system, reporting it to the local police; there was the campus judicial system, which meant going to the office of the dean of students; and there was civil litigation."

Brzonkala opted to go to the dean of students because she would not have to face her attackers. The next day she filed a complaint with Tech's disciplinary panel for students.

At the first judicial board hearing, Crawford was acquitted because he had an alibi. Teammate Cornell Brown claimed he was with Crawford elsewhere that night, although he later refused to make that claim to the grand jury. The board found Morrison guilty of "sexual assault," based on his offensive "diseases" remark. He was suspended for two semesters but appealed the ruling, claiming that his "due process rights" were denied, and that the suspension was "unduly harsh and arbitrary." According to a May 22 letter to Brzonkala from Dean of Students Cathryn Goree, Morrison's appeal was denied.

He then retained attorney David Paxton, a big gun from nearby Roanoke. Paxton combed the facts and discovered an eye-popping glitch. Tech, it seems, had made a printing error. The word "rape" had been omitted from a description of sexual violence in the original printing of the 1994–95 student code of conduct contained in the university rule book.

The rule book was later reprinted with the missing word added. But by then it was too late because, Paxton argued, Morrison couldn't have known from reading the first printing that rape was included in Tech's sexual assault policy.

So on July 21 a second board hearing was held. Though he was on summer break, Morrison returned for the hearing. This time, he was found guilty of "abusive conduct," a lesser charge than sexual assault, again stemming from his "diseases" remark. The board confirmed his suspension.

Brzonkala received a letter from the board saying, "This action was taken because the preponderance of evidence provided during the hearing supports a finding of guilt."

The letter was dated August 4. Strangely, on August 3, Coach Beamer told reporters at a Big East Conference media day that Morrison would return for the fall football season.

Apparently, Beamer knew something that Brzonkala didn't. The decision to reinstate Morrison was made solely by the Tech provost, Peggy Meszaros. Meszaros had concurred with the "abusive conduct" finding, but in a letter to Morrison copied to Beamer, she reduced Morrison's punishment to a one-hour session with a Tech affirmative-action counselor. "While you were convicted of a serious charge," she wrote, "it is my determination that the sanction is excessive when compared with any other cases where there has been a finding of the Abusive Conduct Policy."

Brzonkala and her parents said they never received a letter informing them of Morrison's reinstatement. Brzonkala, who was home for the summer, read about it in the Washington *Post*. This development clinched her decision not to return for the fall semester. "Obviously," says Brzonkala, "they wanted to brush this under the rug."

"It was outrageous," her father says. "Had I sent my daughter back, without her ever knowing that Morrison was still there, she could have run into him in any dark stairwell. No one tried to call. Nobody wrote us a letter. If he were not on the football team, I guarantee he would have been gone. What was this, another printing error?"

In September, Kenneth Brzonkala confronted the dean of the university about Morrison's reinstatement and was told nothing could be done. At the beginning of November, Christy Brzonkala took her story to Terry Padalino, the editor in chief of the student newspaper, the *Collegiate Times*. Padalino says that when she heard it, she immediately sat down to tap out an editorial: "Something stinks in Blacksburg," she wrote. "For more than a year, a young woman, once a student at Virginia Tech, has been recovering from an assault she claims was made against her in the bedroom of a linebacker for Tech's 13th-ranked football team.... Her Tech college career is all but over. Morrison, on the other hand, is having a banner year as a member of the Big East Champion Hokies."

Padalino interviewed Beamer, but Meszaros did not return numerous phone calls. "She wouldn't see us," says Padalino, "even though we went to her office."

Nor could Padalino reach Morrison or Crawford, who also refused through their lawyers to talk to *Ms*. For two weeks, Padalino sat on the editorial and a front-page story that was to accompany it: "It was a week before the final football game of the season. Because it was a big game, we decided to wait so that it wouldn't look as if the game was her motive in coming forward."

On November 28, 1995, the *Collegiate Times* hit the streets with a thud that reverberated all over campus. In her editorial, Padalino demanded that Meszaros be "severely disciplined for her heartless aiding and abetting of this malicious cover-up."

Soon after, an open forum was held for students, faculty, and townspeople in the student union building. About 250 members of the community, most of them angry, heard Meszaros read a 25-minute statement.

Brzonkala did not attend, but Leslei Syner, who had just formed a group on campus called Women Against Rape, was there to do the cross-examining of Meszaros. Syner said, "You do not have printed rules against murder, but does that mean you would condone killing?"

Many assumed that the university was coddling a star athlete. The Hokies were, after all, a top-ranking team in 1995, with only one loss. But in the months following, the pig-skinners would also rack up an astounding 21 arrests, six convictions, and four dropped charges. The team was filling the dockets of the Blacksburg courthouse, with Morrison and Crawford in the lead. Morrison was arrested on charges of being drunk in public and petty larceny. Crawford was arrested twice, once for hitting a service-station attendant with his car and once for the rape and attempted sodomy of another Tech student. The latter was settled out of court. This litany of crimes prompted Washington *Post* columnist Tony Kornheiser to wonder if the Hokies were in training for "the Convict Bowl."

Crawford was expelled because of the latest rape charge, and Morrison, whose deferred suspension was never enforced, finished college in 1999.

Now Christy Brzonkala's case rests with the Supreme Court. If VAWA is upheld by the Court, Brzonkala wins the right to have her case reheard by the first judge who ruled VAWA unconstitutional. The suit seeks $4 million from Morrison and Crawford and $4.3 million from Virginia Tech. The combined punitive damages equals the amount the university received for its 1995 appearance in the Sugar Bowl. Brzonkala also sought damages from the university for violating Title IX, which bars sexual discrimination by universities that receive federal money. According to the Associated Press, in late February Virginia Tech settled that suit, paying Brzonkala $75,000.

Brzonkala may go back to college but never to Tech. She says she's tired of being a poster child. "I am so over the cause," she says. "But it will be easier to sleep at night knowing all this is behind me."

Patrick Tracey is a freelance writer based in Washington, D.C.

From *Ms.* Magazine, April/May 2000, pp. 53–61. ©2000 by *Ms.* Magazine. Reprinted by permission.

SILENT
NO MORE

Survivors of sexual abuse can begin to heal the pain of the past by speaking out

BY ROBIN D. STONE

My journey from victim to survivor began when I was about 9 years old. My younger sister and I were sleeping over at an uncle's house in the country. I adored my uncle, and I curled up on his lap to watch the late-night movie. Everyone else was asleep when, sometime later, he led me by the hand to a dark corner of his house. There he fondled my growing breasts and rubbed my crotch. When he was finished, he sent me to bed, warning me never to tell anyone what he had done. "The incident," as I now refer to it, was five minutes of confusion, horror and profound embarrassment. Its impact has lasted a lifetime.

Like many children who've been violated and warned to keep quiet, I did as I was told. Through years of family gatherings and church functions, I kept my distance from my uncle as I built a wall of silence around myself. Inside it, my secret began to take root in my life, and as a tree's roots slowly conform to their surroundings, so was I shaped by my inability to give voice to what had happened to me. Deep down, I believed that I had done something to deserve what

happened, and even as I wrestled with that, there were periods when I managed to convince myself that it was really no big deal. Still, I decided that I shouldn't get too close to men, or anybody else for that matter. Even God was not exempt. I remember thinking that if God really existed, he wouldn't have let my uncle touch me.

Though some may find it difficult to understand how five minutes can forever affect the course of a life, those who have been sexually violated know all too well the residue of humiliation and helplessness that the experience leaves behind. Not telling about the abuse only compounds its effects. Indeed, some find that secrecy can become a way of life. Kristen (name has been changed), whose older cousin repeatedly forced her to have intercourse with him from ages 9 to 12, says, "There was a real connection between my not telling about the abuse and withholding other things about my life as well. You become good at hiding because you fear that if you don't, others will be able to see the shameful truth of what happened to you."

Sooner or later, though, the secret must be reckoned with, because the silence that helps us cope in the beginning can lead to anxiety, depression, addiction, memory loss, cancer, promiscuity and sexual and reproductive problems. "There's a mind-body-soul connection," explains Maelinda N. Turner, a Vancouver, British Columbia, social worker with a degree in divinity who has worked mostly with Black and Latino clients. "It may sound New-Agey, but if emotions aren't released, they hide in the body as disease."

A Quiet Epidemic

Because sexual violence—being forced or coerced to perform sexual acts—is fueled by the abuser's need for power and control, those who have less power, such as children, are often more vulnerable. Indeed, children under 12 make up about half of all victims of sexual assault. And not surprisingly, the rates of rape and other forms of sexual assault are higher in poor and urban areas, where so many feel powerless. As a result, experts say,

Healing the Hurt

By Iyanla Vanzant

1. Talk to someone. Find someone you trust and let them know what happened. Tell them exactly how you feel. Do not participate in the conspiracy by remaining silent.

2. Keep a journal of thoughts and prayers. Even after talking, the thoughts continue to circle in your mind. Write down what you think and feel, then write a prayer to have those thoughts and feelings healed.

3. Avoid asking yourself why. Asking why deepens the wound and feeds the feelings of shame and guilt. An unanswered why shifts the responsibility onto your shoulders.

4. Keep your body moving. The trauma of sexual abuse gets locked in the muscles and tissues of the body. You must exercise to free yourself of the effects of the emotional and mental trauma. Dancing, swimming or yoga can help you rebuild and regain a healthy relationship with your body.

5. Talk to yourself. Learn to love yourself by creating powerful, loving affirmations that support and encourage you. Affirmations let you know that you are still okay.

6. Rehearse the confrontation. Write out what you would say to your abuser, and write the response you believe the abuser would have. Keep writing both sides of the story until you experience peace. Repeat this exercise as many times as necessary.

7. Realize it was not your fault. Whether you were abused as a child or an adult, avoid blaming your appearance, behavior, inability to escape, lack of retaliation or fear for the violation.

8. Don't run from the memories. You only delay your healing when you avoid, deny or resist the memory of the experience. Instead, draw a picture that represents what you feel. When you are done, burn it!

9. Create a safe place. Choose a place in your home that you can decorate with comforting objects, or go to a park or some other easily accessible location. Claim it as a safe haven. When you go to your safe place, sit quietly, pray, meditate or just hold loving thoughts about yourself.

10. Get professional help or support. Do not deny yourself healing support and encouragement. Find a counselor, therapist or support group with whom you can continue to explore and share your thoughts and feelings.

Black women have a disproportionately higher risk of assault.

In recent years, even as overall crime rates have fallen, the incidence of rape and sexual abuse has risen. At least one in four women, and one in six men, will experience some form of sexual abuse in their lifetime. And according to some estimates, as many as one in four young women on college campuses will become a victim of rape or attempted rape, although half of those violated won't think of it as such. That's partly because almost 70 percent of rape and sexual-assault victims know their offender as an acquaintance, friend, relative or intimate partner, and we're loath to see people close to us as rapists. Think about it: If a mugger beats a woman as he steals her purse, she'd report that to the police. But if an associate rapes a woman after she has invited him up for a drink, she thinks about the line of questioning ("You did

invite him up, didn't you?") and decides to keep it to herself. The bottom line: Fear often keeps us quiet and can even keep us from admitting to ourselves that we have been criminally violated. There's the fear of what people will think and what they'll say. There's the fear of retaliation. The fear that you won't be believed. Fear that you'll jeopardize existing relationships. Fear that somebody will go to jail. Fear that you'll be alone. And fear that you actually invited it. The fear can be so overwhelming that many victims of abuse actually repress the memory as a way of coping.

So why are we so reluctant to talk about sexual violence? Well, first we'd have to be willing to talk about sex, which many of us find uncomfortable. "We're certainly not the only group that's silent regarding abuse," says Gail E. Wyatt, Ph.D., author of *Stolen Women: Reclaiming Our Sexuality, Tak-*

ing Back Our Lives (John Wiley & Sons). "But we're the only group whose experience is compounded by our history of slavery and stereotypes about Black sexuality, and that makes discussion more difficult."

Because so few of us tell, nobody knows how big the problem of sexual violence really is. All statistics are based only on *reported* assaults, and, according to the 1999 National Crime Victimization Survey from the U.S. Department of Justice, sexual assault is reported only about 28 percent of the time, making it the least reported violent crime in the United States. Untold numbers continue to suffer in silence, sleepwalking through their days, alive but not truly living, compressing their feelings so they won't feel pain.

For survivors of sexual abuse, there is no one formula for recovery, but every path to healing ultimately requires that

Safeguarding Our Children

Few of us actually teach our children how to protect themselves from sexual abuse, despite the fact that 67 percent of all reported victims of sexual assault are under 18, according to a recent Department of Justice survey. How do we empower our kids to defend themselves, and to create an environment in which they'll feel free to tell us anything? Here are ways to start:

Give children the appropriate vocabulary so that words like *vagina, breast* and *penis* aren't foreign to them. Naming intimate body parts helps your child claim them in a healthy way.

Respect their boundaries. If Aunt Sally wants a kiss and your little one resists, don't force the issue. Children pushed to submit to affection may begin to feel that grown-ups' demands are more important than their own physical limits.

Teach them about inappropriate touching. "Say to your child, 'Nobody should touch you there,' or 'Nobody kisses you on the mouth,'" says New York clinical psychologist Dorothy Cuningham, Ph.D. Introduce concepts gradually, starting around age 3 and depending on your child's ability to understand. But don't put off talking about inappropriate touching, Cunningham warns. Toddlers can be the most vulnerable.

Encourage children to express their feelings. "You can't have closed communication and then expect it to be open if there's sexual misconduct," Cunningham points out. "Invite your children to talk to you. Don't just ask 'How's school?' Ask 'How's your teacher?' and 'What did you do today?' Get a sense of their relationships and friendships." Give feedback so your child knows you're listening and responsive. And don't be afraid to ask direct questions. For example, you might periodically ask your child "Has anyone ever tried to touch you in a way you did not like, or asked you to touch them in a way that made you uncomfortable?" One woman, abused by an older relative for years during her childhood, says that if her mother had asked her a direct question, her painful secret would have come out.

Teach children that it's okay to question authority—especially those in authority who make them feel uncomfortable. This can be a challenge for those of us raised to "do as you're told" by grown-ups. But children should never feel that they have no choice.

Know your child. "If you're tuned in, you know when she's upset," Cunningham says. If a once-carefree child becomes moody, withdrawn and unresponsive, don't dismiss it as phase. If your child suddenly doesn't want to go to Uncle Fred's house, pay attention. If your youngster becomes preoccupied with mature sexual concepts, don't assume it's just something picked up at school. Question your child gently, and above all, let her know you love her unconditionally.

—R.S.

---

we speak out about the ways in which we have been violated. On the following pages, three women (names and identifying details have been changed) give voice to their stories of abuse and silence—and they discover, in the telling, a way to finally move beyond the secrets that have haunted them for so long.

Dangerous Games

Stephanie, a 31-year-old artist, rarely makes her way from her East Coast home to the rural midwestern town where she grew up. Home reminds her of the "games" she and her two sisters used to play with their father. "When Mama was away, Daddy would put us on his lap and feel us up," says Stephanie, the middle sister. "He'd call us into his room one at a time. He'd start with a hug or a tickle, and then he'd touch my breast. We knew what was happening. My sis-

ters and I had a code. We'd say, 'Okay, in five minutes, you've got to come and get me.'" Throughout the girls' childhood, their father would call the eldest sister the most often. Today that sister escapes the pain of those memories through the use of illegal drugs and alcohol. Stephanie's youngest sister struggles with overeating. On the surface, Stephanie, who is single, seems highly functional compared with her sisters. She is full of energy and has a host of friends and a calendar packed with theater dates, parties and book-club meetings.

When I ask Stephanie how she feels about what her father did to her and her sisters, she seems surprised. She has never thought much about it, she says, adding, "What's done is done." But she quickly contradicts herself. "Things have built up over the last few years," she admits. "I'm at the point where I hate

when my father even answers the phone. Yet when I do go home, I don't want him to know that I feel uncomfortable. He's this old man and he does love me. It's all bizarre."

Stephanie believes her abuse is to blame for her struggle to become truly intimate with men. "For a long time, I didn't like to be touched," she says. "It made me feel kind of helpless." Her sisters, too, have had trouble sustaining relationships. Neither has ever married, but each has a child.

"The great wound of sexual abuse," explains social worker Maelinda Turner, "is that it leads you to believe you're not worthy to celebrate the gifts of the power of your sexuality without fear, question or judgment." I ask Stephanie if she and her sisters have ever considered talking with a professional. She shrugs: "I feel like you're supposed to just go on with your life."

Turner sees patterns typical of sexual-abuse victims in Stephanie and her sisters. "You can find ways to escape from the pain," she explains. "Work, drugs, food. You can be successful, smart and busy, but eventually it sneaks up on you. At some point you need to slow down and deal with what happened and how it has affected your life."

She stresses that unless their father gets counseling, the sisters have to contend with the fact that when their children are around him, they, too, will be in danger. That concern became quite real a few years ago, when one sister suspected their father had begun to abuse her 6-year-old son. Her fear for her son led her to finally confront her father about the abuse she and her sisters had suffered. As the secret tumbled out, her mother reacted with disbelief. "You all must have done something," she said lamely, apparently not knowing how else to respond. Stephanie's father insisted nothing had happened with his daughters or his grandson, and her mother let the issue drop. Stephanie's sister, dismayed by her parents' denial and needing to protect her son, now avoids her parents' home.

That episode was the first and last time the sisters ever openly discussed the abuse with their parents. Turner believes that the entire family will need to go into therapy if real healing is to occur, but she acknowledges that it is unlikely that Stephanie's parents will ever move past their denial. Mothers who can't acknowledge their daughters' abuse have often been abused themselves, she reflects. Until they can deal with their own demons, they can't help their daughters. "It's like a cancer," Turner says. "If your grandmother had it and your mother had it, you're susceptible."

As for her father, Stephanie is resigned. "People are who they are," she says. "Rather than have him live out his last days being miserable, I've made a conscious decision to make him feel comfortable." A soft sigh escapes her as she adds: "That just leaves me waiting until he dies."

Sex, Money, Drugs

Evelyn's eyes say she's 50. In fact, she is only 35. She grew up in a comfortable home in New York City with her parents, sister and two brothers. When she was 10, her brother's teenage friend began to creep up to her bedroom to fondle her. He'd give her candy to keep silent. Evelyn finally threatened to tell when he pressured her to "let him put his thing in me." Then he left her alone. In junior high, she fell into a clique of girls who regularly visited the principal's office. "We let him feel us up, and he gave us money and good grades," she says. The principal was fired when one of the girls became pregnant and told. No one else in the clique breathed a word.

At 16 Evelyn befriended a man who owned a neighborhood store. He invited her into the basement for drugs and sex. Not long after, she got pregnant and dropped out of school to have his child. She was in the ninth grade and could barely read. "I was always used to a man taking care of me," she says. At 18 she met Benny, who fed her crack habit and then beat her. Desperate to escape him, Evelyn left her baby with her mother and took off on her own. Soon she was prostituting to buy crack. "It didn't matter what they did to me," she says of the countless tricks she turned. "I just wanted my money."

Author Gail Wyatt, a professor of psychiatry at UCLA, observes that by the time Evelyn was a teenager, she had been conditioned to see herself as a sexual object and sex as a means to an end. Evelyn's case is extreme, Wyatt notes, but in all sexual relationships it's important to ask, "Is my body just being used to get me something?"

Evelyn quickly sank into a miserable routine of sex, violence and drugs that consumed two decades of her life and drained her self-worth. In crack houses she would often emerge from her haze naked and bruised, knowing she had been raped. "I was too afraid to go to the cops," she says. "Why would they believe me? I wanted to die. I asked God why I wasn't dying." She was too ashamed to tell her family she needed

help: "I didn't want them to see me; I didn't want to disgrace them."

Indeed, her unwillingness to reveal to her family her earliest incidents of abuse—first by her brother's friend, then by the principal and later the store owner—may have led to Evelyn's pattern of abusive sexual encounters. As Wyatt observes, family dynamics are frequently at the root of our silence around issues of sex and sexuality. "An abuse victim's decision not to tell says a lot about whom they trust, their loneliness and isolation," she explains. "Sometimes there's an emotional distance in the family. It's difficult to talk about sex if you're not talking in general. And abusers will tell you they can sense vulnerable, needy kids."

Evelyn, still vulnerable and needy as an adult, eventually entered an upstate treatment program, where her pattern of abusive sexual encounters continued: She had sex for money with men on staff. She got caught and kicked out and headed back to the streets. Eventually she landed in Project Greenhope, a Manhattan rehabilitation and drug-treatment residence for women who've had trouble with the law. More than a year later, she's clean and fortunately AIDS-free, and through counseling she's coming to understand the roles sexual abuse and silence have played in her life. Soon she will be on her own, and with only $117 a month in welfare, she will need to find a job and a home. "I'm learning to love myself, but I'm scared to death," she admits. "I've never paid a bill in my life."

While Wyatt applauds Evelyn's efforts so far in turning her life around, she cautions that Evelyn will need long-term psychotherapy to help her reclaim her own power over her body: "This young woman was conditioned to give her power away," Wyatt says, adding that Evelyn needs to develop positive relationships with women, perhaps other graduates of her treatment center, and steer clear of the temptations of old friends and habits. She encourages Evelyn to avoid sexual relationships altogether until she gets in touch with her own sexuality. "This is not just about sex," Wyatt says. "This is her whole life."

Longing for Nurturing

Behind Kim's fiery spirit and quick wit is a wounded, still grieving young woman. She's overweight, but she has "too many other things to work on" besides dropping pounds. She's single and often lonely, though she has a boyfriend of seven years. Before him, by her own account, she had a string of mostly empty sexual relationships, 40 in all. "I used to confuse sex with love," she says. Now 34, she still finds it hard to believe that a man could want more than sex from her, saying, "I'm afraid people will leave if they see the real me."

Kim can identify exactly when these feelings of worthlessness began. Her stepfather started fondling her during bath time when she was about 7, and by the time she was 11 he had graduated to intercourse. "I went from crying to just giving in to fighting to get him away from me," she says. She felt she had no choice but to remain silent: Her stepfather had warned that if she told her mother, a prominent southern political activist, he'd kill them both. To prove his point, he'd sharpen his knives and clean his gun in front of Kim.

And so she endured routine rapes by the man who was supposed to be taking care of her while Mommy was out saving the world, beatings when she threatened to tell, and a pregnancy and horrifying miscarriage that she suffered through alone at age 16. "I knew my stepfather was the father," she wrote in a journal, "and just like everything else he had done to me, I could not tell anyone about it."

When Kim was 19, her stepfather pressed one time too many for sex. She resisted and he slapped her, and in her anger she found the courage to tell her mother. Kim was stunned when her mother responded by accusing her of seducing her stepfather and ordered her out of the house. Forced to live with friends and family for a while, Kim eventually moved out on her own. Many years later, she would learn that her mother herself had been sexually abused by a relative. Through therapy she would come to understand that her mother had no inkling of how to protect or support her daughter. At the time, though, Kim was devastated.

"Sometimes I think I shouldn't have said anything," Kim says through tears. "I paid a price: I had to change my life. I had no degree, no job, no skills, nobody but me. What I've lived through is incomprehensible. I lost a good part of my life." She tries to describe the physical and psychological impact of her past: "I constantly have indigestion. When I'm afraid, I want to throw up. I'm always waiting for the other shoe to drop, for something to rock my semblance of being normal."

Dorothy Cunningham, Ph.D., a clinical psychologist with a private practice in New York, explains that Kim's situation was made worse by her mother's denial: "When a parent refuses to accept what's going on, they're often thinking about what it could do to their career and to their family," Cunningham says. "It took a lot of courage for Kim to say this happened, and the mother left her child to heal herself."

Kim has been trying to do just that. Now working toward her college degree, she has been in therapy for years, though she admits she doesn't go as often as she should. "Sometimes it's too hard," she says. Yet therapy is crucial to Kim's healing process, Cunningham says. "There's a loss of innocence, a loss of childhood and family," she explains, and Kim needs to mourn that loss. Therapy can be a safe place to grieve.

Cunningham also sees in Kim a woman who needs to get angry. "People who stay in victim mode blame themselves," she says. "They see themselves as bad and dirty. In some ways that's safer than unleashing the anger that's inside. You need to give yourself permission to be angry. Say 'I deserved to be listened to; I deserved protection.' When you're a victim, you don't feel like you deserve anything. When you're angry, you're moved to action; you're empowered."

One of the most difficult memories for an abuse victim to deal with is the sensation of physical pleasure that she may have experienced. Even now, Kim struggles to understand how she could have felt pleasure while being raped. "It was like looking forward to a lover," she says, her voice almost a whisper. "And

as much as I looked forward to it, it repulsed me too."

As disturbing as Kim finds this aspect of her abuse, her experience is not uncommon. "It's very difficult for many to accept," Cunningham confirms. "You can be terrified and confused but still have an orgasm. Kim should know that her body did what bodies are supposed to do—it responded to touch. That's how bodies are made. She needs to know she's not a perverted soul."

Seven years ago, after Kim's stepfather died, she began to reach out to her mother. But their conversations often spiral into accusations and tears. Though she still longs for the nurturing that she feels she missed while growing up, Kim recognizes that she is more likely to get it from supportive friends and family members than from her mother. "She is what she is," Kim sums up, "but I still love her. And I know I'm going to be okay."

Common Ground

While every experience of sexual abuse is different, some common therapeutic themes emerge: We need to understand the role of power in our relationships, and hold our abusers accountable for their actions. And we must learn to treat ourselves kindly as we work to come to terms with what happened. "You can't mark progress or breakthroughs," Maelinda Turner says of the healing process, "but you can look back six months or a year and know that you're in a different place."

My own healing took years. I was 21 when my mother and stepfather finally sensed my discomfort around my uncle and gently encouraged me to tell them about it. My parents were surprisingly calm, and I felt enormous relief that I could finally let go of my secret. But when my mother called my uncle to confront him, he denied everything, which left my parents to decide whom they should believe. Fortunately for me, they believed their daughter. Some heated family discussions followed, and it was eventually agreed that a few relatives should be informed so they'd know not to leave their kids vulnerable. My uncle steered clear of me, and life went on.

But even after I shared my experience with my parents, I didn't really deal with the *effects* of it for another 12 years. During that time, the 9-year-old girl in me was still feeling a 9-year-old's feelings. And so, about four years ago, with the help of a psychotherapist, I began the hard work of untangling the secret from my life, pulling up its deeply rooted feelings of shame and fear and self-doubt.

When I look back on my experience, I see that the most difficult aspect of my abuse was not the telling, of what happened to me—it was carrying the burden of silence for all those years. In my own journey toward healing, I'm learning to counter the 9-year-old's thoughts that even now sometimes play in my mind. I'm learning not to be afraid of inviting attention by speaking up or standing out or even by writing. I'm learning that I didn't deserve what happened to me, and that I have a right to be angry at my uncle. I'm also learning that I can have warm, close relationships.

I married a man whose love was strong enough to breach the wall I'd built around myself, and who understood why I needed to take this healing journey. We have a young son who is my heart and joy, and I'm doing work that fulfills me. I used to wonder where I might be if not for what happened in that dark corner so many years ago. But I now see that in spite of what happened, I'm embracing life, moving out of the long shadow of silence and doing what I can to help myself, and others, heal. And like so many survivors, I carry on.

GETTING HELP

If your child tells you she has been abused, assure her that she did the right thing in telling and that she's not to blame for what happened. Offer her protection, and promise that you will promptly take steps to see that the abuse stops. Report any suspicion of child abuse to your local child-protection agency or to the police or district attorney's office. Consult with your child's physician, who may refer you to a specialist with expertise in trauma. A caring response is the first step toward getting help for your young one.

If you know a sister who has been sexually assaulted, encourage her to seek out a group or individual therapist who is trained to counsel her. These resources can help:

BOOKS

Surviving the Silence: Black Women's Stories of Rape by Charlotte Pierce-Baker (W.W. Norton & Co., $23.95).

I Never Called It Rape: The Ms. Report on Recognizing, Fighting and Surviving Date and Acquaintance Rape by Robin Warshaw (HarperPerennial, $13).

I Never Told Anyone: Writings by Women Survivors of Child Sexual Abuse edited by Ellen Bass and Louise Thornton (Harper-Collins, $13).

I Can't Get Over It: A Handbook for Trauma Survivors by Aphrodite Matsakis, Ph.D. (New Harbinger, $16.95).

ORGANIZATIONS

Rape, Abuse and Incest National Network (RAINN), 635-B Pennsylvania Ave., S.E., Washington DC 20003; (202) 544–1034; (800) 656-HOPE (hot line directs you to a crisis counselor). Or contact the group on-line at rainn.org or rainnmail@ aol.com.

Association of Black Psychologists, P.O. Box 55999, Washington DC 20040; (202) 722–0808.

National Association of Black Social Workers, 8436 W. McNichols St., Detroit MI 48221; (313) 862–6700.

National Black Women's Health Project, 600 Pennsylvania Ave., S.E., Suite 310, Washington DC 20003; (202) 543–9311.

Survivors of Incest Anonymous, P.O. Box 190, Benson MD 21018; (410) 893–3322.

Men Can Stop Rape, P.O. Box 57144, Washington DC 20037; (202) 265–6530 or mencanstoprape.org.

Robin D. Stone, editor-in-chief of essence. com, is writing a book about Black women survivors of sexual abuse. She is reachable by E-mail at womenwise@aol.com.

THE Last SEXUAL TABOO

We live in an age of free condoms, how-to videos, and graphic advice on how to please your man. So how come we still have a problem when a girl just wants to have fun—BY HERSELF?

by judith newman

UNDER THE RUBRIC "THINGS I FIND EROTIC," DOLPHINS AND BEANIE BABIES DO NOT RATE HIGH. WHICH IS WHY THESE CHEERFUL KNICKKNACKS IN KIM BIBB'S LIVING ROOM LOOK SOMEWHAT OUT OF PLACE NEXT TO HER DISPLAY TABLE OF PLASTIC PENISES. The penises are… well, let's put it this way: Any woman who believes Size Doesn't Matter clearly isn't in the sex-toy business. • I'm in Bibb's modest tract home near Huntsville, Alabama, because she is hostessing a Saucy Lady party, which I'm told is like a Tupperware party, only with "romance enhancers": lubes, ticklers, vibrators. "So… it's a Schtupperware party!" I offer brightly. Ten women stare at me in baffled silence. Alabama: not the best place to try out Yiddish puns. • The party is educational. "Honey, when was the last time your man raved about how tight you are?" asks Saucy Lady founder and high-octane pitchwoman B.J. Bailey, in what I pray is a rhetorical question. "If he ain't begging for it, it's 'cause you're not Kegeling enough! He's just floppin' around in the Grand Canyon!" B.J., auburn-haired and cheerleader-pretty at 46, preaches 50 Kegels a day and plenty of orgasms. "If you have a headache, oh honey, the best thing you can do is have an orgasm!" she exclaims, as she demonstrates a pink, lifelike behemoth that's rotating and whirring menacingly. Then she pulls out a slim wand that buzzes like a weed whacker. She runs it gently over her face. "When it was illegal to sell these," she says, "I said it was really good for your sinuses." • Illegal? Well, yes. In most states of the union, a Saucy Lady party would be just a night of tacky fun. But here in the buckle of the Bible Belt, if lawmakers have their way, a gathering like this could land B.J. in jail—one year of "hard time" plus a $10,000 fine for each vibrator she sells. In 1998, the Alabama legislature banned

the sale of sex toys—"any device designed or primarily marketed for the stimulation of human genital organs." (It's perfectly legal to use them). Outraged, Bailey and six other women decided to sue. In 1999, a federal judge ruled the law unconstitutional. But here it is, 2001, and an appeals court has ordered him to take another look at the case. If Bailey's lawyers can't come up with some convincing arguments, the sex-toy business could become illegal again.

Women fighting for the right to bear dildos may not seem like the world's noblest political crusade. But that's just why I came to Alabama: I had heard about the ban and the ensuing legal fight, and I wanted to understand why anyone, anywhere, would feel passionately enough about a mechanized piece of plastic to literally make a federal case out of it.

I mean, I'm a pretty sophisticated gal. I came of age in the 1970s; I went to my share of women's groups in college, where with a speculum and a mirror and a great deal of wine we oohed and aahed over how beautiful our cervixes were. (Okay, actually, I couldn't bring myself to look. But I drank the wine.) More recently I chortled over the *Sex and the City* episode where good-girl Charlotte became so addicted to her vibrator her friends couldn't get her to leave her apartment. In other words, *I got it*. At least I thought I did.

But sitting in Bibb's living room, I realize there are some things I don't get at all.

These cheerful moms—homemakers and factory workers, married and divorced, young and not-so, churchgoers all—are as different from Charlotte and her Manolo-obsessed friends as Fifth Avenue is from the local mall. Yet far from being repressed, they talk—and talk and talk—about their vibrators with a fondness

B.J. Bailey figures that about 80,000 women have attended her Saucy Lady parties. If the residents of Huntsville are this attached to their BOBs (that's battery-operated boyfriends), what does that say about the rest of America?

usually reserved for small pets. I had to wonder: If the women of Huntsville are this attached to their BOBs (that's battery-operated boyfriends), what about the rest of America? Have we secretly become a vast vibing culture? How? When? Why?

And no matter how big the network of vibe lovers has grown, why were any of them in this room? These days, anyone can buy—or sell—sex toys in the privacy of her own home; thank the Internet for that. Surely B.J., so clever and energetic, could figure out a way around the ban, even if it meant giving up parties like this one.

But as the evening winds down, it becomes clear: The party *is* the point, or a big part of it. B.J. doesn't want to go underground. She wants to be able to stand in her living room and tell women exactly what is so great about vibrators, and just how good they can make you feel. "I do believe that the Lord gave us the ability to enjoy our bodies for a reason," says B.J., who attends church every Sunday, has held many Baptist-only Saucy Lady parties, and believes fervently in angels. "Part of my job is to tell people that God wants us to have pleasure."

Eventually the party breaks up, and one by one the women head to the bedroom with B.J. to buy their treats in private. The rest of us bond in the kitchen over Crock-Pot chili and Snickerdoodles. "Can't wait to get home," murmurs one plump, wide-eyed customer who hasn't uttered a word all evening. She examines the contents of her brown paper bag thoughtfully. "Wonder if my husband's still awake?"

When B.J. (her name is Brenda Joyce; she adopted the nickname "because I knew men would remember it") is finished with her other Saucy Ladies, she takes me aside and presses something into my hand—a "Lil' Beaver." It's a ring of plastic that fits over a penis, with a vibrating "tickler" positioned in the right place.

Apparently I look tense.

I glance down at the little guy. How could I have thought a vibrator is just about getting off? No; it's about taking matters, literally and figuratively, into your own hands. A job may be stressful, backbreaking, tedious; children may be demanding and unruly; a mate inconsiderate, bored, or boring—or maybe there's no mate at all. There's not much in life a girl can count on to give her pleasure. But a vibrator? A vibrator delivers.

IT'S HARD TO IMAGINe, but from the days of the ancient Greeks until just a few decades ago, the female orgasm was considered not so much a vehicle of pleasure as a means to prevent illness—specifically, hysteria (or "womb disease"). Plato referred to the uterus, in which the condition was thought to originate, as "an animal inside an animal"; symptoms might include fainting, nervousness, insomnia, loss of appetite, and, most insidious, the tendency to be very cranky. The preferred remedy was sexual intercourse, though exercise (horseback riding, anyone?) sometimes worked, too.

Of course, defining sexual frustration as female pathology did not encourage men to become unselfish lovers. Nor did it encourage women without partners to take care of themselves. No; a disease requires a doctor or other caring medical professional. If symptoms were severe enough, the recommended treatment was to "massage the genitalia with one finger inside, using oil of lilies, musk root, crocus, or similar," the physician Pieter van Foreest wrote in a 1653 medical text. (And *we* can't even get doctors to make house calls.)

"It wasn't sex," says historian Rachel Maines, author of the eye-opening 1999 book *The Technology of Orgasm: Hysteria, the Vibrator, and Women's Sexual Satisfaction*. "It was just like the breaking of a fever." Nor was it considered fun for doctors; genital massage was time-consuming, messy, and hard on the wrists. So American physician George Taylor's 1869 invention was most welcome: a patented steam-powered vibratory machine called "The Manipulator" that was about the size of a dining room. It came with a warning that treatment of female complaints should be "supervised to prevent overindulgence."

By the early 1900s, companies saw the advantages of marketing portable vibrators to women themselves—talk about an untapped market—and ads began to pop up in places where other household appliances were sold. One manufacturer plied its wares in *Woman's Home Companion*: "American Vibrator may be attached to any electric light socket, *can be used by yourself* in the privacy of dressing room or boudoir, and furnishes every woman with the very essence of perpetual youth." (The emphasis was in the original.) In a 1918 Sears, Roebuck catalog, under the heading "Aids That Every Woman Appreciates," were a sewing machine, an electric fan and radiator, a household mixer, and a vibrator: "very useful and satisfactory for home service."

In fact, it was not until the 1920s, when sex toys began showing up in early stag films, that the jig was up for doctors and "decent" housewives. Vibrators lost their respectability, and physicians lost an easy source of revenue. The diagnosis of hysteria, on the other hand, remained in the American Psychiatric Association's official manual until 1952.

THE WOMAN WE HAVE to thank for taking machine-aided orgasm out of the closet again is an artist and educator named Betty Dodson. Her book, *Liberating Masturbation; A Meditation on Selflove* (later renamed *Sex for One*), appeared in 1974. This was more or less the moment when the feminist revolution collided with the sexual revolution—which, at least in the beginning, was a lot more liberating for men than for women. Dodson turned masturbation into a cottage industry, holding workshops that taught

> "I faked orgasms until I was 28 years old," B.J. tells me. "I thought touching yourself down there was nasty and dirty and wrong. I thought you had to do it through men." Her first vibrator changed her life.

women exactly what to do. (She even sold videotapes of some of her workshops. Let's just say that I never made such good use of the fast-forward button. At the end, everybody hugged.) Pent-up demand led sex educator Joani Blank to open Good Vibrations, a San Francisco store geared especially to women, in 1977. Innumerable retail operations followed.

One thing did not follow, however: a nation of glowing, satisfied women. Twenty-five years after Dodson made the scene, researchers surveyed thousands of women about their sex lives, and published the dismaying results in the *Journal of the American Medical Association*. Nearly 43 percent said they had some form of sexual dysfunction, including lack of desire, insufficient lubrication, difficulty reaching orgasm, and pain.

For many years, B.J. Bailey belonged to this unfortunate sisterhood. "I faked orgasms until I was 28 years old," she tells me as we cruise downtown Huntsville in her cherry red Dodge Durango. "I thought touching yourself down there was nasty and dirty and wrong. I thought you had to do it through men—they'd get you there, it's up to them. But lots of 'em don't." B.J.—thrice-married, a mother, and a grandmother—is quiet for a moment. "I'm not proud I slept with a lot of men. You sleep with enough of 'em, and people call you a whore. Well, I didn't want to be a whore; I just wanted to have an orgasm."

Her first husband was so physically abusive—hitting her, shoving her head in the toilet bowl, stealing her glasses so she couldn't drive away—that when she did finally escape, "I left with only a diaper bag, a suitcase, and my eight-month-old baby. I weighed 98 pounds." Her second husband was a descent, kind man, but their marriage eventually broke up, partly because of health issues with her son, who had a heart problem, and partly for reasons she'd rather not discuss in print.

Oddly, Bailey doesn't remember how she got her first vibrator, or from whom, but she knows it was a plain penis-shaped seven-incher, and she knows she figured out what it was good for. So by the time she met her third and current husband, Daniel, she had learned to have an orgasm by herself. "I was honest with him—at first. I said, 'I've never had an orgasm with a man.' But that was before we went to bed together. The first time, I did fake it. And he turned to me and said, 'I know you faked it. You don't ever have to do that again.'" And she didn't.

Yet here, too, vibrators helped enormously. "We don't always use them, but sometimes when I have a little trouble getting over the top, you know, it's Dan who'll say to me, 'Honey, why don't you get out one of your toys.'" I start to tell B.J. she's lucky to have married such a mensch, but then I think about the Schtupperware pun and decide to skip it.

She began her business ten years ago. At the time she lived in California, where she worked as a secretary. She'd been invited to several FUN (For Us Now) parties, a local sex-toy-in-

the-home enterprise, and she'd had a great time. Recruited by the company, she plunked down $1,200 on her credit card to buy merchandise for her own FUN party. "At first I thought, 'No way in hell will I speak about sex in front of strangers!' But I was good. And I realized I was helping lots of women. I thought, 'If I've had a problem with this, maybe other folks do, too.'"

Soon after, when her husband got laid off from his job and they moved to Huntsville, she realized that if the ladies of Southern California needed a little spice in their lives, her new neighbors needed it that much more. Nearly 80,000 Saucy Ladies later, she figures she's right.

N O ONE IS SURE how many women today own vibrators. But in the 1996 "Sex in America" survey conducted by the University of Chicago's National Opinion Research Center, 20 percent of those polled called sex toys either "very" or "somewhat" appealing. That percentage is probably quite conservative, since respondents were often interviewed in the company of their spouses and children. A recent online survey by xandria.com, a sex education Web site, puts the number closer to 87 percent—but hey, these are people visiting a site whose motto is "Sex. Education. Life. Pleasure."

One thing is certain: Among aficionadas, there's a "buy one, collect 'em all!" mentality. In my informal survey of friends, acquaintances, and total strangers who inexplicably agreed to answer my nosy questions, I rarely found a vibrator user who owned just one.

"Now let's see… I've still got my first one, the trusty five-incher I got 15 years ago as a gag gift," begins Janet L., 36, an unmarried customer service associate at a store near Huntsville and a steady Saucy Ladies customer. "Then there's the Wand, the Super Egg, the Silver Bullet, the G Spot vibrator, the Ultimate Beaver… just six! I use different ones for different times, depending on my mood. You keep the favorites under your pillow."

Indeed, vibrators are a heartwarming example of American consumerism at its best: We're a country that likes choice. Even in a relatively small outfit like Good Vibrations, there are 130 models to choose from. Charlotte's *Sex and the City* model was the Rabbit Pearl, which consists of a large (always large) pink shaft ringed with nubbly pearls. The shaft gyrates. "My boyfriend gets jealous when he sees this—he can't gyrate," says Katie, a health educator in Seattle. On the outside, positioned to hit the clitoris, is a bunny with rapidly flicking ears. Apparently the ears make all the difference. (And you don't have to worry about what they think of your thighs.)

Some vibrators are shaped for penetration, some not; some models last a long time, some don't. One classic, the powerful plug-in Hitachi Magic Wand, was designed to ease sore muscles. A few years ago the manufacturer decided to phase it out, prompting a run on the product. Wisely Hitachi started making it again. "My friends call it the Hitachi Hammer of God," says Abigail C., 41, a San Francisco computer analyst.

B.J.'s personal favorite is the Super Egg—small, ovoid, "with this tickly nub on the end that hits just the right spot. It gets you from 0 to 60 like *that*." The Ultimate Beaver is a close second—it's like the Rabbit Pearl only with a, um, beaver. A good starter vibrator is the Jelly 6/12 inch: "It's flexible and angled to help hit your G spot," says B.J., who keeps various models along with lubricating cream and other paraphernalia in a gift basket in her bedroom. And then there's the Cadillac of vibrators, which B.J. calls the Queen. It comes from Japan (read: superior craftsmanship), has a steel shaft that will never wear out, numerous speeds, great gyrating action—and costs $150. "If you have $150 to spend on one of these, you don't need a man!" B.J. jokes.

You can always count on B.J. to get to the crux of the issue. As one of her customers—a big, buxom blonde with a laugh like a tractor pull—puts it; "Some guys around here, if it ain't attached to them, they get scared." Yet most of the Saucy Ladies—and if experts are to be trusted, most women in general—enjoy using their vibrators with their partner. They certainly don't view plastic as a substitute for flesh and blood. "I do not mean to imply that electric-, diesel-, or steam-powered orgasms are preferable to penis-, hand-, or tongue-powered ones," says Lisa E., a writer in Denver. "That's like asking me to rate cheesecake vs. cheeseburgers vs. grilled ahi with a sesame wasabi glaze. They're all good." Plenty of women disagree with even this. "Vibrators are *too* easy," one friend says. "You don't have to do any work. You don't even have to fantasize!"

The smart woman introduces BOB to her mate gently. "If you want your partner to get into the vibrator as much as you do, your attitude has to be, 'Honey, look what we've got?'—not 'Look what I've got, and it can do your job,'" says Jane Greer, a marriage and sex therapist in New York City and author of *Gridlock: Finding the Courage to Move On in Love, Work and Life*. "The idea is to share. The benefit to him is that he can do something that feels great for you or with you. Let it be an extension of him, not competition."

Often, though, the thrill has nothing to do with sharing. "Anytime a woman can control her own pleasure and her own life, it's empowering," says Stephanie B., a Web site producer in Alabama. Stephanie, who was discouraged from touching herself when she was growing up—"My mother didn't like the idea of tampons"—got her first vibrator at 21 and has amassed quite a collection since. "I get to choose how often I have an orgasm, what type. And vibrators teach me about my body. If I didn't masturbate or use vibrators, it would be harder to tell my mate how to give me pleasure. You masturbate, you use a vibrator, and you know. It's like, 'Oh honey, hit right there!'"

Plenty of women simply can't have an orgasm any other way. Betty Faye Haggermaker, 51, took pleasure for granted during most of her 20-plus-year marriage. After a hysterec-

tomy, though, it vanished, a turn of events that is not uncommon. A vibrator gave her back the capacity to enjoy sex.

Haggermaker, a 51-year-old florist who lives near Huntsville, is not by nature an activist. But when she heard about the ban, she joined the lawsuit. "If you can't buy a vibrator, what's the government gonna tell you you can't do next?"

OH YES: THE BAN. In this day and age, why would a legislature prohibit the sale of vibrators? One possibility: Alabama just likes to ban things. This is, after all, a state that still has many "dry" counties and some of the highest taxes on a bottle of liquor anywhere in the nation. If sex education is offered in schools at all, it must be taught from an abstinence perspective, and no illegal activity can be mentioned. (Oral sex, aka sodomy, outside marriage is outlawed in Alabama, too.)

Amy Herring, one of two local attorneys working with the ACLU on the case, has her own theory. "The ban was part of a larger antiobscenity law meant to crack down on girlie bars and X-rated videos," she tells me over barbecued pork, vinegar slaw, and hush puppies. "The sex-toys part was a few lines buried in a 50-page bill. Frankly, we're pretty sure Tom Butler"—the state senator who sponsored the bill—"never even noticed it."

Lots of other people say the same thing. (As for Butler himself, he didn't return repeated phone calls to his office and home.) But if he did make a mistake, he didn't back down. When Herring and others pointed out that doctors and sex therapists routinely prescribe vibrators for patients suffering from sexual dysfunction, the Democrat, who's also a pharmacist, told the *Huntsville Times*: "I don't care what they call it, therapeutic or whatever. Some of it's just trashy."

Herring, 46 and much-married (currently, to a pleasant man 13 years her junior), met B.J. in the early nineties at one of her parties. "I had a ball. I bought some stuff, then bought some more stuff. I used them with my husband. I don't care if you print this. I was sexually dysfunctional. I could be a plaintiff in this suit."

She cares about the case so much she's not collecting a fee, instead taking out a second mortgage on her farm to keep her office going. But then, she's not representing just B.J. and her co-plaintiffs—a woman who owns a local "novelty" shop called Pleasures, Haggermaker, and four other vibrator users. She's representing all womankind and, by extension, all Mankind, too. "We have an opportunity to bring about an important expansion of the right to privacy," Herring says. "If we put on a trial, it's going to be like the Scopes monkey trial, only about sex instead of evolution."

Alabama isn't the only state to ban vibrators. Louisiana overturned its law last year, but prohibitions still stand in Georgia, Mississippi, Tennessee, and Texas, where you are only allowed to own six "obscene devices." (Six. How do you suppose they came up with that number? Five, you're a law-abiding citizen; seven, you can be hauled off to jail?)

Alabama attorney general Bill Pryor's defense of the ban has been noticeably tepid. "[I]t is my constitutional duty to defend the laws of Alabama when these laws are challenged in court," he said in a faxed statement. "The obscenity reform law… does not, in my judgment, violate any provision of the U.S. Constitution."

What about the right to privacy? First of all, there is no right to privacy in the Constitution. The right is inferred from what the Supreme Court assumed the Founding Fathers meant to say, or might have expected for themselves. Second, says the ACLU's New York—based attorney Mark Lopez, "the sexual right to privacy is recognized in the context of reproduction only"—that is, the right to decide whether or not to procreate. Sex for pleasure alone, with or without toys, is not protected under federal law—yet.

U.S. District Judge Lynwood Smith spent nearly a hundred pages trying to justify overturning the ban on other grounds. The 11th U.S. Circuit Court of Appeals didn't buy his reasoning and told him to take another look at the case. But the conservative court didn't reinstate the law. Instead, it ordered Smith to consider whether the Constitution *should* protect "every individual's right to private sexual activity"—in other words, sex for its own orgasmic sake.

Smith must decide, the court said, "whether our nation has a deeply rooted history of state interference, or noninterference, in the private sexual activity of married or unmarried persons." Basically, says Lopez, the court wants to know what the Founding Fathers would have thought about vibrators.

"I can tell you exactly what they would have thought!" Herring says with a hoot. "The Founding Mothers would have used them! This is why women went to spas! If you were 'hysterical,' they put you in this bath with these water jets, and you got that warm and fuzzy feeling."

For a moment, the laughter fades from her voice. "Hey, if I were living in the 18th century, I'd be hysterical, too," she says. "Otherwise, I might never have an orgasm. For much of this country's history, that's how it was. The only reliable way for a woman to receive sexual pleasure was to be hysterical."

T HERE ARE PLENTY OF other issues to be sorted out in the Alabama case. Why pick on vibrators and not ribbed condoms or books like *Sex for One*, which are clearly also "designed or marketed as useful primarily for the stimulation of human genital organs"? How, with the Internet, can a ban be enforced? B.J. Bailey finds the law's implicit sexism especially irritating. "Do you hear anyone arguing about cracking down on Viagra sales?" she fumes. "And everybody knows guys use it not just for medical reasons, but for fun. Some women use vibrators because it's the only way they can have an orgasm. But for others… Well, is there a problem with ladies having fun?"

If, in the end, the courts don't support B.J., she figures she can take her case to a wide public. The story of her life has been optioned by a major Hollywood production company; the working title is *Can't Find Me Love*.

"I want someone like Dana Delaney to play me—or Susan Sarandon!" she says. "She plays strong, powerful women. Sarandon would know how important it is for a woman to be in charge of her sexuality."

Ultimately, this is what keeps B.J. and the Saucy Ladies fighting: not just the right to privacy, not just the right to have some fun, but the right to decide what fun *is* and to share it with anyone they want to—or with no one at all. These are rights that most American women assume we won decades ago. Apparently, we were wrong.

Think of the sex-toys suit as a call to arms. "This isn't just about orgasms," B.J. says. "This here's about power."

Judith Newman is a writer in New York City.

From *Health* May 2001, pp. 142-144, 146, 148, 150. © 2001 by Health. Reprinted by permission.

LUST AND REVENGE ON WALL STREET

The sex was consensual and, in the high-hormone world of Wall Street, hardly unusual. So why did a blue-chip brokerage firm fire a hotshot trader and his former lover?

By Allison Glock

By the time it happened, the flirtation had been simmering for months. Wall Street trader Tom Hudson had noticed his coworker Gabrielle Katz straightaway. It would have been difficult not to. Katz, then twenty-three, is a petite brunette with creamy skin, swollen lips, and doe eyes that make her look like a blend of Elizabeth Taylor and Winona Ryder. She has the tight little body and the big open smile (with dimpled cheeks, even), and at Goldman Sachs, where she worked as a desk manager, she was irresistible honey for a whole horde of broker bees.

More than a few of them had asked Katz out, but she refused. She had a boyfriend. Which was probably for the best, at least as far as Hudson was concerned, because he had a wife.

Then, in June 1998, Goldman Sachs held a client outing—an overnight white-water rafting trip replete with booze-fueled corporate bonding. The day was spent impressing clients and downing gin and tonics, and by 11:00 P.M., everybody was slaphappy. It was then, at the end of the day, that a bleary-eyed Hudson and Katz found each other in the dark, fell into each other's arms, and made love with the unique fervor of people who know in their hearts that they are doing something very wrong.

"It was so powerful," Katz says now, eating a fish steak at Olives NY, a restaurant in Manhattan. "We had been fighting the temptation for so long. I was so drawn to him. And I couldn't stand myself because of it."

As Hudson explains, "I wasn't in love. It was more like a drug addiction, only magnified."

The temptation was intense, and so for a time, against their better judgment, Hudson and Katz dated. It was a private, grown-up affair, without operatic drama, focused and adult and consensual—minus, of course, the consent of Hudson's wife. The couple met at Katz's apartment once a month for four months. And then, as with most affairs, it ended. As compelling as their chemistry was, neither Katz nor Hudson wanted a full-on relationship. A one-night stand is an indiscretion. Affairs are a commitment, necessitating lying and willful blindness and new underwear, and, as such, they quickly become exhausting.

"We both knew there was no future in it," Hudson says. "I broke it off. I said, 'We shouldn't have done it, and we can't do it anymore.' I had been married five years. I didn't want to throw that away. It's a big leap to leave a marriage. I wasn't willing to make that leap."

"I cried my eyes out," Katz says. "But I got over it. It was what had to be done, and I was proud of him for doing it because I knew I couldn't."

By February 1999, Hudson and Katz—who both worked on the "bad bank debt" desk—had parted amicably, they say, and gone about their jobs at Goldman Sachs as if nothing important had ever passed between them. They remained distant friends, but the heat was gone. And then, Tom Hudson was unexpectedly pulled from a morning meeting. "I was directed to a conference room. I remember the blinds were down. It was very dark. There was a round table in the center, but no one was sitting down. I walked in and saw my boss, John Urban [who declined to comment on the case], as well as a person from Compliance. They asked if I was having a relationship with Gabrielle Katz." Hudson says he explained what happened, how he had, for a brief time, cheated on his wife. "I told them the affair had ended months prior, he recalls. He also informed them that he'd confessed the relationship almost a year before to Bob O'Shea, a partner but not his direct supervisor. (He's since left the company and did not respond to a request for comment.) "They said, 'Fine,' and sent me home."

The next day, they were both fired. Hudson says he was told it was because of the affair, while Katz says her bosses were less direct: They asked about Hudson—she declined to answer—but also made reference to her lack of "team spirit." Goldman Sachs contends, in response to a lawsuit Hudson eventually filed, that he wasn't let go because of the extramarital relationship per se, but because he failed to report it to his superior and lied when asked about it. (Katz is not part of the suit, and Goldman officials refused to comment on her.)

Katz took the news with an acquiescent shrug, heading home to North Carolina for a conciliatory coddle from Mama, but Hudson was less compliant. His shock was outweighed only by his indignation, and he became lit with rage. "I was fired four months after any romantic involvement with Gabrielle," he explains angrily. "I was told by Bob O'Shea that if I wanted to have a relationship with her, it was okay; she would just need to be moved off the desk to avoid the appearance of impropriety." (And, in fact, Katz says she was subsequently moved from the desk where the traders sat and into a cubicle, though she wasn't transferred out of Hudson's department.) A Goldman source disputes this version of events, however: Hudson told O'Shea the relationship was over, and he was then given a memo instructing him to inform his superior if it resumed.

Hudson's dismissal certainly didn't have anything to do with his contributions to the company's coffers. He was an earner. "I worked years to get my position at Goldman. It wasn't my job; it was my *career*. My numbers were great." Indeed, in the two years he worked for the company, he says he earned at least $20 million in profits for Goldman, and just three weeks before his termination he'd been awarded $5 million in stock options in conjunction with the company going public. Often, Hudson says, when Goldman fires people, they're given a few months with a desk and a phone to find work elsewhere. Fornicators, it seems, have to leave the next day.

"There are certain things you come to expect in this country, certain basic rights and freedoms," he says with exasperation. "Is an affair really grounds to fire somebody? I mean, is it?" Hudson sighs. "There are times in your life where you see it changing. You're on the outside looking in. That day was one of those moments for me. Everything has changed. Absolutely everything."

Wall Street is not known for its sexual scrupulousness. In fact, the profession is far more famous for its licentiousness, so much so that two prime-time dramas premiered last year showcasing the sordid lifestyles of the trading desk's young and randy. (One episode of *The $treet* even featured two colleagues getting it on in the corporate john.) "You're young, you have a lot of money, and you're in a chaotic, stressful environment," explains a

former Sachs broker. "It doesn't take long before you start thinking you can do pretty much whatever you want."

Predictably, "whatever you want" often translates into sex, drugs, and rock 'n' roll. Many brokers live large, snorting the proverbial lines off the hookers' cleavage before speeding off in gleaming Porsches to $1,000 chophouse dinners in the Hamptons—the latest Dave Matthews screaming from the hopped-up sound system, irritating the headaches of the catalog-model wives tanned and trussed by their sides.

There is a testosterone fog over Wall Street, a schoolyard pressure to be a man, and infidelity, if not explicitly encouraged, is certainly not viewed as anything to be ashamed of. Kowtowing to the wife, well, that's something different. "Cheating isn't a story we haven't heard before," says a broker from J. P. Morgan. "People get involved with each other on the desk all the time. Come summertime with the interns, it's a free-for-all."

SCORES IS TO WALL STREET WHAT BADABING IS TO TONY SOPRANO'S CREW.

He continues, "We move millions of shares. The better the time we show people, the bigger the order. We make a killing, and it's so much cash that a lot of guys don't know what to do with it, so they act up."

But Hudson is not exactly what you would call a player. He is handsome enough, but his hairline creeps back at the corners, and his body is soft, his face broad. A clot of chest hair winks out from under his polo shirt. And while he is funny, he is not snarky like those smooth, well-pressed, hair-gelled, "Hey baby" chest bumpers you see at Scores, a Manhattan strip club that's to Wall Street what Bada Bing is to Tony Soprano and his crew. Hudson isn't one of those guys who go through women like popcorn and uses the word "dude" even though they're well into their thirties.

After word got out that he'd been fired for adultery, his identity at Goldman Sachs changed, friends still at the company told him. He was no longer that nice "Tommy dude"; he became Tommy Lee. Former colleagues whispered that he'd had sex in the conference room, by the watercooler. They said that there was an explicit video circulating that showed studmaster Tom in a Goldman Sachs three-way with Katz and another woman. "It was ridiculous," Hudson says. "That's a video I, for one, would love to see."

The other consequences of his dismissal were less amusing. "When I tried to find work elsewhere, everyone wanted to know the real reason I got fired. Infidelity seemed so implausible." Hudson was asked if he'd altered the books. If he'd stolen money. If he'd done anything else truly reprehensible, which on Wall Street means anything to do with misappropriating cash. "I kept saying, 'No, no, no!' But no one believed me."

Not only was he unemployed and unable to cash in the $5 million in stock options Goldman Sachs had allocated him, his wife divorced him. Hudson found himself alone, disparaged, and homeless (his wife got the apartment). So he did what many lost souls do when they feel helpless and vengeful. He called a lawyer.

Manhattan litigator William Roth has been in practice twenty-three years and has never seen a suit like Hudson's. "It's a change," he enthuses about the case. "We're making new law. I have no idea how it will turn out."

In brief, Hudson is suing Goldman Sachs for $100 million for wrongful termination, based partly on New York Labor Law 201-d, which states "Unless otherwise provided by law, it shall be unlawful for any employer… to discharge from employment or otherwise discriminate against an individual… because of… an individual's legal recreational activities."

"The question," Roth says, "is whether sex is seen as a recreational activity. No less an authority than the *Harvard Law Review* says it is 'the world's oldest recreational activity,' but will a jury feel the same way?"

Hudson feels sure they will. He's already lost once in court. Judge Beatrice Shainswit ruled that even if the facts he alleges are true, no law protects adulterers against discrimination—though she seemed to suggest the trader may have another reason to be angry, if not to sue: "[P]laintiff's discharge appears more likely to have been motivated by the prospect of paying him a multimillion-dollar bonus if he stayed than by any mid-twentieth-century devotion to the ideals of home, hearth, or truthfulness."

Hudson is appealing the decision, but his main claim remains that he was discriminated against by his boss, Urban, who let it be known around the office that he condemned not only infidelity but also homosexuality because they violated his religious beliefs, according to the suit. "I just want the truth to come out," Hudson says sternly. "Nobody gets fired in Wall Street for this. I worked for a hypocritical fundamentalist Christian; he made partner."

He takes a breath. "We went with Bob O'Shea to a strip club; he's married," Hudson goes on, adding that several in their party had lap dances. "I guess the rules are different for partners."

"Men's clubs would not exist without Wall Street— find me another market so totally price insensitive," says an ex-Goldman employee. "I was told at a lunch with a former Goldman partner that what it takes to succeed on Wall Street is the willingness to do whatever the client wants. He said he used to take clients to the hot-dog stand and then straight into a porno shop. He said this with pride."

"Make no mistake," adds still another Goldman veteran, "the desk is a coarse, crude, and disgusting place."

In its defense, the company argues in its appellate brief that Hudson was shown the door because employees must inform their superiors about any affairs that may create "a conflict of interest" or the "appearance" of one. Though Hudson wasn't Katz's direct supervisor, he could have influenced her performance reviews and pay, the company says, since they worked in the same department and he was above her in the corporate hierarchy. And, again, Goldman also claims that he lied about the relationship, telling O'Shea it was over, though Hudson denies that.

At the time Hudson was working at Goldman, the employee handbook didn't require relationship reporting, but workers were told about it in orientation sessions and other internal meetings, a Goldman source said. Indeed, one current employee and one alum told ELLE they remember being advised not to date co-workers without notifying the boss, and signing a paper acknowledging that they'd heard and understood the rules. But Hudson and Katz say they can't remember ever being given such instructions, and that they certainly didn't sign anything.

Legal experts say cases like Hudson's are rare. "Perhaps that's because it takes a lot of chutzpah to get caught cheating and then go to court anyway," says Eugene Volokh, a professor at UCLA Law School who's an expert in employment law.

He thinks Hudson has an uphill battle, since he, like many workers, was what's known as an "at-will" employee, meaning he could essentially be fired for any reason. "Adultery may be permissible grounds for firing," Volokh says. "So might chewing gum. Hudson has to show discrimination. As a general matter there is no 'right to fairness.'"

WALL STREET JOKE: IF YOU'RE NOT ON YOUR SECOND WIFE, YOU'RE ON YOUR THIRD.

Plus, under the law, adulterers—unlike racial minorities, women, and gays—don't have any explicit protection against discrimination. As Volokh puts it, "There's not a tremendous amount of discrimination against adulterers. It's not like blacks before the civil rights movement."

Jeffrey Rosen, associate professor at George Washington University Law School and author of *The Unwanted Gaze; The Destruction of Privacy in America*, is sympathetic on Hudson but also hesitant to assign victory: "People may care about invasion of privacy in the abstract, but then they don't rally in specific cases. It may be the case that adulterers don't have a political constituency. It could be that they can't shoehorn adultery into a protected interest. We have protections for all sorts of discrimination at work, but adultery doesn't seem to be one of them."

Or as one of the former Goldman employees says, "What happened to Tom sucks. If you look at what they paid him versus what he earned the company, they got a steal. I'm not saying what he did is morally right, but you don't fire a guy over it. The joke on Wall Street is if you aren't on your second wife, you're on your third. It's a loose environment. Anything goes."

The "anything goes" climate is on vivid display any given night at New York Dolls, a strip club near Wall Street with enough broker clientele that a NASDAQ ticker glows on the mirror behind the topless girls—perhaps letting the traders know at any moment just how long a lap dance they can afford. One recent evening, a trader dropped one hundred dollar bill after another for the privilege of a blond's nearly naked company. She rubbed her bare nipples against his chin and bent over his knees, while he sat transfixed in his pinstriped suit and blue dress shirt. His wedding ring glistened under the blacklight as he stuffed another hundred in her lace garter.

The dancers at Dolls are top-shelf and smart enough to recognize money tables when they come in. "Brokers spend some cash," says a dancer I'll call April. "They love the Champagne Lounge"—a special room where, for $350 an hour, the men can hand-pick dancers and have greater privacy. "I have so many Goldman business cards at home," she says. "They all want to go on dates. Please. I use them for stock tips."

"Lia," another Dolls dancer, offers further insight. "Brokers are always asking me to do some lines of coke. They're always drunk or hopped up. They grab your ass. They ask all of us out. I say, 'But you're married.' And they say, 'So?'"

While some might argue that buying a lap dance, though base and vaguely pathetic, is not the same as sleeping with a co-worker, it does seem improbable that a company that would reimburse expenses incurred while groping bare-assed beauties on your lunch hour would find it a fireable offense to dip your pen into the corporate well. Sure, infidelity—or, to take Goldman Sachs's position, lying about it—isn't high on anyone's list of honorable activities, but shouldn't there be a difference between what isn't nice and what you can lose your job over? Bill Clinton got to keep his, after all.

In fact, romance has a distinguished history of originating in office contacts. As one judge wrote in a 1949 case, "There comes a point where this court should not be ignorant as judges of what we know as men."

"I still think Goldman Sachs is a great company," Hudson says wistfully. "It's not me against them. But the issue deserves to be fully vetted in court. I'm not proud of what I did, but it shouldn't have cost me my career."

A month before he's due to file his appeal, Hudson is having dinner with Katz. They've found a unique bond with each other, both having been fired and publicly disgraced. Hudson first called Katz in July of 1999, shortly after his wife filed for divorce. "I needed a friend," he says. "And she was one of the ones I had left."

"I comforted him over the loss of his marriage," she confides. "It was an odd role."

By autumn, the two were sharing an apartment. "We've been together ever since," Katz says. And, as her 4-carat Harry Winston ring testifies, they plan on staying that way. (Hudson eventually got another job at a smaller investment-banking firm, though he was laid off in February.) "At first I had crippling guilt," Katz says. "I felt something was wrong with me. Now it's more surreal. When we have fun together, a lot of that weird stuff about how we came to be goes away."

"If we hadn't been fired, we wouldn't be together," Katz says.

"Ironic, isn't it?" Hudson adds.

"It's not exactly a fairy tale," Katz laughs. "But it works."

When asked if she's concerned about Hudson's capacity for monogamy, she is quick to answer. "I don't think it's in Tom's nature to cheat. It was a special case with us." She pauses and looks at the ceiling. "Of course, I have to think that, don't I?"

"The funny thing about love," Hudson says, reaching for Katz's hand, "is that it isn't always something you can put your arms around. Every relationship has issues. Thankfully, ours are all in the past."

PREGNANT? YOU'RE FIRED!

DESPITE LAWS THAT ARE SUPPOSED TO PROTECT PREGNANT WOMEN, GROWING NUMBERS OF MOMS-TO-BE ARE FINDING THE WORKPLACE ANYTHING BUT FAMILY-FRIENDLY. HERE'S HOW TO MAKE SURE THIS DISCRIMINATION DOESN'T HAPPEN TO YOU

BY STEPHANIE B. GOLDBERG

In 1995, Janet Rau, now thirty-two, was a rising star at Applebee's restaurant in suburban Atlanta. She was promoted to general manager after just a year and a half on the job. "I was the first female to hold that position within the franchise," says Rau. "In many ways, I was an experiment for them."

That March, she informed her district manager that she and her husband planned to start a family. "I didn't want to spring it on him as a surprise," she says. At her performance review in September, Rau says the manager remarked: "That's when I knew you weren't one hundred percent committed to your job."

Later that month, Rau announced her pregnancy. Rather than congratulate her, the district manager said glumly: "We'll just have to deal with it." Rau was upset, but figured her boss simply needed some time to get used to the idea. A few weeks later, she experienced uterine bleeding

and took a week off. When she returned, things were never the same. In November, her boss demoted her to second assistant manager—two levels down from her previous post —and transferred her to another location. "It was devastating," she says.

Rau's boss gave her an odd explanation for the demotion—her restaurant had not performed successfully during the Atlanta Olympics. While that was true, Rau says the real reason the establishment lost business was its location in Cobb County, which had been ruled out as an Olympic site because it had an anti-gay resolution.

"You're doing this because I'm pregnant," she told him.

He denied it. But Rau, angry, started looking for legal help. A friend referred her to Atlanta attorney Nancy Rafuse (who, coincidentally, was pregnant herself). The lawyer agreed to represent Rau and filed a claim with the Equal Employ-

ment Opportunity Commission (EEOC) against the owner of the Applebee's franchise for discrimination. From that point on, "it was very clear that they were going to make her so miserable she would just leave the job," says Rafuse.

Rau was denied promotions and reprimanded for missing work to care for her sick husband. She says the last straw came when an employee she had fired for pushing and threatening her was rehired by the company a week later. "I was afraid for my safety—and for the safety of my unborn child," says Rau, who resigned in 1998.

In August 1999, a jury decided that Rau had been discriminated against and awarded her $1.8 million in damages. Because federal law limits the amount of damages to $300,000, the award was later reduced to that amount plus $34,000 in back pay.

Rau, who is now a marketing consultant, contends the suit was never about money. "I knew I had done a good job, but invariably, doubts start creeping in," she explains. "To have a jury listen to the facts and draw the same conclusion I did is wonderful."

WHEN THE LAW IS NOT ENOUGH

Surprisingly, what happened to Rau is not uncommon. According to the EEOC, from 1992 to 1999, pregnancy discrimination complaints increased by 23 percent. This is in spite of the Pregnancy Discrimination Act (PDA) of 1978, which makes it illegal for companies with fifteen or more employees to hire, fire or withhold promotions on the basis of pregnancy or related conditions such as miscarriage.

Once women have children, "employers mistakenly have a sense that they aren't going to be as productive," says one expert

---

In addition, under the Family Medical Leave Act (FMLA), which went into effect in 1993, workers who have been employed for at least a year at companies with fifty or more employees are allowed to take up to twelve weeks of unpaid leave annually for family-related medical situations, such as the birth of a child. They must be reinstated when they return to work—or placed in comparable positions in terms of pay, status and benefits.

So why is pregnancy discrimination still happening? According to experts, employers can find ways around the laws by claiming that hiring, firing and promotion decisions were made for valid business reasons. "Discrimination has become more subtle," explains Sandhya Subramanian, policy counsel for the National Partnership for Women & Families, an advocacy group in Washington, D.C. She says the sto-

ries she hears today are on the order of: "I got pregnant and I felt pressure to leave my job. Then I was terminated, and I'm convinced it had something to do with my pregnancy."

Some employers view pregnancy as a problem because they assume that once women have children they won't work as hard as they used to. "They mistakenly have a sense that workers aren't going to be as useful or productive," says Subramanian. Often, it comes down to corporate culture, adds Marcia Bram Kropf, vice president of Catalyst, a New York City research and advisory group that promotes the advancement of women in business. "Many industries grew up around the assumption that husbands work, wives stay home with the children and workers should be free to travel or stay late without any advance notice," says Kropf. "And if you're not doing that, you're not going to be seen as committed to your work—even if you're outproducing your co-workers."

Bonnie Kerzer, a thirty-six-year-old sportswear designer and mother of two in Brooklyn, New York, was a victim of that outdated thinking about motherhood. After she announced her pregnancy in 1992, the president of the manufacturing company where she had worked for two years became unfriendly to her, Kerzer recalls. Three days before she was due back at work from maternity leave, "he called to tell me my job had been eliminated," she says. "I couldn't believe it."

The company claimed her services were no longer needed, but Kerzer was suspicious—especially when they hired another person to perform duties similar to hers. A former colleague confided to her that the president of the company had once remarked that Kerzer's pregnancy "was a sign that she was lazy." Kerzer was outraged.

She began looking for an attorney. "I had to see about eight different lawyers before I could find one who would take my case on contin-

gency," she says. "It's not easy to file suit. You need to be very persistent."

In 1998, she received a settlement from her employer, the terms of which are confidential. "It would have been so easy to give up," she says. "But I knew I had been wronged and that I had to continue to fight."

PUSHING THE LIMITS?

When it comes to accommodating pregnant workers, some companies say that they're forced to bear too heavy a burden. Take the case of the Chicago-area auto leasing company that fired Regina Sheehan, a purchasing agent, in 1994, when she was five months pregnant. Sheehan, now forty-three, was fired several months before she was to take her third maternity leave in three years.

According to Sheehan, the company made no secret of its hostility toward her pregnancies. During her third pregnancy she had to take a three-week disability leave because she was at risk for a miscarriage. When she returned, she was told by her supervisor, "Gina, you're not coming back after this baby."

Although her performance reviews had been satisfactory, Sheehan was closely monitored by the company to see if she was meeting her performance goals. When she was terminated, a supervisor told her: "Hopefully, this will give you some time to spend at home with your children."

"I was hysterical," says Sheehan. "I was going through a difficult pregnancy, and we really needed my income." She contacted a lawyer and filed a claim with the EEOC.

Her case went to trial in 1997. A jury awarded her $30,000 in back pay and attorney's fees, but the matter wasn't concluded until more than a year later, when the verdict was upheld on appeal.

Anita Blair, a lawyer and president of the Independent Women's Forum, a conservative group headquartered in Arlington, Virginia, believes that women like Sheehan are

THE **SMART WAY** TO NEGOTIATE A MATERNITY LEAVE

- DO YOUR HOMEWORK. Before springing the news on your boss, find out how other women have been treated. "You're likely to have problems if performance is evaluated by the notion that you have to be physically present at work to be a productive employee," says Cynthia Thompson, Ph.D., associate professor of business at Baruch College, in New York City.
- GIVE AS MUCH NOTICE AS POSSIBLE. By law, you're required to give notice at least thirty days prior to your departure. However, the experts recommend going beyond that. "Our research shows that women who experienced the fewest problems with maternity leave were more likely to have given their employers sufficient notice," says Ellen Galinsky, president of the Families and Work Institute, in New York City.
- DEFINE YOUR GOALS. Before talking to your boss, decide how long you want to be away and how available you want to be to your co-workers.
- PUT YOURSELF IN YOUR EMPLOYER'S SHOES. At the same time you notify your employer of your pregnancy leave, outline a plan for handling your work while you're away, suggests Cindia Cameron of 9-to-5, The National Association of Working Women.
- GET ALL INFORMATION ABOUT YOUR LEAVE IN WRITING. This avoids misunderstandings and puts you on much sounder footing if you have to contemplate legal action in the future.
- STAY IN TOUCH WITH YOUR BOSS WHILE YOU'RE ON LEAVE. It will be better for your career, says Cameron, "and it reduces the shock of returning to the office."

For more information, call the 9-to-5 Hotline at 800-522-0925.

expecting too much from their employers. "That person is gone three months of the year and is getting full-time benefits for part-time work," says Blair. "It's not simply a problem for management, but it also demoralizes the other employees who have to cover for her."

As difficult as it may be for companies to handle one employee's three maternity leaves in three years, the law is the law, other experts contend. "It's disruptive in the sense that [companies] are used to an individual's habits and now they have to break in another person," acknowledges Houston employment lawyer Beatrice Mladenka Fowler. "But legally, their responsibilities are clear."

"Society is still catching up with the law," adds Subramanian. "Many employers are ignorant of their obligations, and a lot of people are unsure of their rights or hesitant about taking advantage of them."

FIGHTING BACK

If you suspect that you are a victim of pregnancy discrimination, keep notes of conversations with managers and document any reduction of responsibilities. If you plan to discuss your situation with your human resources department, you may want to consult an attorney, since your remarks can have legal consequences later.

Then, contact the EEOC promptly. From the day you experience a discriminatory act, such as denial of pregnancy leave or termination, you have 180 to 300 days to file a claim with the regional office of the EEOC, depending on your state. If your state or municipality has its own civil rights agency (you can find this out by calling the NOW Legal Defense and Education Fund, in New York City, at 212-925-6635), you may want to file a charge with them first and then file a complaint with the EEOC.

The agency will investigate your complaint. More than half of all claims filed are dismissed—nearly 55 percent in 1999—for lack of evidence.

Regardless of the EEOC ruling, you can still get your day in court by requesting a right-to-sue letter from the agency. From a practical standpoint, however, a lack of EEOC certification "can hurt a lot," according to staff attorney Yolanda Wu of the NOW Legal Defense and Education Fund. "It might make it harder for you to get an attorney, and the defendant would certainly use the fact in court to try to prove you have a weak case."

The good news is that after overcoming so many hurdles, you're likely to prevail in court. Jury Verdict Research, a Horsham, Pennsylvania, company that maintains a database of jury awards, analyzed pregnancy discrimination verdicts and settlements from 1993 to April 2000, and found that 61 percent of the plaintiffs won, receiving median awards of $56,360.

An alternative to litigation is private mediation, in which a neutral party hears both sides and makes a decision. Because it's a private proceeding, it's quicker, cheaper, more informal than litigation and more conducive to preserving relationships (this is especially useful if you plan to return to work at the company). If you don't like the mediator's decision, you can disregard it and file a lawsuit.

Preparing yourself emotionally for litigation is important, too. Many lawyers discourage women from bringing suit because these cases are so difficult to win.

Kathleen Williamsen, a thirty-one-year-old art teacher and the mother of a sixteen-month-old daughter, was turned down by two attorneys before she found one who would represent her. Williamsen filed a claim last year with the EEOC over her treatment by the Sewanhaka Central High School District, in Elmont, New York. She says she received good performance ratings during 1997, her first year of teaching. But then she got pregnant. "The thinking is that you're not as accessible once you have children," says Williamsen. "That you won't stay as late or work as hard."

Within a week of her announcement in October 1998, Williamsen received her first unsatisfactory performance review. Several more followed. Matt Jacobs, the president of her local teachers' union, claims never to have seen such a blatant turn-around in performance evaluations. "Her performance was not just good—it had been outstanding," he says.

Williamsen transferred to another school for the fall 1999 semester. She was denied tenure and lost her job this past January. She is now suing the school district.

"I try not to be bitter," Williamsen says. "I have my dignity and the knowledge that I did the right thing."

Is it cool to be a VIRGIN?

Two and a half million teenagers have pledged not to have sex until marriage. We found two of them but only one kept her promise.

BY SARA GLASSMAN ADDITIONAL REPORTING BY MARGIE BORSCHKE

Vanessa Schafer and Kirsty Douglas have never met or heard of each other. They live 2,000 miles apart, but the two have a lot in common. They are both 17 and will be seniors at large public high schools this fall. They have been cheerleading since they were little. After school, you can usually find them at practice, and on Friday nights, they're probably cheering for their schools' basketball or football teams. And, they've both taken pledges promising not to have sex until they get married, which is why we're writing about them.

They made their vows of abstinence in school. Vanessa, who lives in Arizona, had a weeklong sex-ed course called Passion and Principles, a statewide abstinence-only program paid for by the government as part of her 11th-grade-curriculum. In ninth grade, Kirsty, of South Carolina, had a one-day workshop run by the Christian youth abstinence organization True Love Waits. Hers was coed.

In both of their classes, the emphasis was on not having sex at all, and staying a virgin for health and moral reasons. Passion and Principles talked about condoms, but only in terms of their failure rate. About a third of sex-ed classes nationwide primarily teach this "abstinence until marriage" message.

One presentation from the class really sticks out in Vanessa's mind. There was a big heart made out of construction paper at the front of the room, she says. "The teacher asked a question like, 'How much of your heart goes to the guy you had sex with?' And girls would tip off the whole thing or a big chunk. Then a guy came in and just tore a little piece of it. I was shocked! It's a lot more special for a girl than a guy."

On the last day of the course, Vanessa's teacher passed out white cards with black and purple lettering that said, "Save Sex for Your Mate: Believing that true love waits, I make a commitment to myself, my family, those I date, and my future mate to be sexually pure for the day I enter marriage." Students were instructed to sign it if they agreed.

Vanessa scribbled her name at the bottom of the card. "I had my mind set that I was gonna not have sex till marriage, so I signed it," she says. Under her signature is a quote from the New Testament, "Love is patient, love is kind." Vanessa carries the card in her wallet at all times.

Abstinence promoters think pledges will make teenagers more committed because they'll feel like the thing to do is to stay a virgin. They're hoping that famous pledge signers like Jessica Simpson and self-proclaimed virgins such as Britney Spears and Anna Kournikova will up the movement's cool quotient. However, studies show that the larger the number of kids taking pledges at a school (either because that's what everyone's doing, or the pledges are part of a required sex-ed class), the less meaningful and effective they tend to be.

At the end of Kirsty's class, all 100 students signed the pledge. Others who were known to be promiscuous just didn't attend the workshop. One girl who didn't go already had a reputation as a hoochie. She *couldn't* have pledged, says Kirsty.

Then all of the pledgers wrote their names on Popsicle sticks and glued them onto a poster that was displayed outside of the school for a week. It was a lot like what True Love Waits did in 1994, when it displayed more than 210,000 pledge cards on the National Mall in Washington, D.C.

"All of a sudden it just happened–oh gosh, we had sex."

Some of the girls in Vanessa's class had already had sex, but they were encouraged to pledge, too. Like one of Vanessa's close friends, who's also a cheerleader. "She could still pledge her secondary virginity," says Vanessa. "When you wait to have sex again until you're married."

Card or no card, Vanessa had always known that she wouldn't have sex before she got married. Although she studies the Bible on Sundays with her grandfather, she doesn't consider herself very religious. It's her family's past that has had the strongest influence on her decision. My mom got pregnant when she was 18 and had my older brother, she says. She didn't marry that guy; she married my dad instead. I don't want to ruin my kid's life from my mistake. My brother was lucky because my dad is like his dad.

Vanessa wears an abstinence ring on her wedding-ring finger. She asked her mom to buy it for her last Christmas. "It's sterling silver and has a heart that stands for love with a key inside, and then a cross that represents God goes through them," she says. "It's like I really wanna give my heart to that special guy that I have sex with."

Kirsty says she and her friends would gossip about sex, but she still planned to wait. "People would be talking about who they slept with this weekend, or about other people, and I'd always say, 'That's horrible! Oh gosh, I'm definitely not going to have sex until I'm married,' " says Kirsty.

Then there were the boys....

Vanessa officially started dating Nate in December 1999, at their school's winter formal. They'd known each other for about five months, but they had been going out with different people. When they both became single, Vanessa asked Nate (who's really buff and has spiky brown hair and brown eyes) to the dance. "He was the nicest guy I knew, and I really didn't want to go with anyone else," she says. "But I liked him more as a friend." When he dropped her off at home that night, Nate touched Vanessa's face and kissed her while they were standing by his car.

On Vanessa's Sweet 16 birthday on February 6, 2000, Nate gave her a CD player, a dozen roses, and tons of balloons (to be sure she got plenty of attention in the school hallways).

From the very beginning, Vanessa had told Nate how she felt about having sex. After she pledged she showed him her card. He was into it. Nate's a born-again virgin: he's decided not to have sex again until he's married. "He doesn't pressure me or anything like that. He knows that I don't wanna have sex yet," she says.

Kirsty met blond-haired, blue-eyed, football player Taylor at church. "I'd always had a crush on him," she says. So her friend invited him to her Sweet 16 party on January 21, 2000. "But I still didn't really think he would come," she says.

He did. Later, on the night of the party, Taylor, Kirsty, and a few others were in the hot tub in her aunt's yard. "I kept thinking, If only I could hug him or something!" she says. "I took a picture with him, and then we kissed."

They started going out. The subject of her TLW pledge didn't come up, but they never crossed a certain line when they were fooling around. "He's so sweet that he just never even tried to have sex with me," says Kirsty.

On Valentine' Day, Kirsty went to Taylor's house. "He gave me a box of rose petals with a bracelet, a teddy bear, and a card," she says. Then they went out to eat.

On that same day, Nate gave Vanessa two dozen roses during her third-period math class and a gold heart necklace with an amethyst, her birthstone.

By summer, both couples were celebrating six-month anniversaries. Vanessa and Nate made out, of course, but they'd stop themselves before having sex. "When I would start to feel guilty about what we were doing, I'd just be like, Okay, let's go bowling or see a movie to get our minds off of it," says Vanessa.

Not surprisingly, Kirsty and Taylor also hung out a lot that summer. They saw each other practically every day. Sometimes they went swimming at Taylor's aunt's pool or the lake, or they'd go out to eat at a local steakhouse or see movies.

Then one evening in June, they had the house to themselves (as they often did). After watching the movie *Hope Floats* (Kirsty's favorite), they messed around in her room. "We got carried away," says Kirsty. "All of a sudden it just happened— oh gosh, we had sex." Ironically, she had lost her pledge card some time before. (She and Taylor wanted their names changed for this story, and Kirsty didn't want her picture taken.)

After Taylor left, Kirsty turned on the television to *Jerry Springer,* which featured pregnant teenage girls. "It scared the crap out of me!" she says. "I thought, I don't know anything about sex. What if I got pregnant? And I cried."

According to a recent study, people who take abstinence pledges when they are 16 or 17 (Kirsty was 14, and Vanessa was 16) are more likely to wait to have sex—up to 18 months longer. But when they do lose their virginity, there's a bigger chance that they won't use contraception because they haven't learned about it—in sex ed at school or anywhere else. Kirsty and Taylor hadn't ever talked about having sex. Luckily, when it happened, Taylor had a condom, which is 97% effective in preventing STDs and pregnancy, but *only* when used correctly and consistently. This is hard to do without learning how.

"I was worried about having a baby. Then I also felt really guilty about losing my virginity," Kirsty says. "I was distracted in school and couldn't think about anything else." A month later, she was at the mall with her mom and went to the bathroom. She was *really* relieved to discover she had gotten her period. Kirsty was lucky—four out of every 10 girls get pregnant at least once before they turn 20.

Kirsty started taking the Pill. About two weeks after she got her period, she and Taylor had sex again. "At least I'm using protection. But there's always that one chance," she says. (She remembers hearing that in her True Love Waits class.)

The two started having sex more often—like every day. "I went crazy, I guess," she says. "Sometimes it was really romantic, and other times it was like, yeah, we're done." Like many girls who take pledges, Kirsty still had sex, but felt horribly guilty about it. She would go through periods of up to a month where she wasn't into it at all. "I would tell Taylor, who never pressured me, [that] he just doesn't understand how it is to be a girl; I'm [only] 16 and I don't want a baby. That would ruin everything."

Kirsty's best friend, who pledged with her, didn't wait for a wedding ring either. And she suspects that most of her teammates on the cheerleading squad had all broken their pledges. "I think the summer hit and we were older and kind of all got corrupted," Kirsty explains. It's still not something the whole team discusses. "Some of the cheerleaders are prudes and definitely wouldn't approve," she says.

Vanessa's team also avoids the topic. Vanessa and her friend haven't broken their pledges yet, but Vanessa's also not totally sure about the girls on her squad. I know that some of them have had sex, but we just don't talk about it. So maybe a pledge didn't make abstinence the popular thing to do after all.

It's unclear what difference the pledges made for Kirsty and Vanessa. Kirsty's still conflicted about breaking her pledge. "I signed and I promised myself I would wait until I got married," she says. "But then I'm also glad I didn't because I love him." Whether or not it has anything to do with her pledge, Vanessa stands firm in her decision to wait.

The number of teens graduating from high schools as virgins has gone up from 46% to 50% since 1990. Nobody's really sure if abstinence pledges played a role in this. Another thing: More teens are experimenting with oral sex as an alternative to losing their virginity, but it isn't safe, at least when it comes to transmitting some STDs. Three million teens contact STDs every year. And 25% of new HIV cases in the U.S. are found in people ages 13 to 19. Even scarier is that 58% of them are girls. So waiting can be a good thing, with or without a pledge. But the really important thing is that when you do decide to have sex, you know how to protect yourself. Sex-ed classes at your school can, and should, help you learn how to do just that.

For more information about safe sex, contact your local Planned Parenthood at 800-230-PLAN or www.planned-parenthood.org. For more information about True Love Waits, go to www.truelovewaits.com.

From *Your Magazine*, August 2001, pp. 156-159. © 2001 by Gruner & Jahr USA Publishing. Reprinted with permission of the author Sara Glassman. Additional reporting by Margie Borschke.

Naked Capitalists

The men and women in the San Fernando Valley who produce 'adult' videos are not the gold-chained creeps of your fantasies. They're as American as consumerism, presiding over a $10 billion business that gives millions of viewers exactly what they want.

By Frank Rich

In late January 1998, during the same week that America first heard the ribald tale of the president and the intern, *Variety* tucked onto Page 5 a business story that caused no stir whatsoever. Under a Hollywood dateline, the show-biz trade paper reported that the adult-video business "saw record revenues last year" of some $4.2 billion in rentals and sales.

It soon became clear to me that these bicoastal stories, one from the nation's political capital and the other from its entertainment capital, were in some essential way the same story.

In the weeks that followed, Washington commentators repeatedly predicted that the public would be scandalized by the nonmissionary-position sex acts performed illicitly in the White House. But just as repeatedly voters kept telling pollsters that they weren't blushing as brightly as, say, Cokie Roberts. The *Variety* story, I realized, may have in part explained why. An unseemly large percentage of Americans was routinely seeking out stories resembling that of the president and the intern—and raunchier ones—as daily entertainment fare.

The $4 billion that Americans spend on video pornography is larger than the annual revenue accrued by either the N.F.L., the N.B.A. or Major League Baseball. But that's literally not the half of it: the porn business is estimated to total between $10 billion and $14 billion annually in the United States when you toss in porn networks and pay-per-view movies on cable and satellite, Internet Web sites, in-room hotel movies, phone sex, sex toys and that archaic medium of my own occasionally misspent youth, magazines. Take even the low-end $10 billion estimate (from a 1998 study by Forrester Research in Cambridge, Mass.), and pornography is a bigger business than professional football, basketball and baseball put together. People pay more money for pornography in America in a year than they do on movie tickets, more than they do on all the performing arts combined. As one of the porn people I met in the industry's epicenter, the San Fernando Valley, put it, "We realized that when there are 700 million porn rentals a year, it can't just be a million perverts renting 700 videos each."

Yet in a culture where every movie gross and Nielsen rating is assessed ad infinitum in the media, the enormous branch of show business euphemistically called "adult" is covered as a backwater, not as the major industry it is. Often what coverage there is fixates disproportionately on Internet porn, which may well be the only Web business that keeps expanding after the dot-com collapse but still accounts for barely a fifth of American porn consumption. Occasionally a tony author—David Foster Wallace, George Plimpton and Martin Amis, most recently—will go slumming at a porn awards ceremony or visit a porn set to score easy laughs and even easier moral points. During sweeps weeks, local news broadcasts "investigate" adult businesses, mainly so they can display hard bodies in the guise of hard news. And of course, there is no shortage of academic literature and First Amendment debate about pornography, much of it snarled in the ideological divisions among feminists, from the antiporn absolutism of Catherine MacKinnon and Andrea Dworkin to the pro-porn revisionism of Sallie Tisdale and Susie Bright.

I'm a lifelong show-biz junkie, and what sparked my interest in the business was what I stumbled upon in *Variety*—its sheer hugeness. Size matters in the cultural marketplace. If the machinations of the mainstream TV, movie and music industries offer snapshots of the American character, doesn't this closeted entertainment behemoth tell us something as well? At $10 billion, porn is no longer a sideshow to the mainstream like, say, the $600 million Broadway theater industry—it is the mainstream.

And so I went to the San Fernando Valley, aka Silicone Valley, on the other side of the Hollywood Hills, to talk with the suits of the adult business. I did not see any porn scenes being shot. I did not talk to any antiporn crusaders or their civil-libertarian adversaries. I did not go to construct a moral brief. I wanted to find out how some of the top players conduct their business and how they viewed the Americans who gorge on their products.

Among other things, I learned that the adult industry is in many ways a mirror image of Hollywood. Porn movies come not only in all sexual flavors but also in all genres, from period costume dramas to sci-fi to comedy. (One series is modeled on the old Hope-Crosby "Road" pictures.) Adult has a fabled frontier past about which its veterans wax sentimental—the "Boogie Nights" 70's, when porn was still shot only on film and seen in adult movie theaters. (The arrival of home video revolutionized porn much as sound did Hollywood.) Adult also has its own *Variety* (Adult Video News), its own star-making machinery (the "girls" at Vivid and Wicked are promoted like bygone MGM contract players), its own prima donnas and cinéastes. It has (often silent) business partners in high places: two of the country's more prominent porn purveyors, Marriott (through in-room X-rated movies) and General Motors (though its ownership of the satellite giant DirecTV, now probably to be sold to Rupert Murdoch), were also major sponsors of the Bush-Cheney Inaugural. Porn even has its own Matt Drudge—a not-always-accurate Web industry gossip named Luke Ford, who shares his prototype's political conservatism and salacious obsessiveness yet is also, go figure, a rigorously devout convert to Judaism.

I didn't find any porn titans in gold chains, but I did meet Samantha Lewis, former real-estate saleswoman and current vice president of Digital Playground, whose best-selling "Virtual Sex" DVD's are, she says, "the Rolexes and Mercedeses of this business." I talked with Bill Asher, 38, the head of Vivid, who is an alumnus of Dartmouth and U.S.C. (for his M.B.A.) and Lawry's (the restaurant chain). I listened to the story of John Stagliano, who was once a U.C.L.A. economics major with plans "to teach at the college level" but who instead followed his particular erotic obsession and became Buttman, the creator of hugely popular improvisational cinemavérité porn videos that have been nicknamed "gonzo" in honor of the freewheeling literary spirit of Hunter S. Thompson. A political libertarian, Stagliano was for a while a big-time contributor to the Cato Institute.

If the people who make and sell pornography are this "normal"—and varied—might not the audience be, too? It can't be merely the uneducated and unemployed who shell out the $10 billion. And it isn't. Porn moguls describe a market as diverse as America. There's a college-age crowd that favors tattooed and pierced porn performers; there's an older, suburban audience that goes for "sweeter, nicer, cuter girls," as Bill Asher of Vivid Pictures puts it. There is geriatric porn (one fave is called "Century Sex"), and there's a popular video called "Fatter, Balder, Uglier." Oral sex sells particularly well in the Northeast, ethnic and interracial videos sell in cities (especially in the South), and the Sun Belt likes to see outdoor sex set by beaches and pools.

Yet such demographics are anecdotally, not scientifically, obtained. So few Americans fess up when asked if they are watching adult product, says Asher, "that you'd think there is no business." But in truth, there's no business like porn business. Porn is the one show that no one watches but that, miraculously, never closes.

"Porn doesn't have a demographic—it goes across all demographics," says Paul Fishbein, 42, the compact and intense man who founded Adult Video News. "There were 11,000 adult titles last year versus 400 releases in Hollywood. There are so many outlets that even if you spend just $15,000 and two days—and put in some plot and good-looking people and decent sex—you can get satellite and cable sales. There are so many companies, and they rarely go out of business. You have to be really stupid or greedy to fail."

He points me toward the larger producers whose videos top AVN's charts and have the widest TV distribution. There are many successful companies, but some of them cater to niche markets (like gay men) that as of yet haven't cracked the national mass market of TV, where pay-per-view pornographic movies, though priced two or three times higher and not promoted, often outsell the Hollywood hits competing head to head. In a business with no barrier to entry—anyone with a video camera can be a director or star—there are also countless bottom feeders selling nasty loops on used tape. Whatever the quality or origin of a product, it can at the very least be exhibited on one of the 70,000 adult pay Web sites, about a quarter of which are owned by a few privately held companies that slice and dice the same content under different brands.

Fishbein has a staff of 62 to track it all. He seems smart, sensible and mercurial—in other words, just like any other successful editor. And like almost everyone else I met in porn, he says he fell into it by accident. While a journalism student at Temple University in his hometown,

Philadelphia, he managed a video store and found that customers kept asking him how to differentiate one adult tape from another. It was the early 80's, and the VCR was starting to conquer America, its popularity in large part driven (as the Internet's would be later) by the easier and more anonymous access it offered to porn. Prior to home video, pornography had a far smaller audience, limited mainly to men willing to venture into the muck of a Pussycat Cinema—the "raincoaters," as the trade refers to that dying breed of paleo-consumer. The VCR took porn into America's bedrooms and living rooms—and, by happenstance, did so at the same time that the spread of AIDS began to give sexual adventurers a reason to stay home. There is no safer sex than porn.

As adult titles on tape proliferated, Fishbein started a newsletter to rate them. Other video-store owners, uncertain about which porn films to stock, took a look. Now, some 18 years later, Fishbein runs an empire that includes 10 Web sites and spinoff journals like AVN Online. He also stages trade shows and presents the AVN Awards in Vegas in January. An issue of AVN can run in excess of 350 slick pages, much of it advertising, in which a daunting number of reviews (some 400 a month) jostle for space with sober reportage like "For Adult, Ashcroft Signals Circle the Wagons Time." Fishbein has a soft spot for porn veterans like Al Goldstein, the 65-year-old paterfamilias of Screw magazine who writes a column for Fishbein's main Web site, AVN.com, in which Goldstein sometimes rails against the new corporate generation of pornographers who have no memory of the daring and sacrifice of their elders. "Al Goldstein took 19 arrests for this business," Fishbein says reverently.

Though he embodies the corporatization of porn, Fishbein exudes a certain swagger. "I'm here by accident, and now that I'm here, I'm proud of what I do," he says. "My mother sits at my awards table each year when girls accept awards for oral sex. Sex sells and it drives the media, and it always has. Billboards, movies, ads, commercials. It's what we're thinking about at all times of the day. We're told it's bad, and it manifests itself as political debates."

Fishbein assures me that he has no "naked girls running through the office," and alas, he is right—though a staff member does wander in with a photo to ask, "Was that the naked sushi party?" But there's a pleasant buzz and bustle about the place— one I associate with journalism. "This could be a magazine about pens and pencils," Fishbein says. Maybe.

The browsers on the two computers behind his desk are kept on CNN.com and AVN.com, which is modeled on CNN's as a (porn) news portal. The décor of his large, meticulous office is mostly movie memorabilia. A film buff as well as a news junkie, Fishbein is a particular fan of the high-end comedies of Woody Allen, Albert Brooks and Preston Sturges, and he could be a highly articulate, slightly neurotic leading man out of one of them. He speaks glowingly of having just taken his 12-year-old stepdaughter to "Yi Yi." Does he watch the movies that AVN reviews? He flinches. "I haven't watched an adult movie without fast-forwarding since I saw one in a theater at 18. I watch them for business reasons. My wife and I don't watch them for entertainment. It is hard for me to look at it as more than product."

Many of the top porn producers are within blocks of Fishbein's office in the utterly anonymous town of Chatsworth—an unhurried, nondescript sprawl of faded strip malls, housing developments and low-slung (and usually unmarked) business complexes that look more like suburban orthodontic offices than porn factories. Everyone in the business seems to know one another. "There's a certain camaraderie among those who are on the fringe of society, a similarity to outlaws," Fishbein says. Yet he seems like any-

thing but an outlaw; he was about to fly off to the Super Bowl and then a skiing vacation. I ask if organized crime is a factor in today's porn world. "When I got here, I heard there were mob companies," he answers. "But I've never even been approached by a criminal element. I've never been threatened or bribed. So if it ever existed, it's part of the history of the business." He almost sounds disappointed.

Russell Hampshire, who owns one of the biggest companies, VCA Pictures, did do time in jail—nine months in 1988 for shipping obscene videotapes across state lines to federal agents in Alabama. Somewhat more prosaically, he is also a graduate of McDonald's Hamburger U., which he attended while running McDonald's franchises in El Paso in the 70's. It's business training that came in handy in the porn biz. "I learned about inventory, buying the proper insurance, doing everything by the book, not taking shortcuts," he says.

Hampshire, who runs VCA with his wife of 10 years, Betty, has an Oscar Madison look—Hawaiian shirts, gym shorts and a baseball cap. I wouldn't want to get on his bad side. He's big and leathery and sounds like Lee Marvin as written by Damon Runyon. Asked why the sign outside says "Trac Tech" instead of VCA, he says he wants to stay "as innoculous as possible."

He has been in the business since 1978 and waxes nostalgic for the early video days, when you could transfer a prevideo Marilyn Chambers classic to cassette and sell it wholesale for up to a hundred bucks. Now his top movies wholesale for $18 or $19, sometimes lower. "There used to be only 10 to 12 titles to choose from in a video store," he says. "Now there are thousands of titles." A typical release may sell only 2,000 units or less—7,500 would be a modest hit—but thanks to TV and international sales, Hampshire says he makes money "on every title." Though the total income from a hit is pocket money by Hollywood standards, Hollywood should only have such profit margins. An adult film that brings in $250,000 may cost only $50,000 to make—five times the original investment. Production locations are often rented homes, shooting schedules run less than a week, and most projects are not shot on the costly medium of film. There are no unions or residuals. Marketing costs are tiny, since quote ads run in AVN and skin magazines, not in national publications or on TV. Most economically of all, porn movies don't carry the huge expense of theatrical distribution: video killed off adult movie theaters far more effectively than it did regular movie theaters.

Still, Hampshire resents the lower overhead of porn's newcomers: "I have 80 employees. I have a 100 percent medical plan for everyone's family—dental and vision care too. Some of my guys have been working here 17 or 18 years. And I'm up against amateurs with $800 Handicams." He also grouses about the new administration in Washington, as many in the industry do, fearing there could be a replay of the war on porn during the Reagan years, when Attorney General Edwin Meese called for restrictions on live sex shows and the dissemination of pornographic materials. "I like the rest of Bush's cabinet—just not Ashcroft," Hampshire says.

With the company's in-house press rep, a former preschool teacher named Mischa Allen, in tow, Hampshire takes me on a tour of VCA's 40,000-square-foot operation, proudly showing off the state-of-the-art video-editing bays, the room containing 3,000 video-duplication decks (churning out 400,000 tapes a month) and the prop room in which I spot a neon sign for "Bada Boom" from the set of the recent "Sopornos 2." The mechanized assembly line on which the tapes are boxed and shrink-wrapped is as efficient as that for bottling Coke.

But more than anything, VCA resembles the corporate headquarters of a sports franchise. Only on close inspection do I realize that a towering glass case full of what look like trophies in the reception area in fact contains awards such as the 1996 Best Group Sex Scene, bestowed upon the "Staircase Orgy" from "New Wave Hookers 4." Hampshire, an avid golfer and bowler, has lined VCA's corridors with his collection of autographed sports jerseys, the latest from Tiger Woods. On one wall are plaques of appreciation from the Hampshires' philanthropic beneficiaries, including a local school to which they donate video equipment and free yearbook printing.

Hampshire's own office is spacious, outfitted with leather furniture, but—characteristically for the business—looks like a bunker. Above his desk is a console of TV screens tuned into the feeds from security cameras. Incongruously, this inner sanctum's walls are festooned with another variety of pompously framed "collectibles"—autographed letters and photographs from Anwar Sadat, Menachem Begin, Jimmy Carter and Richard Nixon. Hampshire says they're all copies, but he points to a melted-looking clock and says, "I've got Salvador Dalis all over the place—authentic Salvador Dalis." He also shows off a vintage group photo of Murder Inc.

But Hampshire describes his existence as considerably more mundane than Bugsy Siegel's. He almost never goes to a set, where the hurry-up-and-wait pace makes it as "boring as Hollywood." He ticks off his duties: "Dealing with distributors and OSHA rules and regulations. I have to write reviews of all my department heads and decide raises."

As I leave his office I notice still another framed artifact: a Bronze Star for "exceptionally valorous action on 12/8/67" while serving as a Company C rifleman in combat in Vietnam. The citation says that Hampshire "continually exposed himself to hostile fire" while saving the lives of his fellow soldiers.

It's the only thing that seems to embarrass him. "I buried it for so long," he says. "When I first came out here, I was ashamed to say anything because people might say I'm a bad person."

ALMOST EVERY ADULT COMPANY IS pursuing innovative media, preparing for Internet broadband and interactive hotel-room TV. At Wicked Pictures' newly revamped Web site, for instance, a visitor can cross-index a particular porn star with a sexual activity, then watch (and pay for) just those scenes that match. Digital Playground's "Virtual Sex" DVD's resemble video games in how they allow the user to control and inject himself into the "action."

As in nonadult video, DVD is cutting into videocassette sales—even more so in adult, perhaps, because DVD's have the added virtue of being more easily camouflaged on a shelf than cassettes. Hampshire is particularly proud of VCA's DVD technology. With his vast catalog, he is following the model of Hollywood studios by rereleasing classics—The Devil in Miss Jones 2," "The Opening of Misty Beethoven"—in "Collectors Editions," replete with aural commentaries from original stars like Jamie Gillis. As with Hollywood's DVD rereleases, they are pitched at nostalgic consumers in the "boomer-retro" market. "These aren't 'adult'—they're pop culture now," says Mischa Allen.

But VCA aims far higher than merely recycling golden oldies. In a windowless VCA office, I meet Wit Maverick, the head of its DVD production unit. He is 37, and with his blue Oxford shirt, goatee and glasses, he could be a professor somewhere—perhaps at Cal Arts, where he got a masters in film directing. He ended up at VCA, he says, because it was "the best opportunity to push the envelope of technology."

Maverick knocks mainstream studios for providing only a linear cinematic experience on their DVD's. "There's a great hubris in Hollywood," he says. "They think the way the director made the film is the only way the story can be told. We have a lot more humility. If a viewer wants something different, we give it to him." As an example he cites "Being With Juli Ashton," VCA's take on "Being John Malkovich." The viewer, Maverick says, "can go inside the head of the person having sex with Juli Ashton, male or female. He can choose which character to follow. He can re-edit the movie. Would James Cameron let anyone do that with 'Titanic'?

"I feel like filmmakers 100 years ago," Maverick continues. "It's a great technology, but we still don't know what to do with it. A hundred years from now I want grad students to read what I've done on DVD the way I read about D.W. Griffith."

WIT MAVERICK COLLABORATES ON HIS DVD's at VCA with Veronica Hart, 44, one of the business's most prominent female executives and, before that, a leading porn star of the late 70's and early 80's.

Universally known as Janie—her real name is Jane Hamilton—she is typical of the mostly likable people I met in the porn world. She combines hardheaded show-biz savvy and humor with an utter lack of pretension and even some actual candor—a combination unheard of on the other side of the hills.

"The difference between us and Hollywood," she elaborates, "is money and ego. We deal with thousands of dollars, not millions. In mainstream, people are more cutthroat and pumped up about themselves. We're just like regular people—it has to do with exposing yourself. If you show something this intimate, there isn't a lot you can hide behind. You're a little more down to earth. We're not curing cancer. We're providing entertainment."

Hart studied theater at the University of Nevada in her hometown, Las Vegas. After acting leads in plays by Pinter and Lorca—as far east as Kennedy Center's annual college theater festival—she passed through the music business in En-

gland and worked as a secretary at Psychology Today magazine in New York before ending up in movies like "Wanda Whips Wall Street." While we are talking in her office she looks up Veronica Hart's 100-plus performing credits on the Internet, including some non-hard-core B movies with faded mainstream actors like Farley Granger and Linda Blair. "In this one I played a stripper," she says while scrolling down the list. "That was a real stretch."

She pulls back from the computer screen and sums up her career: "I was lucky enough to be a performer in the golden age of porn cinema. I'm no raving beauty, and I don't have the best body in the world, but I look approachable. And I've always really enjoyed sex." More recently, she played a cameo as a judge in "Boogie Nights," but she disputes that movie's historical accuracy about porn's prevideo age. "We never shot in L.A. back then, only in New York and San Francisco," she says. Indeed, adult exactly mimicked movie-industry history—beginning in New York, then moving west.

In 1982, at the top of her career, Hart fell in love and left the business. "AIDS had just started up, and I lost every gay person I knew," she says, listing close friends who worked on the production side of the straight-porn business. She had two sons and helped support her family in part by stripping. Though not intending to re-enter porn, eventually she did, as a producer and director.

Hart has been in adult longer than anyone I met and has done "everything" in it, she jokes, "including windows." She warns me that "any blanket statement about the business is meaningless" because it's so big that "every conceivable type of person" can be found in it. "You'll find someone who's into it to provide spiritual uplift and educational self-help" she says. "And if you want to find rotten, vicious, misogynistic bastards—you'll find them. You'll find everyone who fits the stereotype and everyone who goes against the stereotype. In the loop and dis-

posable-porno section of our business, you'll find the carnival freak-show mentality. There has to be a geek show somewhere in our society. What ticks me off is that all of adult is classified according to the lowest that's out there. We've always been legal. Child molestation has never been in mainstream adult. We've always policed ourselves. There's no coerced sex. But there are little pipsqueaks who get their disgusting little videos out there. There's a trend in misogynistic porn, and it's upsetting. I've been in the business for more than 20 years, and I helped make it possible for these guys to make these kinds of movies. I don't believe that's what America wants to see."

As for her own movies, Hart, like many of her peers, is preoccupied with the industry's biggest growth market—women and couples. The female audience was thought to be nearly nil when consuming pornography required a visit to a theater, an adult book store or the curtained adult section of a video store. But now hard core is available at chains like Tower (though not Blockbuster), through elaborate Web sites like Adultdvdempire that parallel Amazon and by clicking a pay-per-view movie on a TV menu (where the bill won't specify that an adult title was chosen).

The Valley's conventional wisdom has it that women prefer more romance, foreplay and story, as well as strong female characters who, says Bill Asher of Vivid, "are not only in charge of the sex but the rest of the plot." Hart isn't sure. "Just because women like romance doesn't mean we want soft sex," she says. "We want hot and dirty sex just like anybody else. For instance, many women love the fantasy of being taken—but how do you portray it without sending a message to some guys to abduct?"

Hart, who thought of herself as a sexual pioneer when she was a porn performer, finds that there is no shortage of women who want to appear in adult now. She never has to search for new talent; willing performers call her "from all over the country." The men? "They're props."

Today's porn stars can be as temperamental as their Hollywood counterparts, or more so. "I assume Sarah Jessica Parker and Kim Cattrall show up on the set on time," said Paul Fishbein rather tartly when I asked about Jenna Jameson, the industry's reigning It girl of recent years. Though he was trying to give her a free vacation as thanks for her work as host of the recent AVN awards, Jameson wasn't returning his calls. "In adult, they don't show up and don't care," Fishbein says. "Lots of girls in this business—and guys, too—are dysfunctional. The girls get here at 18 and aren't mature. They do it because they're rebels or exhibitionists or need money. They think they're making real movies and get really upset when they don't win awards or get good reviews."

Some porn directors have similar pretensions. They can receive grandiose billing—A Brad Armstrong Motion Picture"—and are sometimes grudgingly indulged with a "big budget" project ($250,000 tops) made on film, even though sex scenes are far harder to shoot on film (with its trickier lighting and shot setups) than on video—and even though adult films are almost never projected on screens. "We have our own Brad Pitts wanting to make 'Seven Days in Tibet,'" said one executive. Performers are paid at fairly standardized rates—by the day or sex scene, as much as $1,000 per day for women, as little as $200 for men. The contract girls at Vivid and Wicked sign for $100,000 and up a year, in exchange for which they might make nine movies, with two sex scenes each, over that time, along with any number of brand-boosting promotional appearances at consumer conventions and video stores. The top stars double or triple that figure by running their own subscription Web sites, marketing autographs (along with less innocent mementos) and most lucratively, dancing in the na-

tion's large circuit of strip clubs at fees that can top $10,000 a week.

But porn stars have an even shorter shelf life than Hollywood's female stars and fare worse in love. Though H.I.V. and drug testing, as well as condom use, are rigorous at the top adult companies, one producer asks rhetorically, "Who wants to date a woman who's had sex with 60 people in two months?"

Since I've rarely found actors to be the most insightful observers of the movie business, I wasn't eager to sample the wisdom of porn stars. But I did seek out Sydnee Steele, a newly signed Wicked contract girl who is by many accounts a rarity in the business—she's happily married. Her husband is Michael Raven, 36, a top adult director. They met in Dallas in the early 90's, when she was a jewelry saleswoman in a shopping mall and he was a car salesman who sold her a mariner blue Miata. Eventually they drifted into the local swingers' scene. (One porn worker would later tell me, "Texas, Florida and Arizona are where all the swingers and strippers come from, though no one knows why.")

"The industry looks up to our relationship," Raven says when I meet the couple, now married nine years, at Sin City, another production company in Chatsworth. Avid porn fans in Texas, they migrated to the Valley to turn their avocation into a livelihood. Like many of the directors and male performers in the business, Raven is a somewhat lumpy everyman, heading toward baldness and sporting a meticulous goatee. A Kandinsky poster decorates the Sin City office. "I've gotten jealous on occasion," Raven allows. "I'm not jealous of her because of sex in movies; I'm jealous when her work takes her away from me. I get lonely if she's gone two weeks on the road."

"Sometimes I'm too tired for my husband," Steele says. "We love what we do, but it's hard work—lots of 12-hour days." By now, I've watched some of what she does and find it hard to square the rapacious star of "Hell on Heels" with the

woman before me, who is softer-spoken, prettier and considerably less animated than her screen persona. Maybe she can act.

The daughter of a college professor, Steele comes from what she calls a "'Leave It to Beaver' nuclear family," Raven from a religious one. "I've leaned toward the right in my politics," he says, "but I'm bothered by the Republicans' association with the religious right. I know from my experience of religious people that those who protest and scream the loudest usually have the biggest collection of adult under their bed." He wishes they'd protest violent entertainment instead: "In video games, you're supposed to destroy, maim and dismember an opponent. But if one person is giving pleasure to another in adult, that's evil. Sex on TV is more destructive than hard core. You can depict a rape on TV—we don't touch that subject."

Like his wife, Raven is increasingly recognized by strangers—largely because "Behind the Scenes" documentaries about his movies appear on DVD's and on cable erotic networks, much like Backstory features on American Movie Classics. But Raven no longer stays in contact with his own family. And Steele's parents, she says, "don't totally know what I'm doing and don't ask. We don't lie, but they've never really been told."

The secrecy among porn people is so prevalent that it's a running, if bittersweet, gag in a made-for-the-Internet TV series called "The Money Shot" that Paul Fishbein of AVN is producing as a lark. If you care to sample only one product of the adult industry, this is it—and the episodes can be seen free in streaming video on a nonporn site, moneyshot-the-series.com. But be warned, its rating clocks in at about PG-13. "The Money Shot" is a roman à clef comedy, much in the spirit of HBO's classic "Larry Sanders Show," about daily life in the adult biz, as it filters into the offices of an AVN-like publication called "Blue Movie Guide." In a rather poignant episode titled "The

Parents Show," one character dolefully concludes, "Nobody in this business tells their folks nothing."

Bryn Pryor, 33, is the director and a writer of "The Money Shot." He's an AVN staff member who arrived in the Valley after nine years in the theater, much of it children's theater, in Arizona. "The Money Shot" hits his friends where they live. "Porn is legal now, but it has the mentality of other businesses, like prostitution and gambling, that started with organized-crime connections," he says. "People approach it as if they've done something wrong. If our customers project shame, than you must be doing something wrong. Everyone at AVN writes under a pseudonym. We have people here who don't want anyone to know their real name." Variations on this theme were visible everywhere I went in the Valley. Receptionists at porn companies tend to answer the phone generically: "Production Company" or "Corporate Office."

Typifying this ambivalence is Steve Orenstein, 38, the owner of Wicked Pictures. He made his accidental entrance into the porn business through his mother—who got him a part-time job when she worked as a bookkeeper at an adult-book distributor and he was 18. But he does not seem eager to reveal his calling to his 9-year-old stepdaughter.

"Being in the business you walk that line all the time—do you say what you do or not?" he says. Orenstein has revealed his true profession to only a handful of people whom he and his wife have met on the PTA circuit. "I'm comfortable with what I do," he says, "but I don't want parents of our child's friends saying their kids can't play with her because of it." His stepdaughter has noticed the Wicked logo on his shirt. "She knows I make something only adults can see."

The Orensteins have spoken to a therapist about the inevitable day of reckoning with their child. "The counselors say don't tell her yet," he says, "don't overexplain." But surely she'll guess by adolescence? Orenstein, a slight, nervous man with a reputation as a worrier, merely shrugs. For the moment, he's more concerned about protecting the child from prime-time television, citing a recent episode of the sitcom "The King of Queens" on CBS. He recalls: "The guy's rolling off his wife, and my 9-year-old asks, 'What do they mean by that?' Should I be letting her watch it?"

Russell Hampshire's gambit is to tell strangers he's in "the video-duplication business." Allen Gold, a VCA executive with daughters ages 1 and 3, says he's "in the DVD business." Paul Fishbein doesn't bring either AVN or adult product into his house. Michael Raven and Sydnee Steele have decided for now not to have children.

I ask Veronica Hart, whose two teenage sons are at magnet schools for the highly gifted, what they have made of her career. "It's horrible for them," she says. "I'm their loving mommy, and nobody likes to think of their parents having sex and being famous for it. I'm not ashamed of what I do. I take responsibility for who I am. I chose. From the time they were kids, my stripping gear was washed and hanging in the bathtub. At the same time I apologize to my kids for how the choices in my life have affected them. They're well adjusted and can joke with me about it: 'I know I'm going to spend the rest of my life on the couch.'"

No wonder the porn industry has its finger on the pulse of American tastes. Not only do its players have a lifestyle more middle class than that of their Beverly Hills counterparts, but in their desire to keep their porn careers camouflaged in a plain brown wrapper, they connect directly with their audience's shame and guilt. Still, the next generation of porn consumers and producers alike may break with that puritan mindset. The teenagers who grew up with cable and the VCR "come to the table already saturated with sex," says Bryn Pryor. "They've never known a time without Calvin Klein ads and MTV. By the time they see porn, they've already seen so many naked people they're pre-jaded."

This may explain why Americans are clamoring for ever more explicit fare. In mainstream TV, sex is no longer sequestered on late-night public access shows like "Robin Byrd." At HBO, Sheila Nevins, the highly regarded executive in charge of its nonfiction programming, has been stunned by the success of sexual documentaries like "Real Sex," now in its 11th year, and "Taxicab Confessions." Focus groups complain to HBO that another hit series, "G-String Divas," doesn't go far enough. "They know what really happens in a strip club," Nevins says, and find HBO's version "too R-rated." Though HBO, known for its heavy promotions of "The Sopranos" and "Sex and the City," spends nothing to advertise its sex series, they always are among the network's most watched. "I can do all the shows I want about poverty in the Mississippi Delta," Nevins says, "but this is what hard-working Americans want to see. At first we were embarrassed by the sex shows, and producers didn't want their names on them. Now we have Academy Award producers, and their names can't be big enough."

At Playboy, Jim English, the head of its TV division, and his boss, Christie Hefner, have felt the heat. Its Playboy and Spice channels have been squeezed from both sides in the cable-satellite marketplace. The softer, if X-rated, cuts of hard-core movies that it runs are no longer much more explicit than regular cable programming at HBO, Showtime ("Queer as Folk") and MTV ("Spring Break"). Even the Learning Channel (with "Bra Wars" and "Wild Weddings") and the History Channel (with its four-part "Sex in the 20th Century") are testing the waters. Meanwhile, erotic networks like Hot and Ecstasy, which run XX films, are cannibalizing Playboy's audience from the other end of the erotic spectrum. The result: This summer Playboy plans to start "Spice Platinum Live," which edges toward XXX. (I'll leave the codified yet minute clinical distinctions separating X, XX and XXX to your imagination.)

Even in an economic downturn, everything's coming up porn. Newly unemployed dot-com techies who can't find jobs in Silicon Valley are heading to Silicone Valley, where the work force is expanding, not contracting. "Vivid overall has doubled, tripled revenues and profits in the past couple of years," says Bill Asher. While he says there's no such thing as a Hollywood-style "home run" in porn—unless another celebrity like Pamela Anderson turns up in a sex video, intentionally or not—he sees potentially "a tenfold jump" in profits as distribution increases through broadband and video-on-demand. (Porn executives are no less fuzzy than Hollywood's as to when this might be.) "There are opportunities here that Paramount will never have in terms of growth," Asher says. "Our product travels well internationally and is evergreen. Five-year-old product is still interesting to someone; it's not yesterday's news like a five-year-old Hollywood blockbuster. Our costs are relatively fixed. As there's more distribution, 90 cents of a dollar hits the bottom line." The absence of adult retail stores in conservative pockets of the country is no longer a barrier. "You can get a dish relatively anywhere," Asher says, "and get whatever you want."

When Vivid took over and expanded the Hot Network in 1999, Asher says, "there was no outcry. We got thank-you letters and sales boomed. We put up two more channels in months. Cable companies were begging for them. It doesn't take a genius to do this. Literally the customers say, I like what you've got—give me some more of it." Entertainment-industry executives not directly involved in the adult business confirm its sunny future. Satellite and cable companies have found that the more explicit the offerings, the more the market grows. AVN re-

ports that TV porn may actually be increasing video-store sales and rentals rather than cannibalizing them—by introducing new customers to the product. Though some cable companies say they don't want adult, only one of the country's eight major cable providers, Adelphia, forbids it. The others are too addicted to the cash flow to say no. The organized uproar that recently persuaded a teetering Yahoo to drop its adult Web store—but not its gateways into other adult sites—is the exception, not the rule.

And despite a rumor that one porn mogul keeps a Cessna waiting at Van Nuys airport to escape to Brazil if there's a government crackdown, the odds of that look slim. Too many Fortune 500 corporations with Washington clout, from AT&T to AOL Time Warner, make too much money on porn—whether through phone sex, chat rooms or adult video. At the local level, the Supreme Court's 1973 "community standard" for obscenity may be a non sequitur now that there's a XX national standard disseminated everywhere by satellite and the Web. A busted local video retailer in a conservative community can plead that his product is consistent with what the neighbors are watching on pay-per-view—as one such owner successfully did in Utah last fall.

Should John Ashcroft's Justice Department go after porn, smart betting has him pursuing shadowy purveyors of extreme porn on the Internet (though it's not clear that the actionable stuff originates in the United States) and child pornography, all of which is condemned by the professional adult industry. "No one in this business will complain if Ashcroft goes for the kid angle," Fishbein says.

Jim English of Playboy suggests that one way to meet the typical American porn audience en masse is to accompany him to a live broadcast of a hit Playboy show called "Night Calls 411." Fittingly, "Night Calls" is televised from a studio in Hollywood, right by the old Gower Gulch,

where low-budget studios long ago churned out early features in bulk much as the adult business does now.

Two underclad hostesses, Crystal Knight and Flower, intersperse wisecracks and sex tips with viewers' phone calls. Though only a few callers get on the air, as many as 100,000 try to get through, with still more deluging the show with "Miss Lonelyhearts" e-mail.

It's not "Larry King Live," but in some ways it could be an adult version of the "Today" show, whose fans cross the country with the hope of being in view as the camera pans Rockefeller Center. The "Night Calls" devotees go further: many of them are engaging in sex when they call. "Having sex is not enough of a turn-on in America—you have to be on TV too," jokes English. The callers often ask that the hosts talk them through to what The Starr Report called completion, and the women oblige—hoping for slam-bam speed so they can move on to the next caller. I'm struck by how much the male and female callers alike mimic porn performers, with their clichéd sex talk and over-the-top orgasmic shrieks. The adult audience apes its entertainers as slavishly as teenagers do rock idols.

By now, I've become intimately familiar with the conventions of adult entertainment, having asked those I met in the business to steer me to their best products. I've watched Wicked's "Double Feature," a multiple winner of AVN awards, among them Best Comedy, and found it full of erudite cinematic references, including a campy spoof of Ed Wood films. I've seen Vivid's new "Artemesia," a costume drama set in 16th-century Italy and given AVN's highest rating; it is laced with high-flown ruminations on the meaning of art, somewhat compromised by the tattoos on the performers. From Video Team, a company specializing in interracial porn, there is a thriller called "Westside" with a social conscience reminiscent of "West Side Story," a soundtrack that features music by Aaron Copland and a take on the drug wars that wouldn't be out of place in "Traffic."

It's no wonder, though, that Stagliano's gonzo, in which the performers just get it on, has such a following. All the plot and costuming and set decoration and arty cinematography—why bother? The acting—who needs it? (In "Flashpoint," Jenna Jameson, cast as a female firefighter, sounds the same when sobbing over a colleague's death as she does in coital ecstasy.) The films are tedious, and I'm as tempted to fast-forward through the sex scenes as the nonsex scenes. No matter what the period or setting, no matter what the genre, every video comes to the same dead halt as the performers drop whatever characters they're supposed to be assuming and repeat the same sex acts, in almost exactly the same way, at the same intervals, in every film. At a certain point, the Kabuki-like ritualization of these sequences becomes unintentionally farcical, like the mu-sical numbers in a 30's Hollywood musical or the stylized acrobatics in a martial-arts film. Farcical, but not exactly funny. All the artful mise en scène in the world cannot, for me anyway, make merchandised sex entertaining or erotic.

I tell Bryn Pryor of AVN and "The Money Shot" my reaction. He's a professional porn critic. Is this the best that adult has to offer?

"The top of the heap in porn is the bottom in mainstream," he says. "The sad fact is that while consumers are more aware than they've ever been, nobody cares if it's a good movie, and we all know that. They care if it's hot in whatever subjective way it's hot to them. Most porn directors don't even watch the sex; they just direct the dialogue. They tell the camera people they want three positions and then go off and eat."

He continues: "Porn is not a creative medium. Everyone in the porn industry says he's on the way to something else, like waiters and bar-tenders, but it may be that most of us belong here. If we were really good, we'd be doing something else."

Pryor envisions a day when adult and Hollywood will converge, but in a sense that's already the case. If much of porn ranges from silly to degrading, what's the alternative offered on the other side of the hills? The viewer who isn't watching a mediocre porn product is watching—what? "Temptation Island"? W.W.F.?

Moralists like to see in pornography a decline in our standards, but in truth it's an all-too-ringing affirmation of them. Porn is no more or less imaginative than much of the junk in the entertainment mainstream—though unlike much of that junk, it does have an undeniable practical use. In that regard, anyway, there may be no other product in the entire cultural marketplace that is more explicitly American

Frank Rich is an Op Ed columnist for *The Times* and a senior writer for the magazine.

Carnal Knowledge

A preacher woman's mantra—'No more sheets!'—has shown millions of single sisters a spiritual path toward personal integrity, self-respect and living in fulfillment and peace with our God-given sexuality

BY MICHELLE BURFORD

If you didn't happen to join 17,000 folks attending Bishop T. D. Jakes's 1998 singles' conference in Dallas, let me fill you in on the now famous "No More Sheets" sermon delivered by a 42-year-old preacher woman known as Prophetess Juanita Bynum. In offering her message, this sister dipped into her private business in a way few ministers ever have before. Through shouts and waving handkerchiefs, she riveted the audience with a nakedly honest account of her own struggles with her physical longing for a man and rampant lustful pursuits—and she even trotted out a few bedsheets to make her point. By the end of the session, the crowd of sisters of every age was on its feet chanting her mantra: "No More Sheets! No More Sheets! No More Sheets!"

Bynum's sermon on unhealthy sexual obsessions was so forthright, fiery and Sojourner Truth-ful, the videotaped recording (Juanita Bynum Ministries, $20) is now widely known among Black women as, simply, the video. The tape was soon followed by a book, *No More Sheets: The Truth About Sex* (Pheuma Life Publishing, available for $19.99 at pneumalife.com).

The video alone has sold more than a million copies and spawned a revolution of sorts among Black women—including *No More Sheets* video parties in sisters' living rooms not unlike the ones that heralded the video release of *Waiting to Exhale*. There's something undeniably real about Prophetess Bynum's words—especially when she's talking about sex: She has been there, done that and knows whereof she speaks.

After her parents raised her and her four siblings in a toe-tappin', tambourine-bustin' Pentecostal church in Chicago, Bynum, still a virgin at 21, married and moved to Port Huron, Michigan. But her marital partnership unraveled "inch by inch,"

she says, and her husband left her after only a year and a half. "I married for sex—and for what the man looked like," she admits. "Everybody told me he wasn't right, but I was screamin', 'I'm in love. I can change him.' "

The pain of their 1983 separation precipitated a collapse that put Bynum in the hospital for three weeks. After her divorce became final in 1985, she fell into a series of sexual escapades. More than one sugar daddy lured her with smooth talk and promises of material generosity—but the serial drama in her life left her more scattered and even emptier than her failed marriage. "I got tired of men with their hands in my underwear," she confesses on the video. "It was too expensive."

If Juanita Bynum's inner life back then was stormy, her work life was gagging for its last breath. She had struggled in odds-and-ends gigs while she was married. Desperate to anchor her finances and her emotions after her messy divorce and her subsequent unhealthy attachments, she reached out for the life jacket of welfare. In 1990 she moved from Michigan back to her hometown of Chicago and went to beauty school to become a hairdresser, a job that helped her get off public assistance after two years. She then left the beauty business to become a flight attendant for the now-defunct Pan American Airways, the company that transferred her to where she lives these days—New York City.

It was in 1991, when Pan Am went belly-up, that Juanita, emotionally buoyed and spiritually resuscitated after attending the New Greater Bethel Ministries in New York, decided to get back to what she dubs her "call"—preaching. She had sampled it previously at 17 and 18, when she was still living under her parents' roof. "My friends said that God shut Pan Am down because I

> # "'As much as my heart wanted Mr. Got-It-Together," says Prophetess Juanita Bynum, "my spirit could only attract somebody who was as messed up as I was. I knew I had to work on myself."

wouldn't go and preach," she says. "I know God was saying that this was my destiny, but I didn't want to hear it."

Ten years ago she finally stopped ignoring that prompt. Through her church, Juanita began speaking, as she had done as a teenager, in small venues of 50 or so women around the country. In 1996 she met the Pentecostal evangelist Bishop T. D. Jakes (author of the 1994 inspirational best-seller *Woman, Thou Art Loosed!*), and he invited her to the singles' conference in Dallas that year. Though Jakes knew little about Juanita's own ministry or personal life, the bishop told her he felt God had something momentous for her to say. Indeed, the message she had prepared to deliver at a small women's breakfast went over so well that he invited her to address the much larger group who would show up that evening for the main event.

Two years later on the night she delivered the "No More Sheets" message to yet another singles' conference audience, Bynum hadn't even penned her sermon beforehand. "When I got on that platform," she says, "that message had a voice of its own. It wasn't from me—it was from God." If you eye her closely on the video, you can sense she is winging it: With the organ pipin' up in the background, Juanita sprints from one corner of the stage to the other and leads the audience in a round of call and response, hurling out rhetorical questions like "How can you help someone if you don't tell anybody where you been?" and "Can I get at least one sister in here to just be honest tonight?"

When Juanita walks into the Manhattan hotel suite where I interview her, she's sporting all black, a sharp blazer and cute heels. Somehow she appears a tad more buttoned-up than the video made her seem. But about 52 seconds into our chat, the arms start flailing and the voice starts rising and the neck starts rolling—and I know there has been no mix-up. By the end of our time together, Prophetess Bynum's trademark authenticity has turned even me, the original Doubting Thomasina, into a true believer.

Michelle Burford: In *No More Sheets*, you hit on two of the hottest topics for Black women: God and sex. Sisters responded by buying up you video into the millions!

Juanita Bynum: And some of them literally run up to me and fall onto my chest in tears, thanking me! Angela Bassett came up to me and said, "I read your book three times, and it changed my life." Then I talked to Mary J. Blige on the phone, and she said *No More Sheets* turned her around.

Burford: I loved a point you made in your video: A women who has slept with a lot of men has, in a spiritual sense, married each of those men. Then when the right man for her comes along, that woman has no emotional space for him.

Bynum: That's one reason I'm not remarried to this day. People often ask me, "Do you want to marry again?" I tell them, "I'll get married when I get *single*."

Burford: And how long does it take to "get single" after you've had a series of sexual relationships?

Bynum: That depends on how many relationships you've been in, and the depth and length of time of each. When a woman ends a relationship, she still carries the man's residue—and she's subconsciously still trying to please him. In a relationship I was in after my divorce, I found myself always washing the dishes right after I ate—because the man I'd been with *previously* wanted that. I was still under his influence. I wasn't ready to date again because I wasn't healed.

Burford: Take me back to the time right after your marriage ended. What were you feeling?

Bynum: I felt like a failure as a woman. When you put together a home with your own hands, and then it comes apart, you ask yourself, *What didn't I do to make it work?* Then you start feeling like you weren't attractive or sexy enough. You think, *Maybe I didn't have a good enough body.* You go through all these head trips. But I've learned that after you've been hurt, you can't just focus on your hurt—you have to look at the lesson in it. When you baby-sit the hurt, you never learn the lesson. You have to say, "Okay, God, what is the message here?"

Burford: When did you do that?

Bynum: After my divorce. That's when I started my relationship binge. Because I was hurting so badly, I was out to prove there wasn't anything wrong with me. So instead of keeping my focus on the lesson, I detoured to one man after another.

Burford: But exactly when did you sit with yourself and think about the lesson in your hurt?

Bynum: After this so-called binge. Sometimes I would look back at some of the men I was with and say, "What in the world was I thinking?" It was crazy! What I finally realized was that an aura surrounds every woman who has been damaged. I had actually been *attracting* certain men. I had always wanted an executive, a businessman—and a man of God—to want me, and he wouldn't. The only kind of brother who could bond with me was someone with a soul like mine: troubled, messed up and full of insecurities. As much as my heart wanted Mr. Got-It-To-gether, my spirit could only attract somebody who was where I was. I knew I had to work on myself. Now I don't get play from hoodlums. And I no longer need a man who will buy me a new dress or furniture. I've got lamps. I've got a couch. I've got a stove. I don't have to subject myself to a man's disrespect simply because he bought me a living-room set.

Burford: A woman's posture is completely different when she enters a relationship not needing money from a man.

Bynum: And once you get past material things, you can go directly into a relationship saying, "I need a friend." We marry for a couch and we call sex love, but when the sex gets low and the couch gets old, we don't have a friend. That's why I don't have the same criteria for a mate that I once had. I used to think a man had to throw a big rock on my finger.

Burford: That mentality hinders so many widows.

Bynum: It causes us to miss out on fulfilling relationships. What about the guy who works for Amtrak? He may not make much money, but he pays his bills on time and has excellent credit. He has integrity, he's kind, and he knows how to be a friend. But sisters walk past that kind of man, because he isn't a CEO. When you do that, it's a sign that you're not healed. A man is not less because he has worked at the steel mill for 20 years. Ain't he still a good man?

Burford: But if you're a wounded woman, you can't even *see* that kind of man. You attract a man who's willing to exploit your vulnerabilities.

Bynum: Yes. And a wounded woman also attracts a man who has not gotten himself together enough to be the best choice for *anybody*—but he knows that she can't do any better. And because she has been hurt, she wants to be validated by a man. From the start, she sees things about him that she knows she doesn't like, but she's too needy to move on. His credit is shot, and he has no integrity, but in the eyes of a depressed and slapped-up woman, he's a hero—until the woman begins to heal and make better choices. That's what happened to me.

Burford: You say that the amount of time it takes a woman to heal is connected with the length and depth of the relationship she has been in. During your series of relationships, how long did each usually last?

Bynum: From six months to a year. And at the time, many of my friends constantly told me, "You've got to forget your last relationship. You've got to move on and find the right one." That was such a wrong concept. What do you do with your emotions while you're going from one person to the next? My friends treated my divorce like it was a car accident: After an accident, you have to get in the car and drive so you won't fear driving. But that doesn't work in relationships.

Burford: Racing into another relationship never solves anything.

Bynum: It only camouflages the pain. At a glance, you look like you have a wonderful relationship, and you're back in the swing of life. But if somebody looked at you on the inside, they'd say, "That girl is hurting."

Burford: So how do you know when you're completely over a man?

Bynum: Once nothing inside you aches when you think of him. You can even see him in the store and say, "How you doin'?" without feeling pain.

Burford: Deep down, did you know you weren't ready to date again after your divorce?

Bynum: I knew. But I was afraid to be alone. If you took a poll across the nation, you might be surprised at how many women are afraid to be in a room by themselves or just sit alone.

Burford: That's because when you turn off the TV and send the children into another room, you have to face yourself. And when you've never done that, it's scary.

Bynum: We're afraid of truth. And when sisters see brothers marrying White women, some of us feel an extra pressure to seek Black men's acceptance. So if a brother comes along who doesn't have his act together, we put up with him. Yet we don't enter these relationships totally unaware of what we're getting into. We're just willing to keep the less desirable things in our blind spot. Then when the newness of a relationship wears off, what's in our blind spot comes to the forefront. But it has always been there. And deep in our subconscious, we knew it from the beginning.

Burford: But we *choose* to ignore it?

Bynum: We do. We're driven more by what we want than by what we need.

Burford: And sometimes, we just feel desperate.

Bynum: Exactly. And I had to ask myself this question in one of my moments alone: *What if it's not meant for me to marry again? What would I do?* And I've decided that staying singe would be okay. I am already fulfilled.

Burford: During your man binge, did you think you'd be unfulfilled if you weren't in a relationship?

Bynum: I didn't know who I was. And when you don't know who you are, you will join up with anybody.

Burford: Many sisters will read this story and say, "Stop the madness, Juanita—sex with a lot of men is not a bad thing." What would you say to these women?

Bynum: I'd ask each one of them this: Do you know who you are without a man? Sisters are seeking ecstasy through sex, which is why they have so many partners. They want an out-of-this-world experience. But they're getting nothing but a fleshly experience.

Burford: And in relationships, two halves do not make a whole. To make things work, you have to come into a partnership knowing that the other person can never completely fulfill you.

Bynum: That's it! And sex with a lot of men is just a bad idea. You're taking your emotions through unnecessary swings: You can't have sex with someone *without* drawing your emotions into it. Physically, men are built as sexual *projectors*, whereas women's bodies are designed to *receive*. A man ejaculates; a woman carries that ejaculation.

Burford: So when you have sex with a man, what does he leave with you?

Bynum: His world. His experience. His scars. And many men take advantage of the moment to have an ejaculation with no regard for what they're leaving inside women. It's rape of the soul.

Burford: What does that mean for the sister who has slept with 30 men in the last five years?

Bynum: Her soul is a highway—just a place for traffic. The walls of her spirit no longer have the strength to house a real relationship. I always tell myself, *You can go ahead and have some sex—but is it really worth the ten minutes of "Ah, ah, ah"? Is the man really your destiny?* When I break it down like that, the whole thing sounds weak.

Burford: And in these times, you also have to ask yourself whether the brother has AIDS.

Bynum: And will it be worth it to see him two years from now with his wife and kids, while you're still with nobody? *Uh-uh*.

Burford: You've said that part of the power in your message comes from living with integrity when you're not in the pulpit. When it comes to men and sex, how do you maintain that integrity?

Bynum: When I meet a guy who my spirit tells me isn't right, I don't date him. I say, "Honey, don't waste your money on me. Bread and chicken are too expensive these days."

Burford: And do you tune out TV shows and movies that are filled with sex?

Bynum: Oh, yes. Everything we do is a delayed result of what we've already done. If I watch a sexual movie, the images plant a seed in my mind that has a chance to stay there and grow.

Burford: What's the end result of living outside of integrity for years?

Bynum: Disaster. When you lack integrity, you are never in line with yourself. I believe I can come across with power as a preacher because I work to maintain my character when I'm not preaching. If you use your rent money to get your weave done, if you steal from the company you work for or if you always make excuses for being late, then you don't have the strength to project when it's time for your message to be heard.

Burford: One last question: What are you passionate about?

Bynum: I have a passion for compassion—and it's driven by where I've been. If I close my eyes right now, I can see myself in the snow, wearing a black $2 coat and tennis shoes with no socks, waiting to get my $76 in food stamps. I can see myself in the hospital after my nervous breakdown, crying and throwing myself against the walls of the padded cell they put me in. When I remember the process it took to get myself from there to where I am today—and then I see a sister with no hope—I'm driven to get to that sister. I believe that the pain in each of our pasts gives us an opportunity to help others. If I honestly tell somebody what has happened to me, then maybe that person will be transformed.

Michelle Burford is an ESSENCE editor-at-large.

A DISEMBODIED 'THEOLOGY OF THE BODY'

John Paul II on love, sex & pleasure

Luke Timothy Johnson

Papal teaching on human sexuality has received some positive reviews recently. A number of these have appeared in the journal *First Things*. In "Contraception: A Symposium" (December 1998), Archbishop Charles J. Chaput, O.F.M. Cap., declares that Pope Paul VI has a lock on the title of prophet because, in *Humanae vitae*, he was right. In the same issue, Janet E. Smith thinks that people who regard the papacy's condemnation of contraception to be based on the "artificial" methods employed simply have not acquainted themselves with the richness of papal teaching. In particular, she says, "those who appreciate precise and profound philosophical reasoning should read Karol Wojtyla's *Love and Responsibility*," while offering a strong recommendation also for "the extensive deliberations of Pope John Paul II." Even more recently, Jennifer J. Popiel ("Necessary Connections? Catholicism, Feminism, and Contraception," *America*, November 27, 1999) states that "unlike many women, I find the church's doctrinal statements on contraception and reproduction to be clear and compelling," and argues that Natural Family Planning is fully compatible with feminism, since "only when we control our bodies will we truly control our lives."

George Weigel joins this chorus of praise in his biography of John Paul II, *Witness to Hope* (Cliff Street Books, 1999). Under the heading, "A New Galileo Crisis," Weigel traces the pope's systematic response to the "pastoral and catechetical failure" of *Humanae vitae* in a series of 130 fifteen-minute conferences at papal audiences beginning on September 5, 1979, and concluding on November 28, 1984. The conferences were grouped into four clusters: "The Original Unity of Man and Woman," "Blessed Are the Pure of Heart," "The Theology of Marriage and Celibacy," and "Reflections on *Humanae vitae*." These talks were brought together under the title *Theology of the Body: Human Love in the Divine Plan* (Pauline Books and Media, 1997).

Weigel himself considers John Paul II's work to be a "theological time bomb" that may take almost a century to appreciate fully, or even assimilate. It "may prove to be the decisive moment in exorcising the Manichaean demon and its deprecation of human sexuality from Catholic moral theology," because the pope takes "embodiedness" so seriously. Weigel considers these conferences to have "ramifications for all of theology," and wonders why so few contemporary theologians have taken up the challenge posed by the pope. He is surprised as well that so few priests preach these themes and only a "microscopic" portion of Catholics seem even aware of this great accomplishment, which he considers to be "a critical moment not only in Catholic theology, but in the history of modern thought." Weigel provides three possible reasons for this neglect: the density of the pope's material, the media's preoccupation with controversy rather than substance, and the fact that John Paul II is himself a figure of controversy. It will take time to appreciate him and his magnificent contribution.

Is Weigel right? Have the rest of us missed out on a theological advance of singular importance? Can the claims made for the pope's *Theology of the Body* be sustained under examination? Recently, I devoted considerable time (and as much consciousness as I could muster) to reading through the 423 pages of the collected conferences, and I have reached a conclusion far different from Weigel's. For all its length, earnestness, and good intentions, John Paul II's work, far from being a breakthrough for modern thought, represents a mode of theology that has little to say to ordinary people because it shows so little awareness of ordinary life.

I want to make clear that I am here responding to the theological adequacy of papal teaching. I do not dispute the fact that in some respects papal positions can legitimately be called prophetic. Certainly, John Paul II's call for a "culture of life" in the name of the gospel, against the complex "conspiracy of death" so pervasive in the contemporary world, deserves respect. Likewise, the pope's attention to the "person" and to "continence" stand as prophetic in a time of sexualized identity and rationalized permissiveness. It is small wonder that those worried about moral confusion in matters sexual would want to accept all the papal teachings, since some of them are incontestably correct.

> *John Paul II's work, far from being a breakthrough for modern thought, represents a mode of theology that has little to say to ordinary people because it shows so little awareness of ordinary life.*

But I want to ask whether we ought to make some distinctions even where the pope does not, whether while approving some of his positions we can also challenge others. Weigel is correct in noting that these conferences are dense and difficult to read—what must they have been like to hear? But Weigel fails to note how mind-numbingly repetitive they are. He does not seem to notice that the pope only asserts and never demonstrates, and that he minimizes the flat internal contradictions among the conferences. For example, on October 1, 1980, the pope declares that a husband cannot be guilty of "lust in his heart" for his wife, but a week later, in the conference of October 8, he states confidently that even husbands can sin in this fashion. But beyond such relatively minor deficiencies (how many theological writings are not dense, repetitive, and inconsistent?), the pope's *Theology of the Body* is fundamentally inadequate to the question it takes up. It is inadequate not in the obvious way that all theology is necessarily inadequate to its subject, and therefore should exhibit intellectual modesty, but in the sense that it simply does not engage what most ought to be engaged in a theology of the body. Because of its theological insufficiency, the pope's teaching does not adequately respond to the anxieties of those who seek a Christian understanding of the body and of human sexuality and practical guidance for life as sexually active adults.

If the pope had only made casual or passing comments on the subject in a homily, then a critical response would be unfair. But everything suggests that John Paul II intended these conferences to be read as a "theology of the body" in the fullest sense of the term "theology." The pope uses academic terms like phenomenology and hermeneutics, refers to contemporary thinkers, provides copious notes, and in the very commitment to the subject over a period of five years in 130 conferences, indicates that he wants his comments to be given serious attention. It is perhaps appropriate to offer a number of observations concerning things that someone far removed from the corridors of doctrinal declaration, but not unschooled theologically, and certainly not disembodied, might want to see yet does not find in John Paul II's discourses.

PRELIMINARY OBSERVATIONS

A starting place is the title itself, which, while perhaps not chosen by the author, legitimately derives from his frequent reference to a "theology of the body" and his constant focus on "human love in the divine plan." Surely, though, an adequate theology of the body must encompass far more than human love, even if that were comprehensively treated! The pope cites 1 Corinthians 6:18 approvingly: "Flee fornication. Every sin a person commits is apart from the body. But the one who fornicates sins in his own body." But Paul's rhetorical emphasis cannot be taken as sober description. Do not the sins of gluttony and drunkenness and sloth have as much to do with the body as fornication, and are not all the forms of avarice also dispositions of the body? Reducing a theology of the body to a consideration of sexuality falsifies the topic from the beginning. Of course, an adequate theological phenomenology of the body as the primordial mystery/symbol of human freedom and bondage must include every aspect of sexuality. But it must also embrace all the other ways in which human embodiedness both enables and limits human freedom through disposition of material possessions, through relationships to the environment, through artistic creativity, and through suffering—both sinful and sanctifying. The pope's title provides the first example of the way in which a grander—or to use his word "vast"—conceptual framework serves to camouflage a distressingly narrow view of things.

The pope's subtitle is "Human Love in the Divine Plan," but no real sense of human love as actually experienced emerges in these reflections. The topic of human love in all its dimensions has been wonderfully explored in the world's literature, but none of its grandeur or giddiness appears in these talks, which remain at a level of abstraction far removed from novels and newspapers with their stories of people like us (though not so attractive). John Paul II thinks of himself as doing "phenomenology," but seems never to look at actual human experience. Instead, he dwells on the nuances of words in biblical narratives and declarations, while fantasizing an ethereal and all-encompassing mode of mutual self-donation between man and woman that lacks any of the messy, clumsy, awkward, charming, casual, and, yes, silly aspects of love in the flesh. Carnality, it is good to remember, is at least as much a matter of humor as of solemnity. In the pope's formulations, human sexuality is observed by telescope from a distant planet. Solemn pronouncements are made on the basis of textual exegesis rather than living experience. The effect is something like that of a sunset painted by the unsighted.

The objection may be made: isn't it proper to base theology in Scripture, and isn't John Paul II correct to have devoted himself so sedulously to the analysis of biblical texts, rather than the slippery and shoddy stuff of experience? Well, that depends on how seriously one takes the Catholic tradition concerning the work of God's Holy Spirit in the world. If we believe—and I think we have this right—that revelation is not exclusively biblical but occurs in the continuing experience of God in the structures of human freedom (see Dei verbum, 2.8), then an occasional glance toward human experience as actually lived may be appropriate, even for the magisterium.

As for the pope's way of reading Scripture, the grade is mixed. Certainly he is careful with the texts. Nor does he misrepresent those aspects of the text he discusses in any major way—although he leaves the impression that Matthew's "blessed are the pure of heart" (5:8) refers to chastity, when in fact he knows very well that the beatitude does not have that restricted sense. Even more questionable are the ways John Paul II selects and extrapolates from specific texts without sufficient grounding or explanation. First, he scarcely treats all the biblical evidence pertinent to the subject. His discourses center on a handful of admittedly important passages, with obligatory nods at other texts that might have rewarded far closer analysis, such as the Song of Songs (three conferences) and the Book of Tobit (one). Other important texts are given scant or no attention. A far richer understanding of Paul would have resulted, for example, from a more sustained and robust reading of 1 Corinthians 7, which truly does reveal the mutuality and reciprocity—and complexity—of married love.

Second, John Paul II does not deal with some of the difficulties presented by the texts he does select. For instance, he manages to use Matthew 19:3–9, on the question of marriage's indissolubility, without ever adverting to the clause allowing divorce on the grounds of porneia (sexual morality) in both Matthew 5:32 and 19:9. What does that exceptive clause suggest about the distance between the ideal "in the beginning" evoked by Jesus, and the hard realities of actual marriages faced by the Matthean (and every subsequent) church?

Third, for all of his philosophical sophistication, John Paul II seems unaware of the dangers of deriving ontological conclusions from selected ancient narrative texts. He inveighs against the "hermeneutics of suspicion," but the remedy is not an uncritical reading that moves directly

from the ancient story to an essential human condition. He focuses on the Yahwist creation account in Genesis 2, because that is the account cited by Jesus in his dispute with the Pharisees concerning divorce (Matt. 19:5), and, I suspect, because its narrative texture—not to mention its human feel—allows for the sort of phenomenological reflection he enjoys. But as the pope certainly understands, this creation account must also be joined to that in Genesis 1 if an adequate appreciation of what Jesus meant by "from the beginning" (Matt. 19:8) is to be gained. If Genesis 1—which has God creating humans in God's image as male and female—had been employed more vigorously, certain emphases would be better balanced. John Paul II wants, for example, to have the term "man" mean both male and female. But the Genesis 2 account pushes him virtually to equate "man" with "male," with the unhappy result that males experience both the original solitude the pope wants to make distinctively human as well as the dominion over creation expressed by the naming of animals. Females inevitably appear as "helpers" and as complementary to the already rather complete humanity found in the male. Small wonder that in virtually none of his further reflections on sexuality do women appear as moral agents: Men can have lust in the hearts but not women; men can struggle with concupiscence but apparently women do not; men can exploit their wives sexually but women can't exploit their husbands sexually.

Such tight focus on male and female in the biblical account also leaves out all the interesting ways in which human sexuality refuses to be contained within those standard gender designations, not only biologically but also psychologically and spiritually. What appears in the guise of description serves prescription: human love and sexuality can appear in only one approved form, with every other way of being either sexual or loving left altogether. Is it not important at least to acknowledge that a significant portion of humans—even if we take a ludicrously low percentage, at least tens of millions—are homosexual? Are they left outside God's plan if they are not part of the biblical story? Would not an adequate phenomenology of human sexuality, so concerned with "persons," after all, rather than statistics, take with great seriousness this part of the human family, who are also called to be loving, and in many fashions to create and foster the work and joy of creation?

Even within this normative framework, out of all the things that might be taken up and discussed within married love and the vocation of parenting, John Paul II's conferences finally come down to a concentration on "the transmission of life." By the time he reaches his explicit discussion of Humanae vitae, it is difficult to avoid the conclusion that every earlier textual choice and phenomenological reflection has been geared to a defense of Paul VI's encyclical. However, there is virtually nothing in this defense that is strengthened by the conferences preceding it.

WHAT THE POPE LEAVES OUT

John Paul II is certainly to be appreciated for trying to place the knotty and disputed questions concerning procreation into a more comprehensive theology of the body. But there are a number of things lacking in these conferences and in the various declarations of the pope's apologists. I will simply list some obvious ones without development.

Most important, I would like to see a greater intellectual modesty, not only concerning the "facts" of revelation but also with the "facts" of human embodiedness. In everything having to do with the body, we are in the realm of what Gabriel Marcel called mystery. The body does not present a series of problems that we can solve by detached analysis. The body rather is mystery in two significant ways. First, we don't understand everything about the body, particularly our own body. The means by which we reveal ourselves to others and unite lovingly with others is not unambiguous. The body reveals itself to thought but also conceals itself from our minds. Second, we cannot detach ourselves from our bodies as though they were simply what we "have" rather than also what we "are." We are deeply implicated and cannot distance ourselves from the body without self-distortion. Our bodies are not only to be schooled by our minds and wills; they also instruct and discipline us in often humbling ways. Should not a genuine "theology of the body" begin with a posture of receptive attention to and learning from our bodies? Human bodies are part of God's image and the means through which absolutely everything we can learn about God must come to us.

In this regard, I find much of contemporary talk about "controlling our bodies" exactly contrary to such humility, whether such language derives from technocrats seeking to engineer reproductive processes or from naturalists who seek the same control through continence. I am not suggesting that a lack of continence or temperance is a desirable goal. But self-control is not the entire point of sexual love; celibacy is not the goal of marriage! And it may help to remember, in all this talk of controlling the body, that Dante assigned a deeper place in hell to the cold and the cruel than to the lustful. It can be argued, especially from the evidence of this century, that more evil has been visited upon us by various Stalins of sexless self-control than by the (quickly exhausted) epicures of the erotic. Recognition of the ways in which we suffer, rather than steer, our bodies is a beginning of wisdom.

Along these lines, I would welcome from the pope some appreciation for the goodness of sexual pleasure—any bodily pleasure, come to think of it! Pleasure is, after all, God's gift also. A sadly neglected text is 1 Timothy 6:17, where God supplies us all things richly for our enjoyment. Sexual passion, in papal teaching, appears mainly as an obstacle to authentic love. Many of us have experienced sexual passion as both humbling and liberating, a way in which our bodies know quicker and better than our minds, choose better and faster than our reluctant wills, even get us to where God apparently wants us in a way our minds never could. Along the same lines, papal teaching might find a good word to say about the sweetness of sexual love—also, I think, God's gift. Amid all the talk of self-donation and mutuality, we should also remember, "plus, it feels good." Come to think of it, why not devote some meditation to the astonishing triumph of sexual fidelity in marriage? Faithfulness, when it is genuine, is the result of a delicate and attentive creativity between partners, and not simply the automatic product of "self-control." In short, a more adequate theology of the body would at least acknowledge the positive ways in which the body gifts us by "controlling" us.

As with pleasure so with pain. A theology of the body ought to recognize the ways in which human sexual existence is difficult: how arduous and ambiguous a process it is for any of us to become mature sexually; how unstable and shifting are our patterns of sexual identity; how unpredictable and vagrant are our desire and craving, as well as our revulsion and resistance; how little support there is for covenanted love in our world; how much the stresses of life together—and apart—bear upon our sexual expression. John Paul II and his apologists seem to think that concupiscence is our biggest challenge. How many of us would welcome a dose of concupiscence, when the grinding realities of sickness and need have drained the body of all its sap and sweetness, just as a reminder of being sentient! I would welcome the honest acknowledgment that for many who are married the pleasure and comfort of sexual love are most needed precisely when least available, not because of fertility rhythms, but because of sickness and anxiety and separation and loss. For that matter, a theology of the body ought to speak not only of an "original solitude" that is supposedly cured by marriage, but also of the "continuing solitude" of those both married and single, whose vocation is not celibacy yet whose erotic desires find, for these and many other reasons, no legitimate or sanctified expression, and, in these papal conferences, neither recognition nor concern.

The pope does not examine these and many other aspects of the body and of "human love in the divine plan." Instead, the theology of the body is reduced to sexuality, and sexuality to "the transmission of life." The descent to biologism is unavoidable. What is needed is a more generous appreciation of the way sexual energy pervades our interpersonal relations and creativity—including the life of prayer!—and a fuller understanding of covenanted love as life-giving and sustaining in multiple modes of parenting, community building, and world enhancement.

REVISITING 'HUMANAE VITAE'

John Paul II's conferences and the recent articles I have quoted have meant to defend the correctness of *Humanae vitae,* but paradoxically they remind readers with any historical memory how flawed that instrument was, and how badly it is in need of a fundamental revisiting. George Weigel calls it a "pastoral and catechetical failure," as though the encyclical's deficiencies were merely those of tone or effective communication. John Paul II's biblical reflections, in fact, appear as nothing less than a major effort to ground *Humanae vitae* in something more than natural law; an implicit recognition of the argumentative inadequacy of Paul VI's encyclical. As my earlier comments indicate, I would judge his success as slight. It would be a weary business to take up the entire encyclical again, but it is important at least to note five major deficiencies that require a genuinely theological response rather than enthusiastic or reluctant apology.

In these comments, I will speak of "artificial birth control" only in terms of using a condom, diaphragm, or other mechanical device, mainly because I have considerable unease concerning chemical interventions and their implications for women's long-term health.

> *I would welcome from the pope some appreciation for the goodness of sexual pleasure—any bodily pleasure, come to think of it!*

First, the encyclical represents a reversion to an act-centered morality, ignoring the important maturation of moral theology in the period leading up to and following Vatican II, which emphasized a person's fundamental dispositions as more defining of moral character than isolated acts. I am far from suggesting that specific acts are not morally significant. But specific acts must also be placed within the context of a person's character as revealed in consistent patterns of response. The difference is critical when the encyclical and John Paul II insist that it is not enough for married couples to be open to new life; rather, every act of intercourse must also be open, so that the use of a contraceptive in any single act in effect cancels the entire disposition of openness. But this is simply nonsense. I do not cancel my commitment to breathing when I hold my breath for a moment or when I go under anesthesia. Likewise, there is an important distinction to be maintained between basic moral dispositions and single actions. The woman who kills in self-defense (or in defense of her children) does not become a murderer. The focus on each act of intercourse rather than on the overall dispositions of married couples is morally distorting.

Second, the arguments of Paul VI and John Paul II sacrifice logic to moral brinkmanship. When Paul VI equated artificial birth control and abortion, he not only defied science but also provoked the opposite result of the one he intended. He wanted to elevate the moral seriousness of birth control but ended by trivializing the moral horror of abortion. Similarly, from one side of the mouth, John Paul II recognizes two ends of sexual love, unitive intimacy and procreation. But from the other side of his mouth he declares that if procreation is blocked, not only that end has been canceled but also the unitive end as well. He has thereby, despite his protestations to the contrary, simply reduced the two ends to one. This can be shown clearly by applying the logic in reverse, by insisting that sexual intercourse that is not a manifestation of intimacy or unity also cancels the procreative end of the act.

Third, the position of the popes and their apologists continues to reveal the pervasive sexism that becomes ever more obvious within official Catholicism. I have touched above on the way John Paul II's reading of Scripture tends to reduce the moral agency of women within the marriage covenant and sexual relationships. This becomes glaringly obvious in the argument that artificial birth control is wrong because it tends to "instrumentalize" women for men's pleasure by making the woman a passive object of passion rather than a partner in mutuality. Yet the argument makes more experiential sense in reverse. Few things sound more objectifying than the arguments of the natural family planners, whose focus remains tightly fixed on biological processes rather than on emotional and spiritual communication through the body. The view that "openness to life" is served with moral integrity by avoiding intercourse during fertile periods (arguably times of greatest female pleasure in making love) and is not served (and becomes morally reprehensible) by the mutual agreement to use a condom or diaphragm, would be laughable if it did not have such tragic consequences. And what could be more objectifying of women than speaking as though birth control were something that only served male concupiscence? How about women's moral agency in the realm of sexual relations? Don't all of us living in the real world of bodies know that women have plenty of reasons of their own to be relieved of worries about pregnancy for a time and to be freed for sexual enjoyment purely for the sake of intimacy and even celebration?

Fourth, the absolute prohibition of artificial birth control becomes increasingly scandalous in the face of massive medical realities. One might want to make an argument that distributing condoms to teenagers as a part of sex education is mistaken, but that argument, I think, has to do with misgivings concerning sex education—and a general culture of permissiveness—as a whole. But what about couples who can no longer have sexual relations because one of them has innocently been infected by HIV, and not to use a condom means also to infect the other with a potentially lethal virus? When does "openness to life" in every act become a cover for "death-dealing"? Given the fact that in Africa AIDS affects tens of millions of men, women, and children (very many of them Christian), is the refusal to allow the use of condoms (leaving aside other medical interventions and the changing of sexual mores) coming dangerously close to assisting in genocide? These are matters demanding the most careful consideration by the church, and the deepest compassion. It is difficult to avoid the sense that the failed logic supposedly marshaled in the defense of life is having just the opposite result. If the political enslavement of millions of Asians and Europeans led the papacy to combat the Soviet system in the name of compassion, and if the enslavement and murder of millions of Jews led the papacy to renounce the anti-Semitism of the Christian tradition in the name of compassion, should not compassion also lead at the very least to an examination of logic, when millions of Africans are enslaved and killed by a sexual pandemic?

Fifth, and finally, shouldn't *Humanae vitae* be revisited rather than simply defended for the same reasons that it was a "pastoral and catechetical" failure the first time around? It failed to convince most of its readers not least because its readers knew that Paul VI spoke in the face of the recommendations of his own birth-control commission. The encyclical was, as Weigel calls it, a "new Galileo crisis," not simply because it pitted papal authority against science, but also because the papacy was wrong both substantively and formally. It generated an unprecedented crisis for papal authority precisely because it was authority exercised not only apart from but also in opposition to the process of discernment. Sad to say, John Paul's theology of the body, for all its attention to Scripture, reveals the same deep disinterest in the ways the ex-perience of married people, and especially women (guided by the Holy Spirit, as we devoutly pray) might inform theology and the decision-making process of the church. If papal teaching showed signs of attentiveness to such experience, and a willingness to learn from God's work in the world as well as God's word in the tradition, its pronouncements would be received with greater enthusiasm. A theology of the body ought at least to have feet that touch the ground.

Since God is the Living One who continuously presses upon us at every moment of creation, calling us to obedience and inviting us to a painful yet joyous quest of wisdom, theology must be inductive rather than deductive. Our reading of Scripture not only shapes our perceptions of the world, but is in turn shaped by our experiences of God in the fabric of our human freedom and in the cosmic play of God's freedom. Theology that takes the self-disclosure of God in human experience with the same seriousness as it does God's revelation in Scripture does not turn its back on tradition but recognizes that tradition must constantly be renewed by the powerful leading of the Spirit if it is not to become a form of falsehood. Theology so understood is a demanding and delicate conversation that, like sexual love itself, requires patience as well as passion. If we are to reach a better theology of human love and sexuality, then we must, in all humility, be willing to learn from the bodies and the stories of those whose response to God and to God's world involves sexual love. That, at least, is a starting point.

Luke Timothy Johnson, *a frequent contributor, is the Robert W. Wood-ruff Professor of New Testament at the Candler School of Theology, Emory University. Among his more recent books is* Living Jesus *(HarperSanFrancisco).*

Glossary

Abnormal Anything considered not to be normal, i.e., not conforming to the subjective standards a social group has established as the norm.

Abortifacients Substances that cause termination of pregnancy.

Acquaintance (date) rape A sexual encounter forced by someone who is known to the victim.

Acquired dysfunction A difficulty with sexual functioning that develops after some period of normal sexual functioning.

Acquired immunodeficiency syndrome (AIDS) Fatal disease caused by a virus that is transmitted through the exchange of bodily fluids, primarily in sexual activity and intravenous drug use.

Activating effect The direct influence some hormones can have on activating or deactivating sexual behavior.

Adultery Extramarital sex.

Affectional Relating to feelings or emotions, such as romantic attachments.

Agenesis (absence) of the penis (ae-JEN-a-ses) A congenital condition in which the penis is undersized and nonfunctional.

AIDS Acquired immunodeficiency syndrome.

Amniocentesis A process whereby medical problems with a fetus can be determined while it is still in the womb; a needle is inserted into the amniotic sac, amniotic fluid is withdrawn, and fetal cells are examined.

Anal intercourse Insertion of the penis into the rectum of a partner.

Androgen A male hormone, such as testosterone, that affects physical development, sexual desire, and behavior.

Androgen insensitivity syndrome A developmental condition in which cells do not respond to fetal androgen, so that chromosomally male (XY) fetuses develop external female genitals. There also is a feminization of later behavioral patterns.

Androgyny The presence of high frequencies of both masculine and feminine behaviors and traits.

Anejaculation Lack of ejaculation at the time of orgasm.

Anorchism Rare birth defect in which both testes are lacking.

Aphrodisiacs (af-ro-DEE-si-aks) Foods or chemicals purported to foster sexual arousal; they are believed to be more myth than fact.

Areola (a-REE-a-la) Darkened, circular area of skin surrounding the nipple of the breast.

Artificial embryonation Process in which the developing embryo is flushed from the uterus of the donor woman five days after fertilization and placed in another woman's uterus.

Artificial insemination Injection of the sperm cells of a male into a woman's vagina, with the intention of conceiving a child.

Asexuality A condition characterized by a low interest in sex.

Bartholin's glands (BAR-tha-lenz) Small glands located in the minor lips that produce some secretion during sexual arousal.

Behavior therapy Therapy that uses techniques to change patterns of behavior; often employed in sex therapy.

Benign prostatic hyperplasia (BPH) Enlargement of the prostate gland that is not caused by malignancy.

Berdache (bare-DAHSH) Anthropological term for cross-dressing in other cultures.

Bestiality (beest-ee-AL-i-tee) A human being having sexual contact with an animal.

Biological essentialists Those who believe that sexual orientation is an inborn trait, resulting from biological factors during development.

Bisexual Refers to some degree of sexual activity with or attraction to members of both sexes.

Bond The emotional link between parent and child created by cuddling, cooing, and physical and eye contact early in a newborn's life.

Bondage Tying, restraining, or applying pressure to body parts as part of sexual arousal.

Brachioproctic activity (brake-ee-o-PRAHK-tik) Known in slang as "fisting"; a hand is inserted into the rectum of a partner.

Catharsis theory A suggestion that viewing pornography will provide a release for sexual tension, thus preventing antisocial behavior.

Celibacy (SELL-a-ba-see) Choosing not to share sexual activity with others.

Cervical cap A contraceptive device that is shaped like a large thimble and fits over the cervix and blocks sperm from entering the uterus.

Cervical intraepithelial neoplasia (CIN) Abnormal, precancerous cells sometimes identified in a Pap smear.

Cervix (SERV-ix) Lower "neck" of the uterus that extends into the back part of the vagina.

Cesarean section A surgical method of childbirth in which delivery occurs through an incision in the abdominal wall and uterus.

Chancroid (SHAN-kroyd) An STD caused by the bacterium *Hemophilus ducreyi* and characterized by sores on the genitals, which, if left untreated, could result in pain and rupture of the sores.

Child molesting Sexual abuse of a child by an adult.

Chlamydia (klu-MID-ee-uh) Now known to be a common STD, this organism is a major cause of urethritis in males; in females it often presents no symptoms.

Circumcision Of the clitoris—surgical procedure that cuts the prepuce, exposing the clitoral shaft; in the male, surgical removal of the foreskin from the penis.

Climacteric Mid-life period experienced by both men and women when there is greater emotional stress than usual and sometimes physical symptoms.

Climax Another term for orgasm.

Clitoridectomy Surgical removal of the clitoris; practiced routinely in some cultures.

Clitoris (KLIT-a-rus) Sexually sensitive organ found in the female vulva; it becomes engorged with blood during arousal.

Clone The genetic-duplicate organism produced by the cloning process.

Cloning A process involving the transfer of a full complement of chromosomes from a body cell of an organism into an ovum from which the chromosomal material has been removed; if allowed to develop into a new organism, it is an exact genetic duplicate of the one from which the original body cell was taken; the process is not yet used for humans, but it has been performed in lower animal species.

Coitus (ko-EET-us *or* KO-ut-us) Heterosexual, penis-in-vagina intercourse.

Coitus interruptus A method of birth control in which the penis is withdrawn from the vagina prior to ejaculation.

Combining of chromosomes The process by which a sperm unites with an egg, normally joining 23 pairs of chromosomes to establish the genetic "blueprint" for a new individual. The sex chromosomes establish its sex: XX for female and XY for male.

Coming out To acknowledge to oneself and others that one is a lesbian, a gay male, or bisexual.

Computerized sperm selection Use of computer scanning to identify the most viable sperm, which are then extracted to be used for fertilization of an ovum in the laboratory.

Conception The process by which a sperm unites with an egg, normally joining 23 pairs of chromosomes to establish the genetic "blue-

Glossary

print" for a new individual. The sex chromosomes establish its sex: XX for female and XY for male.

Condom A sheath worn over the penis during intercourse to collect semen and prevent conception or venereal disease.

Coprophilia Sexual arousal connected with feces.

Core gender identity A child's early inner sense of its maleness, femaleness, or ambivalence, established prior to puberty.

Corona The ridge around the penile glans.

Corpus luteum Cell cluster of the follicle that remains after the ovum is released, secreting hormones that help regulate the menstrual cycle.

Cowper's glands Two small glands in the male that secrete an alkaline fluid into the urethra during sexual arousal.

Cryptorchidism (krip-TOR-ka-diz-um) Condition in which the testes have not descended into the scrotum prior to birth.

Cunnilingus (kun-a-LEAN-gus) Oral stimulation of the clitoris, vaginal opening, or other parts of the vulva.

Cystitis (sis-TITE-us) A nonsexually transmitted infection of the urinary bladder.

Deoxyribonucleic acid (DNA) The chemical in each cell that carries the genetic code.

Desire phase Sex researcher and therapist Helen Singer Kaplan's term for the psychological interest in sex that precedes a physiological, sexual arousal.

Deviation Term applied to behaviors or orientations that do not conform to a society's accepted norms; it often has negative connotations.

DHT-deficiency syndrome A condition in which chromosomally male fetuses have underdeveloped male genitals and may be identified as girls at birth. However, at puberty they begin to develop masculine secondary sex characteristics and seem to maintain masculine patterns of behavior.

Diaphragm (DY-a-fram) A latex rubber cup, filled with spermicide, that is fitted to the cervix by a clinician; the woman must learn to insert it properly for full contraceptive effectiveness.

Diethylstilbestrol (DES) Synthetic estrogen compound once given to mothers whose pregnancies were at high risk of miscarrying.

Dilation The gradual opening of the cervical opening of the uterus prior to and during labor.

Dilation and curettage (D & C) A method of induced abortion in the second trimester of pregnancy that involves a scraping of the uterine wall.

Dilation and evacuation (D & E) A method of induced abortion in the second trimester of pregnancy; it combines suction with a scraping of the inner wall of the uterus.

Direct sperm injection A technique involving the injection of a single sperm cell directly into an ovum. It is useful in cases where the male has a low sperm count.

Dysfunction Condition in which the body does not function as expected or desired during sex.

Dysmenorrhea (dis-men-a-REE-a) Painful menstruation.

E. coli (Escherichia coli) Bacteria naturally living in the human colon, which often cause urinary tract infection.

Ectopic pregnancy (ek-TOP-ik) The implantation of a blastocyst somewhere other than in the uterus (usually in the fallopian tube).

Ejaculation Muscular expulsion of semen from the penis.

ELISA (enzyme-linked immunosorbent assay) The primary test used to determine the presence of HIV in humans.

Embryo (EM-bree-o) The term applied to the developing cells when, about a week after fertilization, the blastocyst implants itself in the uterine wall.

Endometrial hyperplasia (hy-per-PLAY-zhee-a) Excessive growth of the inner lining of the uterus (endometrium).

Endometriosis (en-doe-mee-tree-O-sus) Growth of the endometrium out of the uterus into surrounding organs.

Endometrium Interior lining of the uterus, innermost of three layers.

Endorphins A chemical produced by the brain in response to physical intimacy and sexual satisfaction.

Epidemiology (e-pe-dee-mee-A-la-jee) The branch of medical science that deals with the incidence, distribution, and control of disease in a population.

Epididymis (ep-a-DID-a-mus) Tubular structure on each testis in which sperm cells mature.

Epididymitis (ep-a-did-a-MITE-us) Inflammation of the epididymis of the testis.

Episiotomy (ee-piz-ee-OTT-a-mee) A surgical incision in the vaginal opening made by the clinician or obstetrician to prevent the baby from tearing the opening in the process of being born.

Erectile dysfunction Difficulty achieving or maintaining penile erection (impotence).

Erection Enlargement and stiffening of the penis as internal muscles relax and blood engorges the columns of spongy tissue.

Erogenous zone(a-RAJ-a-nus) Any area of the body that is sensitive to sexual arousal.

Erotomania A very rare form of mental illness characterized by a highly compulsive need for sex.

Estrogen(ES-tro-jen) Hormone produced abundantly by the ovaries; it plays an important role in the menstrual cycle.

Estrogen replacement therapy (ERT) Treatment of the physical changes of menopause by administering dosages of the hormone estrogen.

Ethnosexual Referring to data concerning the sexual beliefs and customs of other cultures.

Excitement The arousal phase of sex researchers William Masters and Virginia Johnson's four-phase model of the sexual response cycle.

Exhibitionism Exposing the genitals to others for sexual pleasure.

Exocytosis The release of genetic material by the sperm cell that permits fertilization to occur.

Fallopian tubes Structures that are connected to the uterus and lead the ovum from an ovary to the inner cavity of the uterus.

Fellatio Oral stimulation of the penis.

Female sexual arousal disorder Difficulty for a woman in achieving sexual arousal.

Fetal alcohol syndrome (FAS) A condition in a fetus characterized by abnormal growth, neurological damage, and facial distortion caused by the mother's heavy alcohol consumption.

Fetally androgenized females A condition in which hormones administered during pregnancy caused chromosomally female (XX) fetuses to have masculinization of genitals and perhaps of later behavior patterns, even though they were raised as girls.

Fetishism(FET-a-shizm) Sexual arousal triggered by objects or materials not usually considered to be sexual.

Fetus The term given to the embryo after 2 months of development in the womb.

Fibrous hymen Condition in which the hymen is composed of unnaturally thick, tough tissue.

Follicles Capsules of cells in which an ovum matures.

Follicle-stimulating hormone (FSH) Pituitary hormone that stimulates the ovaries or testes.

Foreplay Sexual activities shared in early stages of sexual arousal, with the term implying that they are leading to a more intense, orgasm-oriented form of activity such as intercourse.

Foreskin Fold of skin covering the penile glans; also called prepuce.

Frenulum(FREN-yu-lum) Thin, tightly-drawn fold of skin on the underside of the penile glans; it is highly sensitive.

G Spot A vaginal area that some researchers feel is particularly sensitive to sexual stimulation.

Gamete intra-fallopian transfer (GIFT) Direct placement of ovum and concentrated sperm cells into the woman's fallopian tube to increase the chances of fertilization.

Gay Refers to persons who have a predominantly same-gender sexual orientation and identity. More often applied to males.

Gender dysphoria(dis-FOR-ee-a) Some degree of discomfort with one's identity as male or female, and/or nonconformity to the norms considered appropriate for one's physical sex.

Gender identity A person's experience of gender feelings of maleness, femaleness, or an ambivalent position between the two.

Gender identity disorder The expression of gender identity in a way that is socially inconsistent with one's anatomical gender; may also be described as gender dysphoria.

Gene therapy Treatment of genetically caused disorders by substitution of healthy genes.

Genetic engineering The modification of the gene structure of cells to change cellular functioning.

Genital herpes(HER-peez) Viral STD characterized by painful sores on the sex organs.

Genital warts Small lesions on genital skin caused by papilloma virus; this STD increases later risks of certain malignancies.

Gestational surrogacy Implantation of an embryo created by the sperm and ovum of one set of parents into the uterus of another woman who agrees to gestate the fetus and give birth to the child, which is then given to the original parents.

Glans Sensitive head of the female clitoris, visible between the upper folds of the minor lips; in the male, the sensitive head of the penis.

Gonadotropin-releasing hormone (GnRH)(go-nad-a-TRO-pen) Hormone from the hypothalamus that stimulates the release of FSH and LH by the pituitary.

Gonads Sex and reproductive glands, either testes or ovaries, that produce hormones and reproductive cells (sperm or eggs).

Gonorrhea(gon-uh-REE-uh) Bacterial STD causing urethral pain and discharge in males; often no initial symptoms in females.

Granuloma inguinale(gran-ya-LOW-ma in-gwa-NAL-ee or NALE) STD characterized by ulcerations and granulations beginning in the groin and spreading to the buttocks and genitals.

Hemophiliac(hee-mo-FIL-ee-ak) Someone with the hereditary blood defect hemophilia, primarily affecting males and characterized by difficulty in clotting.

Hepatitis B Liver infection caused by a sexually transmitted virus (HBV).

Heterosexism The assumption that people are, or should be, attracted to members of the other gender.

Heterosexual Attractions or activities between males and females.

HIV Human immunodeficiency virus.

Homophobia(ho-mo-PHO-bee-a) Strongly held negative attitudes and irrational fears relating to gay men and/or lesbians and their lifestyles.

Homosexual The term that is traditionally applied to romantic and sexual attractions and activities between members of the same gender.

Hormone implants Contraceptive method in which tiny hormone-releasing containers are surgically inserted under the skin.

Hormone pumping A fertility-enhancing technique involving the injection of progesterone into a woman's system.

Hormone replacement therapy (HRT) Treatment of the physical changes of menopause by administering dosages of the hormones estrogen and progesterone.

Hot flash A flushed, sweaty feeling in the skin caused by dilated blood vessels, often associated with menopause.

Human chorionic gonadotropin (HCG) A hormone detectable in the urine of a pregnant woman. Most home pregnancy tests work by detecting its presence in woman's urine.

Human immunodeficiency virus (HIV) The virus that initially attacks the human immune system, eventually causing AIDS.

H-Y antigen A biochemical produced in an embryo when the Y chromosome is present; it causes fetal gonads to develop into testes.

Hymen Membranous tissue that can cover part of the vaginal opening.

Hypersexuality Unusually high level of interest in and drive for sex.

Hypoactive sexual desire disorder (HSDD) Loss of interest and pleasure in what were formerly arousing sexual stimuli.

Hyposexuality An especially low level of sexual interest and drive.

Hypoxphilia Creating pressure around the neck during sexual activity to enhance sexual pleasure.

IImpotence(IM-pa-tens) Difficulty achieving or maintaining erection of the penis.

In vitro fertilization (IVF) A process whereby the union of the sperm and egg occurs outside the mother's body.

Incest(IN-sest) Sexual activity between closely related family members.

Incest taboo Cultural prohibitions against incest, typical of most societies.

Induced abortion A termination of pregnancy by artificial means.

Infertility The inability to produce offspring.

Inhibited sexual desire (ISD) Loss of interest and pleasure in formerly arousing sexual stimuli.

Intersexuality A combination of female and male anatomical structures, so that the individual cannot be defined as male or female.

Interstitial cystitis (IC) A chronic bladder inflammation that can cause debilitating discomfort and interfere with sexual enjoyment.

Interstitial-cell-stimulating hormone (ICSH) Pituitary hormone that stimulates the testes to secrete testosterone; known as luteinizing hormone (LH) in females.

Intracytoplasmic sperm injection (ICSI) A technique involving the injection of a single sperm cell directly into an ovum. It is useful in cases where the male has a low sperm count.

Intrauterine devices (IUDs) Birth control method involving the insertion of a small plastic device into the uterus.

Kleptomania Extreme form of fetishism in which sexual arousal is generated by stealing.

Labor Uterine contractions in a pregnant woman; an indication that the birth process is beginning.

Lactation Production of milk by the milk glands of the breasts.

Lamaze method(la-MAHZ) A birthing process based on relaxation techniques practiced by the expectant mother; her partner coaches her throughout the birth.

Laparoscopy Simple procedure for tubal ligation, involving the insertion of a small fiber optic scope into the abdomen, through which the surgeon can see the fallopian tubes and close them off.

Laparotomy Operation to perform a tubal ligation, or female sterilization, involving an abdominal incision.

Latency period A stage in human development characterized, in Freud's theory, by little interest in or awareness of sexual feelings.

Lesbian(LEZ-bee-un) Refers to females who have a predominantly same-gender sexual orientation and identity.

Libido(la-BEED-o or LIB-a-do) A term first used by Freud to define human sexual longing or sex drive.

Lumpectomy Surgical removal of a breast lump, along with a small amount of surrounding tissue.

Luteinizing hormone (LH) Pituitary hormone that triggers ovulation in the ovaries and stimulates sperm production in the testes.

Lymphogranuloma venereum (LGV)(lim-foe-gran-yu-LOW-ma-va-NEAR-ee-um) Contagious STD caused by several strains of Chlamydia and marked by swelling and ulceration of lymph nodes in the groin.

Glossary

Male erectile disorder Difficulty achieving or maintaining penile erection (impotence).

Mammography Sensitive X-ray technique used to discover small breast tumors.

Masochist The individual in a sadomasochistic sexual relationship who takes the submissive role.

Mastectomy Surgical removal of all or part of a breast.

Ménage à trois(may-NAZH-ah-TRWAH) *See* Troilism.

Menarche(MEN-are-kee) Onset of menstruation at puberty.

Menopause(MEN-a-poz) Time in mid-life when menstruation ceases.

Menstrual cycle The hormonal interactions that prepare a woman's body for possible pregnancy at roughly monthly intervals.

Menstruation(men-stru-AY-shun) Phase of menstrual cycle in which the inner uterine lining breaks down and sloughs off; the tissue, along with some blood, flows out through the vagina; also called the period.

Microscopic epididymal sperm aspiration (MESA) A procedure in which sperm are removed directly from the epididymis of the male testes.

Midwives Medical professionals, both women and men, trained to assist with the birthing process.

Mifepristone (RU 486) A progesterone antagonist used as a postcoital contraceptive.

Miscarriage A natural termination of pregnancy.

Modeling theory Suggests that people will copy behavior they view in pornography.

Molluscum contagiosum(ma-LUS-kum kan-taje-ee-O-sum) A skin disease transmitted by direct bodily contact, not necessarily sexual, that is characterized by eruptions on the skin that appear similar to whiteheads, with a hard seed-like core.

Monogamous Sharing sexual relations with only one person.

Monorchidism(ma-NOR-ka-dizm) Presence of only one testis in the scrotum.

Mons Cushion of fatty tissue located over the female's pubic bone.

Multiplier effect When biological and socioenvironmental factors build on one another in the process of human development.

National Birth Control League An organization founded in 1914 by Margaret Sanger to promote use of contraceptives.

Natural childbirth A birthing process that encourages the mother to take control, thus minimizing medical intervention.

Natural family planning/fertility awareness A natural method of birth control that depends on an awareness of the woman's menstrual/fertility cycle.

Necrophilia(nek-ro-FILL-ee-a) Having sexual activity with a dead body.

Nongonococcal urethritis (NGU)(non-gon-uh-KOK-ul yur-i-THRYT-us) Urethral infection or irritation in the male urethra caused by bacteria or local irritants.

Nonspecific urethritis (NSU)(yur-i-THRYT-us) Infection or irritation in the male urethra caused by bacteria or local irritants.

Normal A subjective term used to describe sexual behaviors and orientations. Standards of normalcy are determined by social, cultural, and historical standards.

Norplant implants Contraceptive method in which tiny hormone-releasing cylinders are surgically inserted under the skin.

Nymphomania(nim-fa-MANE-ee-a) A term sometimes used to describe erotomania in women.

Obscenity Depiction of sexual activity in a repulsive or disgusting manner.

Onanism(O-na-niz-um) A term sometimes used to describe masturbation, it comes from the biblical story of Onan, who practiced coitus interruptus and "spilled his seed on the ground."

Opportunistic infection A disease resulting from lowered resistance of a weakened immune system.

Organizing effect Manner in which hormones control patterns of early development in the body.

Orgasm(OR-gaz-em) A rush of pleasurable physical sensations and series of contractions associated with the release of sexual tension; usually accompanied by ejaculation in men.

Orgasmic release Reversal of the vasocongestion and muscular tension of sexual arousal, triggered by orgasm.

Orgy(OR-jee) Group sex.

Osteoporosis(ah-stee-o-po-ROW-sus) Disease caused by loss of calcium from the bones in postmenopausal women, leading to brittle bones and stooped posture.

Ova Egg cells produced in the ovary. One cell is an ovum; in reproduction, it is fertilized by a sperm cell.

Ovaries Pair of female gonads, located in the abdominal cavity, that produce ova and female hormones.

Ovulation Release of a mature ovum through the wall of an ovary.

Ovum donation Use of an egg from another woman for conception, with the fertilized ovum then being implanted in the uterus of the woman wanting to become pregnant.

Pansexual Lacking highly specific sexual orientations or preferences; open to a range of sexual activities.

Pap smear Medical test that examines a smear of cervical cells to detect any cellular abnormalities.

Paraphilia(pair-a-FIL-ee-a) A newer term used to describe sexual orientations and behaviors that vary from the norm; it means "a love beside."

Paraphiliac A person who is drawn to one or more of the paraphilias.

Partial zona dissection (PZD) A technique used to increase the chances of fertilization by making a microscopic incision in the zona pellucida of an ovum. This creates a passageway through which sperm may enter the egg more easily.

Pedophilia(peed-a-FIL-ee-a) Another term for child sexual abuse.

Pelvic inflammatory disease (PID) A chronic internal infection associated with certain types of IUDs.

Penis Male sexual organ that can become erect when stimulated; it leads urine and sperm to the outside of the body.

Perimetrium Outer covering of the uterus.

Perinatal A term used to describe things related to pregnancy, birth, or the period immediately following the birth.

Perineal area(pair-a-NEE-al) The sensitive skin between the genitals and the anus.

Peyronie's disease(pay-ra-NEEZ) Development of fibrous tissue in the spongy erectile columns within the penis.

Pheromones Human chemicals, the scent of which may cause an attraction or behavioral change in other individuals.

Phimosis(fye-MOE-sus) A condition in which an abnormally long, tight foreskin on the penis does not retract easily.

Placenta(pla-SENT-a) The organ that unites the fetus to the mother by bringing their blood vessels closer together; it provides nourishment for and removes waste from the developing baby.

Plateau phase The stable, leveled-off phase of sex researchers William Masters and Virginia Johnson's four-phase model of the sexual response cycle.

Polygamy The practice, in some cultures, of being married to more than one spouse.

Pornography Photographs, films, or literature intended to be sexually arousing through explicit depictions of sexual activity.

Premature birth A birth that takes place prior to the 36th week of pregnancy.

Premature ejaculation Difficulty that some men experience in controlling the ejaculatory reflex, which results in rapid ejaculation.

Premenstrual syndrome (PMS) Symptoms of physical discomfort, moodiness, and emotional tensions that occur in some women for a few days prior to menstruation.

Preorgasmic A term often applied to women who have not yet been able to reach orgasm during sexual response.

Prepuce(PREE-peus) In the female, tissue of the upper vulva that covers the clitoral shaft.

Priapism(pry-AE-pizm) Continual, undesired, and painful erection of the penis.

Progesterone(pro-JES-ter-one) Ovarian hormone that causes the uterine lining to thicken.

Prolapse of the uterus Weakening of the supportive ligaments of the uterus, causing it to protrude into the vagina.

Promiscuity(prah-mis-KIU-i-tee) Sharing casual sexual activity with many different partners.

Prostaglandin Hormone-like chemical whose concentrations increase in a woman's body just prior to menstruation.

Prostaglandin- or saline-induced abortion Used in the 16th–24th weeks of pregnancy, prostaglandins, salt solutions, or urea are injected into the amniotic sac, administered intravenously, or inserted into the vagina in suppository form to induce contractions and fetal delivery.

Prostate Gland located beneath the urinary bladder in the male; it produces some of the secretions in semen.

Prostatitis(pras-tuh-TITE-us) Inflammation of the prostate gland.

Pseudohermaphrodite A person who possesses either testes or ovaries in combination with some external genitals of the other sex.

Pseudonecrophilia A fantasy about having sex with the dead.

Psychosexual development Complex interaction of factors that form a person's sexual feelings, orientations, and patterns of behavior.

Puberty Time of life when reproductive capacity develops and secondary sex characteristics appear.

Pubic lice Small insects that can infect skin in the pubic area, causing a rash and severe itching.

Pubococcygeus (PC) muscle(pyub-o-kox-a-JEE-us) Part of the supporting musculature of the vagina that is involved in orgasmic response and over which a woman can exert some control.

Pyromania Sexual arousal generated by setting fires.

Rape trauma syndrome The predictable sequence of reactions that a victim experiences following a rape.

Refractory period Time following orgasm during which a man cannot be restimulated to orgasm.

Resolution phase The term for the return of a body to its unexcited state following orgasm.

Retrovirus(RE-tro-vi-rus) A class of viruses that reproduces with the aid of the enzyme reverse transcriptase, which allows the virus to integrate its genetic code into that of the host cell, thus establishing permanent infection.

Rh factor A blood-clotting protein agent whose presence or absence in the blood signals an Rh+ or Rh- person.

Rh incompatibility Condition in which a blood protein of the infant is not the same as the mother's; antibodies formed in the mother can destroy red blood cells in the fetus.

RhoGAM Medication administered to a mother to prevent formation of antibodies when the baby is Rh positive and its mother Rh negative.

Rhythm method A natural method of birth control that depends on an awareness of the woman's menstrual/fertility cycle.

RU 486 A French abortion drug; a progesterone antagonist used as a postcoital contraceptive.

Sadist The individual in a sadomasochistic sexual relationship who takes the dominant role.

Sadomasochism(sade-o-MASS-o-kiz-um) Refers to sexual themes or activities involving bondage, pain, domination, or humiliation of one partner by the other.

Satyriasis(sate-a-RYE-a-sus) A term sometimes used to describe erotomania in men.

Scrotum(SKROTE-um) Pouch of skin in which the testes are contained.

Selective reduction The use of abortion techniques to reduce the number of fetuses when there are more than three in a pregnancy, thus increasing the chances of survival for the remaining fetuses.

Self-gratification Giving oneself pleasure, as in masturbation; a term typically used today instead of more negative descriptors.

Semen(SEE-men) Mixture of fluids and sperm cells that is ejaculated through the penis.

Seminal vesicle(SEM-un-al) Gland at the end of each vas deferens that secretes a chemical that helps sperm to become mobile.

Seminiferous tubules(sem-a-NIF-a-rus) Tightly coiled tubules in the testes in which sperm cells are formed.

Sensate focus Early phase of sex therapy treatment, in which the partners pleasure each other without employing direct stimulation of sex organs.

Sex addiction Inability to regulate sexual behavior.

Sex therapist Professional trained in the treatment of sexual dysfunctions.

Sexual aversion disorder Avoidance of or exaggerated fears toward forms of sexual expression (sexual phobia).

Sexual differentiation The developmental processes—biological, social, and psychological—that lead to different sexes or genders.

Sexual dysfunctions Difficulties people have in achieving sexual arousal and in other stages of sexual response.

Sexual harassment Unwanted sexual advances or coercion that can occur in the workplace or academic settings.

Sexual orientation A person's erotic and emotional attraction toward and interest in members of one or both genders.

Sexual surrogates Paid partners used during sex therapy with clients lacking their own partners; only rarely used today.

Sexually transmitted diseases (STDs) Various diseases transmitted by direct sexual contact.

Shaft In the female, the longer body of the clitoris, containing erectile tissue; in the male, cylindrical base of penis that contains three columns of spongy tissue; two corpora cavernosa and a corpus spongiosum.

Shunga Ancient scrolls used in Japan to instruct couples in sexual practices through the use of paintings.

Smegma Thick, oily substance that may accumulate under the prepuce of the clitoris or penis.

Social learning theory Suggests that human learning is influenced by observation of and identification with other people.

Sodomy laws Laws that, in some states, prohibit a variety of sexual behaviors, often described as deviant sexual intercourse. These laws are often enforced discriminatorily against particular groups.

Sonograms Ultrasonic rays used to project a picture of internal structures such as the fetus; often used in conjunction with amniocentesis or fetal surgery.

Spectatoring Term used by sex researchers William Masters and Virginia Johnson to describe self-consciousness and self-observation during sex.

Sperm Reproductive cells produced in the testes; in fertilization, one sperm unites with an ovum.

Sperm banks Centers that store frozen sperm for the purpose of artificial insemination.

Spermatocytes(sper-MAT-o-sites) Cells lining the seminiferous tubules from which sperm cells are produced.

Spermicides Chemicals that kill sperm; available as foams, creams, jellies, or implants in sponges or suppositories.

Sponge A thick polyurethane disk that holds a spermicide and fits over the cervix to prevent conception.

Spontaneous abortion Another term for miscarriage.

Staphylococcus aureus(staf-a-low-KAK-us) The bacteria that can cause toxic shock syndrome.

Glossary

Statutory rape A legal term used to indicate sexual activity when one partner is under the age of consent; in most states that age is 18.

STDs Sexually transmitted diseases.

Sterilization Rendering a person permanently incapable of conceiving, usually by interrupting passage of the egg or sperm.

Suppositories Contraceptive devices designed to distribute their spermicide by melting or foaming in the vagina.

Syndrome(SIN-drome) A group of signs or symptoms that occur together and characterize a given condition.

Syphilis(SIF-uh-lus) Sexually transmitted disease (STD) characterized by four stages, beginning with the appearance of a chancre.

Systematic desensitization Step-by-step approaches to unlearning tension-producing behaviors and developing new behavior patterns.

Testes(TEST-ees) Pair of male gonads that produce sperm and male hormones.

Testicular cancer Malignancy in the testis that may be detected by testicular self-examination.

Testicular failure Lack of sperm and/or hormone production by the testes.

Testosterone(tes-TAS-ter-one) Major male hormone produced by the testes; it helps to produce male secondary sex characteristics.

Testosterone replacement therapy Administering testosterone injections to increase sexual interest or potency in older men; not considered safe for routine use.

Toucherism Gaining sexual gratification from the touching of an unknown person's body, such as on the buttocks or breasts.

Toxic shock syndrome (TSS) An acute disease characterized by fever and sore throat, and caused by normal bacteria in the vagina that are activated if tampons or contraceptive devices such as diaphragms or sponges are left in for long periods of time.

Transgenderists People who live in clothing and roles considered appropriate for the opposite sex for sustained periods of time.

Transsexualism A strong degree of discomfort with one's identity as male or female, characterized by feelings of being in the wrongly sexed body.

Transvestite An individual who dresses in clothing and adopts mannerisms considered appropriate for the opposite sex.

Trichomoniasis(trik-uh-ma-NEE-uh-sis) A vaginal infection caused by the *Trichomonas* organism.

Troilism(TROY-i-lizm) Sexual activity shared by three people.

Tubal ligation A surgical cutting and tying of the fallopian tubes to induce permanent female sterilization.

Umbilical cord The tubelike tissues and blood vessels originating at the embryo's navel that connect it to the placenta.

Urethra(yu-REE-thrah) Tube that passes from the urinary bladder to the outside of the body.

Urophilia Sexual arousal connected with urine or urination.

Uterus(YUTE-a-rus) Muscular organ of the female reproductive system; a fertilized egg implants itself within the uterus.

Vagina(vu-JI-na) Muscular canal in the female that is responsive to sexual arousal; it receives semen during heterosexual intercourse for reproduction.

Vaginal atresia(a-TREE-zha) Birth defect in which the vagina is absent or closed.

Vaginal fistulae(FISH-cha-lee *or* -lie) Abnormal channels that can develop between the vagina and other internal organs.

Vaginismus(vaj-uh-NIZ-mus) Involuntary spasm of the outer vaginal musculature, making penetration of the vagina difficult or impossible.

Vaginitis(vaj-un-NITE-us) General term for inflammation of the vagina.

Vas deferens Tube that leads sperm upward from each testis to the seminal vesicles.

Vasa efferentia Larger tubes within the testes, into which sperm move after being produced in the seminiferous tubules.

Vasectomy(va-SEK-ta-mee *or* vay-ZEK-ta-mee) A surgical cutting and tying of the vas deferens to induce permanent male sterilization.

Voyeurism(VOYE-yu-rizm) Sexual gratification from viewing others who are nude or who are engaging in sexual activities.

Voluntary surgical contraception Sterilization; rendering a person incapable of conceiving with surgical procedures that interrupt the passage of the egg or sperm.

Vulva External sex organs of the female, including the mons, major and minor lips, clitoris, and opening of the vagina.

Western blot The test used to verify the presence of HIV antibodies already detected by the ELISA.

Wolffian ducts(WOOL-fee-an) Embryonic structures that develop into male sexual and reproductive organs if male hormones are present.

Yeast infection A type of vaginitis caused by an overgrowth of a fungus normally found in an inactive state in the vagina.

Zona pellucida(ZO-nah pe-LOO-sa-da) The transparent, outer membrane of an ovum.

Zoophilia(zoo-a-FILL-ee-a) Bestiality.

Zygote An ovum that has been fertilized by a sperm.

SOURCES

Sexuality Today: The Human Perspective, Kelly, Gary F., Fifth Edition, 1995. Dushkin/McGraw-Hill, Guilford, CT.

Pregnancy, Childbirth, and Parenting (Wellness), 1992. Dushkin/McGraw-Hill, Guilford, CT.

Index

Index

Test Your Knowledge Form

We encourage you to photocopy and use this page as a tool to assess how the articles in *Annual Editions* expand on the information in your textbook. By reflecting on the articles you will gain enhanced text information. You can also access this useful form on a product's book support Web site at *http://www.dushkin.com/online/*.

NAME:

DATE:

TITLE AND NUMBER OF ARTICLE:

BRIEFLY STATE THE MAIN IDEA OF THIS ARTICLE:

LIST THREE IMPORTANT FACTS THAT THE AUTHOR USES TO SUPPORT THE MAIN IDEA:

WHAT INFORMATION OR IDEAS DISCUSSED IN THIS ARTICLE ARE ALSO DISCUSSED IN YOUR TEXTBOOK OR OTHER READINGS THAT YOU HAVE DONE? LIST THE TEXTBOOK CHAPTERS AND PAGE NUMBERS:

LIST ANY EXAMPLES OF BIAS OR FAULTY REASONING THAT YOU FOUND IN THE ARTICLE:

LIST ANY NEW TERMS/CONCEPTS THAT WERE DISCUSSED IN THE ARTICLE, AND WRITE A SHORT DEFINITION:

We Want Your Advice

ANNUAL EDITIONS revisions depend on two major opinion sources: one is our Advisory Board, listed in the front of this volume, which works with us in scanning the thousands of articles published in the public press each year; the other is you—the person actually using the book. Please help us and the users of the next edition by completing the prepaid article rating form on this page and returning it to us. Thank you for your help!

ANNUAL EDITIONS: Human Sexuality 02/03

ARTICLE RATING FORM

Here is an opportunity for you to have direct input into the next revision of this volume.
We would like you to rate each of the articles listed below, using the following scale:

1. **Excellent: should definitely be retained**
2. **Above average: should probably be retained**
3. **Below average: should probably be deleted**
4. **Poor: should definitely be deleted**

Your ratings will play a vital part in the next revision.
Please mail this prepaid form to us as soon as possible.
Thanks for your help!

RATING	ARTICLE	RATING	ARTICLE
	1. Child Sex Trade Rises in Central America		37. The Last Sexual Taboo
	2. AIDS Has Arrived in India and China		38. Lust and Revenge on Wall Street
	3. AIDS: 20 Years of Terror		39. Pregnant? You're Fired!
	4. The New Gender Wars		40. Is It Cool to Be a Virgin?
	5. Parasites in Prêt-à-Porter		41. Naked Capitalists
	6. Never Too Buff		42. Carnal Knowledge
	7. "The Uniform for Today Is Belly Buttons"		43. A Disembodied 'Theology of the Body': John Paul II on Love, Sex & Pleasure
	8. The Second Sexual Revolution		
	9. Man Power		
	10. Male Sexual Circuitry		
	11. The Science of Women & Sex		
	12. Sex, Drugs & Rock 'n' Roll		
	13. Improved AIDS Treatments Bring Life and Hope—At a Cost		
	14. Too Much of a Good Thing		
	15. Why Are We Gay?		
	16. The Five Sexes, Revisited		
	17. The New Flirting Game		
	18. Passion Flowers		
	19. Are You Connecting On the Five Levels of Sex?		
	20. Explosive Sex: The Surprising Turn-On You Can't Ignore		
	21. Satori in the Bedroom		
	22. How to Rediscover Desire		
	23. What's New in Contraception? Understanding the Options		
	24. What You Need to Know About RU-486		
	25. Childless by Choice		
	26. How Old Is Too Old to Have a Baby?		
	27. Birth of a Father: Becoming Dad		
	28. Baby, It's You! and You, and You …		
	29. Which Babies? Dilemmas of Genetic Testing		
	30. Are Boys the Weaker Sex?		
	31. Too Sexy Too Soon		
	32. The Secret Sex Lives of Kids		
	33. Sexual Passages		
	34. Married With Children		
	35. Christy's Crusade		
	36. Silent No More		

(Continued on next page)

ABOUT YOU

Name

Date

_____

Are you a teacher? ❏   A student? ❏
Your school's name

_____

Department

_____

Address   City   State   Zip

_____

School telephone #

_____

YOUR COMMENTS ARE IMPORTANT TO US!

Please fill in the following information:
For which course did you use this book?

_____

Did you use a text with this ANNUAL EDITION?   ❏ yes ❏ no
What was the title of the text?

_____

What are your general reactions to the *Annual Editions* concept?

_____

Have you read any pertinent articles recently that you think should be included in the next edition? Explain.

_____

Are there any articles that you feel should be replaced in the next edition? Why?

_____

Are there any World Wide Web sites that you feel should be included in the next edition? Please annotate.

_____

May we contact you for editorial input?   ❏ yes ❏ no
May we quote your comments?   ❏ yes ❏ no